RAPPROCHEMENT ACROSS THE HIMALAYAS

RAPPROCHEMENT ACROSS THE HIMALAYAS

Emerging India-China Relations in Post Cold War Period - (1947-2003)

Keshav Mishra

KALPAZ PUBLICATIONS
Delhi-110052

RAPPROCHEMENT ACROSS THE HIMALAYAS

Emerging India-China Relations in Post Cold War Period - (1947-2003)

Rs. 790

ISBN: 81-7835-294-X

Published in 2004 in India by
Kalpaz Publications,
C-30, Satyawati Nagar, Delhi-110052
E-mail : Kalpaz@hotmail.com

Laser Typesetting at : Shree Vaishnavi Creations, Delhi
Printed at : Mehra Offset Press, Delhi

Contents

Preface

Few relationships are as important for peace and stability in Asia as between India and China. India-China relations have moved a long way since the brief but bitter war in 1962. New contours in the bilateral relations were visible in 1976, when in a major diplomatic initiative, both sides agreed to resume ambassadors in their respective capitals. This marked a positive beginning. The early eighties witnessed a realisation among the political leadership of both sides to tackle the border issue, a highly emotive as well as intractable problem.

The process of India-China rapprochement received a great impetus by Prime Minister, Rajiv Gandhi's historic visit to China in December 1988. This process was further boosted by Prime Minister, Li Peng's visit to India in December 1991. This manifested a growing confidence on the part of the political leadership of both sides to tackle all the issues which had bedeviled the relationship between the two Asian giants. The new found political maturity was reflected in multifaceted cooperation between the two countries including the constitution of the Joint Working Group to resolve the vexed issue of border.

An endeavour has been made in this study to delineate the changing contours of India-China relationship from 1963 to 1991, in terms of bilateral, regional and international perspectives. The first chapter traces the background of India-China relations from 1947 to 1962. The second chapter deals with the period of stalemate in the bilateral relations from the year 1963 to 1975. The third chapter seeks to study the process towards rapprochement in Sino-Indian relations during the years 1976 to 1991. The fourth chapter studies the South Asian context of India - China relationship. It deals with the interaction between China and other South Asian nations i.e. Pakistan, Nepal, Bhutan, Sri Lanka and Bangladesh, which constitutes an important factor in the India-China relationship. The fifth chapter encapsulates the international political setting, which considerably affected India-China interaction. The sixth comprises the conclusions of the study.

In finishing the thesis, I owe a lot to many individuals and institutions whose invaluable assistance is unforgettable. I owe a tremendous debt of gratitude to my supervisor, Prof. Nancy Jetly for patient supervision, thoughtful counsel and constant spurring. Since the inception of this research work, she took keen interest in the progress of the work and with her incisive criticism gave constructive suggestions at every stage of the work. I take this opportunity to acknowledge heartfelt thanks to her.

I am extremely thankful to all my teachers of South Asian Studies, whose enlightening lectures on South Asian Affairs enabled me to tackle my research. I sincerely thank Dr. Qian Wenzhong of Department of History, Fudan University, Shanghai for extending all cooperation during my stay over there. Further I wish to thank Shri Shiv Shankar Singh the then Director of Higher Education, U.P. Dr. R.V. Singh, Assistant Director and Dr. A.K. Shahi for their help in granting me study leave for one year. My sincere thanks to my friends – Ashish, Sushil, Shakeel, Ajitabh, Rahul, Saurabh, Sanjay, Satish and Shekharji for all their help. The constant encouragement of Dr. Satyendra Nath in many ways helped me to finish this work.

The undiminished love, affection of my parents and sisters have proved to be a constant source of sustenance and inspiration in my life's various endeavours. This Ph.D. research was no exception. I would be failing in my duty if I do not specially thank my wife, Vani and my daughter, Vidisha for patiently enduring my long hours of work at home and offering me inspiration.

I am thankful to the staff members of JNU Library, NMML, IDSA, New Delhi and Fudan University Library, Shanghai Public Library, Shanghai and National Library, Beijing for allowing me to use their facilities. I am thankful to Jawaharlal Nehru Memorial Fund, New Delhi for giving me scholarship to visit China for one year which helped me to collect primary source material for the study. I am also thankful to the UGC for providing me financial assistance.

The Post Cold War Period has witnessed significant developments in the bilateral relations between India and China. After the disintegration of Soviet Union, both Asian Powers realised the urgency of stabilizing the borders and further improve overall bilateral relations in an uncertain world order. India and China were compelled in many ways by the prevalent circumstances and contemporary historical forces to construct the edifice of rapprochement. As a result of the India-China Summit level talks of 1993 and 1996, the overall bilateral relations resistered alround improvement.

A combination of factors brought about brief breakdown in the process of rapprochement in 1998. However, the process of India-China rapprochement was irreversible. From the beginning of 1999, the Asian giants restored the dialogue mode in a more substantive and meaningful manner. In the present ongoing phase, a more mature India outlined a friendly framework for engagement with China. At the political level, as a result of Prime Ministerial Summits of 2002 and 2003, the overall bilateral relations registered upward trend. A more confident and assertive India, gradually veered towards realism and was no more guided by idealism.

The present study analyses the emerging pattern of India-China rapprochement in the Post Cold War Period. It argues that the permutation and combination of bilateral issues in the backdrop of regional context and dynamics of evolving global setting were major inputs in the overall India-China rapprochement. The first chapter deals with the construction of rapprochement from 1992 to 1997. The second chapter seeks to study the period of breakdown of India-China engagement in the year 1998. The third chapter analyses the attempts to reconstruct rapprochement from 1999 to the present phase. The fourth chapter studies the regional context of India-China relationship. It analyses the interaction between China and other South Asian nations, i.e., Pakistan, Nepal, Bangladesh etc, which in turn influences the overall India-China Rapprochement. The fifth chapter encapsulates the evolving global setting, which also shaped in some ways the India-China rapprochement. The sixth chapter comprises the conclusions of the study.

The author has benefited a lot from discussions and interactions at the Institute for Defence Studies and Analyses, New Delhi. He would like to record his sincere thanks to former Director (Retd) Air Commodore Jasjit Singh and the Deputy Director, Commodore Uday Bhaskar and Colleagues of China and East Asia Cluster.

I also express my gratitude to the Kalpaz Publications, for undertaking the publication of this book.

Keshav Mishra

1

Historical Background (1947-1962)

India and China, the two giants of Asia are inheritors of age old, great civilizations and are neighbours. India-China relationship, although essentially bilateral in nature, is compounded and even shaped greatly by external factors of regional and global settings.[1] Although both countries initiated the process of nation building generally from late forties, i.e., 1947 and 1949 and respectively, the models of their development as well as political system was not similar. While India followed the path of parliamentary democracy, mixed economy and non-alignment; China adopted one party rule of Communism, state controlled economy and joined Communist Camp of Soviet Union. However, different political systems did not come in the way of flowering of relationship between India and China in the era of anti-imperialist and Pan Asiatic Sentiment.

In 1947, when India became independent, the nationalist Kuomintang government was in power in China, India established diplomatic relations with China in 1948 and sent K.M. Panikkar as its first ambassador. Military defeat of the Kuominatang government at the hands of the Communists led to the establishment of the People's Republic of China on 1st October, 1949. Soon thereafter, the Government of India extended official recognition to it on 30th December, 1949.[2] Thereby, India became one of the first non-communist states to recognise the People's Republic of China. The Chinese communists, on the other hand, were unhappy about India's policy of non-alignment. Mao Zeedong openly stated that throughout the world, one sided either towards imperialism or with socialism and a third road did not exist. He said: "... sitting on the fence will not do nor there a third road... We oppose the illusions about a third road".[3] During this period, the Chinese continued to ignore the fact that India was an independent country and called Nehru a hireling of Anglo-American imperialism. Prime Minister Jawaharlal Nehru on his part, persistently viewed Indian independence and the Chinese revolution as parallel expressions of resurgent Asian nationalism. In a oft quoted statement in Parliament, Nehru visualised China as the third great power in tomorrow's world but hastened to add that India was destined to be the fourth.[4] He was aware that in New Asia, China and India were destined to play vital and perhaps competitive leadership roles. But the architect of India's China policy, Nehru wanted the two emerging Asian great nations to be friendly to each other. As a result, India's efforts for localising the conflict in Korea, its advocacy of China's entry in the United Nations and its consistent support to China on the question of integration of Taiwan with the Mainland led to appreciation for India's role in the Chinese mind. There were exchanges of state visits by the Prime Ministers of China and India. Between June 1954 and January 1957, Zhou En Lai paid four visits to India. Prime Minister Jawaharlal Nehru visited China in October 1954 and 1956.[5]

The issue of Tibet, however, stood in the way of cordial neighbourly relations. Tibet issue was a British legacy and the Britishers recognised the Chinese suzerainty, if not sovereignty, over Tibet subject to internal autonomy and British presence in Tibet. Independent India thus inherited from British the right to keep a political agent at Lhasa, maintain trade agencies at Gyantse, Gartok and Yatung, maintain postal and telegraph offices along trade route upto Gyantse and station a small military detachment to ensure safety of the British routes.

India after independence also acknowledged suzerainty of China over Tibet, subject to Tibet's status as an autonomous unit. New Delhi, therefore was surprised when the Chinese leadership declared that "liberation of Tibet was one of the basic tasks of the People's Liberation Army". The Chinese army moved into Tibet on 7 October, 1950.

India sent three notes to China and stressed that the settlement of the Tibet problem should be effected by peaceful negotiation adjusting the legitimate Tibetan claim to autonomy within the framework of suzerainty.[6] China, on its part, questioned India Interference in the internal affair. In May 1951, a treaty was signed between China and Tibet, whereby China's suzerainty over Tibet was accepted and its hold over Tibet's trade, communication system and external affairs was recognised. Thus, this treaty brought Tibet into China's fold, which was described as the "motherland", though it guaranteed Tibet's regional autonomy.[7]

India subsequently tried to impart impetus to improve its relations with China, in the light of the peaceful turn of events in Sino-Tibetan Relation. The efforts on the part of both sides led to the signing of "India-China Agreement on Trade and Intercourse" in 1954. Accordingly, India renounced the traditional position it had enjoyed in Tibet as inheritor in British treaty rights. The agreement provided for the establishment of Chinese trade agencies in New Delhi, Kalimpong and Calcutta, while

India retained its trade agencies in Yatung, Gyantse and Gartok travel regulations and trade routes for pilgrims and visitors from either country were also laid down.[8] India also agreed to withdraw within six months its military escorts in Tibet and hand over the post and telegraph services and rest houses owned by it in Tibet to the Chinese authorities. In the preamble to the agreement the two countries reaffirmed that they would abide by the famous five principles 'Panchsheel': mutual respect for each other's territorial-integrity and sovereignty, mutual non-aggression, mutual non-interference in each other's internal affairs, equality and mutual benefit and peaceful coexistence. India viewed Panchseel as a major step towards world peace. It was this aspect that Nehru emphasised while presenting the Agreement to Parliament on 15 May 1954, he said: "By this Agreement, we ensure to a very large extent peace in a certain area of Asia. I would earnestly wish that the area of peace could be spread over the rest of Asia and indeed over the rest of the world".[9] Subsequently, bilateral relations between India and China were marked by the Hindi-Chini-bhai-bhai phase till it rapidly deteriorated from the late fifties.

China's imposition of centralised state structure provoked a Tibetan national uprising in 1959. This resulted in the exodus of the Dalai Lama, Tibet's preeminent religious leader and about 100,000 others to India, where they were given sanctuary.[10] A large section of Indian public opinion criticised Chinese denial of autonomy and repressive military measures against the Tibetans. India also took exception to Chinese allegations about India being a "centre for collusion with imperialism against Tibet". China responded with outrage and initiated a steady build up of army in Tibet. After China crushed the Tibetan uprising India's relations with China deteriorated further.

The undemarcated border of some 2500 miles in mountainous terrain proved to be an insuperable barrier to India-China amity. The India-China boundary has been divided into three sectors: firstly, the western sector, which comprises the boundary of Kashmir (Ladakh region) with Xinjian and of Kashmir with Tibet region of China. Secondly, the middle sector, which consists of the borders of Himachal Pradesh and Uttar Pradesh with Tibet, and finally the eastern sector consisting of border of North East Frontier Agency, now Arunachal Pradesh with Tibet. Small border clashes began from mid and late fifties, first in the middle sector, then in the western sector of Ladakh, where the Chinese constructed a road linking Xinjiang to Tibet across the Aksaichin plateau, and finally in the eastern sector along the McMahon line.[11]

The first white paper on India-China relations, presented to the Parliament in September 1959, revealed that differences existed between both sides on the border issue. The border issue was raised in 1954 by Prime Minister Nehru when he drew the attention of Zhou Enlai to certain maps published by China which showed an incorrect boundary alignment between the two countries and incorporated large areas of Indian territory within China. The Chinese Premier replied that those maps were reproductions of old Kuomintang maps, which the communist regime could not revise due to lack of time. It was in December 1958 that Nehru pointed out in a letter to his Chinese counterpart that continued misrepresentation of Indian border in Chinese maps needed to be taken up urgently. In reply, the Chinese Premier, Zhou-en-Lai claimed some 40,000 square miles of Indian territory in the western and eastern sectors. Zhao's explanation for the claim lay in his review of the history of British imperialist expansion into the Himalayas.[12] Thereby, he challenged India' position that the boundary between the two nations, in most parts, was sanctioned by specific agreements and stated that historically no treaty or agreement had ever been signed on the India-China boundary between the Chinese Central government and the Indian government.

Nehru on his part, reiterated that India' boundary with China had been settled for centuries by history, geography, custom and tradition. Rejecting China's claims to large areas of Indian territory, he indicated his willingness, however, to discuss any disputes over minor alignments. But China went ahead to further aggravate situation and intruded forty miles deep into Indian territory in the Ladakh region and near the Kongka Pass on 20 October, 1959, resulting in heavy Indian casualties. As a result, government came under attack for its failure to take effective action against China's violation of India's sovereignty and territorial integrity. The Indian government consequently, decided to place the entire frontier in direct charge of the army. Meanwhile, on 7 November 1959 Zhou proposed that in order to maintain the status quo on the border:-

1. the armed forces of both the countries to withdraw 20 kilometers from the McMahon Line on the east and from the Actual Line of Control in the West; and
2. the armed personnel of the two sides should not be sent into the demilitarised zone;
3. the two Prime Ministers should hold talks on the border and other issues in the immediate future;
4. status quo should be maintained.[13]

Nehru put forward his own set of proposals suggesting as an interim measure that Indian personnel should withdraw to the west of the international boundary in the Ladakh region as shown in their maps, similarly the Chinese personnel should be withdrawn to the east of the international boundary as shown in their maps. This would create a no-man's land as the two lines were separated by long distances.[14]

In April 1960, the Chinese Prime Minister, Zhou Enlai, visited India for six days and held discussions with Nehru and other Indian leaders. It was a serious attempt to settle the border issue but, unfortunately, both sides could reach neither an agreement on the boundary dispute nor an understanding about the nature and scope of the boundary problem. In April 1960 Premier Zhou Enlai put forward six point proposal which could serve to a mutually acceptable solution. The six points were the followings:-

1. Boundary disputes existed between China and India.
2. A line of actual control existed up to which each side exercised administrative jurisdiction.
3. In determining the border, certain geographical principles such as water sheds, river valleys and mountain passes shall be equally applicable to all the sectors of the boundary.
4. Settlement of the border should take into account the national feelings of the two peoples towards the Himalayas and the Karakoram Mountains.
5. Pending a settlement both sides should keep to the line of actual control and should not put forward territorial claims as pre-conditions.
6. Each side should refrain from patrolling along all sectors of the boundary.[15]

The Indian approach, on the other hand, stressed the following:-

1. There is a traditional and customary boundary between India and China.
2. China had never questioned the boundary and in fact had accepted and acquiesced in what India had always taken to be this traditional and customary alignment.
3. The Sino-Indian boundary has already been delimited either formally or through a historical process.
4. India has traditionally exercised administrative control up to the boundary and China should desist from disturbing the status quo as it has done since 1959.
5. Marginal adjustments for rectification of the boundary could be made by mutual agreement, if found necessary after consultations.[16]

Both sides, however, agreed that officials would examine all the historical evidence, on which each side had based its claim including documents, records and maps and submit report for the consideration of the two governments. The officials of the two sides met in three sessions between 15 June to 12 December 1960 to "explore and examine the factorial material" each possessed. The officials, however, failed to reach consensus on any of the fundamental issues on the agenda. The strong differences in respect of the boundary between the two countries were further reflected, when in December 1960, after several weeks of fruitless talks, two divergent reports were published by the two sides. Though India's case was strong, well argued and was widely appreciated, yet, it failed to break the stalemate on the contentious border issue.[17]

Meanwhile, tension on the borders continued unabated, as there were fresh instances of Chinese violation of Indian territory. Nehru maintained that while India was building up its defence position, it would not indulge in any adventurist action. The Indian forces set up a large number of forward posts in Ladakh to safeguard India's frontiers and move to forward areas which had remained unoccupied earlier. This move, begun in 1960, was crystalised into a 'forward policy' at a high level meeting held on 2 November 1961 and it was then decided that Indian forces should fill the gaps along the India-China border upto the international boundary, particularly in Ladakh, by setting up forward posts.[18] Afterwards, Nehru made a proposal to China on 14 May 1962 that both sides withdraw to the west and east of the lines shown in their respective maps in the Ladakh region of western sector. Nehru also offered to permit the Chinese to use the Aksaichin road for civilian purposes, pending negotiation and settlement of the boundary. China rejected both the proposals and continued its pressure on the border. In the meantime, India-China agreement of 1954 lapsed on 3 June 1962, as India maintained that no negotiations could be carried out unless China withdraw its forces from the Indian territory and restored the status quo as it existed in 1954.

While the formalities of exchanging notes was going on between the both sides, the People's Liberation Army, suddenly on 8 September 1962, marched across the well established McMahon Line in eastern sector. The Indian government now set up a new army corps under the Eastern Command to fight the Chinese aggression. The Chinese invasion on 20 October 1962 all along the border from eastern sector to western sector changed the entire complexion of India-China relations. Apparently, the Indian forces were completely overwhelmed and Indian posts across the entire border fell in the Chinese hands. On 24 October premier Zhou Enlai put forward his three point proposals for ceasefire:

1. Pending a peaceful settlement both parties would respect the line of actual control between the two sides along the entire Sino-Indian border and the armed forces of each side would withdraw twenty kilometers from this line and disengage.

2. Provided the Indian government agreed to this proposal, China would withdraw its frontier guards in the eastern sector to the north of the line of actual control, while both China and India would simultaneously undertake not to cross the line of actual control in the middle and western sectors.
3. Talks between the two Prime Ministers would be held once again to seek a friendly settlement.

Rejecting the proposals Nehru replied on 27 October that India would welcome any Chinese representative to discuss further measures to facilitate a peaceful settlement, provided China reverted to the position as it prevailed all along the boundary prior to 8 September 1962. Zhou Enlai replied that by the line of actual control he meant basically the line existing on 7 November 1959.[19]

A state of national emergency was proclaimed on 26 October 1962. On 8 November Nehru moved a resolution in Parliament recording the resolve of the Indian people to "drive out the aggressor from the sacred soil of India, however, long and hard the struggle may be" and it was passed unanimously. Meanwhile, the uneasy lull on the border was broken again on 15 November 1962 when China launched a massive attack in the eastern sector. However, on 21 November 1962, the Chinese government announced a unilateral ceasefrire along the entire border and withdrawal of its troops to positions 20 kilometers behind the 1959 line of actual control. Further, the Chinese government suggested to Indian government that the officials of the two sides should meet to discuss the 20 kilometers withdrawal of their armed forces to form a demilitarised zone, the establishment of civilian check-posts and the return of captured personnel.[20] Nehru stated that although the Chinese declaration was a unilateral one, in so far as the ceasefire was concerned, India would accept it and do nothing to hamper it.

The latest research in China gives an inside view of how major decisions about India were made by Mao Zedong between 1959 to 1962[21] General Lei Yingfeng served in various capacities in the Supreme Command and in his memoirs, one chapter deals exclusively with the Sino-Indian conflict, where he recalls the sequence of events leading up to the armed conflict of 1962. The Chinese military measures in anticipation of the armed conflict with India were put in place by the Summer of 1962, at least a few months before 20th October. It would appear that it was the clash on 8 September, 1962 at Dhola in the eastern sector, which convinced the Chinese leadership that a military engagement was inevitable. [22] On 6th October 1962, the order was sent to the Chinese border forces:

"If the Indian army attacks, hit back ruthlessly . . . if they attack, don't just repulse them, beat back ruthlessly so that it hurts".[23] The decision to teach India a lesson in a brutal way was Mao's and was to a considerable extent determined by his unique perception.

After the war came to an end, the scene shifted to diplomatic front and from 10 to 12 December, the conference of six non-aligned nations Srilanka, Burma, Cambodia, Egypt, Ghana and Indonesia met in Colombo. Without taking any stand on the wrongs and rights of conflict, the six Afro-Asian nations called on both India and China to settle their dispute peacefully by evolving a ceasefire formula. The ceasefire formula, evolved by the conference and later known as the Colombo Proposals, attempted to provide an equitable and fair basis for further negotiations between the two nations. In the western sector, the proposals stipulated Chinese withdrawal twenty kilometers of the traditional customary line as claimed by China without any corresponding withdrawal on the Indian side. The area thus vacated was proposed to be a demilitarised zone to be manned by civilian posts of both sides. In the eastern sector, the line of actual control recognised by both the governments was to be treated as a ceasefire line. With regard to the middle sector, the proposals recommended the status quo to be maintained.[24] On 6th October 1962, the order was sent to the Chinese border forces.

India accepted these proposals after seeking some clarifications. The clarifications made it clear that India could move right upto the McMahon line except for civilian post in Thagla Ridge and Longjee. The Chinese government initially accepted the proposals in principle as a preliminary basis of talks with the Indian government, later rejected it and asked for negotiations without preconditions. China questioned India's right to move its forces upto the McMohan line and the setting up of its civilian posts in the demilitarised zone in the western sector. India-China relations predictably ended in a stalemate. The Chinese invasion was a personal blow to Jawaharlal Nehru, the architect of India's China policy. As Nehru admitted: "We were getting out of touch with power realities in the modern world. We were living in an artificial atmosphere of our own making and we have been shocked out of it."[25] From now onwards, foreign policy planners became more responsive to security needs and greater importance was attached to defence preparedness.

A number of scholars have criticised Nehru's China policy, particularly, India's defeat in 1962 conflict and were of the opinion that whereas the Chinese leadership single-mindedly pursued a policy which was in their national interests, Nehru failed to protect India's national interest. The ideas of 'Hindi-Chini-bhai-bhai', world peace and Asian solidarity could be no viable substitutes for the concrete national interest and power projection. Nehru, was also criticised for his Tibet policy, where he failed to strike advantageous bargains with Zhou Enlai. If the Indian case on the border rested on legal evidence, the Chinese wanted a political settlement on the basis of their large claims on Indian territory. Thus, what was locked in combat was not merely the borders of India and China but also the power ethos, the rivalries inherent in the revival of Asia's two largest nation states. Mutual misperceptions only aggravated the crisis. The Chinese also failed to understand Nehru's domestic political compulsions, i.e., he was criticised for pursuing flexible policy towards China.

On balance, it can be maintained that Nehru's policy of seeking friendship with China was sound notwithstanding the debacle of 1962. At the initial stage, India could ill afford to follow a policy other than that of peaceful coexistence. Towards this end, Nehru sought security through the policy of friendship with China. His failure lay in his inability to anticipate the immediacy of massive Chinese invasion. Further, Sino-Indian relationship got intermeshed with developments in international politics. Globally China perceived Indian role as a part of international conspiracy against itself. Beginning in the 1960's, China perceived India as an adversary associated with western imperialism in aiding and abetting rebellion in Tibet. At the same time, from late fifties relations between USSR and China was marked by rifts. The détente between the United States and the Soviet Union further reinforced the seize mentality of Beijing. China thus felt isolated and threatened. Moreover, in this period a close and cordial relationship between India and Soviet Union was developing. Predictably, China was unhappy over this and last straw came in the shape of Moscow's neutrality on Indian-China border dispute. China struck India, when both USA and Soviet Union were engaged in the Cuban missile crisis in 1962. At this crucial juncture both superpowers could ill-afford to divert their attention. China announced ceasefire hastily before a sizable international assistance could be set afoot for India. It is clear that hostility with China was a part of Beijing's broader perception of a global anti-Chinese conspiracy. Consequently, this created an extremely complex situation on Sino-Indian border that defied solution in a purely bilateral framework for a long time.

II

The Chinese interest in South Asian region primarily stems from the fact that the Autonomous provinces of Tibet and Xinjiang share borders with many South Asian nations and China being an emerging Asian power naturally desired its influence in the region. Once China's control over Tibet in October 1950 was complete, India's vulnerability from the Himalayan region was quite clear. Though India did its best to avoid becoming involved in a conflict with China over Tibet at the same time, India was not oblivious of security threat with regard to other Himalayan kingdoms viz. Nepal, Bhutan and Sikkim. India, which had inherited its treaty obligations from British India, went ahead with its policy of consolidating the northern frontier. On 8th August, 1949, India and Bhutan signed a treaty at Darjeeling replacing the previous ones signed by British government in 1865 and 1910. This treaty guaranteed internal autonomy to Bhutan and it agreed to be guided by the advice of the Government of India in regard to its external relations which also included matters of defence.[26] In view of the fact that there was a 190 miles of common frontier between Bhutan and Tibet, India took up the responsibility of helping Bhutan in the improvement of its defences and in the building up of strategic roads linking it with India.

Nepal is the northern gateway to the Indian Gangetic plains, therefore, it is strategically important for India. Jawaharlal Nehru recognised this fact and announced in the parliament as early as on 6 December, 1950, that:

Our interest in the internal conditions of Nepal has become still more acute and personal, in view of the development across our borders, in China and Tibet. Apart from our sympathetic interest in Nepal, we are also interested in the security of our own country. From time immemorial, the Himalayas have provided us with a magnificent frontier... we cannot allow that barrier to be penetrated for it is also the principal barrier to India. Much as we stand for the independence of Nepal, we cannot allow anything to go wrong in Nepal or permit that barrier to be crossed or weakened because that would be a risk to our security.[27]

The Indo-Nepalese treaty of peace and friendship which was signed on 31 July 1950 in Kathmandu defined the basis of India-Nepal relations[28]. It included provisions on security incorporated in articles 2 and 5 and explained in paras, 1,2 and 5 of the letters exchanged with the treaty.[29] Nepal established its diplomatic relations with China in 1955 only after India and China signed agreement over Tibet in 1954. Nepal and China signed a new treaty in September 1956 by which the annual tribute of Rs. 10,000 sent by Lhasa to Kathmandu was dropped, extra territorial rights enjoyed by Nepal were abolished and Chinese sovereignty over Tibet was recognised by Nepal.[30] Thus the Nepalese government settled its interest in Tibet with China more or less on the same line as the Indian government had done in order to develop friendship with China.[31] As Sino-Indian relations worsened from 1959 Nepal tried to fish in the troubled water and make overtures to China.

China in consonance with its new South Asian policy tried to wean Nepal away from Indian influence. Zhou Enlai paid an official visit to Kathmandu in the last week of April 1960. It was noteworthy that Zhou's visit to Kathmandu had been preceded by his visit to New Delhi where his discussions with Nehru on the border issue were unsuccessful. On 28 April 1960, he signed a treaty of peace and friendship with Nepal reaffirming the faith of the two countries in the five principles of peaceful coexistence.[32] It was during this visit that Zhou Enlai, in an address to a group of Nepali businessmen in April 1960, mentioned the possibility of linking Kathmandu with Lhasa by road.[33] B.P. Koirala, Prime Minister of the democratic regime stated clearly that he did not regard the proposed Kathmandu-Lhasa road as an economic proposition and that Nepal had no interest in building strategic roads. Predictably B.P. Koirala had no intention of taking any step which India might consider dangerous to its security. China took another step to embitter Nepal's relations with India, when during B.P. Koirala's visit in Beijing in March 1960, China proposed to conclude a non-aggression pact with Kathmandu. A non-aggression pact with China would have indicated and perhaps implied fear of aggression of Nepal by India. Therefore, Nepal refused to sign the Pact.[34] Thus during the B.P. Koirala's premiership China failed in its move of sowing the seeds of discord between India and Nepal.

China was more successful in establishing close relations with Nepal once king Mahendra dissolved the democratic government of B.P. Koirala in December 1960 and relations between India and Nepal gradually deteriorated. China geared its diplomacy to exploit the situation to the detriment of India with whom it had now a direct confrontation in the Himalayas. The Chinese Vice Premier acclaimed king Mahendra's leadership while welcoming the Nepalese delegation to the joint committee on boundary in Beijing in early February 1961.[35] China showed a friendly gesture to Nepal by taking a lenient view of its boundary claims and on 6 February 1961 it was announced in Beijing that agreement on general delineation of the border between the two countries had been reached.[36] Further, in September-October 1961 King Mahendra paid a state visit to China. The most important event which took place during King Mahendra's visit to China was the conclusion of an agreement on the Kathmandu-Kodari road.[37] The road agreement marked a great victory for Chinese diplomacy in Nepal. China continued to further its offensive of embittering

India's relations with Nepal. The Chinese Vice Premier, Marshall Chenyi, declared on 4 October 1962 that "in case any foreign army makes the fool hardy attempt to attack Nepal—China will side with the Nepali people."[38]

It was notable that Chenyi's statement preceded the India-China war of 1962 by two weeks. Further, the Chinese demanded the withdrawal of Indian technicians from Nepal's northern military check-posts for stopping the use of Gurkhas by India against China during 1961-62 and even later.[39] Following the 1962 India-China war when the Indian troops fell into the Chinese hands. China repatriated the arrested Indian Gorkha soldiers to Nepal. It was a calculated move to humiliate India and to create a friendly sentiment for China in Nepal. Thus during the 1961-62 period China in tune with its new South Asian policy of countering India's role in the region improved its position in Nepal to a considerable extent.

As for Sikkim, attempt was made to bring it closer within Indian sphere of influence. Treaties between British India and China of 1890 and 1893 gave the British position of protectorate over Sikkim. India inherited these treaties and had the right to send a political officer to assist the king of Sikkim in the administration. A treaty was signed on 5 December 1959, between India and Sikkim under which Sikkim's old position as an Indian protectorate was recognised and while confirming the internal autonomy of Sikkim, India was authorised to take up the responsibility of Sikkim's external affairs, communications and defence.[40] India was also permitted to station troops in the state, build airfields and roads.

As for Sino-Pak relations, China's reaction to Pakistan's recognition of January 4, 1950, was slow. The reasons were obvious. Unlike, India which looked upon the emergence of a new China as a great feat of the spirit of Asian nationalism, Pakistan had shown no special enthusiasm about new China. Pakistan, by 1954 also signed mutual defence assistance agreement with the United States and joined American sponsored Southeast Asia Treaty Organisation (SEATO) and the Baghdad Pact, which was later to become the Central Treaty Organisation (CENTO). Pakistan, however, also utilised the Bandung Afro Asian Nations Conference in April 1955 to cultivate China where Pakistan's Prime Minister, Mohammad Ali Bogra, met the Chinese Premier Zhou-En-Lai. On 23 April 1955, Zhou said Mohammad Ali Bogra had told him that Pakistan had not joined SEATO and other military alliances on account of its fear of China and it would not be involved in a future war between the United States and China.[41] The Bandung Conference revealed firstly that China and Pakistan, with different political ideologies could have a limited working relationship. Secondly, that China and India were rivals for influence in the Afro-Asian world and finally that Pakistan's role could be utilised by

China not only against India but also against the Soviet Union, whose influence China wanted to dilute among the Afro-Asian countries.[42]

However, between October 1958 and 1959, Pakistan under Gen Ayub Khan pursued an extremely pro West policy and Pakistan's relations with China began to deteriorate. In early 1959 Ayub proposed to India a joint defence of the sub-continent against an external threat.[43] On 21 July 1959 China sent a strong protest note to Pakistan government, in which it listed several causes of Chinese grievance against Pakistan. Among the important issues on which Pakistan was alleged to have adopted unfriendly attitude were Pakistan's voting pattern in the United Nations regarding People's Republic of China's entry into UN, reception to the Taiwanese Haj Mission and Pakistan's attitude towards the Tibetan question. In 1959, Pakistan supported a resolution by Ireland and Malaya in the United Nations, which deplored the forcible denial by China of fundamental rights and freedoms to the Tibetan. The protest note ended with the lines ".... Since the Ayub government came to power, the Pakistan government's hostile attitude towards China has become even worse than before".[44]

However, by late fifties China reassessed its role in South Asia because of a number of occurrences: tension along the Indian-China border, the 1959 rebellion in Tibet, the growing estrangement between China and the Soviet Union over bilateral issues and the question of peaceful coexistence with the west. These events were taken note of by the policy makers in Pakistan. Therefore, in October 1959, when Ayab Khan repeated his proposal of the joint defence of the sub-continent, he also said that Pakistan would approach China to redefine the border between the Pakistan occupied Kashmir and Chinese Xinjiang.[45] The Chinese refusal in 1960 to discuss with Indian officials the boundary between China and the Pakistan occupied part of Kashmir was an important move on Beijing's part to bring Pakistan close to China. China had of course as already mentioned kept its option of friendship with Pakistan open since Bandung Conference.

By 1960-61 the actions and statements made by leaders of both Pakistan and China showed the mutual willingness to improve relations between China and Pakistan. In 1961 when the question of Chinese representation came up before the United Nations, Pakistan supported in the General Assembly a Soviet draft resolution which sought to accord Communist China its due place in the United Nations. It was Pakistan which formally approached Beijing for boundary demarcation in its diplomatic note of 28 March 1961.[46]

It was on 3 May 1962 that Pakistan and China formally announced their intention to define the boundary between China's Xinjiang and Pakistan occupied Kashmir. The two sides agreed to conduct negotiations so as to attain an agreed understanding of location and alignment of this boundary and to sign on this basis an agreement of a provisional nature. Indian protests dated 10 May 1962 were rejected by both Pakistan and China.[47] Formal talks opened in Beijing only on 12 October 1962, just a week before China's massive invasion on India, when a procedural agreement on boundary negotiations was said to have been reached by two sides.[48] It was within a brief period of about two months that the two sides sorted out all the complex issues of location and alignment of the boundary and were ready to sign a full fledged boundary agreement.[49] A strong protest from India dated 31 December 1962 repudiated firmly the validity of any agreement involving Indian territory between parties who have no legal or constitutional locus stand in respect of this territory.[50] India contended that Pakistan had surrendered 13,000 square miles of Indian territory.[51]

There is no doubt that the "speedy attainment of agreement", to use the words from the Sino-Pak joint Communiqué of 26 December 1962, was made possible and facilitated by the India-China Conflict, which inclined Beijing to give up delaying tactics and respond quickly to the Pakistan's desire for a border agreement by making some concessions. That this was the case was confirmed by Bhutto himself.[52] The boundary agreement between China and Pakistan was signed in Beijing on 2 March 1963 by the foreign ministers Chenyi and Z.A. Bhutto. The Conclusion of the boundary agreement with Pakistan, after China's boundary agreement with Burma and Nepal was presented by Chenyi "as example for settling issues in a friendly way between countries with different social systems".[53] He blamed India for not being interested in seeking a peaceful settlement of the boundary question with China in its bid to obtain arms assistance from the imperialists which poses a serious menace to the peace of Asia.[54]

The India-China war was a water-shed in Pakistan-China entente. Pakistani reaction to the Sino-Indian war of 1962 was anti-Indian. Firstly, Pakistan held India responsible for the conflict. Secondly, Pakistan argued that the Sino-Indian war was local and limited conflict. Finally, Pakistan's reaction to western arms supply to India in the wake of Chinese attack turned into resentment against the USA and Britain.[55] The Chinese attack on India convinced Pakistan that break between China and India was final. Similarly the Chinese were sure that Pakistan would not submit to Western pressure to resolve its differences with India and there would not be an eventuality of India and Pakistan forming a joint front against China- a possibility about which China was hither to apprehensive.[56] Thus, Pakistan and China draw close to each other shed mutual suspicion and went on to establish an extremely close relationship after India-China war of 1962.

Similarly with Bhutan, China tried to limit India's influence. The 'special relations' which the treaty of 1949 established between Bhutan and India were not accepted by China. The question of Sino-Bhutanese boundary, the Chinese leaders claimed, did not fall within the scope of Sino-Indian talks held in 1960-61.[57] The Tibet revolt of 1959 and its aftermath opened the eyes of the rulers of Bhutan to the realities of the Chinese menace and Bhutan sealed its borders with Tibet in 1960. In 1961 China made offer of assistance to Bhutan for its economic development which was rejected by the king Jigme Dorji Wangchuk.[58]

Bhutan declared neutrality during the India-China conflict of 1962. Its territory was not attacked by China. However, Chinese claims on the entire eastern district of Tashignong and pockets of north eastern and north western Bhutan were not withdrawn.[59] An area in the east, northwest of Tawang and on the trijunction of Bhutan, India and Tibet, was encircled for 'settlement in future discussion' by the Colombo Powers when they submitted proposals to China and India.[60] As with Pakistan and Nepal, China tried to develop close relationship with Sri-Lanka as well. For Sri Lanka, China being the most populous country and a growing economic and military power, had to be befriended. Moreover, in trying to erode Indian per-eminence Sri Lanka wanted to encourage the involvement of external powers, who for their own reasons, had differences with India. In this context as a Sri Lankan Scholar has noted, from the point of view of small states of South Asia, a stronger presence of China as a counter veiling force is a desirable phenomenon in view of the growing and unquestionable supremacy of India in the region.[61]

The bilateral relations between Sri Lanka and China were affected by the prevalent international situation and the ideological orientation of the ruling party in Sri Lanka. During the initial phase of post independent year (1948-1956), the UNP was in power and Sri Lanka was aligned to the west. A significant development in their bilateral relations occurred in 1952 when Sri Lanka concluded the Rubber-Rice Agreement with the People's Republic of China. Economically it was very beneficial for Sri Lanka, because it not only provided a ready market for surplus rubber, but also to import the much needed rice at below the world market prices. This agreement proved advantageous for Sri Lanka and irrespective of the ideological orientation of the ruling party, the agreement has been renewed every five years.[62]

When SLFP assumed power in 1956 SWRD Bandaranaike and Sirimavo Bandaranaike brought about a definite shift in Sri Lanka's foreign policy. As part of this shift, diplomatic relations with the People's Republic of China was established and mutual political, cultural and trade relations were expanded.[63] The bilateral ties were further cemented during Premier Zhou Enlai's visit of Colombo in 1958.[64] When the Sino-Indian conflict broke out in October-November 1962, Sirimavo Bandaranaike took the initiative to summon the Colombo conference of a few non-aligned countries to mediate in the India-China dispute. It may be noted here that Sri Lanka's neutrality in Sino-Indian war was not seen in India as a friendly act.

Therefore, by 1962 China had a formidable presence in the South Asian region and its sole motive was to contain India's influence in the region.

III

India-China relations were also influenced to a considerable extent by the global political configurations. In 1947, when India became an independent country under the able guidance of Jawaharlal Nehru, it adopted nonalignment as fundamental tenet of its foreign policy. People's Republic of China, on the other hand, seeing the main contradiction as being between socialism and capitalism, joined the Socialist Camp led by the USSR. Initially, China attacked nonalignment because in its opinion, one leaned either towards imperialism or towards socialism and a third road did not exist.[65]

Later on, China modified its view regarding India's policy of nonalignment. Apparently, China appreciated India's serious efforts for localising the conflict in Korea, India's support of China's representation in the United Nations, her approval of China's view on the question of integration of Taiwan with the mainland and India's opposition to the Japanese Peace treaty. India's position on these international issues which deeply concerned China, had a positive impact on India-China relations. In June 1954 while visiting India, Zhou Enlai acknowledged that, "India has made valuable contributions to the efforts of bringing about an armistice in Korea... This position of India is of great significance for safeguarding peace in Asia.[66]

As the Korean war progressed, India's position slowly established the credibility of non-alignment among the communist camp, particularly

USSR and China. The Soviet Union acknowledged India's contribution in ending the Korean war. Further, India's image of non-aligned power gained ground when India declined US military aid and Nehru declared in the Parliament on 23 December 1953 that the United States had subverted the area of peace and brought Cold War to the Indian borders by turning Pakistan into her military ally.[67]

This change in the Soviet out-look has to be viewed in the context of overall Soviet policies which were primarily geared to meet the Western challenge. In fact, Soviet foreign policy was increasingly dominated by the US factor, including Sino-US confrontation. The Socialist Camp of USSR and China held US imperialism to be their principal adversary with which ideological confrontation was inevitable.

However, towards the end of 1950's the international political situation began to change. Three factors were introduced into the international politics. Firstly, the US Soviet Cold War was giving way to conflict cum cooperation between the two. Though the Soviet Union considered US imperialism as its principal enemy, it was not prepared for confrontation with it. Moscow therefore partially strove for a détente with the West. Secondly the non-alignment come to be regarded by both the Super Powers as a factor of peace and stability, and thirdly, the Sino-Soviet rift was widening.[68]

During the early fifties nonalignment was not considered by US as helpful in the containment of communism. The USSR also regarded it as subservient to western imperialism. Mid-fifties onwards the Soviet Union no more viewed it with suspicion, nor did the US consider it immoral. In fact, now it came to be regarded as a factor of peace and stability in the world. India became a beneficiary of a change in the attitude of the Super Powers. Naturally, it caused concern to both Pakistan and China.

The Sino-Soviet differences, which were simmering since the late fifties, widened in sixties. The Chinese were opposed to the Soviet line of 'Peaceful Coexistence', 'Soviet development through Parliamentary Path' and the Soviet attitude towards the nationalist bourgeoisie. The Sino-USSR entente broke own in the late fifties when the Soviet Union decided on the strategy of peaceful coexistence with the United States, inherent in which was also the strategy of keeping the power and influence of the Chinese Community Party in check. Mao's concurrence with the twentieth CPSU Congress strategy was ruled out. Because this implied, in the first stance, placing some of the vital unfulfilled Chinese ambitions, the liberation of Taiwan and acquisition of the security council seat in cold storage and secondly China's acceptance of the nuclear tutelage of the

Soviet Union.[69] The twentieth Party Congress represented the major turning point in Sino-Soviet relations in the Post Stalin era. It set the stage for several of the major elements of conflict that have since appeared: between China and Soviet Union differences over global strategy, over intra-bloc relations, over the pace and scope of destalinization, over the permissible diversity of methods used in building socialism and communism and over the fundamental question of Socialist leadership.[70] In the meantime, the Sino-Soviet differences over the question of boundaries between the two countries became serious.[71] Further, India became an important issue between the Soviet Union and China. For political purposes the Sino-Soviet differences accentuated the differences between India and China.

At the same time, USA viewed India and China as two competitive models for nation building among the developing countries in Asia and Africa. The Eisenhower administration fancied the competition syndrome between India and China in the context of the Cold War and wanted democratic model of India to succeed against socialist model of China. The coming of the Kennedy administration brought a slight shift in the US policy towards India. Kennedy held the view that India and China were competitors in a struggle for the economic and political leadership of Asia.[72] Kennedy had considered India as "the hinge of fate in Asia". When he became President, he committed greater economic aid to India for its third five year plan. In June 1961 the United States had agreed to give India $1045 million in development loans during the first two years of the third five year plan.[73] China sought to establish "an inseparable link" between the anti-Chinese feelings in India and US aid to India. China charged India of becoming a part of the anti-Chinese schemes of US imperialism.

The rift between China and USSR occurred at a time when Indo-Soviet relations were growing friendly since the mid-fifties. Soviet Union encouraged India to play a leading role for the promoting of world peace. China did not like favourable Soviet attitude towards New Delhi and got annoyed over the Soviet attitude towards the Sino-Indian border skirmishes of 1959. The Indian position on the border dispute received rather unexpected support from the Soviet Union in September 1959. As a noted analyst has put it, the Soviet support persuaded Nehru that no flexibility in his basic stand on the border was called for. It was indirect Soviet support of Indian behalf that immediately hardened the Chinese position on the border dispute.[74] The Chinese could not reconcile to the fact that Moscow could not discriminate between a fellow communist country and a non communist country. Moreover, between September

1959 and February 1961, the Soviet Union pledged $500 million for India's Third Five Year Plan projects. Beginning in sixties, Soviet Union started selling military hardware to India and in 1961 it even sold transport planes for use in Ladakh evidently against China. In the middle of 1962, it was announced that India would purchase ten squadron of MIG-21 fighters and it was also disclosed that Soviet Union would build factories in India for the manufacture of the MIG aircraft.[75]

Furthermore, China was opposed to the grant of the Soviet aid to the non-socialist countries. It pleaded that such aid should be excessively given to the socialist countries.[76] China objected to Soviet aid to India due to Chinese perception that India was being helped to become an effective competitor to China and that it was unfair that India was benefiting from both the blocs.

The border dispute between India and China if seen in isolation may be essentially interpreted as a territorial question between two nation states. However, if viewed against the background of the positions taken by the Soviet Union and China, it may be wrong to delink it from its doctrinaire aspect. The Chinese believed that the Sino-Indian differences had arisen as a result of the Indian government's compromise with domestic reaction and imperialism and that this was inevitable due to the class nature of the Indian ruling classes. Later during the exchange of polemics with the Soviet Union, the Chinese revealed that "one of the important differences of principle between the Soviet leaders and ourselves turns on the Sino-Indian boundary question."[77] China considered it wrong for the Soviets to "maintain strict neutrality" on the frontier dispute and felt that far from being neutral, Soviet statements actually censured China and Were biased in India's favour. China referred to the fact that Khrushchev had rejected the notion that the Sino-Indian dispute had anything to do with ideology. He regarded it as nationalist dispute, in which China displayed a narrow nationalist attitude. Finally the Soviets implied that China had deliberately escalated the conflict on the eve of Khruschev's visit to the United States in order to subvert the chances of détente.[78]

It should also be remembered that China attacked India in October 1962 when both the Super powers were engaged in Cuban missile crisis. By the time the crisis was resolved, China had declared a unilateral ceasefire. China perceived Indian support by both USA and USSR as being encircled by hostile forces. Feeling isolated and showing a seize mentality, the Chinese were concerned about support of imperialist forces on twin issues of Tibet and territorial dispute with India. Consequently, as some scholars have pointed out China decided to militarily attack

India. [79] This step was also necessitated by the fact that China wanted to show to world that it is independent from Soviet led socialist camp and could show its own strength by defeating its Asian rival.

It is quite clear from the foregoing that India –China relations were influenced as much as by bilateral issues as by regional and international political configurations. Further, bilateral issues between India and China were linked with both the South Asia factor as well as global political setting. Thus, the combination of bilateral, regional and interaction factors influenced India-China relations during the years under survey culminating in the outbreak of 1962 conflict, which eventually froze relations between the two powerful neighbours for almost two decades.

References

1. S.P. Seth, "Sino-Indian Relations: Problems and Prospects", *Asia-Pacific Community* (Tokyo), Fall 1984, p. 68.
2. A. Appadorai and M.S. Rajan, *India's Foreign Policy and Relations* (New Delhi, 1985) p. 114.
3. *Selected Works of Mao Zedong*, Vol. IV (Beijing, 1969), p. 415.
4. *Jawaharlal Nehru Selected Speeches,* Vol. IV, Publications Division, Ministry of Information and Broadcasting, Government of India (New Delhi, 1964), p. 278.
5. Appadorai and Rajan, n. 2, p.117.
6. For the text of the notes exchanged between India and China on Tibet, See Chankya Sen, ed, *Tibet Disappears* (Bombay, 1960), pp. 69-77.
7. *Ibid,* pp. 78-81.
8. For text see, *Foreign Policy of India: Texts of Documents, 1947-64* (New Delhi, 1966), p.198.
9. *Lok Sabha Debates,* Vol. 5, 1954, Col. 7496.
10. For details see John F. Avendon, *In Exile from the Land of the Snows* (New York, 1986), pp. 65-133.
11. Surjit Man Singh and Steven I. Levine, "China and India: Moving Beyond Confrontation", *Problems of Communism* (Washington), 38 (2-3), March and June 1989, p. 31.
12. This point of view is documented by British writers, See Neville Maxwell, *India's China War* (Bombay, 1970), See also Alastiar Lamb, *The India-China Border: The Origins of the Disputed Boundaries* (London, 1964).
13. Quoted in T. Karki Hussain, *Sino-Indian Conflict and International Politics in The Indian Sub-Continent, 1962-66 (New Delhi,* 1977), p.121.
14. *Ibid.*
15. *Beijing Review* (Beijing), no.18, 3 May 1960, p.18.
16. T.S. Murty, *Paths of Peace: Studies on the Sino-Indian Border Dispute* (New Delhi, 1987), p.122.

17. D.K. Banerjee, *Sino-Indian Border Dispute* (New Delhi, 1975), pp. 22-21. For China's claims in the eastern, middle and western sector respectively, see, Banerjee, pp. 25-27.
18. Appadorai and Rajan, n.2, p. 136.
19. Quoted in Nancy Jetly, *India-China Relations, 1947-77: A Study of Parliament's Role in the Making of Foreign Policy* (New Delhi, 1979), p. 173.
20. Quoted in T. Karki Hussain, n.13, pp. 23-24.
21. For details see, General Lei Yingbeng, *My days as Military Staff in the Supreme Command (*Jiangxi, 1997).
22. Quoted in C.V. Ranganathan and Vinod C. Khana, *India and China: The Way Ahead After "Mao's India War"* (New Delhi, 2000), p. 24.
23. Roderick Macfarquhar *The Origins of Cultural Revolution in China* Vol.3, (Oxford, 1997), p. 307.
24. Nancy Jetly, n. 19, p. 201.
25. *Jawaharlal Nehru Selected Speeches,* Vol. IV, p. 230.
26. S.P. Vamra, *Struggle For the Himalayas* (New Delhi, 1971), p. 58.
27. Jawharlal Nehru, *India's Foreign Policy*, Publications Division (New Delhi, 1971), p. 436.
28. For the text of the treaty, see n. 8, pp. 56-58.
29. For the letters see, *Hindustan Times* (New Delhi), 4 December 1959.
30. For the text of the treaty see, A.S. Bhasin, ed., *Documents on Nepal's Relations with India and China*, 1949-66 (New Delhi, 1960), p. 183.
31. S.K. Jha, *Uneasy Partners: India and Nepal in the Post Colonial Era* (New Delhi, 1975), p.106.
32. For the text of the treaty see, A.S. Bhasin, n. 30, pp. 205-206.
33. *Asian Recorder* (New Delhi), 21-27 May 1960, p. 3329.
34. *Statesman,* (Calcutta), 26 April 1960.
35. S.D. Muni, *Foreign Policy of Nepal* (Delhi, 1973), p. 119.
36. *Times of India,* (New Delhi), 7 February 1961.
37. *Asian Recorder,* 3-9 December 1961, p. 4298.
38. New China News Report (Beijing), 6 October 1962. [hereafter NCNA]
39. S.D. Muni, n. 35, pp. 122-123.
40. For the text of the treaty see, n.8, pp. 37-40.
41. George M. Kahin, *The Asian-African Conference: Bandung* (Cornell, 1956), pp. 57-58
42. P.L. Bhola, *Pakistan-China Relations: Search for Politico Strategic Relationship (Jaipur 1986),* p. 69.
43. *Ibid,* p. 80.
44. *Beijing Review*, no. 30, 28 July 1959, p. 18.
45. P.L. Bhola, n. 42, p. 81.
46. *Ibid,* p. 90.
47. J.P. Jain, *China, Pakistan and Bangladesh* (New Delhi, 1974), p. 55.
48. *Ibid,* p. 59.
49. *Ibid,* p. 67.

50. *Ibid*, p. 66.
51. G.W. Choudhary, *India, Pakistan, Bangladesh and The Major Powers* (New York,1975), p. 179.
52. J.P. Jain, n. 47, p. 67.
53. With Burma the Chinese conceded McMahon Alignment on the Burmese territory.
54. J.P. Jain, n. 47, pp. 68-69.
55. P.L. Bhola, n. 42, p. 91.
56. *Ibid,* p. 92.
57. *Report of the Officials of the Government of India and the People's Republic of China on the Boundary Question* (New Delhi,1961), p- CR-156.
58. V.H. Coelho, *Sikkim and Bhutan* (New Delhi, 1969), p. 78.
59. *China Pictorial*, first published in July 1958 and protested by India.
60. Surjit Mansingh, "China-Bhutan Relations", *China Report*, (New Delhi), 30,2, 1994, p. 179.
61. Mahinda Werake, "China and South Asia: Some Historical Perspective", in S.Kodikara, ed, *South Asian Strategic Issues: Sri Lankan Perspectives (New Delhi,1990),* p. 65.
62. L.M. Jacob, "Sri Lanka-China Relations", in Ramakant ed, *China and South Asia* (New Delhi,1988), p. 159.
63. V. Suryanarayan, Sri Lanka's Policy Towards China, *China Report*, 30:2, 1994, p. 206.
64. *Ibid.*
65. *Selected works of Mao Zedong*, n.3 p. 415.
66. Quoted in T. Karki Hussain, n. 13, p. 4.
67. *Lok Sabha Debates*, Vol. 14, 1953, Col. 2981.
68. P.L. Bhola, n.42, p. 82.
69. Donald S. Zagoria, *The Sino-Soviet Conflict, 1956-1961* (Princeton, 1961), p.35.
70. *Ibid,* p.40.
71. P.L. Bhola, n.42, p.83.
72. John F. Kennedy, *Strategy of Peace* (New York, 1961), p.142.
73. Richard P. Stebbins, *The United States in World Affairs* (New York, 1961), p. 208.
74. Bhabani Sen Gupta, *The Fulcrum of Asia,* (New York, 1970), pp. 128-129.
75. Devendra Kaushik, *Soviet Relations with India and Pakistan* (New Delhi, 1971), pp. 66-67.
76. Donald S. Zagoria, n.69, p. 262.
77. "The Truth about how the leaders of the C.P.S.U. have allied themselves with India against China", *Beijing Review* no.45, 8 November1963, p. 19.
78. *Ibid.*
79. C.V. Ranganathan and V.C. Khanna, n. 22, pp. 21-24.

2

The Period of Stalemate (1963-1975)

Following the conflict of 1962, India-China relations were frozen into a state of hostile coexistence. Although both nations continued to maintain diplomatic relations these were at a lower level. The border conflict dealt a heavy blow to the sentiment of friendship between the two countries. As a result, the diplomatic impasse continued for a long period.

In the beginning of 1963, the Sri Lankan Prime Minister Mrs. Bandaranaike visited China with the mandate of the Colombo Powers. The Premier, Zhou Enlai expressed appreciation for the Afro-Asian mediators who were making sincere efforts to be of assistance to both sides.[1] The government accepted the proposals in principle as a preliminary basis of talks with the Indian government. It however raised two points of interpretation of the proposals. First, that the stipulation about the Indian troops maintaining their existing military position should be applicable to the entire border and not to the western sector alone. Secondly, China was prepared not to set up civilian posts in vacated places under dispute provided Indian troops or civilian personnel did not reenter those places. The areas were Thagla/Chedong in the east, Barahoti/wu-je in the middle and the areas in the western sector. It was stated that the two-point interpretation would not prejudice the positions of India and China on their border alignment. The Indian government might have its own difference of interpretation which could be resolved during discussions.

Later the Sri Lankan Premier, Mrs. Bandaranaike arrived in New Delhi in January, 1963 to appraise the Indian leaders of the implications of the Colombo proposals. The representatives of United Arab Republic and Ghana also joined in the talks at the end of which a communique was issued. The communique indicated that India had received satisfactory clarifications on the substantive parts of the proposals. Nehru told them that he would place the proposals and their clarification before the Indian Parliament for consideration. India's final response to the proposals would be held in abeyance till the Parliament studied them fully. Later, the Colombo proposals as clarified were accepted in principle by the Indian government.[2] But the clarifications given to India were ,substantially different from China's interpretation of the proposals.

On China's part, there was strong criticism of the Indian attitude both towards the border dispute as well as the proposals of the mediator nations. The Chinese media stated that where as the Chinese were keen to avert any resumption of conflict, India had failed to reciprocate the Chinese goodwill. The Indian leaders including Nehru were asserting in their bellicose speeches that the fundamental conflict with China had not ended and that war efforts must not be slackened.[3] The Chinese also reacted unfavourably to the manner in which India had come to interpret the Colombo proposals. In the opinion of China, the purpose of the Colombo conference was to promote direct negotiations between China and India. The proposals were merely for the consideration of the two governments. The Chinese government was not obliged to accept them in toto. India on the other hand believed that its acceptance of Colombo proposals was in the interest of peace, even they fell short of the Indian demand for the status quo. It seemed to be a strange form of logic for China to reject the proposals because India had accepted them. India maintained that in refusing them, China was motivated to retain "at least partially the gains of its latest aggression".[4] In the light of a continued clash of views, the Colombo proposals were shelved and diplomatic stalemate persisted between India and China.

In his first address to the Parliament after conflict with the China, on 18th February 1963, the President reiterated Indian government's resolve to strengthen the defences and economic infrastructure in the context of China's past betrayal. Referring to China's intransigent stand on the Colombo proposals, he stated that India, "committed as it is to peaceful methods, will always endeavour to solve disputes peacefully, in accordance with honour and freedom. But whatever may happen, we cannot and will not submit to dictation backed by military force."[5] In March 1963, Chinese Premier Zhou En lai declared that the Chinese government's stand for direct negotiations would not change. If India owing to the needs of its internal and external politics was not yet prepared to hold talks, China was willing to wait with patience.[6] Meanwhile, political parties, Swatantra Party, Jana Sangh, Socialist Party advocated aggressive policy towards China and criticised Nehru's China policy. Nehru declared in the Parliament that India would continue to work for an honourable settlement. He further stated that, nothing prevented India from strengthening its defence while keeping the door open for an honourable peaceful settlement. He strongly resisted the suggestion of breaking off diplomatic ties with China and maintained that the gesture though brave would be quite unwise.[7]

In April 1964 Nehru suggested that India was prepared to surrender its claim to establish an equal number of civilian posts as the Chinese had in the demilitarized zone. He however hoped that it was for China to make the proposal. "No such approach has been made and therefore the position remains the same as before".[8] Nehru stated in the AICC meeting on 17 May 1964 that India had taken the lead in accepting the Colombo proposals as well as the suggestion of considering the vacation of the post as a basis for starting negotiations, and it was now upto China to take further initiative for direct talks with India.[9] Nehru's initiative was however, not reciprocated by China.[10] The bilateral relations remained unchanged in the Post-Nehru period.

The first important parliamentary discussion on external affairs after Nehru's demise took place on 25 September 1964. The new External Affairs Minister, Swaran Singh initiated the discussion and regretted that China continued to take a "negative and intransigent attitude towards the Colombo proposals". He categorically stated that India was willing to enter into negotiations with China in the "manner envisaged in the Colombo Proposals", should the latter withdraw its seven posts in the demilitarized zone in Ladakh. He further stated that "we have thus gone to the farthest limit possible within the ambit of the Colombo Proposals in order to enable negotiations to take place between the two countries". The minister, however, declared: "we shall not go to the conference table on Chinese terms and we shall not give up our rights in territory which was illegally and by force occupied by China. It is for China to give evidence of her sincerity to reach a settlement which she has singularly failed to do so far".[11]

Throughout the year 1964 both countries alleged border intrusions into each other's territories and lodged protests. China continued to negatively potray India's image. On 16 October, 1964 China exploded atom bomb and conducted its first nuclear test.[12] With China going nuclear, India's threat perception increased manifold. The Members of Parliament warned that the entire context of India's defence strategy and foreign diplomacy had changed with China emerging as a nuclear power.

The Member of the Lok Sabha stated that "the Chinese explosion cannot be ignored; it cannot be written off; it cannot be played donw; it is of major signaificance. We are the country for which it has the most immediate importance".[13] Prime Minister Shastri realised the gravity of the issue and stated in the parliament that India could not simultaneously raise its voice against nuclear warfare and weapons and also go in for atom bomb which, interalia, would add heavily on state exchequer. He was of the opinion that India's policy towards nuclear weapons was advantageous to the nation, and the government would keep the threat in mind, but it would not take any decision in a hurry that only with an atom bomb it could defend itself against China.[14] In December, 1964 Prime Minister Shastri stated that in view of continued intransigence any question of negotiations with China did not arise, the Indian government would continue to believe "in the pursuit of peace and in settlement by mutual discussions provided always that such discussions can be held consistently with the honour and dignity of the country". Replying to the non-communist opposition's demand for a categorical assurance that not an inch of land would be surrendered to China, Shastri said: "we are not going to give up our Indian territory. But it is true that the Colombo proposals are there and we have to keep them in mind".[15]

In the meantime, in December 1964, Premier Zhou Enlai stated that the Indian demand of withdrawal of China's civilian posts was entirely unreasonable. He further stated that China had not given up its sovereignty over the 90,000 sq.kms of territory south of McMahon Line. Reacting to Zhou's contention an Indian official spokesman said that "what Zhou En-lai has now done is to bolt and bar the door completely".[16] In the first analysis of Shastri regime by the Chinese media, the Indian government was characterised as a dictatorship of the big bourgeoisie and big landlords which had stripped of "its own masks of democracy and socialism".[17] The Chinese held that since his assumption of power, Shastri had followed Nehru's domestic and foreign policies and the Indian government was "becoming more and more a protégé of U.S. imperialism begging for its aid and working for its global strategy.[18]

The year 1965 witnessed one of the lowest ebbs in India-China bilateral relations due to Pakistan factor. The Sino-Pak boundary protocol involving territory in Jammu and Kashmir was signed on 26 March 1965. India termed the protocol as "legally invalid and politically mischievous". In the summers, the Indian government condemned the Chinese support of Pakistani aggression in the Rann of Kutch and termed "the Chinese government's stand of Pakistan's aggression in the Rann of Kutch as a reflection of its familiar technique of trying to change the established frontiers of states through the use of military force — China has emerged as the greatest disruptive force in Asia..."[19] In September, 1965 when war broke out between India and Pakistan, China supported Pakistan. To pressurise India, China even accused India of intruding into China's territory. To exacerbate the tension, China sent a three day ultimatum, demanding that India should dismantle all aggressive military structures it had allegedly built in the Sikkim border. An aggressive China rejected India's proposal to send an independent observer to the Sikkim border. The Indian Premier Shastri refuted Chinese allegations and termed its stand on Indo-Pak conflict as "nothing but interferences calculated to prolong and enlarge the conflict". Subsequently on 22 September when ceasefire was declared between India and Pakistan, Chinese ultimatum was quietly withdrawn. During September, October and November many border incursions and clashes took place on the India-China border. On 19 September, the Chinese troops ambushed and killed three civilian personnel of an Indian patrol in Tsaskur in the Ladakh Sector. Later, on 20 and 21 September, troops also intruded into the Sikkim border at Nathula and Dong Chula.[20] On 13 November, Chinese troops opened fire on two Indian outposts across Dong Chula on the Sikkim border and killed one Indian soldier.[21] Both nations exchanged diplomatic notes and lodged strong protests.

The Indian Defence Minister, Y.B. Chavan conceded that since 15 September, China had intruded across the border, or the line of actual control on 33 occasions.[22] Throughout the year the Chinese Government maintained, in an intensified form, its hostility towards India. Developments during the year revealed, even more clearly than before, that the India-China border question was not merely a territorial issue but an instrument forged by China to bring about a political confrontation between the two countries and to apply protracted military pressure on India.[23]

Although no major armed clash took place on the border in 1966, Chinese aggressive activity kept the tension simmering on the border. China not only reiterated its territorial claims on the western and eastern sectors of the border, but also carried out a series of minor intrusions across the border. In February, Defence Minister Chavan informed the Parliament that during December 1965 January 1966 the Chinese committed as many as 27 violations.[24] When Mrs. Indira Gandhi assumed the post of Prime Minister after the sudden death of Lal Bahadur Shastri, Premier Zhou Enlai sent message to Madam Gandhi greeting her on the assumption of the post of premier.[25] In January, 1966 China lodged protest with the Indian government against its alleged interference in China's internal affairs by using the question of Tibet. China expressed concern over Dalai Lama's anti-Chinese activities in India.[26] Earlier, when an unofficial delegation came from Taiwan to take part in some celebration programme on Mahatma Gandhi's birthday, not only did China lodged a protest, but also charged India with efforts to create two China "under the instigation of the U.S. imperialism". Again in March, 1966 when Minister of Economic Affairs of Taiwan visited New Delhi to attend United Nations Economic Commission for Asia and East Pacific, China protested the Indian government's provocation against the Chinese people.[27] The Chinese note alleged that the Indian government has become unscrupulous in following Washington's policy of hostility to China and its plot to create "two China's".

China continued hostile propaganda against India. The Chinese Media tried to present a lurid picture of conditions in India. The reports described the Indian economy as a Semi-Colonial economy dependent on foreign aid and the Indian experiment in economic development a failure and "a negative example for the advancing people in Asia, Africa and Latin America." This brought to the surface some of the ideological bitterness and sense of rivalry the Chinese Government has been harboring towards India. The Chinese aim was to hold up to Asia and Africa the Chinese example as the only model worthy of imitation and challenged India's development of economy through peaceful democratic methods.[28] In April, 1966 when Mrs. Gandhi visited U.S.A, her exercise was termed as "the art of begging". She told an American audience that China entered into 'conflict' with India because of its efforts to develop in democratic socialism and India served as a "strong example of democracy" for the Asian countries. The Chinese media reacted that the 'prosperity' and 'democracy' was a euphemism for famine and arrests of the innocent which India now enjoyed.[29]

Meanwhile, on 9 May, 1966 China successfully conducted a thermo-nuclear bomb. Over which a number of Member of Parliament voiced their concern. In Lok Sabha during the discussion on Demands for Grants of Ministry of External Affairs, M.L. Sondhi of Janasangh stated that "to meet the nuclear threat from China it is my submission that India can undertake a test explosion. We must enter the nuclear comity; otherwise, we shall be working in foreign affairs at our peril".[30] The Minister of State of External Affairs, Shri B. R. Bhagat intervened in the debate and stated that:

The situation is such that it is China which has to change its policies. They have to change their posture of hostility. We have adopted a policy of reciprocity and firmness without giving any provocation towards China. If and when China changes her policy towards us, we shall not be found wanting in working a proper response to it.[31]

Mrs. Gandhi however, stated in Parliament that China's nuclear explosion did not justify a revision in the Government's policy of not developing nuclear energy for non-peaceful purposes:

I myself fail to understand how our production of one or two bombs will help us. Many other questions arise out of them. Furthermore, the belief that China can attack any country with nuclear weapons with impunity, I think is a misconceived one".[32]

From mid-1966 onwards, the internal condition of both India and China was in a state of continuous flux. China was in the midst of socio-economic upheaval and acute leadership struggle during the cultural Revolution phase (1966-69). In India, the new Prime Minister, Mrs. Gandhi was an untried and untested leader. There was the spectre of famine due to widespread drought conditions which did not occur because of food assistance from the U.S.A. In the midst of this all, the 1967 parliamentary elections severely weakened the central leadership, where the ruling congress party of Mrs. Gandhi was returned to power with a reduced majority. China's foreign policy remained dormant during the phase of Cultural Revolution but this did not stop the Chinese from extending its support to the so-called national liberation movements in the third world by exhorting them to replace the legitimate regimes. Accordingly, China started exploiting two basic weaknesses in the governance of India. One was the inability to integrate the tribal peoples of the northeast into the mainstream of Indian life. Another was the failure to ameliorate the condition of the rural peasantry and landless labourers in the lower Ganges Valley.[33] Sensing the weakness as an opportunity, China openly supported Naga and Mizo insurgents and encouraged them to rise in revolt against India. The Naxalbari uprising in West Bengal provided a golden opportunity to the Chinese to recommend the Maoist path for the Indian revolutionaries.[34]

India-China relations further deteriorated in June 1967 with the expulsion of two Indian diplomats from Beijing on alleged charges of "espionage activities".[35] The Indian External Affairs Minister stated that the list of charges of alleged spying was a "tissue of lies". On 14 June, the minister referred to the humiliating treatment accorded to the Indian diplomats by the Red Guards who had been physically assaulted. He further stated that the Chinese Government had violated the "ordinary rules of diplomatic usages" and had also broken its own "pledge of conducting the diplomats safely across to border".[36] Later in a daring and surprise action, China put the entire staff of the Indian Embassy and their families in Beijing under seige in the embassy's compound. India immediately lodged a strong protest and warned China that should the seige of the Indian Embassy not be lifted "within 4 hours", India would take appropriate counter measures. On 19th June, India did the same to Chinese embassy staff at New Delhi and immediately the next day China lifted the seige of the Indian Embassy in Beijing India responded on 21 June by lifting restrictions on the movement of the Chinese staff and sent back two Chinese diplomats from India.[37]

The winter of 1967 witnessed skirmishes on India-China border. On 11 September, Chinese troops attacked Indian troops on the Sikkim border across the Nathula and opened heavy mortar and artillery fire. After repeated Indian protests and proposal for ceasefire, by 15 September there was a virtual cessation of all hostile activity. The Chinese again fired heavily on the Indian positions at Chola, on 1 October and both sides suffered casualties. On 10 October, Chola again witnessed exchange of heavy fires between Indian and Chinese troops. The Indian Defence Minister informed the Parliament that Indian losses in the two border incidents were 88 killed and 163 wounded, while the Chinese casualties were estimated to be 300 killed and 450 wounded in Nathula firing, and 40 in Chola. The minister assured that the government was keeping a close watch on developments across the borders having a bearing on India's security, and those were accordingly taken note of in the defence plans.[38]

By the end of 1967, in a discussion on external affairs, Mrs. Gandhi stated:

China continues to maintain an attitude of hostility towards us—carries on anti-Indian propaganda not only against the Indian Government but against the whole way of our democratic functioning and even our national integrity. But I would like to say that we do not harbour any evil intention towards the Chinese people, and we do hope that a day will come when they will also realise that it is in the interests of all the countries of South East Asia that we should be friends and that each country should be able to devote its strength to solving the very major problem of combating poverty and backwardness".[39]

This was a flexible approach adopted by Mrs. Gandhi regarding relations with China.

The Presidential address on 12 February 1968 underscored India's desire to seek normalisation of relations with China. "We have always wished the Chinese people well— The principles of mutual respect, non aggression and non-interference alone provide a durable basis for international relations. On our part, we seek restoration of our relations with China on these principles".[40] The Government of India in a subtle manner indicated that should China not interfere in India's internal affairs, or provoke any aggression, India would be willing to normalise relations with China. However, China did not respond immediately. As usual the Chinese media carried out propaganda against India. India however remained was increasingly concerned with China's blatant interference in its internal affairs. As Prime Minister, Mrs. Gandhi stated in Parliament,

What happens internally in other countries cannot be a subject matter of public comment—our difference with China arose mainly from the fact that China is not prepared to accept this elementary code of international conduct. The day they accept it, we would have gone a long way towards normalising our relations[41].

She further stated: in foreign affairs there are no set positions—what are permanent and set are certain values and interests on which we cannot compromise.[42] The farsighted statements of Mrs. Gandhi apparently indicated that despite Chinese intransigence, India was moving towards creating a favourable climate for ending the stalemate in India-China relations.

On 1 January 1969, Premier Gandhi stated at her Press Conference that the Government of India was prepared to "try and find" a way of solving the dispute with China without insisting on its acceptance of the Colombo proposals as a precondition.[43] The President, Zakir Hussain, stated further in his address to the parliament on 17 February:

It is our firm belief that the disturbed image of our country which China projects through its ideological prisms will succumb to the realities of the situation. Government have expressed more than once with frankness and sincerity their desire to have friendship of relations with China.... consistent with our sovereignty, territorial integrity and on the basis of absolute non-interference in each other's internal affairs.[44]

On 8 April, 1969, External Affair Minister Dinesh Singh outlined the Government's China policy in the Lok Sabha:

Our policy is based on friendship and cooperation. We do not wish to interfere in the internal affairs of others— The policies of China will have to change one day— we have a long frontier with China. We would like to reduce tension along this frontier.[45]

Now, Chinese foreign policy was marked by a more relaxed profile. In 1969 China witnessed the end of infamous cultural revolution. Moderation was the keyword in Chinese internal and external policies. Following the ninth National Party Congress in April, China stated that regarding boundary question "Government have consistently stood for negotiations through diplomatic channels to reach a fair and reasonable settlement. Pending a settlement, the status quo of the boundary should be maintained and conflict avoided—".[46] As a result, Chinese diplomats started attending some receptions in other capitals given in honour of visiting Indian dignitaries. The atmospherics further improved, by the end of the year when, both the Indian and Chinese diplomats exchanged greetings and attended receptions hosted by their respective missions. This led to a limited than at thaw diplomatic level.

The government of India stated in no uncertain terms that "with China it will be our effort to keep our doors open for resolving our differences by discussions provided they are prepared to respect our sovereignty and territorial integrity,"[47]

In his address to the Parliament on 20 February 1970, the President reiterated his government's desire to conduct its relations with China on the "principle of mutual respect of each other's sovereignty and territorial integrity and non-interference. We expect China to respect our rights to pursue own domestic affairs and foreign policy".[48] On 1 May 1970, during the May Day parade at Beijing, in response to India's overtures, Chairman Mao Zedong shook hands with the Indian charged affaires the Tiananmen Rostrum stated that "India is a great country. The Indian people are a great people— we should be friendly".[49] Mao's smile signaled China's intention to normalise India-China relations. Nothing concrete, however, emerged from chairman Mao's famous smile. China went ahead with its propaganda inciting armed rebellion in India and continued to aid and abet the insurgents in north east. In late 1970 informal contacts between the Indian and Chinese diplomats in many third countries capitals were reported and opened up the possibility of resumption of dialogue between the estranged neighbours.

However, the hopeful pointers of 1970 evaporated as quickly as they had appeared. This was due to the growing separatist movement in East Pakistan. China not only supported the military junta and its role in East Pakistan but also tried discreetly to moderate Yahya Khan's brutal policy toward East Pakistan but without success.[50] China alleged that "weighed down with difficulties at home and abroad, the reactionary Indian Government has embarked on a mad course of arms expansion and war preparations—to carry out an expansionist policy towards its neighbour--"[51] China continued to step up unfriendly acts against India. On 12 April, Chinese Premier, Zhou Enlai sent a message to Pakistan President Yahya Khan, reiterating Chinese support to the people and Government of Pakistan in their struggle to protect their national sovereignty and political independence.[52]

Inspite of virulent anti-Indian Chinese propaganda; India played it cool and maintained a low profile. India again took initiative to start a dialogue with China, when its ambassador in Moscow met twice with his Chinese counterpart in May 1971, to discuss the terms of restoration of diplomatic representation to the Ambassadorial level. The Indian Premier wrote a letter to her Chinese counterpart in July, appraising him on the situation in East Pakistan and proposed meetings at any level acceptable to China.[53] In the Indian Parliament, the External Affairs Minister, Swaran Singh stated that while India was willing to normalise relations with China, normalisation did not depend upon one party alone: "If and when the Government of the People's Republic of China is willing and ready to take concrete steps towards normalisation, we shall be equally ready and willing to do so". He welcomed the change in the style of China's diplomacy which had been in evidence of late and hoped that it would also lead to a "change in substance".[54]

After its initial propaganda, China reacted cautiously against the Indo-Soviet treaty in August 1971. China sent positive signals and invited. India to participate in the Afro Asian Table Tennis Tournament to be held in Beijing in November. India did not lag behind and removed the police post outside the Chinese embassy, which had been posted there since June 1967. In October, 1971 India among other countries joined and voted on the question of restoration of the lawful rights of the People's Republic of China in the United Nation.[55] On 27 October, Indian Premier greeted Chinese Premier, Zhou Enlai in a personal letter and expressed India's desire for "working in close cooperation with China in the interest of peace and progress in Asia and throughout the world".[56] In the United Nations, Mr. Samar Sen, Permanent Representative of India welcomed restoration of the Chinese seat and mentioned about Zhou Enlai's reply to Mrs. Gandhi, which concluded with the words: "May friendship between the peoples of China and India grow and develop daily".[57]

But due to rapid developments in East Pakistan, India-China relations could not witness much improvement. Later on, China set aside cautious approach and alleged that India acted as sub super power. China's acting foreign minister, Chi Pengfei, expressed concern at the present tension in the sub-continent and criticised India's crude interference in Pakistan's internal affairs. On 3 December, Indo-Pak conflict broke out on the eastern and western fronts. China accused India of launching a "large scale" attack on Pakistan.[58] China used its newly acquired membership of the United Nations, particularly the security council to the hilt and its permanent representative, Huang

Hua mobilised international diplomatic pressures against India.[59] But compared to 1965 war, during this round of Indo-Pak conflict, China played overall a rather limited role. China sent three protest notes to India and two notes accused India of intrusions in the Chinese territory in December, 1971. But the government of India rejected protest notes and stated Chinese charges as baseless. The Government of India Stated that

We do not wish to provoke China unnecessarily and are willing to normalise relations with her on a basis of equality, mutual respect and non interference in internal affairs. We hope that sooner, rather than later, China will show a positive and constructive response. Normalisation of relations between India and china, we believe, would strengthen peace and security, promote progress and lessen tensions in Asia.[60]

The Bangladesh crisis, undoubtedly impeded the process of normalisation of relations between India and China. China refused to accept the emergence of a new power balance in the region. When the Simla Agreement was concluded between India and Pakistan in July 1972, China reacted favourably. But India regarded China's attitude towards Bangladesh as not very encouraging. In a Parliamentary debate on international affairs in December, the minister of external affairs conceded the lack of Chinese response to India's repeated offer of negotiations. He expressed the hope that China would "appreciate the desirability and the necessity of normalising relations with India so that the two countries—can live as good neighbours".[61] In March 1973, China, sent a new charge d'affaires to New Delhi, after a lapse of nearly 18 months and this was a positive step. Further, some improvement on the diplomatic front was noticeable and increased contacts between the Indian and Chinese diplomats were reported from many world capitals. China also toned down anti-Indian propaganda in a limited way. In April, China invited an Indian team to play in a Table Tennis Tournament to be held at Beijing in August.

As moves were being made to gradually improve India-China relations, the political crisis in Sikkim again put India and China into another round of diplomatic confrontation. After the fifth general elections in January 1973, Sikkim witnessed breakdown of law and order because of tension between pro-chogyal and anti-chogyal parties. In April, following a request from the Chogyal, the Indian government sent its army to maintain law and order in Sikkim, later on Sikkim's administration was taken over by the Indian Political officer in Gangtok. In September 1974, the Indian government made Sikkim an associate state of India by thirty-fifth Constitutional Amendment Bill. Finally, the

Indian government formally announced Sikkim as its twenty-second state on 23 April, 1975.[62] For India, the question was that of Continuous lurking danger in one of its most sensitive border areas. The conferment of full fledged state in April, 1975 served the needs of the Sikkimese people, (which was evident by holding a referendum on the verger issue raised by the Assembly.) The popular mandate came in through a direct reference to the people who overwhelmingly voted in favour of the merger. It also served India's interests as it prevented a threat developing in this region. As a full fledged state of the Indian Union, all internal and external factors could be taken care of within the overall rational policy.[63] The Chinese government accused India of taking over the administration of Sikkim. On 11 September, 1974, the Chinese government issued a statement condemning India for "annexing Sikkim in a colonial way" and declared that China would absolutely not recognise India's annexation of Sikkim.[64] China landed the incident as an effort to found a general Indian empire "with the support of the Soviet Union".[65] India's position was articulated by Mr. Jaipal, India's Permanent Representative at United Nation's General Assembly, who stated that I feel it necessary to place on record the facts, while making it clear at the same time that Indo-Sikkimes relation are not a matter for discussion at the U.N. The people of Sikkim did not have adult suffrage and their elected representatives did not participate in the administration of Sikkim. The ruler agreed to the holding of free elections to Legislative Assembly of the people. Thereafter the Assembly adopted a democratic constitution for Sikkim . . . it is natural and free political evolution of the people of Sikkim in the direction of internal democracy and closer links with neighbouring India. This is entirely in accordance with the wishes of the people of Sikkim as expressed in their elections. The Chinese allegation that India has annexed Sikkim is therefore, clearly mistaken.[66] For India, Sikkim's merger went a long way in strengthening Indian security in the Himalayan region. Now onwards, China-Sikkimese border turned into China-India border.

On 18 May, 1974, the Indian government announced that India had carried out an underground peaceful nuclear explosion, China did not react directly. The Chinese media, published Pakistan. Premier's statement in Lahore on 19 May that his country would never succumb to Indian nuclear blackmail Pakistan "will not compromise the right to self-determination of the people of Jammu and Kashmir. Bhut to further said: "Nor will we accept Indian hegemony or domination over the sub-continent".[67] China pointed out that despite facing economic troubles, the Indian government was raising military spending.[68] India's position was stated by Ambassador R. Jaipal at the International Atomic Energy Agency in Vienna that :

India did not violate any international treaty or agreement. In the light of India's categorical declaration that it does not intend to manufacture nuclear weapons, it cannot legitimately be regarded as posing a nuclear threat to any state. [69]

Further in March 1975, China interfered in the internal affairs of India by commenting adversely on the agreement reached between Indian Premier, Indira Gandhi and Sheikh Abdullah on 24 February, 1975 whereby Kashmir now became a constituent unit of the Union of India with Sheikh Abdullah serving as the Chief Minister of the state. China commented that; the Indian government violated the U.N. resolutions and international agreements —— took new expansionist steps on the question of the accession of Kashmir to further deprive the Kashmir people of their right to self-determination and gobble up the Kashmir region".[70] The hostile propaganda about India continued unabated in the Chinese media throughout 1975. More seriously, on 20 October 1975 there was an incident at Dulong La in the eastern sector of the border and four Indian soldiers were killed. The Government of India lodged a strong protest about this intrusion into Indian territory and the ambush staged by Chinese soldiers.[71] However, both countries showed maturity in keeping the protests in a low key.

Simultaneously, both countries kept the door open for normalisation of relations. In January 1975 a Chinese table - tennis team made a long tour through India in the course of which 'ping pong diplomacy' occupied head lines in the newspapers. In February 1975, Chinese Vice Premier, Chen Xidian stopped in Calcutta on his return from Nepal King Birendra's coronation and announced his government's readiness to hold talks with India.[72] Participating in a parliamentary discussion on foreign affairs, the Minister of External Affairs, Y.B. Chavan reiterated that:

Inspite of what China has or has not done India continued to have an open mind on the question of improving its relations with China and had repeatedly made known its desire and willingness to do so: unfortunately this cannot be a one way affair as well— the Chinese have shown no real change in attitude.[73]

Later, Prime Minister Mrs. Indira Gandhi stated in 1975:

We Want better relations with China. Much to our disappointment, the last two decades have failed to fulfil our initial hope . . . we began with mutual confidence and good will, but the events of the 1950s brought tension and misunderstanding . . . It would be an over-simplification to regard this merely as the result of a border dispute. Simultaneous or subsequent developments – such as China's systematic Support of Pakistan against India, her provocative criticism of India for alleged subservience to the United States and later the Soviet Union, and her persistent, though futile efforts to promote internal subversion – leave us no option but to infer that the border dispute was the outcome of a more complex policy which was aimed at undermining India's stability and at obstructing her rapid and orderly progress. After the cultural revolution, conditions seem more tranquil and there appears to be a new orientation of China's policies. We wonder whether this new mood will also be reflected in China's policy towards India.[74]

During the period between 1963 to 1975, India-China relations were largely frozen. At the diplomatic front, the period witnessed a stalemate which was difficult to break despite India's flexible approach. Further, the internal and external events factors and forces of both countries prevented improvement of bilateral relations. China and India alleged that the other nation was interfering in their internal affairs, the outbreak of naxalbari movement and insurgency in northeast in the case of India and Taiwan as well as Tibet issue in case of China. The estranged neighbours held and projected negative images of each other. All these factors created an atmosphere of India-China cold war which proved difficult to defrost.

References

1. *Beijing Review* (Beijing), no. 2, 11 January 1963, p. 16.
2. *White Paper*, Vol. IX, Ministry of External Affairs, Government of India (New Delhi, 1963), p. 106.
3. *Beijing Review*, no. 3, 18 January 1963, pp. 5-6.
4. *White Paper*, Vol. IX, 1963, p. 17.
5. *Lok Sabha Debates*, Vol. 13, 1963, Cols. 12-14.
6. *White Paper*, Vol. IX, p. 4.
7. *Lok Sabha Debates*, Vol. 19, 1963, Cols. 2191-2217.
8. *Ibid*, Vol. 29, 1964, Cols.107-09.
9. Quoted in Nancy Jetly, *India-China Relations, 1947-1977: A Study of Parliament's Role in the Making of Foreign Policy* (New Delhi, 1979), p. 223.
10. *Beijing Review*, no. 23, 5 June 1964, p. 4.
11. *Lok Sabha Debates*, Vol. 34, 1964, Cols.3789-90.
12. *Beijing Review*, no. 42, 16 October 1964, Special Supplement, pp. ii-iii.
13. *Lok Sabha Debates*, Vol. 35, 1964, Cols—1239-40.
14. Ibid, Cols. 1564-73.
15. Ibid, Vol. 37, 1964, Cols. 6702-11.

16. *Hindustan Times* (New Delhi), 1 January 1965.
17. *Beijing Review*, no. 4, 22 January 1965, pp. 5-6.
18. *Ibid.*
19. *Foreign Affairs Record*, Ministry of External Affairs (New Delhi), 1965, pp.100-101.
20. Quoted in Nancy Jetly, n. 9, p. 233.
21. *Ibid.*
22. Quoted in Nancy Jetly, n. 9, p. 236.
23. *Annual Report 1965-66*, Ministry of External Affairs, Government of ndia (New Delhi), p. 2.
24. *Ibid.*, p. 237.
25. *Beijing Review*, n. 6, 4 February 1966, p. 4.
26. *Ibid.*, no. 2, 7 January 1966, p. 3.
27. *Ibid.*, no.15, 8 April 1966, p. 14.
28. *Annual Report 1965-66*, Ministry of External Affairs, p. 3.
29. *Beijing Review*, no.15, 8 April 1966, pp. 30-31.
30. *Lok Sabha Debates*, Vol. 15, 1968, Col – 2305.
31. *Ibid.*, Col- 2367.
32. *Ibid.*, Vol. 55, 1966, Col.15716.
33. Quoted in Surjit Mansingh, *India's Search For Power*, New Delhi, 1984, p. 202.
34. *Beijing Review*, no.29, 14 July 1967, p. 26.
35. *Ibid.*, no.25, 16 June 1967, p. 39.
36. *Lok Sabha Debates*, Vol. 4, 1967, Cols.5408-10.
37. Quoted in Nancy Jetly, n. 9, pp. 248-49.
38. *Lok Sabha Debates*, Vol. 9, 1967, Cols. 65-66.
39. *Selected Speeches of Indira Gandhi*, Vol. 1, Publication Division, Ministry of Information and Broadcasting (New Delhi, 1974), pp. 400-401.
40. R.K. Jain, *China-South Asian Relations*, 1947-80, Vol. 1 (New Delhi, 1981), p. 378.
41. *Lok Sabha Debates*, Vol. 15, 1968, Cols. 2680-85.
42. *Ibid.*
43. *Times of India* (New Delhi), 2 January 1969.
44. *Lok Sabhas Debates*, Vol. 24, 1969, Col. 23.
45. Quoted in Surjit Mansigh, n. 33, p. 204.
46. *Beijing Review*, Special Issue, 28 April 1969, p. 27.
47. *Annual Report 1969-70*, Ministry of Defence, Government of India (New Delhi), p. 1.
48. *Lok Sabha Debates*, Vol.36, 1970, Col.12.
49. GengNien, Sino-Indian Relations: Retrospect and Prospect, *South Asian Studies* (Beijing), no. 3-4, 1981, p. 3.
50. G.W. Choudhury, *China in World Affairs* (Colarado, 1982) pp. 254-55.
51. *Beijing Review*, no. 12, 20 March, 1970, p. 29.
52. Quoted in R.K. Jain, n. 40, Vol. II, pp.115-16.
53. Quoted in Nancy Jetly, no. 9, p. 267.

54. *Annual Report 1971-72*, Ministry of External Affairs, p. 27.
55. *Beijing Review*, no. 44, 29 October 1971, p. 6.
56. *Annual Report 1971-72*, Ministry of External Affairs, p. 27.
57. Speech by Samar Sen, Permanent Representative of India to the United Nations, in *Beijing Review*, no. 49, 3 December 1971, pp. 44-45.
58. *Beijing Review*, no.50, 10 December, 1971, pp. 6-7.
59. *Ibid*, pp. 7-8.
60. *Annual Report 1971-72,* Ministry of External Affairs, p. 29.
61. *Lok Sabha Debates*, Vol. 21, 1972, Cols. 170-172.
62. *Foreign Affairs Reports (New Delhi)*, Vol. 24, no. 9, September 1975, pp. 140-56, See also B. S. Das, *The Sikkim Saga* (New Delhi, 1983).
63. Quoted in B.S. Das, *The Sikkim Saga,* p. 79.
64. *People's Daily* (Beijing), 11 September 1974.
65. *Indian Express* (New Delhi), 22 April 1975.
66. Jaipal's Speech at U.N. General Assembly on 20 October, 1974 cited in *Strategic Digest* (New Delhi), IV, no-11, November 1974, p. 65.
67. *Beijing Review*, no. 22, 31 May 1974, p. 27.
68. *Beijing Review*, no. 25, 21 June 1974, pp. 18-19.
69. Text of the statement by R. Jaipal at the IAEA Board in Vienna on India's Nuclear Explosion in *Strategic Digest*, IV, no.6, June 1974, pp. 57-58.
70. *Beijing Review*, no.12, 21 March, 1975, p. 28.
71. Quoted in Surjit Mansingh, n. 34, p. 246.
72. *Ibid.*
73. *Lok Sabha Debates*, Vol. 51, 1975, Cols-294-5
74. *Selected Speeches of Indira Gandhi,* Vol. III (New Delhi: 1984), p. 633.

55. *Annual Report 1972–73*, Ministry of External Affairs, p. 24.
56. [illegible] *Review*, no. 40, [illegible] October 1971, p. 4.
57. *Annual Report 1973–74*, Ministry of External Affairs, p. 24.
58. [illegible] *Review*, no. 49, [illegible] December 1973, pp. 13–14.
59. [illegible], no. 50, 14 December 1973, pp. [illegible]
60. Ibid., [illegible]
61. *Annual Report 1973–74*, Ministry of External Affairs, p. 26.
62. [illegible], vol. 21, 1975 [illegible], pp. [illegible]
63. [illegible] *Review*, vol. 24, no. 2, September 1975, pp. [illegible] [illegible] (New Delhi, 1975).
64. [illegible]
65. *Patriot* (New Delhi), 11 September 1974.
66. [illegible] 23 Aug. 1975.
67. [illegible] General Secretary of [illegible] 1974 and [illegible] 11 September 1974, p. 5.
68. [illegible] 1 May 1975, p. [illegible]
69. [illegible] 1976 [illegible], pp. 14–15.
70. [illegible] in Vienna [illegible] Nuclear [illegible], vol. 24, no. 6, June 1974, pp. 17–18.
71. [illegible] 12, 21 [illegible] 1974, p. 18.
72. Quoted in [illegible], p. 24.
73. Ibid.
74. [illegible] 1975, [illegible]
75. [illegible] (New Delhi, 1983), p. [illegible]

3

Towards Rapprochement (1976-1991)

In the mid – seventies, significant changes took place in both Chinese and Indian internal politics. These political changes provided an opportunity for the new leaders of both nations to reassess and reorient their policies towards each other amidst the changed context of international relations. In China Mao Zedong and Zhou Enlai passed away and the ultraleftist clique – the Gang of Four was purged in 1976. Deng Xiaoping became the Supreme Chinese leader. Deng started to push forward the programme of Modernisation. In order to concentrate on domestic modernisation, China took steps to improve relations with the neighbours, as peaceful borders was necessary for the modernisation.

Meanwhile there was also some reassessment of India's new role and status in China . India's refusal to sign Soviet sponsored Asian Collective Security treaty went down well and convinced Chinese experts about India being independent power. The Chinese also recognised the fact that India had become the most important power centre in South Asia after 1971, and that no combination of other South Asian countries could balance India. Therefore, demand for the improvement of India – China relations gradually became strong.

The first reason was Chinese perception that Indo-Soviet friendship was linked with India-China hostility, and improvement of India-China relations was seen as being conducive in distancing India from the Soviet union. It was necessary for China to create a positive atmosphere for India-China bilateral relations in the face of Sino-Soviet confrontation and India-Soviet friendship. It was eloquently proved when the Soviets reminded India of various Chinese hostile activities and warned that the real Chinese objective was to weaken Soviet-Indian friendship.[1]

The second was related with China's security considerations on its western front, especially in Tibet. Political unrest and ethnic strife kept the situation in Tibet far from normal. The Dalai Lama and thousands of refugees from Tibet were living in Indian territory. Security on the western front apparently required India's cooperation and this meant improved India-China relations.

Finally, the American defeat in the Vietnam war and its growing domestic crisis forced the United States to reduce its presence in East Asia. Chinese leaders were concerned about Soviet efforts to fill the power vacuum by proposing the Asian Collective Security regime. Vietnam began to lean towards Soviet Union and took steps to bring all Indo-China under its own control, excluding Chinese influence there. Under such circumstances, it was imperative for China to take steps diplomatically to stabilise India-China relations in order to foil the perceived Soviet designs in the Asia-Pacific region.

During the Lok Sabha debate on Demand for Grants of Ministry of External Affairs for the year 1976-77, a member of Communist Party, Shri Samar Mukherjee stated that :

> We want that Government of India should take a policy decision to improve relations with China. The Government of India should send an Ambassador to China of their own and create an atmosphere so that some dialogue can be started with China and relations can be improved.[2]

Intervening in the debate the Minister of External Affairs Mr. Y.B. Chavan, stated that :

> In the case of China, we should try to make some efforts to improve relations. I hope there will be some response. I do not want to say anything more than that. We should make efforts, because these are two land masses living together for centuries. Geography has put us near each other. I do not think we can select our neighbours.[3]

On 15 April 1976, External Affairs Minister, Y. B. Chavan, announced in the Lok Sabha appointment of Shri K.R. Narayanan as India's Ambassador to the People's Republic of China. He further informed the House, that the initiative for raising the level of India's diplomatic representation in Beijing would be followed by a similar move by the Government of the People's Republic of China.[4]

India's initiative was universally welcomed and was a significant step forward in improving relations with China. The Indian Ambassador to China assumed his duties in July 1976; China responded quickly and Chen Chao-yuan was appointed PRC's Ambassador to India in July, 1976. In his first official statement, the Chinese Ambassador stated that full normalisation of Sino-Indian relations through joint efforts was in full accord with the interests of the people of the two nations, and expressed the hope that the friendship between the two nations would grow further and the bilateral relations would improve.[5] In September,

1976 when Mao Zedong died, Premier, Mrs. Gandhi extended condolences. She sent a message to her Chinese counterpart stating, "Mao was an eminent statesman who led the resurgence and progress of the Chinese people".[6]

In the general election of 1977, the Janata Party defeated the ruling congress Party. China welcomed inauguration of the first non-congress union government. The Chinese premier, Hua Kuo-feng sent a congratulatory message to his new Indian counterpart, Morarji Desai and hoped that, "the traditional friendship between the peoples of China and India would develop".[7]

There was some hope in China about a reorientation in India's foreign policy at this time. Apparently it seemed that the Janata Government's commitment to "genuine non-alignment" encouraged China. Afterwards China started sending feelers to India. A delegation of the Chinese People's Association for Friendship with Foreign Countries led by Wang Bingnan, visited India in March, 1978 at the invitation of the All India Dr. Kotnis Memorial Committee. Wang met the Prime Minister, Morarji Desai and other dignitaries during the visit of the delegation.[8] In his meeting with External Affairs Minister, Wang conveyed an official invitation to Indian External Affairs Minister Shri Atal Behari Vajpayee to visit China.[9] Later, Huang Hua, the Chinese Foreign Minister formally reiterated the invitation to Vajpayee to visit China. Vajpayee in principle accepted the invitation maintaining that the visit would materialise "at an appropriate time after careful and adequate preparation.[10]

China and India, however, had different positions as to the modus operandi of normalisation of relations. In the words of a noted expert:

> India continued to reiterate its desire to work for removing irritants in order to tackle mutual problems in a climate of mutual respect and dignity, but stressed that resolution of the boundary question was central to the restoration of confidence and full realisation of normalisation between the two countries. China maintained, on the other hand, that the boundary question was a complex one bequeathed by history and efforts needed to be made to improve bilateral relations seeking common ground and reserving differences. This would, in turn, generate a favourable atmosphere for the resolution of the dispute when time would be ripe for its settlement.[11]

Indian External Affairs Minister Shri A.B. Vajpayee visited China in February, 1979, where he exchanged views with Chinese leaders on normalisation of Sino – Indian relations. Vajpayee identified the border problem as the key obstacle to normal Sino-Indian relations and made it clear that India considered its resolution essential. Chinese Vice Premier Deng Xiaoping said: "We should seek common ground while reserving our differences. As for the boundary question, we can solve it through peaceful consultation. This question should not prevent us from improving our relations in other fields".[12] Foreign Minister, Huang Hua held talks on three occasions with his Indian counterpart. In his meeting, Vajpayee referred to China's support to Naga and Mizo insurgents in north-east region. He received satisfactory assurances for stopping such support from the Chinese government.[13] The five principles of peaceful co-existence were reaffirmed as the basis of normalisation of bilateral relations and settlement of the border dispute.

However, the positive momentum of Vajpayee's visit was halted by China's at tack on Vietnam while the Indian External Affairs Minister was still in China. Vajpayee cut short his visit and hurried back home. In the face of intense public pressure, particularly harsh criticism in parliament, the Government of India's stance towards the Chinese armed attack became harder and it finally denounced the Chinese action as an aggression against Vietnam. In terms of concrete gains, the Chinese assurance of stopping support to insurgency in northeast and the friendly gesture of reopening the two Hindu holy places, Kailash and Mansarovar (inside Tibet) to Indian pilgrims was one step forward in bilateral relations.

Notwithstanding the developments in Vietnam, Chinese anticipation of a basic change in India's foreign policy with the coming into power of the Janata government proved to be wrong. China underestimated Indian nationalism and the fact that in India no political party was prepared to make any substantial compromise on the border issue. Thereby, India demonstrated that it was in no hurry to force the pace to suit the Chinese interests. In July, 1979 the Janata regime collapsed in India and Mrs. Indira Gandhi staged a recomeback to power in January 1980.

By the beginning of 1980's, China was moving away from the old rigidities of Maoist era. The Chinese Premier, Hua Guofeng, on 15 January, 1980 extended warm congratulations to Mrs. Gandhi, on her assumption of the office of premiership.[14] Further, on 26 January 1980, Huang Hua attended India's Republic Day Celebration at the Indian embassy in Beijing. This was the first time in 20 years that the Chinese foreign minister had graced the annual event. Hua stressed that, "the present turbulent and tense international situation places a greater obligation on both China and India to promote mutual understanding and cooperation."[15]

The turbulent and tense international situation, which the Chinese foreign minister was referring to started in the late 1970s; the Iranian and Afghan revolutions, followed by the entry of Soviet troops into Afghanistan; disturbed the existing strategic balance in West Asia and South Asia. The Soviet Union also succeeded in bringing Indo-China within its sphere of influence with Vietnam as its ally. India and China differed considerably on the issues of Afghanistan and Vietnam's role in Cambodia.

Yet both the countries had been realising for some time the need to get away from a conflictual relationship and to reduce the tensions. Mrs. Gandhi soon realised that any policy of leaning toward the Soviet Union would not serve India's long term security interests. She wanted to reap the benefit of greater diplomatic flexibility by expanding India's ties with the United States, and by seeking improved relations with China. They also agreed that continued efforts to normalise India-China relations would help maintain the strategic balance of the big powers in South Asia. China, on its part, realised that the more it denounced India, the closer it would push towards the Soviet Union. A tactical approach of softening India and thereby diminishing Indo-Soviet relationship could be more fruitful. With the emergence of Deng Xiaoping as the Supreme leader of China and launching of modernisation, this thinking was in consonance with the general thrust of economics taking precedence over politics.[16] China required a peaceful international environment, with emphasis on good relations with its neighbouring countries, for successfully carrying out their economic reforms.

These changes were still in their incipient phase. It was between 1980 and 1984 that the changes gathered full steam. From 1982 onward, since the 12th party congress adopted "independent foreign policy", China began to cultivate balanced relations with both Superpowers U.S.A. and U.S.S.R. China now advocated idea of "peaceful coexistence" and no longer believed that a global war was inevitable. This adjustment in China's relations with the two superpowers was apparently conducive to weakening Soviet opposition to the Sino-Indian thaw and alleviated Indian fear of the American-China-Pakistan axis against India. The development augured well for India-China relationship.

Meanwhile in June 1980, the Chinese leader Deng Xiaoping revived Zhou Enlai's "package proposal" of 1960 by proposing that India and

China settle their border dispute on the basis of the present line of actual control and abandon their respective claims in the eastern and western sectors.[17]

However the package deal was not acceptable to India because it sought to legitimise Chinese occupation of territory in western sector between 1959 and 1962 without offering any territorial compensation to India. Therefore, acceptance of the deal was seen as being tantamount to letting the Chinese retain the territorial gains of the aggression of 1962. Reacting cooly to the proposal, the External Affairs Minister, Shri Narasimha Rao submitted in the Lok Sabha on July 1980 that ways other than the package solution could prove more 'effective'. India, on its part, hoped to settle the border question in a spirit consistent with national honour and interests of both sides on a basis of equality. It, however, considered the fact of the two governments coming to grips with the long standing and complex border problem after a considerable lapse of time as a positive step.[18]

The direct contacts at highest political level took place at Belgrade where both Indira Gandhi and Hua Guofeng attended the funeral of great Yugoslav leader Marshal Tito.[19] This was the first meeting at the Prime Ministerial level between the two countries since Zhou Enlai's visit to India in 1960 and both leaders agreed to continue with the process of improving relations. Both sides stressed that better Sino-Indian relations were essential to peace and stability in Asia and there was need for mutual consultations as also avoidance of confrontation for an amicable solution of their bilateral problems.

Another major step in this direction was the visit of Vice Premier and Foreign Minister, Huang Hua to India on 26 June, 1981. It was the first important visit to India by a Chinese leader since the late Premier Zhou Enlai's visit in 1960. During his New Delhi visit, Huang Hua had extensive talks with Indian leaders on international and bilateral issues, including the border issue. They agreed that friendly and sincere talks would promote mutual understanding reduce differences and increase points of mutual agreement.[20] China agreed that the border was a vital issue that could not be just shelved but had to be resolved, and both sides agreed that their officials should resume the talks on the vexed issue. In a press conference in New Delhi on 28 June, Huang Hua proposed that pending a settlement the two sides should maintain the status quo on the borders and tranquility in the border areas. Hua stated both sides should actively promote contacts and cooperation in all domains. He further stated: "Both China and India are big countries in Asia and both are developing countries. China is willing to develop friendly contacts with India in numerous areas and to study and learn from each other".[21]

II

A tangible gain ensuing from the visit was the decision to hold official level talks regarding both 'bilateral problems and bilateral exchanges', which apparently followed an understanding between the two sides that border settlement, although central to full normalisation of relations, need not be made a precondition for improvement in relations in other areas.[22] Thus the process of normalisation was underway but it was a long and tortuous one.

Problems continued between India and China as was proved by coupled incidents. In October 1981, China refused to give visa to a member of the Indian Parliamentary delegation, TL Rajkumar, Speaker of the Arunachal Pradesh Assembly to an Asian Conference of Parliamentarians on Population and Development. China's official news agency stated that the "So-called Arunachal Pradesh" had been set up in the Chinese territory of some 90,000 square kms. South of the McMahon line which India had "illegally occupied". The Chinese Government had always "resolutely refused" to recognise Arunachal Pradesh, and therefore China could not approve of India sending a person in such a capacity to participate in the conference in Beijing.[23] Only a threat of cancellation of entire Indian delegation's participation in the conference had a desired affect on China and it issued a visa.

The first round of India-China official level talks was held in Beijing from 10 to 14 December, 1981. The talks consisted of three plenary sessions and of subgroup meetings devoted to boundary issue, trade and economic cooperation, cultural exchanges and science and technology. No progress was made in narrowing differences on border questions; rather, both parties were content to restate previously enunciated positions. China expressed its willingness to conclude a comprehensive agreement, involving China's recognition of the McMahon Line as the eastern sector boundary and India's surrender of claims to the Aksaichin. India considered this arrangement unacceptable.[24]

India then suggested that the 1962 Colombo proposals serve as a starting point for negotiations but China stated that Colombo proposals were out dated. India then urged that the various border issues be treated as discrete entities. Such an approach would entail an initial concentration on readily solvable matters, thereby creating a positive atmosphere for discussions on contentious western sector. This plan was rejected by China.[25] Later on, the Indian External Affairs Minister, Narasimha Rao stated, "It was not our anticipation that it would be possible to make substantive progress in the first round we may, however, regard the fact of the meeting itself, the first on this subject in twenty years, as a positive step".[26] The second round of talks was held from 16 to 20 May, 1982 at New Delhi. The leader of the Chinese delegation, Fu Hao emphasised the need to expand cooperation in scientific, technical, and cultural fields. The Indian side clarified New Delhi's bargaining posture on a number of points: the development of Sino-Indian relations in such fields as reciprocal trade would be severely inhibited by absence of progress in the border talks; India regarded the McMahon Line as the boundary in the Easter sector; and India's incorporation of Sikkim was not subject to debate.[27]

The May 1982 discussions were structured along the lines of the first round talks, involving plenary sessions and subgroup meetings on the border issue, cultural relations, science and technology and trade and economic cooperation. China again stressed the need for a comprehensive settlement transforming existing lines of control into permanent boundaries. India on its part, called for a sector-by-sector approach.[28]

The Chinese side proposed five-principles as the basis for settling the border problem and the Indians came out with six working propositions, including besides general principles, some specific procedural and preliminary steps.[29] China suggested that boundary definition should rest on the following concepts: equality, friendly consultations, mutual understanding and accommodation, a fair and reasonable settlement; and a comprehensive solution. India, in turn, submitted the following working propositions; a solution must be found as soon as possible, the solution should be just, taking into account the legitimate interests of both sides, a commonly agreed upon approach and basis for negotiations should be found, the proposals advanced by either side, as constituting an approach to the problem should be considered by the other. It was also held that it was necessary to consider steps to create a propitious atmosphere; and efforts should be made to settle the border issue in each aspects of each sector.[30]

It was clear that progress of normalisation between the two countries remained slow and halting. The Indian Prime Minister, Mrs. Indira Gandhi stated quite frankly that "we cannot pretend that bilateral relations between India and China have been good. The issues between us are most difficult and even emotional. But nothing can be solved without basic goodwill and effort.[31]

Slowly but surely India's position evolved around more or less to the Chinese position that bilateral relations be improved in various spheres while the border issue remained frozen. With options being limited for India, it could only try to maintain the pressure in China to take the border issue seriously. As the President mentioned in his address to the Parliament in 1982, "Further steps have been taken to improve relations with China. Following the visit of the Chinese Foreign Minister during this year, an official delegation went to Beijing to discuss international and bilateral issues including the question of boundary".[32] In October, 1982 Chinese Premier Zhao Ziyang told a delegation of the India-China society that China and India were large Asian countries that could exert great impact on the world. The 1950s was a period of good cooperation, he said, and "the two peoples both miss that period." He further stated: "We will never forget the help they rendered the Chinese people when we were in difficulty. We hope the seeds of friendship sown by them will blossom with beautiful flowers".[33]

In 1983, Mrs. I. Gandhi welcomed a high level delegation led by Zhu Dunan, Vice President of the Chinese People's Association for Friendship with foreign countries. She said there was immense scope for cooperation if only both the countries came closer. The problems between the two could be overcome by creating a "sprit of friendship" she told the Chinese delegation.[34]

The third round of talks was held in Beijing from 29 January to 2 February, 1983. These also yielded no substantial progress on the issue because of differences in positions.[35] The familiar position of China offering a fair deal through its package and India rejecting it out of hand were made. Later on, the Minister of state of External Affairs stated:

> At the official level talks both sides have been able to state their fundamental positions on the boundary question and to make an effort to deal with the differences between them, which remain wide. The have also been able to work out measures for cooperation in cultural and other field's".[36]

In this round, on the boundary question, an attempt was initiated by the two sides to evolve a mutually agreed set of principles to serve as guidelines for future discussions.[37]

The two delegations had a serious exchange of opinions in order to seek common ground. The Chinese delegation put forward a draft containing points common to each country's approach to the boundary issue. Both countries, the draft read, agree on: Adherence to the Five Principles of Peaceful coexistence; the desire for an early settlement through consultations in a spirit of friendship and equality; the need to consider the history, existing conditions and national sentiments of each country; and the maintenance of peace on the border before a settlement is reached. As for India's approach to resolve border issue from sector to sector basis, a Chinese official stated, "it is in favour of a comprehensive settlement, but does not oppose separate discussions on the east, middle and west sectors of the boundary if this may lead to an overall settlement". On how far geographical features like watersheds, river valleys and mountain passes were to be taken into account, the two sides presented different formulations which could not be reconciled during the talks. As a result, final agreement could not be reached on this set of guidelines. A new element introduced in the fourth round of talks related to a general exchange of views on the international situation, which proved to be a useful exercise towards improving mutual understanding.[38] As the Minister of External Affairs, Shri P.V. Narasimha Rao stated in Parliament:

> On the boundary question, detailed discussions were held an attempt was made to evolve a mutually acceptable set of principles to serve as guidelines for future discussions. While some common ground was covered, differences on certain vital aspects remained which would be taken up in the next round of talks. On cooperation and exchanges in other aspects of bilateral relations, the ground was prepared for these contacts during 1984. The exchange of views on the current world situation was a useful exercise resulting in a better understanding of each other's perception of the international situation today".[39]

Undoubtedly, links between the two nations were picking up showing and a more accommodative approach towards each others point of view. But so far as the border issue was concerned, there was no progress.

The fifth round of talks followed in Beijing from 17 to 22 September, 1984. The Chinese delegation was headed by Gong Dafei, adviser to the Foreign Ministry and the Indian delegation by Secretary of External Affairs Ministry K. Natwar Singh. In this round it was reported that differences had been narrowed.[40] What exactly this amounted to was not clear. There was a discernible attempt to find words and phrases more acceptable to both. Chinese vice premier, Wan Li expressed his hope that before agreement was reached on the boundary question, China and India would continue to ensure the tranquility and peace on the border of the two countries. He said the fifth round of talks progressed quite well and the two sides had reached agreement on several issues". It did not matter that there were still some differences existing between the two countries", he said, adding that they could be resolved later.[41]

Later, the Minister of State for External Affairs, Khurshid Alam Khan informed the Parliament that On the boundary question, both sides had directed their efforts at evolving a set of common principles that could serve as a basis for reaching an understanding on a final settlement. Differences on certain aspects had been narrowed down and both sides had agreed to commence substantive discussions on the boundary question during the next round of official level talks.[42]

The assassination of Prime Minister Mrs. Indira Gandhi on 31 October, 1984 "Shocked" China.[43] The Chinese Premier Zhao Ziyang paid tribute to Mrs. Gandhi for her efforts to improve Sino-Indian relations. He further stated: "We hope that the two sides will make efforts to keep this momentum going and try to restore the friendly relationship to the level of the 1950s".[44] Prime Minister, Rajiv Gandhi received Vice-Premier, Yaoyiling on 4 November and reiterated that his government would continue to folow past policies. He also accepted Zhao Ziyang's invitation to visit China.[45]

Due to efforts from both sides, the process of normalisation of India-China relations was not halted by a change of India's political leadership. In his annual address to the Parliament on 17 January, 1985, the President Stated: "Our relations with China have shown improvement. We shall preserve in seeking a solution to the boundary question".[46]

On the eve of the 35th anniversary of the establishment of diplomatic relations, Premier Zhao Ziyang in a message to his Indian counterpart said: "India was one of the first countries to establish diplomatic relations with the PRC. I am pleased to note that in recent years marked progress has been made in the relations between our two countries, thanks to our joint efforts."[47] Rajiv Gandhi in his message noted that India and China were both developing countries with large populations and great future potential. In the "immense tasks" before them, there were many areas in which they could cooperate to their mutual benefit. They could resolve the outstanding problems on the basis of Panchsheel through their joint efforts.[48] In June 1985, China proposed that both sides should reciprocally reopen consulates in Lhasa, Shanghai, Bombay and Calcutta, which had been closed since 1961 and resume the long suspended Sino-Indian border trade.[49]

Prime Minister Rajiv Gandhi was on his part, also keenly interested in speeding up the process of normalisation of ties with China. His first meeting with the Chinese Premier. Zhao Ziyang was in New York in

October, 1985 where both had gone to participate in the 40th anniversary meeting of the United Nations.[50] Both agreed to resolve the border problem. Zhao stated that the border question was a legacy of history, but Mr. Gandhi interjected by stating that it was a key point in their relationship. Both the Premiers agreed that there was need to push forward the efforts to find a solution and to promote friendship between the two countries. Zhao reiterated his country's invitation to Rajiv Gandhi to visit China. Premier Gandhi welcomed the suggestion but stated that such a meeting could be fruitful only if solid preparatory work preceded it.[51]

The sixth round of talks was held n New Delhi from 4 to 11 November, 1985. In this round, both sides adopted a sector by sector approach and explained their respective positions on the Eastern sector of the India-China boundary[52] The two countries stated their views on the substantive issues relating to the eastern sector of the disputed border and decided to discuss in detail, those related to the middle and western sectors in the next round. Further, the Chinese also put forward their long standing claim that the traditional boundary line to the east ran well south of the McMahon Line, that is, the Himalayan crest. Thus, far from the expected break through, China introduced a new element by demanding territorial concessions by India in the eastern sector.[53] The Chinese sources stated: "Both sides had substantive discussions on the boundary and elaborated their respective position on the issue. They agreed that the discussions were useful and conducive to seeking a solution to the boundary".[54] The two sides removed an irritant in bilateral relations by resolving the issue of Indian embassy's property in Beijing seized by the Chinese in 1967. The issue of compensation was also sorted out.

Later informing the Parliament on discussion at sixth round of official level talks, the Foreign Minister, B.R. Bhagat stated:

> The Indian and Chinese delegations held substantive discussion on the India-China boundary questions. Adopting a sector-by-sector approach, both sides clarified their respective positions on the Eastern Sector of the boundary. It was agreed that substantive discussions on the boundary would be continued in subsequent rounds with a view to reaching an early and comprehensive solution covering all sectors of the boundary".[55]

Some five or four days before the seventh round of talks was to open, the news of Chinese intrusion in Arunachal

> Pradesh was published in newspapers. On 18 July, 1986 the Minister of External Affairs, Shri P. Shiv Shankar informed the Parliament: "Honble members are by now aware of the Chinese intrusion in the Sumdorong Chu valley area of Tawang district of Arunachal Pradesh. After verification of the intrusion, we protested strongly to the Chinese government on 26th June, 1936. We stressed that the area of the Sumdorong Chu Valley is clearly south of the McMahon Line and well within Indian territory. We rejected the Chinese response received on 8 July, 1986 that this was a disputed area and on their side of the McMahon line. The McMahon Line constitutes the international boundary in this sector. The Chinese have conveyed that the matter could be discussed 'intensively' at the forthcoming Seventh Round of official level talks in Beijing. We propose to do so".[56]

The seventh round of talks was held from 21 to 23 July, 1986 in Beijing. According to available information, the location of the area in dispute was discussed intensively, but without any resolution of the problem.[57] India's deep concern over the Chinese intrusion in the Sumdorong Chu Valley area of the Tawang district of Arunachal Pradesh was conveyed to the Chinese Side during the talks. India stressed that the Chinese Side should do nothing to aggravate matters and disturb the status quo.[58] The Minister of State of External affairs, Shri K.R. Narayanan, later told the Parliament that:

> At the seventh round of official level talks substantive discussions were continued on the Eastern Sector of the India-China boundary. Thereafter, discussions commenced on the western sector. The Chinese side reiterated that the eastern sector was the area of 'largest depute'. In response, the Indian side clearly enunciated its well known stand that the India-China boundary in the Eastern Sector is the traditional customary line, which has received the additional sanction of treaty and administrative jurisdiction.[59]

Meanwhile, in December 1986, the Indian Parliament approved a bill that conferred full statehood to Arunachal Pradesh.[60] From the Indian standpoint this was only the logical conclusion of a process begun by the British Frontier Agency (NEFA) was made the Union Territory of Arunachal Pradesh in 1971. China, however, saw it as a possible legal erosion of its claim in the eastern sector and accused India of 'deliberately' creating obstacles China lodged a strong protest against this act of India.[61] India, on its part, accused China of interfering in India's internal affairs and reiterated Indian sovereignty over Arunachal Pradesh.

The reports of military exercises in both the eastern and western sectors and of the visit of senior generals to Arunachal Pradesh only heightened tension between the two countries. General K. Sunderjee, the Army Chief organised operation Chequer Board (October 1986-mid March 1987) on the China border under which more than ten army divisions and the air force were involved.[62] The troops fanned out all along the border and took positions. The Chinese reacted by taking positions in dangerous proximity to the Indians. Further China augmented its military presence in eastern Tibet. Almost all the ingredients of a major showdown were fast assembling. In fact, speculation about a second border war between India and China became common place and quite alarming.[63]

However, contrary to what was predicted in some quarters the military conflict did not materialise. The explanation lay partly in the fact that the overt display of military power had effectively neutralised any adventurist step. More important was the fact that hostile intent was conspicuously missing from the high tension that prevailed. Both governments tried to play down the crisis generated by military reinforcements on the borders. In April 1987, a scheduled transit halt of the Defence Minister, K.C. Pant at Beijing was utilised to convey India's manifest desire for peace. Later in June, Indian External Affairs Minister, N.D. Tiwari made a point of stopping in Beijing on his way back to New Delhi from a Non Aligned nations meeting in Pyongyang. The objective of Tiwari's brief talks was officially declared as: "to convey the desire at the political level that we want an improvement of all round relations, that we are determined to seek solutions to the boundary question peacefully through negotiations and that pending the solution, both sides, should do every thing to maintain peace and tranquility".[64]

The events of 1986 and 1987 a new determination to go in for fresh initiative to push forward process of India-China normalisation. India's Minister of External Affairs, Shri N.D. Tiwari stated in the Lok Sabha that it was necessary for both sides to find a solution to the problems peaceful negotiations, consultations and in a manner that ensures the maintenance of peace and tranquility all along the boundary.[65] Prime Minister Rajiv Gandhi stated on 3 March, 1987 in Parliament:

> There has been tension on our border with China. We want a peaceful settlement of the border issue. It will need wisdom and statesmanship. It will need vision and firmness.

> Firmness is included in wisdom . . . It is this perspective that should guide our two countries in seeking a solution to the problem.[66]

Thus Rajiv Gandhi hinted of a new approach in India's policy of improving relations with China.

Rajiv Gandhi's new approach to China was part of the general trend of transition in world politics from hostility and confrontation to détente and dialogue. With the thaw in Sino-Soviet relations, the Soviet leader Gorbachev, who initiated Perestroika and Glasnost in Soviet Union; emphasised China's role in Asian and world affairs and encouraged India's efforts to improve Sino-Indian relations[67]. The cumulative effect of the change in the international and regional climate on India-China relations was distinctly positive.

Subsequently, the eighth round of talks was held from 16 to 18 November, 1987 in New Delhi. The Chinese stated that a fair and reasonable settlement of the border issue could be achieved through friendly consultation and in a spirit of mutual under standing and mutual accommodation. India stressed that time was needed to find a settlement of the border issue due to its complexity.

The New Delhi talks put a formal seal on the general understanding that a political initiative was being seriously considered. There was a growing awareness within the country about the pointlessness of clinging to outmoded positions in the conduct of negotiations which had proved to be sterile in terms of concrete results. There was a general feeling that "it is not the border talks that have to be taken to a higher political level. It is meeting at the highest political level that would lead in time to progress in border talks".[68]

By 1988, Rajiv Gandhi enunciated a new approach in India's policy towards China and replying to a debate in the Lok Sabha, he stated on 20 April:

> With China we have been endeavouring to improve our relations. We are building a climate of trust, looking for a new and productive phase in our relationships. We recognise that the process of normalisation is complex. The border question needs peaceful negotiations. It needs mutually acceptable outcomes and we need to keep in mind the national sentiments in both countries. The maintenance of peace and tranquillity on our borders becomes vital while we talk of long term settlement we are strengthening cooperation in many fields with China. We are glad that the efforts to normalise have been welcomed by all sections of the House. We have accepted in principle that I should visit China on their invitation[69]

The Chinese leadership responded with enthusiasm by early 1988 to the proposal for a visit by the Indian Prime Minister. Talking to the India External Affairs Minister, P.V. Narasimha Rao in New York on 4 October, 1988, his Chinese counterpart, Wu Xueqian told him that Rajiv Gandhi's visit would prove to be turning point in the relations between the two countries.[70]

Later, the Minister of External Affairs, P.V. Narasimha Rao stated in the Parliament in November 1988 :

> The dialogue is an ongoing one pending a lasting peaceful and mutually acceptable solution of the boundary question, it has been agreed that peace and tranquility should be maintained all along the border. Further talks will be held when the Prime Minister visits China."[71]

III

The state visit of Prime Minister Rajiv Gandhi to China in December, 1988 was a definite step towards speeding up the sluggish process of normalisation. Premier Gandhi visited China from 19th to 23rd December, and this was the first visit to China by an Indian Prime Minister in 34 years. Gandhi set the tone by declaring: "it is now time to look to the future, I have come to renew an old friendship".[72] Deng Xiaoping, the top Chinese leader said that "China and India should forget the unpleasant past and set their eyes on the future."[73] Premier LiPeng was Rajiv Gandhi's major interlocutor during the visit, and their discussions focussed on the substantive issue of the border , Tibet, bilateral relations and international situation. Premier Li accepted Gandhi's invitation to pay a return visit to India.

During the visit the two sides had "in-depth discussions" on the Sino-Indian boundary question and agreed to settle it through peaceful and friendly consultations. In his banquet speech, the Chinese Premier, Li Peng dealt with the boundary question by restating the known Chinese position of seeking "a fair and reasonable settlement in a spirity of mutual understanding and mutual accommodation".[74] In reply, the Indian Prime Minister observed that the boundary question needed an enduring solution based on an understanding of each other's point of view which would be in their mutual interest and to the benefit of both peoples.

On 22 December, India and China decided to set up a Joint Working Group (JWG) on the boundary issue headed by the Foreign Secretary on the Indian side and a Vice Minister of Foreign Affairs on the Chinese side. The Joint Working Group was a step forward from that of official level in that it had joint mandate. Further, the JWG was expected to include military personnel and other experts, who were to be directed by political leadership. The Joint Working Group had two important functions. First, to make concrete recommendations for the overall solution of the boundary question. Secondly, the group would ensure that peace and tranquility was maintained in the Line of Actual Control.[75]

The two sides also agreed to develop relations in other fields and to set up a joint group on economic relations and trade, as well as science and technology. The two countries signed three accords on cultural scientific and technological cooperation as well as civil aviation.[76]

But the real gains of Rajiv Gandhi's visit were perhaps more in the intangible category. The long handshake with Deng Xiaoping reflected the intangible new spirit that Rajiv and Deng were trying to infuse into the India-China relationship. As a result, there was a major push forward in the process of India – China normalisation. As Deng told Gandhi that "starting from his visit, China and India will restore friendship between the two countries, peoples and leaders.[77] Rajiv Gandhi himself assessed his visit as a turning point in mutual relations. He admitted that differences still remained but India would like to broaden areas of common interest.

In his annual Address to the Parliament 21 February, 1989 the President stated:

> "With the Prime Minister's recent visit to China, we have embarked on a new and positive phase in our relations with that country. The cordial and constructive discussion held with Chinese leaders have opened the way for a stable, peaceful and mutually beneficial relationship between the two countries. This is a development of great significance for regional and world peace as India and China, together, represent a third of humanity."[78]

While India-China relations looked forward to the future, China's internal situation received a big jolt from the student uprising against the communist leadership. In May-June, 1989 China witnessed outbreak of protest against the anti-democratic nature of the communist regime in Beijing and other important cities. The Government of India declared that it was entirely an internal matter of China. In July 1989, Ghulam Nabi Azad, General secretary of Congress Party met with Jiang Zemin, General Secretary of the Chinese Communist Party. Jiang said he appreciated the Indian government and Congress's attitude of non-interference in China's putting down of the counter revolutionary rebellion.[79]'

The first meeting of the Joint working group was held at Beijing from 30 June to 4 July, 1989 and both sides exchanged views on the improvement of bilateral relations and regional as well international issues of common interest.[80]

Both sides held that while seeking the solution to the boundary issue, the two countries should strive to promote bilateral ties in other fields and to maintain peace and stability in the zones on both sides of the Actual Line of Control.[81] On 8 July, it was announced that India and China had agreed to undertake confidence building exercise and push the process of normalisation of relations between the two countries.[82]

With a view to keep up the momentum generated by the high level political contacts, Chinese Vice Premier, Wu Xueqian came to New Delhi on 11 October, 1989. He held extensive talks with External Affairs Minister, P.V. Narasimha Rao and Prime Minister, Rajiv Gandhi. As Wu stated :

> We can not only strengthen our cooperation and make up for each other's deficiencies in many areas, including economy, science, technology, culture and education, but also enhance, our consultations on the North-South dialogue, South-South cooperation, and number of other international issues- - - - as long as the two sides conduct friendly consultations in a spirit of mutual understanding and mutual accommodation, a mutually acceptable solution can be found.[83]

In his annual address to the Parliament on 12 March, 1990 the President stated :

> The pace of diplomatic exchanges is being accelerated, contributing to the development of mutually beneficial cooperation on the basis of Panchsheel. The foreign Minister of China will be visiting India soon to carry forward the dialogue. We will continue our efforts to find a fair, reasonable and mutually acceptable settlement of the boundary question, consistent with our national interests".[84]

The Chinese Foreign Minister, Qian Qichen visited India in March, 1990.[85] Qian's visit coincided with the 40th anniversary of the establishment of diplomatic relations between China and India. In his talks with his Indian counterpart, I. K. Gujral, Qian agreed that the development of bilateral relations in other fields would create a favourable climate and conditions for a fair and reasonable settlement of the boundary question.[86] The most important point made by Qian on 23 March related to Kashmir. He emphasised the need for a peaceful solution to the Kashmir problem through mutual consultations between India and Pakistan. He hinted that China was against the internationalisation of the Kashmir issue.

Speaking in the Parliament on 9th April, Shri I.K. Gujral said:

> In the broader context, the visit of the Chinese foreign minister last month resulted in a better understanding of the perceptions of both sides on matters of international and regional concern. This was important because both of us face similar problem as continental societies.. Exchange of views and better understanding are themselves of no mean value. In terms of our immediate bilateral interest, I must add that the desire to continue to process of improvement of relations was reiterated by both sides during the visit".[87]

The Joint Working Group held its second meeting on 31 August-1September, 1990 in New Delhi. Both sides agreed on a mechanism under which their military personnel would meet from time to time at an appropriate level to maintain peace in the border areas. At the end of the two days discussions the delegations led by the Chinese vice foreign minister, Qi Huaiyan and the Indian Foreign Secretary, Muchkund Dubey, expressed the hope that by working in a "sincere and forward looking manner it would be possible to establish a basis for settlement of the boundary question as well as for maintaining tranquility in the border areas.[88] The two sides also discussed ways of further improving the bilateral relations and exchanged views on regional and international issues. They noted with satisfaction the growing interaction between the two countries in various fields, including exchanges at the political level.[89]

The nineties unfolded with profound transformation in international politics. Amidst the rapid changing world scenario, both India and China desired a stable relation to face uncertain and ever changing pattern of international politics. The combined effect of international circumstances, regional politics and domestic compulsion, pushed India and China on a closer and irreversible path of rapprochment.

On 21 February, 1991 the President addressed the joint session of the Parliament and stated:

> We have continued the process of seeking a better understanding with China. Our bilateral cooperation has grown and we have also begun to consult each other more closely on international issues. Negotiations in the Joint working group are continuing with a view to resolving the boundary questions in a fair, reasonable and mutually

> acceptable manner. We believe that closer cooperation between India and China will be in the interest of peace and stability in Asia and the world.[90]

The third meeting of the Joint Working Group was held in May 1991 at Beijing. The two sides exchanged views on maintaining peace and tranquility along the border under actual Line of Control.[91]

Later in September, 1991 the Defence Minister, Sharad Pawar stated in the the Parliament:

> There is no tension on our borders with China. In the recent years, China has not taken any such step which can create anxiety or doubt in our minds. Therefore, we will try to develop good relations with China also to ensure mutual development. As far as China is concerned, there is certainly peace on the border and efforts are being made to improve our relations with China".[92]

Chinese Premier, Li Peng paid an official visit to India from 11 December to 16 December, 1991 and it was the first visit to India by a Chinese Prime Minister in 31 years.[93] During the visit, the two governments signed three agreements, i.e., resumption of border trade reopening of consulates in Bombay and Shanghai, and cooperation in peaceful applications of outer space sciences and technology.[94] The two Premiers agreed to give political directions to the Joint-working group in order to facilitate in resolving the border issue. Further, India used this opportunity to convey to China its concern at 'external inputs' to Pakistan's nuclear weapons capacity and missile technology. The Chinese side expressed concern about the continued activities in India by some Tibetans against their motherland and reiterated that Tibet was an inalienable part of Chinese territory. The Indian side reiterated its long standing and consistent position that Tibet was an autonomous region of China and that it did not allow Tibetans to engage in anti-China political activities in India. The two sides positively appraised their cooperation in the fields of trade, culture, science and technology. It was also agreed to hold a cultural festival of India in China and a cultural festival of China in India. The two sides believed that dialogue and exchange of visits between the leaders of the two countries were of major importance to greater mutual understanding and further development of bilateral friendship and cooperation in all fields.[95]

The leaders of the two countries reiterated that efforts would be made to arrive at an early and mutually acceptable solution to the boundary question through friendly consultations. Both sides believed that the talks held so far by the Sino-Indian Joint Working Group on the boundary question had enhanced mutual understanding and agreed that the group should step up its work in search of an earliest possible solution to the boundary questions. It was decided that the next meeting of the joint working group would be held in New Delhi in early 1992 on a mutually convenient date. The two sides agreed to maintain peace and tranquility in the area along the line of actual control pending a final settlement of the boundary question. The also agreed that the periodic meetings between the military personnel in the border areas should be held on a regular basis.[96]

On 20 December, 1991, Prime Minister Narasimha Rao gave a long statement in Lok Sabha, on the visit of Prime Minister of People's Republic of China and stated: "That the visit gained added significance because it had taken place in the context of the ongoing rapid changes in international relations involving a fundamental transformation. He added :

> In our discussions on the international situation. Premier Li Peng and I agreed that the five principles of peaceful coexistence, jointly initiated by India and China in 1954, were essential norms for the conduct of international relations and that all countries, regardless of their size, strength or stage of development, were equal members of the international community. It was our common position that the use of force or threat of force as a means of settlement of disputes should be firmly abjured in international relations. On the outstanding question of the boundary between our two countries, both the Chinese Premier and I were agreed that efforts should be intensified to find an early, fair, reasonable and mutually acceptable solution to this question. We expressed our satisfaction that peace and tranquility had been maintained in the border areas. A number of bilateral agreements have been signed during the visit.. We have agreed to intensify our cooperation in such fields as agriculture, public health, energy and education.. On the issue of Tibet, our long standing and consistent position was clearly reiterated. Tibet is an autonomous region of China and we do not allow Tibetans to engage in anti-China political activities in India. Our respect for His Holiness the Dalai Lama as a religious and spiritual leader remains constant. The approach to such questions should be consensus oriented through political dialogue. The Chinese Prime Minister indicated that all issues except that of the independence of Tibet are open to negotiation with His Holiness the Dalai Lama.[97]

India also conveyed to the Chinese side its concerns about the supply of sophisticated arms and defence technologies to Pakistan and Pakistan's role in fomenting terrorism and subversion in the states of Punjab and Jammu and Kashmir. Narashimha Rao Stated:

> The Chinese Government is opposed to terrorism since it does not solve problems and only sharpens existing contradictions. They have said they do not wish to see conflict and are for the peaceful settlement of differences between India and Pakistan. Our concerns about Chinese arms supplies to Myanmar have also been conveyed.
>
> The issue of human rights figured in our dialogue. I stressed our adherence to the concepts of the indivisibility of all human rights. At the same time, I expressed the view that no country should be denied assistance in the name of human rights. Norms for human rights cannot be determined unilaterally and externally. Primacy should be given to the task of development. The Chinese Premier was of the opinion that the issue of human rights should not be used as a lever for internal in the international affairs of countries.[98]

Commenting on the need for friendship between India and China, the Indian Prime minister reiterated :

China is our biggest neighbour and we are drawn to it both by geographical inevitability and by the tradition of historical interaction. We look forward to the future of our relations with China. Our dialogue must strengthen mutual understanding and enable the peaceful resolution of all outstanding issues. I believe the visit of the Chinese Premier has been an important step in that direction... The approach to this visit was to discuss the border on the one hand and, at the same time, cooperation in other areas of mutual interest there are two categories; one bilateral and the second, in the international field in the common interest of human kind. India and China, as two ancient Civilisations, can do no less. It is their duty to the world. I fervently believe it. This international aspect has always been important and will always be so. But at the present juncture, when the world is in the throes of unprecedented changes I think this particular duty to mankind is also urgent. It brooks no delay. I believe that the future of a vast chunk of humanity, living in developing countries and groaning under Conditions of poverty and want, is at Stake now as perhaps never before. India and China owe this duty to this vast chunk of humanity.[99]

The Prime Minister further stated on the developments on the issue of the border:

> Both the Chinese Premier and I were agreed that efforts should be intensified to find an early, fair, reasonable and mutually acceptable solution to this question. We expressed our satisfaction that peace and tranquility had been maintained in the border areas. We stressed that our differences on the boundary question should be reduced and that we should maintain our contacts with each other in order to provide directions to the Joint Working Group that was set up to deal with this question in 1988... meetings between the military personnel will be held on a regular basis. This was not the case in 1988. Now, these meetings will be held on a regular basis thus making it much easier and much more certain that there will be no breach of peace by any mistake or misunderstanding on the borders".[100]

It was thus clear both sides had taken positive steps to move forward toward the solution of the India-China boundary dispute India had suggested a step-by-step approach to resolve the boundary question. The first step was the stabilisation of the situation on the Line of Actual Control and to delineate it more precisely in those sectors where differences of opinion existed between India and China. The second step was to come to a mutual agreement to maintain peace and tranquility on the Line of Actual Control. The third step was to put in place expanding mutual confidence-building measures which would create an atmosphere of normalcy and peace on the Line of Actual Control, after which both sides could proceed to address the substance of the Sino-Indian boundary question. This approach was mutually agreed upon[101] .

India and China were seriously and sincerely engaged in confidence building measures as far as solving vexed border question was concerned. Undoubtedly the border problem was the key to full normalisation of relationship between India and China. In fact, the events of 1986-87 particularly the Sumdorong Chu Valley incident and subsequent military build up showed how much sensitive and crucial issue border was for normal relationship of India and China. Indeed, it was due to matured handling of this issue by leaders of both sides that things were not allowed to deteriorate and process of rapprochement continued. Admittedly, the process was a slow one, with its phases of ups and downs, but it is important to note that important differences on border issue had not been allowed to cast their shadow on overall progress of rapprochement between India and China.

Considering the sensitivity and complexity of the issue, both sides were following a cautious and step-by-step approach to amicably resolve the border issue.

IV

Economic and trade ties constitute an important aspect in the bilateral relations between India and China. Economic and trade ties between India and China were resumed on an adhoc basis in 1977 after a break of almost fifteen years. Thereafter, the two countries not only reestablished trade but also shipping and banking links at modest levels. Increased economic and technological exchanges improved the general tenor of the bilateral relations. Both India and China, the world's two most populous countries, with vast territories and a variety of natural resources were working hard to eliminate poverty and raising the standard of living of the teeming millions. Thus with their common concern for development, there emerged a new vista for economic interaction. By cooperating in the economic sphere, they could learn from each other's experiences that would not only prove beneficial for the programmes of economic modernisation of both the countries, but would also promote mutual understanding and the development of friendly relations.

To go into the brief history of Sino-Indian trade ties, it is worth recalling that to a large extent, Sino-Indian economic relations have been governed by their political relations throughout history. The brief flowering of friendship during fifties exhibited the initial buoyancy in bilateral trade. The balance of trade was in favour of China. The signing of a trade agreement for eight years in 1954 was a watershed in the bilateral economic relations. As a result of the agreement, (a) bilateral trade agencies were established; (b) payments were effected in rupees or pound sterling; (c) as many as six transit points were specified. The agreement ran upto 1962 and then it was not renewed because of tense relations between the two countries.[102] With the deepening strains in political ties, Sino-Indian trade suffered a setback. The turnover dipped after reaching a peak of nearly Rs.12.7 million in 1959 to Rs. 1.13 million in 1962 and then tapered off to less than Rs.1 million in the next two year, before snapping totally for about a decade and a half, reflecting the then deteriorating political relations between India and China.

With the restoration of full diplomatic relations in 1976, the second phase of Sino-Indian economic relations began. Initially, the main items of export from India were cotton, crude-vegetable materials, iron ore, sugar, barley and tabacco manufactures. While silk, chemicals and compounds, zinc, non-ferrous metals, machinery and transport equipment were principal importing items. The number of products traded between the two countries were few. And it did not add up to even 300 items at the 8 digit standard International Trade Classification (SITC) of over 8,000 items.[103] Apart from this fact, total trade turnover was Rs. 105.61 crores. In 1981-82 the deficit was Rs. 25-58 crores, out of the total trade turnover of Rs. 130.94

cores. Considering the size of the economies of these two big countries, their trade turnover has been insignificant. India's share in China's total trade was 0.4 per cent, while China's share in India's total trade was 0.6 per cent.[104] This can be seen from the table below:

Table 1

Year	*India's exports to China*	*India's imports from China*	*In Rs Total*	*Crores Balance of Trade*
1977-78	1.93	0.63	2.56	1.30
1978-79	24.25	1.71	25.52	23.08
1979-80	20.83	18.91	39.74	1.92
1980-81	23.63	81.98	105.61	-58.35
1981-82	52.68	78.26	130.94	-25.58
1982-83	12.16	105.20	117.18	-92.85
1983-84	5.72	76.79	81.51	-70.07
1984-85	2.12	66.55	68.67	-64.63
1985-86	29.20	141.96	171.16	-112.76
1986-87	14.33	173.34	187.67	-159.00
1987-88	33.73	159.31	193.04	-125.58
1988-89	64.40	132.40	196.80	-68.00

Source: Sino-Indian Trade, Sreedhar (Unpublished Article) in Proceedings of the Seminar on Search for A China Policy, Organised by School of International Studies, JNU (New Delhi, 1988).

The exchange of views over the years enabled both the countries to identify products for exports and joint venture collaboration.[105] Following are some of the important items which have export potential from India: superior grade white leaf tobacco, raw sugar, coffee, wheat, maize, raw cashew nuts, Short and medium staple Cotton, Chromeore, ironware, organic dye stuffs and natural indigo pigments, Paints and Varnishes, Shellac, Railway vehicles, trucks and buses, ships and boats, scooters and mopeds, internal combustion engines, agricultural machinery and Tractors. Among the important potential items for import from China were: Petroleum cooking gas, nitrogen fertilizers, newsprint, vegetable oil, raw silk, ferronickel, aluminum, copper, zinc, lead, mercury antimony, paraffineax, borax and fluorspar. These were some of the products identified at the broader levels of classification.

> Since the resumption of bilateral trade not only were trade delegations exchanged, but there were also regular official talks at the governmental level to expand economic relations between the two countries since 1981. Infact, in the very

> first round of official talks in December 1981 five sub groups were formed to deal with matters concerning boundary, trade and economic cooperation, cultural exchanges and science and technology.[106] Thereby emphasis was sought to be given to increase economic cooperation between India and China. As Minister of External Affairs, Narasimha Rao stated in Parliament in February 1982:

Since the resumption of trade with China in 1977, a number of delegations have been exchanged between the two sides. From the Indian side, HMT, FICCI, MMTC, STC and others including individual businessmen have been sending delegations for discussions. Bilateral trade was also included in discussions between the officials of both sides in Beijing in December. Efforts are underway to increase the volume and diversify the composition of trade. The question of an agreement is not at present under consideration".[107]

In the second round of talks in 1982, the two sides decided to step up economic cooperation. Bilateral trade was also revived during the talks and it was found that the present turnover of $100 million worth of goods exchanged between the two countries was not enough.[108] During the third round of talks in 1983, both sides reviewed the development of bilateral trade and expressed their satisfaction at the steady, though modest growth registered in the past two years. Certain new areas were proposed for economic cooperation which would be explored by both sides.

In the fourth round of talks held in 1983, India and China also agreed to explore ways to step up their trade. In course of the talks India's capabilities in the export of transport equipment, railway equipment, mining transport, ball bearings, wire ropes, dairy plant and thermal power plants were brought to the notice of the Chinese delegation. The Chinese showed interest in import of tanning equipment and technology from India and also in the import of light building materials for high rise buildings. The Chinese side indicated that they have a programme for modernisation of about 3000 industries which could open new opportunities for export of engineering goods to China.[109] Despite the increase in bilateral trade during the preceding few years, both sides felt that the annual trade between the two countries was rather modest. The Indian team stressed that the current balance of trade was against India and to rectify it, China should import some goods from India.

On 15 August, 1984 India and China concluded after thirty years, a new trade agreement to accord each other's commerce the most favoured nation treatment and to boost their bilateral trade. The agreement provided a framework for commerce between the two countries which resumed on adhoc basis in 1977 after a 15 year break caused by the 1962 India-China War. To be automatically renewed after every three years, the agreement required the two countries to give each other's traders the best of terms in respect of customs, duties, taxes and other charges and import-export formalities.[110]

During the fifth round of talks in 1984, Chinese Vice Premier, Wan Lin Sought further strengthening and development of bilateral cooperation in the fields of economy, technology and culture. On 2 March, 1985 an agreement to promote and develop economic and trade relations between the Federation of Indian Chambers of Commerce and Industry (FICCI) and the China Council for Promotion of International Trade (CCPIT) was signed.[111] The two sides also identified specific commodities for import and export. Later, on the invitation of Commerce Ministry, the Chinese Minister of Metallurgical Industry, Li Dongye visited India in August 1985 to explore possibilities of importing certain mineral ores particularly iron ore from India.[112] The Minister of Commerce, Arjun Singh, informed the Parliament that under the Agreement, FICCI and CCPIT had agreed to exchange and distribute information and materials concerning new products, new technologies and new processes in production in their respective countries. The main provisions were: i) to help each other in mutual cooperation in promotion of consultacy services and joint ventures and ii) to assist each other in holding economic and trade exhibitions and specialised fairs in each other's country.[113]

India and China signed a trade protocol on 23rd November, 1985. The protocol provided for exchange of goods of total value of about U.S $ 100-160 million during the 1986. It was to be operative with effect from 1st January 1986.[114] In the beginning, India had a favourable balance of trade with China during 1977-78 and 1978-79. Thereafter, the balance shifted heavily in favour of China. During 1984-85, India's exports to China were only Rs. 2.12 crores as against imports from China worth Rs. 66-55 Crores. The imbalance was expected to be corrected as a result of the fresh protocol. The seventh round of talks held in 1986, expressed satisfaction over the pace of economic cooperation between the two countries.

May 27, 1987 India and China signed in Beijing a second trade protocol envisaging a total trade volume of between $ 150 million and $ 200 million between January 1987 to March 1988. The protocol called for a 35 per cent increase over $ 100-160 million target for 1986.[115] The two sides expressed satisfaction at the growth of trade between the two countries and noted the potential for further growth on a balanced basis.

Throughout the year 1988 efforts continued to be made by both sides to improve economic relations. At the opening of the Indian-China chamber of commerce branch in Calcutta in March 1988, China's Commercial

Counsellor He Wei called for the use of barter, counter trade and counter investment in order to expand trade.[116] The annual bilateral trade protocol was signed in June 1988.[117] Unlike earlier agreements, the 1988 trade protocol set no upper limit on trade. With a view to strengthen economic cooperation between the two countries, a Chinese delegation from the Foreign Investment Administration of the Ministry of Foreign Economic Relations and Trade visited India in June 1988. The Chinese delegation tried to drum up Indian investment in Chinese industrial development and noted the prospects for economic and technological cooperation.[118] Around the same time a delegation from the Federation of Indian chambers of Commerce and Industries visited China to explore opportunities for trade. China decided to import in 1989, 250,000 tones of iron ore. It was 100,000 tones more than the quantity exported to China in 1988.[119] There was also mutual exploration of the possibility of joint ventures and exchanges in new areas.

The most concrete economic fall out of Prime Minister, Rajiv Gandhi's China visit in 1988, was the formation of an India-China Joint Working Group on Trade, Economic Relations and Science and Technology that held its first meeting in New Delhi on 18 September, 1989. Both sides stressed the vast potential for expanding bilateral trade and the need for promoting closer economic ties and cooperation in the areas of science and technology. Zheng Toubin Chinese Minister for Foreign Relations and Trade believed that there were bright prospects for bilateral economic relations. He noted the upward trend in trade but felt that the present level was far below the real potential. Dinesh Singh, Indian Commerce Minister, while expressing gratification at the setting up of the Joint Working Group that reflected the resolve of both sides to strengthen bilateral relations, noted with concern that India had an adverse balance of trade for the past five years and called for remedial measures.[120] The meetings of the Working Group on economic cooperation strengthened bilateral trade as is evident form the table below:

Table 2
Value of Trade Between India and China
(In Rs. million)

Year	*Export to China*	*Import from China*	*Total Trade*	*Balance of Trade*
1989-90	391	658	1049	-267
1990-91	327	556	883	-229
1991-92	1162	526	1688	+636

Source: Directorate General of Commercial Information and Statistics DGCIS, Government of India.

The second meeting of the India-China Joint Group on Economic Relations, Trade, Science and Technology was held at Beijing in February, 1991. The Indian commerce minister, S. Swamy visited China to participate in the meeting and signed a set of agreed minutes and a Sino-Indian trade protocol for outlining the mutual interests in the development of trade.[121] In December 1991, the two countries concluded an agreement to resume border trade after some three decades in a limited way. It was to be confined to one trading point in the middle sector of the India-China border. China was to establish a mart at Pulan in Tibet and India at Gunji in Pithoragarh district of Uttar Pradesh.[122]

By 1991, trade with China increased though it remained a small share of the total value of the external trades of India and China. A brief overview of history of bilateral trade ties shows that during the three years of 1981-83, the average per year value of India-China trade was 29 million US dollars. During the next three years of 1984-86, this annual trade average was 22.6 million US dollars. In the three years between mid 1989 to mid-1992 the annual average value was 42 million US dollars on about 35 percent more than the average for the early 1980s. However, compared to the overall trade value of the two countries, this constituted a very small share. Between September 1989 and September 1990, the value of China's foreign trade was 91,200 million US dollars. In that year the value of China's foreign trade was only 0.07% of the value of India's foreign trade.[123]

To sum up, Sino-Indian economic relations during the period under study moved in parallel with the state of their political relations. Despite all efforts being made to improve economic ties, it should not be overlooked that the trade was still virtually negligible. However, there was considerable potential for increasing bilateral trade.

Apart from economic cooperation, increasing efforts were made to strengthen bilateral relations in the field of science and technology and culture. Indeed, in the first round of official talks in December 1981 separate sub groups were also formed to deal with matters concerning science and technology and cultural exchanges.[124]

In the second round of talks in May1982, India and China decided to step up scientific and technological exchanges. It was decided that an oil delegation, a railway delegation and agricultural experts would be sent by India to China. In turn, China would send to India experts to study wheat breeding and dairy development. A delegation of Chinese scientists would also come to India.[125] During the fourth round of talks in 1983 the two sides felt the need to increase scientific and technological exchanges and thus it was agreed that the Indian delegation on biogas and minihydel power plants would be visiting China and a Chinese team would visit India to study shellac production. The two sides also discussed new proposals during a review of the ongoing programme of bilateral exchanges in science and technology. The new areas included agriculture and irrigation, electronics and communication systems, health, population control, drug research, mining and biotechnology.[126]

In the fifth round of talks in 1984, some areas were identified by the both sides in which they could offer technology to each other. The areas where India could offer technology to China included hotels, engineering goods, transport equipment, thermal power stations, pesticides, plastic and paper China could offer technology to India in biogas plants, mini steel and cement plants, medicine and rice cultivation.[127] During the sixth round of talks in 1985, the subgroup on science and technology decided to exchange delegations in computer industry, agriculture, plasma physics, laser technology and biotechnology.

In 1988 when Premier Rajiv Gandhi visited China, the two governments signed an agreement on intergovernmental cooperation in the sphere of science and technology. Further, the decision to establish a Joint Group on economic relations and trade and science and technology was a step forward in the bilateral cooperation in science and technology.[128] In March 1989 the Agriculture Minister of China. He Kang visited India and along with his Indian counterpart, expressed the common desire for exchange and cooperation in the field of agriculture. A memorandum on agricultural science and technology exchange and cooperation between China and India was signed. Items envisaged in the memorandum included delegation of exchanges, cooperative research, specialised visits and exchange of improved Corp seeds and breeding stocks of poultry, domestic animals and fish.[129] During the historic visit of Chinese Premier, Li Peng to India in December 1991 China and India concluded an agreement on cooperation in the field of outer space sciences. Both sides also agreed to intensify bilateral cooperation in such fields as agriculture, public health and energy.[130] These exchanges not only helped scientific and technological establishments but also pushed forward bilateral relations between India and China.

Thus, economic, scientific and technological exchanges contributed in large measure, in improving bilateral relations between India and China. During the period from 1976 to 1991, cooperation in economic, science and technology and cultural planes continued apace and pushed India-China rapprochement step forward.

To sum up therefore by the year 1991, India-China relations were on upswing. As a result of the summit level talks, India-China relations registered all round improvement. On the border issue, both sides agreed to ensure, peace and tranquility on the Line of Actual Control. Now, both sides were following step-by-step approach to resolve this sensitive issue. Further, to broaden bilateral relations, India and China moved forward to cooperate in the field of economic, science and technology and cultural arenas. As a result of all these developments, the process of India-China rapprochement stabilised firmly by the beginning of the nineties.

References

1. Robert Horn, "The Soviet Union and Sino-Indian Relations", in *Orbis*, (Philadelphia), XXIV, 4, Winter 1983, pp.900-901.
2. *Lok Sabha Debates,* Vol. 60, 1976 Col. 137.
3. *Ibid.*, Col.107.
4. *Ibid.*, Vol. 60, 1976, Col.104.
5. Quoted in Nancy Jetly, *India–China Relations 1947-1977 : A Study of Parliament's Role in the Making of Foreign Policy* (New Delhi,1979) p. 290.
6. *Beijing Review*, no. 42, 15 October 1976, p. 21.
7. *Ibid.*, no.15, 8 April 1977, p. 8.
8. *Beijing Review,* no.13, 31 March 1978, p. 5.
9. Quoted in V.P. Dutt, *India's Foreign Policy* (New Delhi, 1984), p.292.
10. See The Government of India, *Annual Report 1977-78*, Ministry of External Affairs (New Delhi), p. 5.
11. Nancy Jetly, "Sino-Indian Relations: A Quest for Normalisation", *India Quarterly* (New Delhi), 42 (1) Jan-Mar, 1986, p. 55.
12. *Beijing Review*, no. 8, 23 February, 1979, p. 4.
13. *Lok Sabha Debates*, Vol.22, 1979, Col. 247.
14. Summary of World Broadcasting (here after SWB) FE/6321/I, 17 January, 1980.
15. *Beijing Review*, no. 5, 4 February 1980, p. 4.
16. See for details, Harry Harding, *China's Second Revolution* (Washington, 1987).
17. *Far Eastern Economic Review* (Hong Kong), 4 July 1980, pp. 26-27.
18. Quoted in Nancy Jetly, n.11, p. 56.
19. SWB, FEE/6416/I, 10 May 1980.
20. *Annual Report 1981-82*, Ministry of External Affairs, p. 11.
21. *Beijing Review*, no. 28, 13 July 1981, p. 7.
22. Nancy Jetly, n. 11, p. 58.
23. Xinhua (Beijing) 17 October 1981.
24. Jerrold F. Elkin and B. Fredericks, "Sino-Indian Border Talks: The View from New Delhi", *Asian Survey* (Berkeley), Vol. XXIII, no. 10, October 1983, p.1132.
25. *India Today* (New Delhi), 31 January 1982, p. 100.

26. *India and Foreign Review* (New Delhi), XIX, 6, 1982, p. 4.
27. *Patriot* (New Delhi), 19 May 1982.
28. Elkin and Fredricks, n. 24, pp. 1133-34.
29. *Hindu* (Madras) 16 May 1982.
30. Elkin and Fredricks, n. 24, p. 1139.
31. *Foreign Affairs Record,* Ministry of External Affairs, (New Delhi), 1982, pp. 202-203.
32. *Lok Sabha Debates*, Vol. 24, 1982, Col. 11.
33. *Asian Recorder* (New Delhi), 1982, p. 16, 882
34. *National Herald* (New Delhi),13 February 1983.
35. *Ibid.,* 4 February 1983.
36. *Lok Sabha Debates*, Vol. 34, 1983, Col. 84.
37. *Annual Report 1983-84*, Ministry of External Affairs, p. v.
38. *China Daily*, n. 24 October 1983.
39. *Lok Sabha Debates*, Vol. 42, 1983, Col. 12.
40. *Indian Express* (New Delhi), 23 September, 1984.
41. *China Daily*, 24 September 1984.
42. *Lok Sabha Debates*, Vol. 7, 1985, Col. 143.
43. *China Daily* (Beijing) 1 November 1984.
44. *Ibid.,* 2 November 1984.
45. *Beijing Review*, no. 46, 12 November 1984, p. 11.
46. *Lok Sabha Debates*, nol. 1, 1985, Col. 7.
47. *China Daily*, 1 April1985.
48. Indian Express, 1 April 1985, 1985.
49. Nancy Jetly, n. 11, p. 59.
50. Quoted in Surjit Man Singh and Steven I Leveine, "China and India: Moving Beyond Confrontation", *Problems of Communism* (Washington), 38 (2-3), March-June 1989, p. 36.
51. *Hindu* (Madras) 25 October 1985.
52. *Annual Report 1985-86*, Ministry of External Affairs, p. 16.
53. *Hindu*, 11 November 1985.
54. *China Daily*, 13 November 1985.
55. Lok Sabha Debates, Vol. 10, 1985, Col. 34.
56. *Ibid.,* Vol.18, 1986, Cols. 377-78.
57. *Hindu*, 2 August 1986.
58. *Annual Report 1986-87*, Ministry of External Affairs, p. 16.
59. *Lok Sabha Debates*, Vol. 19, 1986, Col. 94.
60. *Hindu*, 10 December, 1986.
61. For full text of Chinese Statement See *Indian Express*, 13 December 1986.
62. Very little exists in the public domain about operation Chequer Board. The only book on the Subject is Ravi Rikhye's, *The War That Never Was* (New Delhi, 1989).
63. Neville Maxwell, *Towards India's Second China-War*, *South* (London) May 1987, pp. 80-83.
64. *Hindu*, 17 June, 1987.
65. *Lok Sabha Debates*, Vol. 27, 1987, Col. 296.
66. *Rajiv Gandhi Selected Speeches and Writings vol. III,* Publications Division Ministry of Information & Broadcasting (New Delhi, 1987), p. 360.
67. *Beijing Review*, no. 49, 5 December 1988, p. 12.

68. Mohit Sen, "India-China: New Possibilities", *Mainstream* (New Delhi) Vol. XXVI, no.18, 13 February 1988, p. 4.
69. *Rajiv Gandhi Selected Speeches and Writings*, Vol. IV, Publications Division (New Delhi, 1988), p. 311.
70. *Times of India* (New Delhi), 6 October 1988.
71. *Lok Sabha Debates* (New Delhi), Vol. 43, 1988, Col. 165.
72. *India Today* (New Delhi), 15 January 1989, pp. 22-29.
73. *China Daily*; 22 December 1988.
74. *Times of India*, 20 December 1988.
75. *Patriot*, 23 December 1988.
76. *Annual Report 1988-89*, Ministry of External Affairs, p. 17.
77. *China Daily*, 22 December, 1988.
78. *Lok Sabha Debates*, Vol. 49, 1989, Col. 14.
79. *Beijing Review*, no. 29, 17 July 1989, p. 7.
80. *China Daily*, 6 July 1989.
81. *Ibid.*
82. *Asian Recorder*, 1989, p. 20, 773.
83. *Asian Recorder*, 1989, p. 20939.
84. *Lok Sabha Debates*, Vol. 2, 1990, Col. 14.
85. *Annual Report 1990-91*, Ministry of External Affairs, p. 22.
86. *Asian Recorder*, 1990, p. 21, 126.
87. *Lok Sabha Debates*, Vol. 3, 1990, Col. 595.
88. *Annual Report 1990-91*, Ministry of External Affairs, p. 23.
89. *Indian Express*, 4 September 1990.
90. *Lok Sabha Debates*, Vol. 14, 1991, Col. 16.
91. *China Daily*, 15 May 1991.
92. *Lok Sabha Debates*, Vol.4, 1991, Col. 449.
93. *Beijing Review*, no.50, 16 December 1991, p. 4.
94. Mira Sinha Bhattacharjea, For a New future, in *Frontline* (Madras), 3 January, 1992, p. 14.
95. See the full text of Sino-Indian Joint Communique in *Beijing Review*, no.52, 30 December 1991, pp. 10-12.
96. *Beijing Review*, no. 52, 30 December 1991, p. 11.
97. *Lok Sabha Debates*, Vol. 7, 1991, Cols. 926-28.
98. *Ibid.*, Cols. 928-29
99. *Ibid.*, Col. 929.
100. *Ibid.*, Cols. 926-927
101. J.N. Dixit, *Across Borders: 50 years of India's Foreign Policy* (New Delhi, 1998), pp. 219-20.
102. R.K. Upadhyaya, "India-China:Rejuvenating Economic Ties". *Mainstream*, New Delhi, Vol. XXIX, no. 51, 12 October, 1991, p. 29.
103. Taranath Bhat, Sino-Indian Economic Relaltions: An overview, *China Report* (New Delhi), Vol.XX, No. 6, November-December 1984, p. 19.
104. R.K. Upadhyaya, n. 102, p. 30.
105. Taranath Bhat, no. 103, p. 21.
106. Nancy Jetly, n. 11, p. 58.
107. *Lok Sabha Debates*, vol. 24, 1982, Col. 122.
108. *Asian Recorder*, 1982, p. 16, 672.

109. *Annual Report 1983-84*, Ministry of Commerce, Government of India, p. 39.
110. *Annual Report 1984-85*, Ministry of Commerce, p. 40.
111. *Asian Recorder*, 1985, p. 18, 255.
112. *Ibid.*
113. *Lok Sabha Debates*, Vol. 10, 1985, Col. 187.
114. *Ibid.*, Vol. II, 1985, Col. 64.
115. *Economic Times* (New Delhi), 1 June, 1987.
116. Surjit Man Singh and Steven I. Levine, n. 50, p. 44.
117. *Lok Sabha Debates*, Vol. 43, 1988, Col. 176.
118. *Economic Times*, 8 June 1988.
119. *Ibid.*, 9 Februrary 1989.
120. *Indian Express* (New Delhi), 19 September 1989.
121. *China Daily*, 14 February 1991.
122. *Frontline* (Madras), 3 January 1992, p. 14.
123. Statistics from the State Statistical Bureau, China's Foreign Trade, (Beijing, 1991).
124. Nancy Jetly, no. 11. p. 8.
125. *Asian Recorder,* 1982, p. 16, 672.
126. *Ibid.*, 1983, p. 17, 511.
127. *Ibid.*, 1985, p.18, 255.
128. *Lok Sabha Debates*, Vol. 49, 1989, Col. 14.
129. *China Daily*, 10 March, 1989.
130. *Lok Sabha Debates*, Vol. 7, 1991, Col. 927.

4

The South Asian Context (1963-1991)

The South Asian dimension constitutes an important factor in the bilateral conflicting perceptions of India and China. The conflicting perceptions of India and China towards South Asia generated tension and further aggravated the bilateral relationship. China, perceived itself as a part of the South Asian region because of geographical contiguity, historical linkage and common heredity with the Mongoloid group of people in India, Nepal and Bhutan. As a result, China considered it natural to get involved in the intra-regional affairs of South Asia. Further, China's interest in the region stemmed from the perception of its security status as well as regional and global roles. India, on the other hand, had its own perception of its role and status in the region. It perceived China as an intrusive power in South Asia and believed that facts of geography, culture and ethnicity, reinforced by economic compulsions, tied the destiny of the South Asian nations much more with India than with China. As such, India viewed China's attempts to forge close relations with its South Asian neighbours as hostile acts. This very briefly sums up the South Asian context of India-China relationship.

Given India's predominant size and power in the region, Indo-Centricity of the region was not surprising. In the beginning, India was the only country in the region, with which China had diplomatic relations. Gradually, even when China opened up with other South Asian Countries, its calculations about India were a major determining factor in its South Asian policy. Secondly, Chinese South Asian policy and approach has been almost totally divorced from ideology.[1] China which was a communist country followed cordial and friendly relations with all South Asian countries, even when none of these countries were under communist rule. In the beginning China followed a policy of friendship with India. At the same time, it extended a hand of friendship to India's major regional adversary, Pakistan which was firmly in the imperialist camp. Even with respect to the smaller South Asian Countries like Nepal, Sri Lanka and subsequently, Bangladesh, China neither stressed the struggle of the working class nor encouraged the peasant masses to rise against their respective governments. Thirdly, China's policy towards South Asia had a global context. China's friendship with Pakistan was not only an extension of a policy of a hostility towards India, but was also an attempt to reduce Pakistan's commitment to United States of America and to prevent it from getting too close to the Soviet Union. From the beginning of sixties, China's South Asian strategy became a function of its long term preoccupation with a perceived Soviet threat.[2]

The India-China conflict of 1962 can be said to constitute a watershed in the history of South Asian relations and the Chinese role therein. China demonstrated her undeniable power vis-à-vis India and this fact impressed Pakistan which hereafter developed closer relations with China. Thus a new dimension to the power politics of the region become operative. Hereafter, Pakistan coordinated its efforts in the diplomatic field with those of China with the object of countering India influence wherever possible. Thus, China became an integral factor in South Asian politics.

II

The close relationship between China and Pakistan in the wake of India-China war of 1962, was further consolidated by the border agreement signed in Beijing on 2 March, 1963 by the Foreign Ministers of China and Pakistan, Chenyi and Z.A. Bhutto.[3]

China and Pakistan agreed to delimit their frontiers by fixing the alignment of the boundary between Xinjiang and Pakistan held Kashmir. Out of the 3,400 sq. miles of territory to which both sides had laid claim, Pakistan received 1,350 sq. miles and China the remaining 2,050 sq.miles.[4] However, a Pakistani spokesman pointed out immediately after the conclusion of the agreement that Pakistan profited by the arrangement since it received 750 sq. miles of territory then under actual Chinese control without surrendering any territory under the actual physical control of the government of Pakistan.[5] Undoubtedly, Pakistan signed the border agreement with a view to embarrass India and to come to an understanding with China in an effort to strengthen its military and diplomatic position vis-a-vis India. Moreover, Pakistan thought that it was likely to get more favourable terms at that particular juncture than at any other time because the Chinese had been branded in the west as an aggressor in their border dispute with India. Chinese were interested in changing this image and presenting themselves as a reasonable and friendly powers.[6]

With the conclusion of the border agreement between Pakistan and China, a new dimension was added to the Kashmir dispute. China recognised the defacto ownership of one third of Kashmir by Pakistan.[7] India reacted srongly and stated that there was no common border between Pakistan and China. India protested to China as well as Pakistan and blamed China more strongly for colluding with Pakistan against India.[8] Prime Minister, Jawaharlal Nehru said in Parliament that China "is directly interfering in Indo-Pakistan relations, and by doing this, seeking to exploit the differences between India and Pakistan on the Kashmir question to further its own expansionist policies".[9] It should be remembered that immediately after the Sino-Indian conflict, Britain and United States pressurised India to open dialogue with Pakistan on Kashmir question and bilateral talks actually began. Nehru rightly stated in Parliament that Sino-Pakistani moves had been 'timed to prejudice the joint talks on Kashmir'.[10] By May 1963, India and Pakistan admitted their failure to arrive at a mutually accepted settlement on Kashmir.

On 17 July 1963, Pakistan's Foreign Minister, Z.A. Bhutto declared in the Pakistan Parliament that an "in the event of war with India, Pakistan would not be alone. Pakistan would be helped by the most powerful nation in Asia."[11] This was clearly a reference to China. In a bid to further strengthen relations with China, both sides signed an air transport agreement on 29 August, 1963. The agreement provided for operation over each other's territories with landing and other necessary facilities.[12] Bilateral relations between China and Pakistan became more close in 1964. Zhou Enlai visited Pakistan in February 1964 and in a joint communique with President Ayub Khan agreed that the Kashmir dispute should be resolved in accordance with the wishes of the people of Kashmir as pledged to them by India and Pakistan.[13]

In 1965 political contacts at the highest level between China and Pakistan increased. In March 1965, President Ayub Khan visited China.[14] In March 1965, the Sino-Pakistan boundary protocol was signed by Foreign Ministers, Chenyi and Bhutto.[15] India construed the signing of the boundary protocol as 'final proof of the fact that motivated solely by their hostility towards India, the Chinese government and the government of Pakistan are opportunistically making use of their unlawful seizure of parts of Kashmir.[16]

Gradually Kashmir became the core issue in the regional politics. China had declared its support for a plebiscite in Kashmir. India was of the opinion that the Chinese attack in 1962 had entirely changed the complexion of Kashmir because Chinese now captured about 15,000 sq. miles of Kashmir's territory. Moreover, by 1963 Sino-pak agreement Pakistan handed over additional territory of 2,000 sq. miles to China.[17]

The continued impasse over Kashmir issue led to substantial deterioration in relations between India and Pakistan. In April 1965, an armed conflict broke out between Indian and Pakistani army in the Rann of Kutch. In September 1965, Kashmir became the cause of a major war between India and Pakistan, in which China pledged its support to Pakistan. On 4 September 1965, the Chinese foreign minister, Chenyi expressed support of the Chinese government for the Kashmiri people's struggle and endorsed the Pakistani version of the escalation of war in Kashmir.[18] Even more important than the verbal support for Pakistan in the war was the increased activity of the Chinese troops on India-China border. This was done with a view to pressurise India to keep a large part of its army on its border with China and took some of the pressure off Pakistan.

On 8 September, the Chinese government charged India with serious border violations on India-China border. It demanded that India must dismantle all the military structures it had illegally built beyond or on the China-Sikkim boundary, withdraw its army and stop aggression against China in the western, middle and eastern sectors of the borders. Otherwise India must bear responsibility for all the consequences therefrom.[19] On 13 September the government of India rejected the Chinese note of 8 September but offered to send on 'independent and neutral' observer to inspect and report on the existence of Indian military structures in Chinese territory beyond the border of Sikkim.[20] The Indian note denied that such structures existed and rejected any link between Kashmir and India-China relations.[21] On 17 September, China demanded again that India dismantle within three days 'all its military works for aggression on the Chinese of the China-Sikkim boundary or on the boundary itself.[22] Otherwise, the Indian Government would be responsible for' all the grave consequences' of its action.

In a statement in the Parliament on 17 September, Prime Minister Lal Bahadur Shastri described the Chinese posture as interference calculated to prolong and to enlarge the conflict.[23] Shastri stated that ".. what China is looking for is not a redress of grievances, real or imaginary, but some excuse to of start its aggressive activities again, this time acting in collusion with its ally, Pakistan".[24] In the Lok Sabha, External Affairs Minister Swaran Singh told the Members that a critical situation has emerged due to China-Pak Collusion: "Beginning as a marriage of Convenience it was nourished by a concern hatred for India and seems to have now become an integral part of the foreign policies of China and Pakistan . . . we have in our preparations and in our attitude keep always this in mind and all our future actions will have to be carefully taken, keeping this dual danger always before us."[25] The crisis eased on 23 September following the ceasefire between India and Pakistan. China climbed down from its provocative posture simultaneously with the acceptance of the ceasefire by Pakistan. China's hostile posture during India-Pakistan war of 1965 proved to Pakistan the value of China as an ally in its conflict with India. The Chinese threats were accompanied by intrusions and armed provocations all along the border. Chinese forces indulged in provocative intruisions at several points in the western, middle sectors and also across strategic passes on the Sikkim-Tibet border. The aggressive military activities on India's border by Chinese troops were intimately connected with Sino-Pak Collusion[26]. For India, this was the first time that it was threatened to face war simultaneously from two fronts.

Even during the subsequent phase of ceasefire and the Tashkent agreement, China persisted in its diplomatic support to Pakistan over the Kashmir question. From mid sixties onwards, China emerged as the major arms supplier to Pakistan. In 1966, on the occasion of its national day military parade Pakistan displayed a number of T-59 tanks and MIG-19 fighter planes which it had received from China. By 1968, China undertook to supply 1000 T-59 tanks, 80 MIG - 19s (F-6s), and 10 Ilyushin - 28 bombers. After 1965, Pakistan received large quantities of Military Supplies from China. These included complete equipment for two infantry division, about 350 tanks, 120 MIG aircraft, two squadrons of IL-28 bombers and large number of artillery pieces, Vehicles, spares for tanks and aircraft, etc.[27] The inward looking posture of China after the outbreak of the Cultural revolution about the mid of 1966 did not affect Sino-Pak relations in any significant measure. Before the fall of president Ayub Khan in March 1969, China seemed to harbour reservations about Pakistan due to Ayub's moves to improve relations with China's adversary, the Soviet Union. Soon after the change in Pakistan's regime, Chinese Premier, Zhou Enlai sent a message to incumbent President Yahya Khan assuring him of China's continued support. Shortly thereafter, Soviet foreign minister, A. Kosygin visited Pakistan and tried to persuade top leadership to join its regional economic and military organisation. Predictably China was anxious to gauge Pakistan's reaction to the Soviet overtures. After a lapse of about two years during the cultural revolution, in 1969 China filled the post of Ambassador to Pakistan with Senior diplomat, Chang Tung. Later Pakistan sent its Chief of Air Force to Beijing and he reaffirmed Pakistan's firm determination not to collaborate with the Soviet Union, in any scheme that would be directed against China.[28] Thus, a little bit of coolness that had crept in the later phase of Ayub era was removed by the end of 1969.

Thus, by 1969 China had carved out a special place for itself in South Asia by developing a very close relationship with Pakistan. Pakistan found this situation as an opportune time to drive a hard bargain with India over Kashmir, and in this respect found China as an ideal lever against India. The stalemate that continued in India-Pakistan relations in turn provided China with an opportunity to exploit Pakistan's susceptibilities against India.

In the 70's, at the regional level, geo-political changes of major significance were to be unleashed in south Asia. While the triangular Sino-USA-USSR relationship had its impact in this volatile region, the deteriorating situation in east Pakistan was fast turning into a flash point between traditional rivals, India and Pakistan. In the 1970 general elections in Pakistan, the East Pakistan based Awami League won an absolute majority in the parliament (167seats out of 317). However, the military ruler, Yahya Khan, paid scant regard to democratic tradition and put off convening the parliament. Despite its major, internal problem, Yahya sought to utilise the prevalent international scenario to the hilt, by acting as messenger between US and PRC. Yahya Khan visited China in November 1970 and met with Maozedong and Zhou Enlai. Pakistan was warmly praised by the Chinese and was provided with 200 million dollars as additional economic aid.[29] The visit concluded with a joint declaration voicing Chinese support for Pakistan on the Kashmir question and Pakistan's reaffirmation of support for a one China policy. It was clear the policy of close relationship with Pakistan would be pursued by China in the decade of Seventies.

Meanwhile the situation within Pakistan deteriorated substantially. The failure of Pakistan's political and military leaders to break the deadlock brought the country to the brink of civil war. Awami league backed by India, openly demanded secession as an independent nation-state and called for a general strike in March 1971. The tragic events in Eastern Pakistan naturally aroused wide concern and sympathy in India. The Yahya regime, however, continued its policy of military repression.[30]

Realising that a confrontation with Pakistan was imminent, India negotiated a Friendship treaty with Soviet Union in August 1971 to neutralise the threat of China's intervention. In addition to its promise of new military assistance, the treaty's most important feature for India was Article Nine which stipulated that neither party would provide any assistance to a power engaged in armed conflict with either of the signatories This had the practical effect of stopping all Soviet assistance to Pakistan.[31] Pakistani rulers saw the gravity of the situation and in early November, Foreign Minister Z.A. Bhutto, led a Pakistani military delegation to Beijing to secure military support. China held that the Indo-Soviet Treaty was actually a military alliance and India was encouraged by massive Soviet military aid.[32]

The Indo-Pakistan war broke out on December 3, 1971. It was waged on two fronts:- in the east and in the west. Following the war, China took a consistent hostile stand against India. China consistently condemned India as having committed "aggression" on Pakistan with the help of Soviet "Social imperialism". In the United Nations, China worked for Pakistan and actively supported the U.S. moves in the Security Council.[33]

The Chinese government demanded that India should be declared aggressor, all countries should support Pakistan and armed forces of both the countries should withdraw to their original position 'so as to create conditions for a peaceful settlement'.

China also sent a note to India accusing it of having sent seven Indian soldiers across the Sikkim border on December 10 to survey Chinese territory; this infiltration was described as severe infringement of Chinese sovereignty.

China pursued a policy that would show all-out support for Pakistan without commitment to military involvement. This led to a policy mix of strong verbal support coupled with material assistance and necessitated keeping a careful watch on the development of the military situation. The verbal support meant virulent pronouncements on different occasions, in particular an active pro-Pakistan, anti-Indian, and even stronger anti soviet show in the United Nations. Simultaneously, China also provided much needed material assistance to Pakistan. After the suspension of arms supply by the United States, China became Pakistan's main source of arms and ammunition and, according to some sources even sent 200 instructors to train Pakistani troops in counter guerrilla warfare.[34]

Following the 1971 war, China had to cope with a new situation in South Asia. Its staunchly, Pakistan, had been cut down to size, completely defeated and India had emerged as the predominant military power in South Asia. The new state of Bangladesh, was oriented toward India and the Soviet Union. China was particularly worried about the possible consequences of India's emergence as the major power in South Asia. Considering this as part of the soviet plan to 'foster India and turn it into a sub-superpower on the south Asia sub continent.[35]

The immediate task ahead for China was to restore a semblance of balance to the regional power structure which had changed after victory of India. When Zulfikar Ali Bhutto, now President of Pakistan visited Beijing in February 1972, Pakistan received generous economic assistance.

In the diplomatic field, the foremost task facing Bhutto was the negotiations with India to secure the repatriation of 93,000 prisoners of war and the evacuation of Indian forces from occupied areas in West Pakistan. In adverse circumstances for Pakistan, the fact that China was stranding firmly behind it was a significant asset. China exercised its first ever veto in the U.N. by barring the admission of Bangladesh to the United Nations on 25 August, 1972.[36]

China's determination to prevent India supremacy in the subcontinent entered a new phase with India's nuclear test on 18 May 1974. In the wake of Indian nuclear test, China assured Pakistan of its "full and resolute support in its just struggle in defence of its national independence and sovereignty against foreign aggression and interference, including that against nuclear threat and nuclear blackmal" China reiterated her consistent position that nuclear weapons should be completely prohibited and thoroughly destroyed and as first step, countries in possession of nuclear weapons should undertake the obligations to be not the first to use nuclear weapons pledging in particular not to use them against non-nuclear weapons countries and supported nuclear weapons free zones.[37]

India's External Affairs Minister, Swaran Singh made a statement in the Lok Sabha on India's Peaceful Nuclear Explosion stating:

The peaceful nuclear experiment which took place on May 18, 1974, represents a step forward on the road to peaceful uses of nuclear energy for the welfare of our people – It is singularly unfortunate that the peaceful nature of this nuclear experiment of ours should be misconstrued and misread in Pakistan. Apprehensions aroused in Pakistan are unfounded. We value our commitment under the Simla Agreement to settle all our differences with Pakistan by peaceful and bilateral ream. India has always supported development of cooperation amongst countries of this region on the basis of sovereign equality. Pakistan's allegations of hegemonistic designs have no basis at all, and are, to say the least, uncharitable.[38]

China gave full and consistent support in the United Nations for Pakistan's proposal for a nuclear free zone in South Asia since it had been brought up in October 1974. The proposal had obvious advantages for China. Firstly, China could demonstrate its support for Pakistan's security. Second, a nuclear free zone would have assured a long run Chinese monopoly of nuclear arms as for as South Asia was concerned. Finally, going beyond its diplomatic assurances on the matter, china probably agreed at a later stage to supply some support to Pakistan's nuclear programme. India was unwilling to accepted any comprehensive nuclear non proliferation arrangements, limited to the Indian subcontinent. A restricted regional arrangement did not address Indian concerns about China or about Superpower nuclear weapons in the Indian Ocean. For this reason, India rejected Pakistan's proposal for a South Asia nuclear weapons free zone comprising just the subcontinent.[39]

In 1976, to consolidate Sino-Pak relations president Z.A. Bhutto visited China. Nothwithstanding a thaw in Sino-Indian relations since 1976, China concentrated on Pakistan as a counterweight to the Soviet Union and India. Even after the death of chairman Mao Ze dong, the post Mao leadership continued to seek close relationship with Pakistan. The change of regime in Pakistan, bringing Gen-Zia-Ul-Haq to power did not affect the course of Pakistan's China policy. His decision to make his first journey outside the Islamic nations to China in December 1977 was also a clear indication that the military regime would continue Bhutto's policy of maintaining close links with China.[40]

The Chinese vice premier Keng Biao's visit to Pakistan in June 1978 at the inaugural ceremony of the 616 Kilometers all - Weather Kara Koram Highway linking Pakistan with China via Gilgit Khunjerab pass and Xinjiang. Underlined the continued closeness between Pakistan and China.[41]

Speaking at the state banquet on 16 June 1978, Keng Bio praised the completion of the Karakoram Highway as 'a crystalization - and outstanding example of close friendship and cooperation between China and Pakistan'.The most important feature of his speech was the declaration that 'What ever the vicissitudes on the international arena, the Chinese government and people will remain your reliable friends in your just struggle to build and defend your country'.[42] Further the close defence relations continued between Pakistan and China. According to the SIPRI Arms Trade Registers, the Chinese deliveries of military equipment to Pakistan in 1972 included 60 F-6 jet fighter bombers, 6 Sanghai II motor gunboats and approximately 100 T-59 tanks worth US # 61, 568,000 (1968 constant prices). In late 1974, Pakistan received another instalment of 159 T-59 tanks and one squadrom of F-6 air craft worth US # 27,135,000. China helped Pakistan to make up the war losses suffered by it in 1971. It helped Pakistan build up a capability for increasing production of arms. Pakistan was the biggest recipient of Chinese military biggest recipient of Chinese military aid amongst non communist countries.[43]

The latest research indicates that the break up of Pakistan in 1971 may have been in the long run the decisive factor in the emergence of Pakistan as a state with nuclear weapon capability. It is possible that Zulfikar Ali Bhutto was able to extract a heavy price from the Chinese for their failure to save Pakistan in 1971. Many analysts of Sino-Pak relations believe that Bhutto was referring to a secret agreement with China regarding assistance to pakistan's nuclear weapon programme when, in his death cell testimony, he mentioned an agreement which he had signed in 1976 after "an assiduous and tenacious endeavour spanning over 11 years of negotiations" and which he describes as "my greatest achievement and contributio to the survival of our people and our nation."[44] Therefore, from India's security point of view the growing relationship of Pakistan and China was undoubtedly a dangerous development.

The growing Sino-Pak defence relations deeply concerned India. Members of Lok Sabha participating in the discussion of the demand for grants of Ministry of Defence noted Chinese arms transfer for the last six or seven years to Pakistan. The members whole spoke included Shri Anant Rao Patil, D. Basumatari and Shri R.B. Singh. They cautioned the government about the dangers to Indian security from two fronts. The Minister of Defence assured the members that Government is preparing to face dangers of Sino-Pak military nexus.[45]

Two developments in 1979-80 had important consequences in South Asia: firstly, the Islamic revolution in Iran and the overthrow of the Shah in early 1979 disturbed the strategic balance in the region. Secondly and more importantly developments in Afghanistan had a deep impact in the entire region. The Soviet presence on the border of Pakistan, also posed threat before China and it has to devise means of coping with this threat. In South Asia, China pursued two pronged strategy, firstly, it supported Pakistan to the hilt to counter soviet threat and secondly, in an attempt to draw India away from Soviet Union, China began to make moves designed to conciliate India.

The decade of eighties saw China developing close relations with Pakistan. As stated early, the Chinese leadership believed that the Soviet invasion in Afghanistan was part of a carefully planned step-by-step scheme for world hegemony.[46] Sino-Pak relationship and Pakistan's geostrategic importance committed China to be responsible for Pakistan's defence.

India was concerned about the massive arming of Pakistan "as a frontline state", India stated that transfer of sophisticated weapons was far beyond Pakistan's legitimate defence needs.[47] The Chinese Premier, Zhao Ziyang paid an official visit to Pakistan in June, 1981. At a press Conference in Rawalpindi on 3 June the Premier said that Pakistan faced a grave military threat because of the hegemonists (USSR) invasion of Afghanistan and that China would fully support Pakistan to strengthen its national defence capability.[48]

In July 1984 Pakistan's Foreign Minister, Sahab Zada Yakub Khan visited Beijing and pointed out that friendship between Pakistan and China was not directed against any country[49]. In May, 1986 Pakistani and Chinese official opened the highest border crossing, i.e., Khunjerab Pass in the world to tourists.[50] India regarded this step as illegal because the pass belonged to Pakistan occupied Kashmir.[51] In September 1986, Foreign Minister Yaqub Khan visited Beijing. During this visit, both sides signed an agreement for Sino-Pakistani cooperation in the area of nuclear energy.[52] Though both sides termed it for the peaceful use, this generated renewed fears in India of covert Chinese assistance to Pakistan's nuclear weapons programme.

India's views were articulated by Ministry of State for External Affairs, Shri Khursheed Alam Khan during Calling Attention Motion in the Lok Sabha. He stated that:

> The non-peaceful dimension of Pakistan's nuclear programme has been a matter of concern for India. Pakistan has been pursuing the objective of acquiring the wherewithal to manufacture nuclear weapons. Reports which have appeared in media have reinforced our apprehensions. We cannot but take into account these developments in our neighbourhood which have grave implications for our security. I wish to assure the House that Government have been keeping, and will continue to keep, a constant vigil on all developments having a bearing on the country's security".[53]

The new Prime Minister's first visit abroad in 1989 was to China in a bid to keep the special link intact.[54] She stated that Pakistan viewed its relations with China as the corner stone in its foreign relations.

In the aftermath of the Tiananmen massacre of June 1989, when China's relations with many countries suffered, Pakistan stood by China. Premier Li Peng's visit to Pakistan in November 1989 also demonstrated Islamabad's support for Beijing at this particularly difficult juncture, Pakistan was the first country to receive one of China's top leaders following the Tiananmen massacre.[55]

Given the predominance of the strategic factor in the relationship, defence was the key area of Sino-Pak cooperation in the eighties. For over two decades Pakistan remained a regular and one of the largest markets of Chinese military hardware. Joint and licensed production of select Chinese weapons in Pakistan and the high level military exchanges and contacts were now well established.[56] According to a study, 'in the twenty five plus years since Beijing began exporting arms to Pakistan, the People's Republic of China became Pakistan's most reliable and extensive supplier of military hardware, transferring military related exports of virtually every description and destined for every branch of the Pakistani military-personnel equipment, ammunition, small arms, mortars, ammoured personnel carriers, tanks, naval vessels, aircraft, missiles and missile technology. Included in this largesse were 1500 tanks, 350 fighter air craft, and 30 naval vessels. Most recently, China provided short – to- intermediate range missiles, capable of carrying a nuclear warhead, as well as active assistance in developing Pakistan's nuclear weapons capability.[57] According to Mushahid Hussain, from 1980, bilateral military transactions were worth over $500 million. The free aid and friendship prices involved in the Chinese arms transfers to Pakistan make a correct assessment of the value difficult. Western estimates are substantially higher. The Stockholm International Peace Research Institute (SIPRI) in its 1992 estimates said that between 1987 and 1991 the total Chinese arms transfers to Pakistan were worth $1,027 million at 1990 constant prices. M. Hussain's study makes this point very clear. After 1980, he wrote: 'The free aid concept of furnishing arms to Pakistan was replaced by supply through purchase from various semi-autonomous Chinese corporations. However, the Chinese were considerate in matters of cost and prices, when it came to dealings with the Pakistan army.[58]

Table: 3
China's Major Conventional Weapons Sales to Pakistan

Year	*Aircraft*	*Armour/artillery*	*Naval vessels*	*Missiles*
1980-83	20 f-6	150 T-59 MBT 50 t-60 lt 50 122 mm MRS	2 Hainan PB 4 Hengue FAC	8 Shshm/SSM 54 SA-2 SAM
1983-85	42 Q-5	150 T-59 MBT Fighters	4 Hwang Fen FAC	16 ShshM 20 CSA/SAM
1986-88	98 Q-5	200 T-59 MBT Fighters	20 Romeno Class Sub	200 portable
1988-89	60 F-7	200 T-59 MBT Fighters	Sub marines	SAM
1990		125 T-59 MBT		M-11 Short Range Ballistic Missile 100 portable SAM

Source: R. Bates Gill, Curling Beijing Arms Sales Orbis, Vol.37, No.3 Summer, 1992, p. 395.

Mutually beneficial cooperation in the development of modern weapons system was another component of Sino-Pak military relationship. The two countries were cooperating in the production of F-7p fighter aircraft at Pakistan's Kamra aeronautical complex. It involved fitting U.S. General Electric F404 engines and U.S. designed avionics and fire control system in an updated air frame of a MIG-21.[59] With China's assistance, Pakistan established indigenous capacity to produce a modern version of the T-69 main battle tank with computarised fire control system, enhanced armour and engine capability.[60]

Reports about China's assistance to the Pakistani clandestine nuclear weapons programme and the supply of M-11 missiles that can carry nuclear warheads revealed the lethal character of the Sino-Pakistani military relations. It created insecurity for the entire region and this issue emerged as a problem in Sino-Indian relations. Throughout the decade there were been regular reports in the media about the Chinese support to Pakistan's weapons programme. These included reliable reports of Chinese technicians being present at Kahuta, Pakistan's first gaseous-uranium-enrichment facility Southeast of Islamabad. There were reports of China's supply of ring magnets and other components to Pakistan. The most serious of these reports was that China transferred to Pakistan a design based on its fourth nuclear explosive device as well as tested or allowed a Pakistani nuclear explosive device to be tested at Lop Nor in Xinjiang.[61]

China supported the overall Pakistani nuclear programme in many ways. In September, 1986 the two countries signed an agreement committing Chinese assistance to Pakistan's nuclear energy sector. Under this arrangement. China sold two mini research reactions to Pakistan in November, 1989 an February, 1990. In November, 1989 China also agreed to sell a 300 megawatt pressurised water nuclear plant. Further in August 1990, Beijing agreed to supply enriched uranium to Pakistan.[62] It is clear from the foregoing that Chinese assistance enhanced Pakistan's overall nuclear weapons programme.

India was justifiably concerned with these negative trends in the region. Even in Lok-Sabha during discussion on the Demand for Grants of Ministry of Defence for the year 1988-89, a ruling member Shri R.S. Sparrow stated that:

> You have to be geo-militarily alert. A Damocles Sword is hanging on the head of India. Coming from China, it is not fair; it is not correct. Why are modern weapons supplied to Pakistan? Why is Sophisticated training being given to Pakistan at Kahuta? This is something which we have to very carefully watch".[63] Another member, Shri E. Ayapu Reddy said that "Contrary to our expectations, the National Security Environment has become more Sensitive today than it was during the last year or the previous year. After the signing of the INF Treaty and Soviet withdrawal from Afghanistan, every one of us expected the de-escalation of tensions, but on the other hand that is not the result. Pakistan is undoubtedly getting sophisticated weapons from America and also from China, almost free of cost. Pakistan is strategic allies of both

> America and China. Apart from that, China and Pakistan have got a common objective so far as India is concerned. Both of them have got territorial ambitions on India".[64]

Therefore, we see that Sino-Pakistan relationship continued to evolve into an autonomous relationship irrespective of India's grave security concerns arising out of Sino-Pak enduring military relations visible in the field of nuclear and missile cooperation. India security analysts maintained that there was a Sino-Pakistani nexus against India, which sought to cap Indian power and influence in the region. The reasoning is that China has supported Pakistan in its core national interests and helped make the latter a formidable military power only to check a potential Indian challenge to Chinese preponderance in Asia. Taken to its logical conclusion, such a line of thinking tends to argue that, as China wants to assert its presence more in the Northeast and Southeast Asian regions, it makes perfect strategic sense to "build up" Pakistan not only to contain and neutralize Indian power, but also to tie India down in subcontinental concerns.[65]

As India's parliamentary standing, committee on Defence, a non-partisan body composed of all the political parties stated in its first report in July 1989, "Nearer home, China is a major Missile power and is also the main source of Missiles and allied technologies for Pakistan. With both these countries we have unsettled boundary disputes and hence there is the need for great attention to this aspect of our Defence preparedness".[66]

III

China also played an active role in the Himalayan region, particularly in Nepal with a view to limit India's influence. In China, Nepal found a balancing force. India did not relish China's presence in the sensitive area which lay within her defence zone. From 1963 onwards, in the context of 1962 conflict India realised the necessity of reaching an understanding with Nepal. Nepal's policy towards China was marked by caution and sophistication. King Mahendra realised that the post 1962 regional environment held dangers and pursued a policy of balanced relationship with both giant neighbours, i.e., India and China.

China, on its part, tried to broadbase its relations with Nepal by giving aid to various projects and emphasising on economic relations. On 19 May 1964, Nepal and China signed a two year trade agreement in Kathmandu.[67] Both countries agreed that the traditional barter trade between Nepalese and Tibetans living within 30 Kilometres of the international boundary would continue. On 2 May 1966, a new agreement on trade and related questions between Nepal and China was signed in

Beijing by the Chinese foreign Minister Chenyi, and Nagendra Prasad Rijal, visiting Minister for Industry and commerce of Nepal.[68] The agreement was concluded on the basis of the 1956 agreement, which it replaced and was to remain in force for a period of six years. It, interalia, provided for the establishment of consulate - General by China in Kathmandu and by Nepal in Lhasa.[69] However, all these agreements could not succeed in substantially increasing the volume of trade between the two countries.

Meanwhile, once India-Nepal relations eased, Nepal felt encouraged to enter into a defence arrangement with India in January 1965.[70] Nepal agreed to receive all of its requirements of arms and ammunition from India and training facilities for Nepalese army was entrusted to India.[71] In 1967. Commander-in-chief of Nepali army and Defence Minister of Nepal made separate visits to India and Nepal obtained most of the desired military equipment.[72] Furthermore, Indian army technical personnel were stationed at checkposts and other strategic locations along the Nepal-Tibet border until 1970. An Indian military liaison group continued to function at Nepali army head quarters in Kathmandu.[73]

With the beginning of cultural Revolution in 1966, the Chinese personnel in Nepal engaged themselves increasingly in political affairs. Chinese construction teams on the Kodari road and other aid projects started showing Chinese propaganda movies to surrounding villages and distributed communist literature and Mao buttons.[74] The worst incident of this period which caused public dispute occurred on 17 June, 1967. On that day, approximately 200 Chinese Embassy Officials and project technicians, gathered at the Kathmandu airport to welcome two of 'Mao's warriors' who had just been expelled from India, they shouted anti-Indian and pro-cultural revolution slogans. This was repeated on 24 June when another batch of Chinese diplomats reached Kathmandu. The Indian government lodged a strong protest against this demonstration and Nepal assured that such incidents would not be repeated.[75]

China on her part, left no stone unturned to discredit India even as it made overtures to Nepal. A commentator of the *People's Daily* stated that "the Chinese people support the people of Nepal in their just struggle against the Indian expansionists, and resolutely support the struggle waged by the people of all countries, that have been subjected to aggression, intervention to bullying by U.S. imperialism, Soviet revisionism and the Indian expansionism.[76] It may be noted here that the Nepalese Prime Minister, Kirti Nidhi Bista lost no time in demanding that Indian operations should ease at Nepalese border checkposts. He also demanded the withdrawal of forty members Indian military liaison group in Kathmandu and Indian wireless personnel along Nepal's northern border attached to checkposts.[77] On 21 July, India's External Affairs Minister, Dinesh Singh told Parliament that India had agreed in principle to the withdrawal.[78]

Thus, in Nepal, China's main aim was to support Nepal's King, provide economic assistance and thereby reduce Nepal's dependence on India. China operated in Nepal in the context of its broad South Asian policy to contain India's influence in the region and indulged in anti-Indian campaign.

China's Nepal policy in the seventies was to use Nepal, both the monarchy and the communists to put pressure on India and also to wean Nepal away from India. This helped Nepal in projecting an image of a separate entity, an ideological and strategic buffer between India and China. Encouraged by King Mahendra's tacit support the Chinese continued their anti Indian campaign. In February 1970 Chinese Premier, Zhou Enlai praised Nepalese monarch for his pro China policy and reiterated China's firm support to Mahendra for his just struggle against foreign interference and for the defence of national independence of Nepal.[79]

By this time, Mahendra began to put some to pressure on New Delhi for a new trade treaty on his terms to replace the 1960 agreement. He endeavoured to mobilise China to pressurise India. In October 1970 he sent Prime Minister Rudra Prasad Giri to China to seek China's assistance. He also appealed to China to help develop transport facilities and industries in Nepal as well as to carry out cotton growing survey at Butwal, 25 kilometers from the Indian border. When New Delhi protested the Nepalese leaders defended the decision to permit the Chinese near the Indian border stating that Indian fears were 'without justification and that India should appreciate the need of other sources of economic assistance to Nepal'.[80]

The new king, Birendra noted the emergence of confident India and new geo political realities in South Asia. The inability of China to prevent the emergence of Bangladesh had aroused concern in Nepal. India under the leadership of Indira Gandhi adopted a more realistic attitude towards it. While it refused to give encouragement to anti-monarchy forces, it expected that Nepal should have due regard for India interests in the Kingdom and should recognise that economic benefits offered by India dependent on reciprocity. In November 1972, the Nepalese Premier visited Beijing to assure the Chinese leaders that Nepal would continue its policy of friendship towards China. Both sides signed a new economic and technical cooperation agreement.[81] China continued to give economic aid to Nepal. Later, King Birendra described premier Bista's visit had enhanced mutual understanding and enlarged the 'areas of cooperation so happily existing between Nepal and China'.[82]

The developments in Sikkim provided the anti-Indian lobby with an opportunity to open a new campaign of vilification against India. India's decision to grant Sikkim the status of an associate state created apprehension in the royal coterie. They perceived the change in Sikkim as a threat to the Nepalese Monarchy. The Chinese press declared that Nepal was the 'next target' of India's 'expansionism' and cited the presence of opposition leaders of Nepal in India.[83]

Nepal and China subsequently began to consolidate their relations.[84] Both sides also signed a new economic agreement providing China to build the 407 kilometre Surkhat road in Western Nepal Meanwhile Birendra intensified his efforts to gain India's acceptance of his foreign policy of equal friendships with India and China. He suggested that Nepal should be recognised as a 'Zone of Peace' China welcomed his proposal because for years Nepal has given China powerful support in international affairs, and 'has always tried to be friendly to China'.[85] But India preferred to remain silent on the issue, quickly knowing the evil purpose behind the proposal.

India also did not support Birendra's proposal of a 'zone of peace' because it ignored the geopolitical realities. India's presence in Nepal did not threaten China's interests, while China's presence in Nepal was detrimental to India.

China continued to encourage Nepal to internationalise Birendra's proposal of a 'Zone of peace' in order to pressurise India At banquets in honour of king Birendra, Premier who visited China, Hua Kuofeng, on 1 June 1976, declared that 'the proposal to declare Nepal a zone of peace reflects the strong desire of the people of Nepal to safeguard their national independence and state sovereignty. The Chinese government firmly support this just propostion. This visit also marked opening of direct air passage between China and Nepal Further, Birendra visited Tibet and became the first foreign head of state to visit the Tibet Autonomous Region of China.[86]

Therefore, we see that king Mahendra throughout the decade of seventies used links with China to put pressure on India. Several steps were taken to encourage contacts with China, i.e., regular mutual visits by dignitaries and delegations and direct air link with Beijing. The Chinese government on its part strongly supported the proposal of a 'zone of peace and encouraged Nepal's efforts to weaken is ties with India. It extended a fair amount of economic and technical aid and encouraged Nepal Tibet border trade. But towards the end of the decade of seventies, the Chinese attitude in South Asia was gradually guided by its improving relations with India.

In May-June 1981, the New Chinese Premier Zhao Ziyang, went to Nepal. This was the first visit by a Chinese Premier Since Zhou Enlai's visit in 1960.[87] Zhao repeated his country's support to Nepal's proposal for declaring the area as a zone of peace. During Li's visit to Nepal in 1984, China announced its agreement to construct the first sector of a high way that would link the west Nepal resort town of Pokhara with the border of Tibet. Beijing undertook the construction of the Pokhara – Mustang road as a 'token of friendship and close understanding' between China and Nepal.[88]

China agreed to provide assistance of 50 million Renminbi for the construction of an international conference centre in Kathmandu. On 26 August, 1987, China and Nepal signed an agreement on air service between Kathmandu and Lhasa, the capital of Tibet.[89]

Once again, from late eighties, 1987 to be precise, it appeared that the Nepalese ruling circle were getting closer to China and distancing, themselves from India. The Chinese advance in participation in projects closer to the Indian border began to cause security concern in India. A specific instance was the contract given in November, 1987 to the Chinese to rebuild a 44-kilometre portion of the Prithvi highway, the main road linking Kathmandu to western and southern Nepal and India. The Chinese were asked to reconstruct the winding mountain road from a point 26 kilometers west of Kathmandu.[90]

While these developments were causing concern in New Delhi, of much greater alarm was the purchase of arms by Nepal from China. In March 1988, the North China Industrial Corporation agreed to sell some $20 million worth of light arms, ammunition, boots and informs and 16 anti-aircraft guns to Nepal.[91] China defended it. From its perspective, military relations were part of normal state-to-state relations. Sovereign independent country such as Nepal had the right to acquire such materials as it deems necessary for its defence, and China had the right to sell such materials. Moreover, China argued the materials sold to Nepal could not in any way be construed as constituting a threat to India. In the Lok Sabha members during a general discussion expressed concern over Chinese exports of arms in India's immediate neighbours including Nepal.[92]

From India's perspective, this was an effort by China to alter the military status quo in the Himalayas. Moreover, Nepal was obligated by the terms of the 1950 Indo-Nepali Treaty of Peace and Friendship, letters exchanged at the time of that treaty, and a further set of letters exchanged in 1965 to purchase arms only from India or from third countries only with India's permission.[93]

Nepal not only refused to heed India's warning not to go through with the purchase but also refused to give guarantees that there would be no further purchases of arms from China and that the weapons already purchased would not be used against India. When Nepal turned insensitive to Indian security; India refused to extend the trade and transit treaties that had expired in March 1988. When those treaties finally lapsed – after two six month extensions – in March 1989, 13 out of 15 border crossing points were closed down.[94] These dealt a severe blow to Nepal's economy.

Nepal expected to be bailed out by China. But Chinese leaders told their Nepalese counterpart not to expect from it to provide an economic alternative to India, saying geographic and financial constraints on China were too great to permit that. But the real reason was subtle change in China's South Asian Policy. By the late 1980s China had moved away from Constant encouragement to Nepal to stand up to India. There was greater realisation in Bnot to unnecessarily provoked eijing conflict in South Asia. Therefore, China advised Nepal to seek a reasonable resolution of its problems with India.[95] Nonetheless, when the crunch came, Beijing gave modest economic support.

China also gave low – key political support. Shortly after the Indian blockade began, a Chinese foreign ministry spokesman expressed concern about the serious difficulties facing the Nepalese people and called on Nepal and India to 'iron out their differences... and resume their normal trade at an early date. He also maintained that land locked countries were entitled to transit through neighbouring countries'.

In the entire episode, Beijing's response was however, mild. The main reason for the Chinese restraint could be the desire to sustain the momentum in Sino-Indian relations resulting from Indian Premier Rajiv Gandhi's December 1988, China visit. After investing a decade of diplomatic energy in Sino-Indian rapprochement, China did not want to risk the still fragile relationship by upholding too forcefully the right to conduct relations with Nepal as it and Kathmandu saw fit.

At the same time, China was not willing to totally give up on the linkages built with the other South Asian countries. During his visit to Kathmandu in November 1989 Chinese Premier Li Peng, reassured his hosts in Kathmandu:

> It has always been China's steadfast policy to develop good neighborly and friendly relations with every country in South Asia. No matter what happens in the international situation, China will always support Nepal and other South Asian countries in their efforts to safeguard independence and sovereignty'.[96] Referring specifically to the Indian-Nepal

> confrontation, Li said that 'as a major country in South Asia', India should be 'more magnanimous and generous' in handling issues with Nepal.[97]

The victory of the democratic movement in Nepal in April 1990 and the acceptance of India's terms by the new Nepal Congress Party led government in June represented a major blow to Chinese influence there. The interim government under K.P. Bhattarai called for the restoration of 'natural' ties with India. India responded by opening the earlier routes on the Indian border for the flow of trade. Even the proposal of a zone of peace was buried.[98] In the joint communique signed in New Delhi by Indian Prime Minister, V.P. Singh and Nepali Prime Minister, K.P. Bhattarai on 10 June, 1990, Nepal pledged to have 'prior consultations with a view to reach mutual agreement on such defence-related matters which in the view of either country could pose a threat to its security'.[99]

However, on balance, Sino-Nepal relations remained close throughout the period under study. The close Sino-Nepal relations had security implications for India.

IV

With Bhutan, China's strategy was to pressurise it to open direct negotiations on the disputed area northwest of Tawang. In 1966 a crisis erupted near the trijunction of Bhutan, Chumbi valley and Sikkim, when Tibetan graziers and Chinese troops entered the Doklam pastures and refused to heed the admonitions of Bhutanese officials to leave. Bhutan stated that the traditional border ran along the water posting Batang La to Sinchel La and asked the government of India to make representations to China.[100] On 30 September, 1966 India sent a note to the Chinese government about 'intrusions' into Bhutanese territory by Chinese herdsmen and patrols and lodged a protest with the Chinese government.[101] An official Chinese statement on the subject denied Indian Government's outcry about Chinese 'intrusions' into Bhutanese territory. It stated that the China-Bhutan boundary had never been formally delimited that China would like to do so 'through friendly consultations' but it was a matter that concerns China and Bhutan alone. The Indian government has no right whatsoever to intervene in it.[102]

The infamous cultural Revolution was at its climax at the time of the Doklam episode and Xinhua news agency went on to accuse India of tightening its control of Bhutan 'under the guise of protection'. There were internal troubles within Bhutan as well. King Jigme Dorji Wang Chuk faced serious coup attempts and his Prime Minister Jigme Dorji was assassinated in 1964. A pro-Chinese lobby that strongly opposed the king's attempts to keep Bhutan closer to India was believed to be involved in Intra-royal family feuds.[103]

Even in Seventies, China pursued its policy of weaning Bhutan away from India. Bhutan joined the United Nations in 1971 and sought to play a more independent role in international affairs China voted in favour of Bhutan's membership of the United Nations. China sent an impressive delegation to attend the coronation of the new king, Jigme Singhye Wangchuk in the summer of 1974. This was a significant event as it was after a period of about a decade and half that Bhutan had sent an official invitation to China along with twenty other foreign countries but China also responded to the invitation by sending a delegation. Naturally the event was played up by Chinese media and was interpreted as having opened a new page in the friendly contacts between Bhutan and China.[104]

The visit of Chinese delegation was interpreted as beginning of renewed efforts on the part of Beijing "to cultivate its relationship with the Bhutanese Government and people'. The event was also significant from another point of view. The Foreign Affairs Minister of Bhutan, Dawa Tshering stated that Article 2 of the treaty of 1949 under which Bhutan was to seek the advice of the Government of India in the conduct of its foreign relations did not make it compulsory for Bhutan to accept that advice.[105]

While wooing Bhutan in 1974-75, China's attacks on India for its 'annexation' of Sikkim reached climax. These accusation found muted resonance in Bhutan because it too faced a problem similar to that experienced by Sikkim, where inundation of Nepali settlers proved so destructive to its Lepcha culture and autonomous princely order. Bhutan's king, however, averted open criticism, personally visited New Delhi and obtained reassurance from Mrs. I Gandhi that India had no design on Bhutan.[106]

It was in 1978-79 that some members of the National Assembly of Bhutan called for closer links with China.[107] These members had expressed certain reservation on the full implications of Article 2 of the treaty of 2949 under which Bhutan was only to seek the guidance of India in the conduct of her bilateral relations.[108] To quote Dawa Tsering. Bhutanese Foreign Minister, 'some National Assembly members felt that if China and India became friends Bhutan would lose all importance to Beijing and New Delhi. They thought we should make our own efforts, to develop ties with China or be left out in the cold'.[109] During the Non Aligned summit in Havana in 1979, Bhutan for the first time took an independent stand on the Kampuchean issue, different from that of India. Bhutan favoured the seating of the ousted Pol Pot regime of Kampuchea while Indian stand was in favour of leaving the seat vacant. The Bhutanese stand went in along with the Chinese stand.

This episode was played up by Chinese media with renewed expression of willingness to establish diplomatic relations with Bhutan and assist its development. However, soon Bhutan again officially stated that it had decided to maintain policy of not seeking diplomatic and trade ties with China.[110] Thus, Chinese attempts to wean Bhutan away from India did not fully succeed in the Seventies.

However, because of the Chinese intrusion of Bhutanese border in 1979 the Druk-Gyalpo stated that "to leave the border undemarcate do would be to the disadvantage of Bhutan in the long run", this was a clear hint that Bhutan was ready to negotiate with the Chinese on the question of the boundary settlement.[111]

With Bhutan, China's relations improved steadily in the eighties. China always questioned India's special relations with Bhutan and expected Bhutan to conduct its own foreign affairs.[112] Chinese misplaced apprehensions about India's special relations with Bhutan proved wrong when Bhutan and China agreed for boundary talks in April 1984 without participation of India.[113] Thus, in April 1984 the first official delegation from Bhutan visited China since the establishment of People's Republic of China in 1949. The Chinese delegation leader, Gong Dafei, Vice Minister of Foreign affairs and the Bhutanese delegation leader Om Pradhan, Bhutanese ambassador to India attended the talks.[114] Chinese Foreign Minister, Wu Xueqian met with the Bhutanese delegation and spoke highly of Bhutan's policy of independence and self reliance, he said, 'China and Bhutan have been friendly to each other since ancient times and there is no conflict of interest between the two countries'. He added, 'so long as the two countries continue their friendly negotiations on the basis of the five principles of peaceful coexistence the boundary question would certainly be settled'.[115]

In April, 1985 the second round of boundary talks were held in Thimphu. During the talks the two sides discussed the principles that should guide the settlement of the border issue. The joint communique said that the second round of talks have made the two countries know each other better and reinforced their friendship. The third round of boundary talks was held in June 1986 at Beijing and both sides continued the process of exchange of views on guiding principles for settling the boundary question. Tashi Tabgyal leader of the Bhutanese delegation said the only problem with China is undefined boundary. Earlier Chinese Foreign Minister, Wu Xueqian told the delegation that the important content of China's foreign policy was to preserve developing good neighbourly relations with adjoining countries and to maintain equality among nations, big or small.[116] The delegation also met with Chinese Premier, Zhao Ziyang, who said, 'It is China's sincere hope to settle the Sino-Bhutanese boundary question at early date. Our boundary question is not so complicated and can be resolved easily'. He further added 'China sets great store by its friendship with Bhutan and will not interfere in its internal affairs'. In 1987 both sides held fourth round of talks in Thimphu.

The fifth round of boundary talks between China and Bhutan was held in May, 1988 at Beijing. In the talks the two sides reached an agreement on the guiding principles for the settlement of the boundary issue, which stipulated that both countries should observe the Five Principles of Peaceful coexistence, treat each other on an equal basis and enter into friendly consultation on the basis of mutual understanding and mutual accommodation with a view to reach a just and reasonable settlement.

The sixth round of talks was held at Beijing in October, 1989. Bhutan's Minister of Foreign Affairs, Dawa Tsering arrived in Beijing and held talks with Chinese Foreign Minister Qian Qichen, who described relations between China and Bhutan as 'very good all along' though the two countries have not yet established diplomatic relations. Tsering said Bhutan cherishes its friendship with China and hopes to further bilateral relations. In a friendly and cordial atmosphere, the two sides consulted each other on the Sino-Bhutanese boundary. The seventh round of talks was held at Thimphu in August, 1990. The meetings were secret and the participants on neither side talked about them in precise terms. On boundary issue, both sides had considerably narrowed down their differences.

Thus, we can safely conclude that Sino-Bhutan relations from 1980 to 1991 had come a long way and had matured. China and Bhutan started official level talks from 1984 and both sides held several round of talks successfully[117]. Though there was no Indian participation in these talks, much to the delight of Chinese, it is worthwhile noting to assume that king Jigme Singye Wang Chuk did not offend against Indian interests or border security and kept the Indian government informed about talks with the Chinese.[118] Thus, Bhutan cared for Indian interests and started negotiations to resolve boundary difference with China.

V

Developing close bilateral relations with Sri Lanka was an important element of China's South Asian policy. The Sri Lankan Prime Minister Sirimavo Bandarnaike visited Beijing in 1963 to explain the Colombo proposals. She was cordially welcomed by the Chinese leaders and effusively praised by the Chinese media for her role as a peace maker. However, the main opposition party, United National Party, criticised the government for not branding China as the aggressor in India-China conflict of 1962. Similarly the maritime agreement signed between China and Sri Lanka, in July 1963, which gave most - favoured nation (MFN) status to each other, also became a serious issue in Sri Lankan domestic politics. The UNP termed it as an evidence of the government pro-China tilt; and since most of the China trade passed through Trincomalee, there were also accusation that Trincomalee has been handed over to China.[119].

When Dudley Senanayake became Prime Minister in 1965 there was a downturn in Sri Lanka-China relations. The UNP government had leanings towards west, it was but natural that relations with China should take backseat. During that period China was in the throes of the cultural revolution and the compulsion conclusions had its effects in bilateral relations.

China's Sri Lankan policy appears to be determined by the Chinese perception of Sri Lanka's place in its global strategy to oppose 'imperialism' and 'social imperialism, i.e., the USA and USSR. We have seen earlier, Sri Lanka was one of the earliest countries to recognise the People's Republic of China and next to Britain, China was the biggest trading partner of Sri Lanka. Among the noncommunist governments of Asia and Africa, Sri Lanka is one of the few countries with which China, except for a few brief periods of low key relations has had excellent diplomatic intercourse. China constituted the principal counter-weight for Sri Lanka against India.

Beijing welcomed the SLFP's return to power in 1970 election as a major partners in United left Front. The radical policies adopted by the Sirimavo Government came in for un stinted praise when a Sri Lankan economic delegation visited Beijing in September 1970.

China's Sri Lanka policy faced a temporary crisis when the first JVP (Janata Vivukti Perumuna) revolt broke out in 1971. Beijing initially adopted a policy of studied silence and Colombo suspected Chinese machinations behind the revolt, lending credence to the suspicion of China's complicity. India was the first country to response favourably to Sri Lanka's appeal for military assistance during the JVP insurrection. Later, China made it clear that it was completely an internal matter to be tackled by the United Front Government.

In a letter to Sirimavo Bandaranaike in May 1971, Zhou Enlai condemned the self styled Gueverists. He added that China was opposed to both 'ultra leftism' and right opportunist in revolutionary struggles.[120]

After this episode, Sri Lanka China relations began to expand. Soon after the prevolt in 1971, Sri Lanka received $ 25 million hard currency from China to tide over the balance of payments difficulties. In June 1972, Sririmavo Bandaranaike made a highly publicised state visit to China and met with Chairman Mao. She said that Sri Lanka was particularly gratified to have the assurance of China of its continued support for Sri Lankan proposal for a peace Zone in the Indian ocean. Both sides also signed agreement on economic and technical cooperation.[121]

Sino-Sri Lankan relationship in the 80's had a strategic dimension considering the geostrategic location of Sri Lanka. Its close proximity to India and the presence of a large Tamil ethnic minority in Sri Lanka, a strong sense of discrimination felt by the Tamils, evoked support from the Indian province of Tamil Nadu, created a strong sense of insecurity. India's support for the Tamil separatists particularly since 1983 aggravated the insecurity. Sri Lanka looked towards China for assistance and support. However, the constraints of China's foreign policy and its limited naval power capability combined with India's formidable military strength, precluded a direct intervention by China on behalf of Sri Lanka. Further, there was a pragmatic realisation in Beijing that a high profile policy would only adversely affect the ongoing process of normalisation of Sino-Indian relations. hence, an analysis of Beijing's reactions on the ethnic conflict makes it clear that China's support to Sri Lanka was on a low key and Chinese media gave a balanced coverage on this issue.[122]

Chinese Foreign Minister, Wu Xueqian visited Sri Lanka in January 1985 and had extensive talks with the Lankan leadership. Wu said that 'the ethnic problem is an internal problem of Sri Lanka and should be solved by the Sri Lankan people themselves'. In November 1985, a3,000 ton Guided Missile Destroyer and supply ship paid a 'friendly visit' to Colombo after a similar visit to Karachi. This was the first time Chinese naval vessels had gone to visit foreign countries since the founding of the People's Republic of China.[123] Li Xiannian, Chinese President visited Sir Lanka in March 1986. He was the first Chinese head of state to visit Colombo since the two countries established diplomatic relations in 1957.[124]

When the India-Sri Lanka confrontation escalated in the summer of 1987, Premier Ranil Wikrama. Singhe visited Beijing to mobilise Chinese support. Beijing again preferred a political solution to the problem. However, it continued to pump arms into Sri Lanka.[125] In one official statement, without naming India, China expressed its disapproval of the bullying actions of big powers and 'interference in internal affairs' of other nations.[126] President Jayawardene summed up China's role as follows: 'They were good friends and gave us military equipments, guns, etc. at reasonable terms. But what could they do? I could not ask them to start a border war in the north to keep the Indians busy. Even if I had, I doubt if they would have done it.[127]

In July 1987, India and Sri Lanka signed a peace pact.[128] Sri Lanka agreed to the introduction of the Indian Peace Keeping Force (IPKF) to maintain civil order, without setting a date for its withdrawal, and the two countries exchanged letters spelling out Sri Lanka's security obligations to India. China did not react. It could not criticise because Lankan government itself agreed for the terms. Privately, however, China's leaders were critical of India's actions. One internal study by the Chinese Academy of social sciences argued that India intervened in Sri Lanka's internal affairs and forced Colombo to sign the various agreements so as to 'control' Sri Lanka and achieve 'regional-hegemony' in South Asia. The article said 'India carved up Pakistan and created Bangladesh. It annexed Sikkim. It has purchased aircraft carriers. It has done every thing to accomplish this objective'.[129] But such views were not expressed openly.

China continued to give Sri Lanka low keyed political support in the conflict over the withdrawal of the IPKF during 1989. From China's perspective, a friendly neighbour such as Sri Lanka, strategically located in the Indian ocean, would be a useful ally in their future activities in the region.

In December, 1990, Chinese Premier Li Peng visited Sri Lanka and held talks with Lankan leaders. Li acclaimed Sino-Sri Lankan relations as a model for developing ties between countries of different social systems and ideologies. In 1991, the gross receipt of foreign loan from China was Rs. 74.2 million and repayment was Rs. 52.5 million. The completion of the Chinese aided Ginganga Flood prevention project in 1982 and the Supreme Court complex in 1987 were two accomplishments in the bilateral relations.

Even Sri Lanka- China military relations continued. Sino-Lanka relations in this crucial area increased in terms of value quantity and quality.[130] According to a recent study, 'since 1989 China's arms transfer to Sri Lanka has risen dramatically. In the 1970's and early 1980's China supplied such weapons as artillery and patrol boats. In the last three years, shipments have included three Y-8 and two Y-12 transport aircraft, a number of Q-5 ground attack jets, regiment of tracked T-85 infantry fighting vehicles, a regiment of Type 59/1 130 mm long range artillery guns, and two advanced Shanghai class gunboats. This surge in its weapon exports to Sri Lanka is thought to make China the largest supplier of arms to that country'.[131] Thus, Sino-Sri-Lankan relations, were expanded in political, economic, cultural and military spheres.

VI

Bangladesh emerged as an independent country in South Asia in December 1971. China's policy towards Bangladesh did not change till the fall of the Mujibur Rahman's government. It was only after Mujib was killed on 15 August 1975 and the new government demonstrated its clear anti Indian tilt, that there was a total change in the Chinese policy. The People's Republic of China recognised Bangladesh on 31 August 1975, fifteen days after the assassination of Mujibur Rahman.[132] This was followed by a joint communique of the ėstablishment of diplomatic relations between China and Bangladesh.

Gradually, Sino-Bangladesh bilateral relations became quite close. From China's point of view, the importance of Bangladesh arose from the basic geographical fact that the latter provides a useful, if not the only useful, territorial over bridge in reaching out to Mynamar and the adjacent areas of south east Asia. A trade route via chittagong, could as well be an added advantage for China's expanding external market. With worsening of relations with India. Bangladesh was constrained to look for diversified sources of assistance and thus reality drove it to build close ties with the western donor countries and the Muslim world as well as China. A perceived threat from India soon became the primary factor in the convergence of interest between Bangladesh and China Hence, Bangladesh gradually embraced China closely as the source of political economic and military support.

During Ziaur Rahman's era, China was being cultivated as a counterbalance against perceived hegenonistsic design of India. It was during Zia's regime that the foundation of close ties between Bangladesh and China was laid and cooperation began in all spheres political, economic, military and cultural.

China began to spoke in extremely assertive tones about regional controversies involving India. In February 1976, China 'condemned India's hegemonic action' regarding Farakka barrage and sharing water of the Ganges. It blamed India's unreasonable Stand for this issue and termed India's action as arrogant and hegemonic'.[133] Later on India and Bangladesh concluded an agreement on Sharing of the Ganga waters at Farakka in November, 1977.[134] In October 1976, the Chinese Foreign Minister stated in United Nations that: We firmly support the reasonable position taken by Bangladesh on the question of sharing the water of the Ganges.[135]

President Ziaur Rahman's visit to China was reciprocated by Chinese vice Premier. Li Hsiennien's visit to Bangladesh in March 1978.
Bangladesh supported Chinese positions on many international issues At

the nonaligned conference in Havana in September 1979, the Foreign Minister of Bangladesh, M. Shamsul Huq, emphasised the right of the Kampuchean people to freely choose a government without any external interference of foreign military presence or intervention".[136] Bangladesh government recognized the Pol Pot regime and opposed Heng Samrin's government. This strengthen the mutual ties between the two friendly nations who continued to share common views on growing number of regional and international issues.

It was during the regime of Ziaur Rahman that enduring relations in the economic field also began to develop. The first formal bilateral contact on economic assistance was made in April 1976. During Zia's visit to Beijing in January 1977, an agreement on Economic and Technical cooperation was signed. Two other agreements were signed when Chinese vice premier Li Hsienien visited Bangladesh in March 1978. The First one was the Economic and Technical Agreement under which China provided 850 million Taka interest free loans, repayable in ten years with a twelve years grace period for the purpose of a Urea factory, a water conservancy plant and some commodity procurements. The second one was a scientific and technological agreement valid for five years, providing for the exchange of expects and expertise on these fields.[137] Further Chinese aid was pledged in the fields of road building, agriculture and rural electrtification. In November 1978, a shipping Agreement was also signed.[138] During the period 1974 to 1979, Chinese foreign aid commitment to Bangladesh was US $ 65.80 million.[139]

Trade relations between Bangladesh and China also began to develop during Zia's regime.[140] During the period, Bangladesh's import from and export to China constituted approximately 3 per cent of the global import and export trade respectively.

The foundation of Bangladesh's close ties on the military front was also laid during Zia's period. Many factors motivated both sides to engage in cooperation in this field. First following the dramatic change in Bangladesh in August 1975, Moscow refused to supply spare parts for military equipment to Bangladesh in 1976. China promptly stepped in to fill in the vacuum. Chinese consideration was guided by the fact that gradually Dacca and Beijing had developed a common strategic perception on the basis of containing India. Second, the liberal nature of Chinese military aid. The terms of China's military aid we are generous, even when arms have been sold commercially. According to a report until 1979/1980 all China arms were supplied free of charge, either as direct grants or as interest free loans.[141] Another study shows that between 1975 and 1979 China supplied 78 percent of Bangladesh's arms imports.[142] This was an incentive strong enough for Bangladesh to be attracted to China's military aid policy. Third for Bangladesh, the Chinese weapons suited the defence forces of Bangladesh. For as a part of Pakistani defence force, they were more accustomed and trained to Chinese brand of weapons than that of any other brands. The inflow of Chinese military aid took place in two forms: weapons and military advisors. China also built arms and ammunication factory in Joydevpur and also took over Bangladesh's soviet built MIG's which Moscow refused to service. Later on China supplied F-6 fighter planes.[143] Thus, by the end of 1979 Sino-Bangladesh relations in various spheres had matured.

The geo-strategic position of Bangladesh is marked by three notable facts, which India cannot ignore. Firstly, Bangladesh with a population of 125 million could not be defined as small nation. Secondly, a friendly Bangladesh is important for unhindered access to strategically important north east India, through the narrow siliguri corridor. Thirdly, China is not a distant neighbour of Bangladesh, because between the north-west corner of Bangladesh and the Souther most point of Tibet's Chumbi valley lies only this very Siliguri corridor. Moreover, as China looks at the possibilities of a naval pressence in the India ocrean, the long Bangladesh coats line along the Bay of Bengal could be an area of interest to it. [144]

In the eighties, China continued to maintain friendly relations with Bangladesh. China in its desire to prove a counter balancing power to India; rapidly improved its relationship with Bangladesh. China also provided Bangladesh with considerable military and economic aid in order to overcome its military weakness and economic poverty.

At politico-strategic level, however, the 'India factor' as a source of unity between China and Bangladesh, seemed to have diluted from mid eighties onwards. A memorandum of understanding was signed between India and Bangladesh in October, 1982 on the question of Ganga water and both sides agreed to work towards a permanent solution.[145] President Ershad was given a clear hint by Chinese leadership during his one of the visits to Beijing that the Bangladesh government could not expect any Chinese support for pillorying India on the issue of river waters. Obviously, that was because in eighties China wanted to improve its relations with India and it no longer wanted to interfere in the bilateral matters among South Asian Countries. Nonetheless, China continued to maintain close relations with Bangladesh.

Of equally great significance, particularly from the Indian standpoint was Sino-Bangladesh linkage in military affairs. During this decade a number of high level military visits took place prominent among these from Chinese side were in January, 1987, Gen. Yang Dezhi, Chief of General

Staff of the PLA and again in 1989 and Chinese Defence Minister Gen. Qin Jiwei in February, 1990. Bangladesh got anti-tank guns, anti-air artillery, MIG-21 class fighters planes battle tanks, and AK-47 rifles.[146] Bangladesh also approached China for upgrading its inland and overseas navigation. The PLA Vice-Admiral Zhenglian Zhong reportedly assured his Bangladeshi counterpart of cooperation in sophisticated management of the navy.[147] It was this aspect of arms transfer in India's neighbourhood which concerned India.

India was concerned with China's military linkages in South Asia. During a debate in Lok Sabha on Demand of Grants of Ministry of External Affairs for the year 1988-89, a member Shri Brajmohan Mohanty stated that:

> "Everybody knows that Bangladesh is now closer to China, Pakistan and USA. China has built up one Chinese Division Inside Bangladesh. China is supervising one ordnance factory in Bangladesh. It is definitely a distressing situation for us. So far as Pakistan and China is concerned, one analysis is that China is not setting the border dispute simply to create an atmosphere of Strenght for Pakistan. Why this combination is a dangerous signal for Indian security and for India's integrity. We must note this.[148]

However, from mid eighties, China was cautious not to antagonise India for its ties-with Bangladesh.

VII

A significant feature in the Chinese policy towards South Asia was its unstinted support for South Asia regional cooperation which came into being as SAARC in 1985. China always supported the idea of regional cooperation in South Asia as a mechanism to promote South-South cooperation. Commenting on the inaugural meeting of SAARC Heads of state, held in Dacca, in 1985, Chinese observers remarked: 'Having suffered serious economic dislocation at the hands of imperialists, the South Asia region inhabited by a population of approximately 1 billion, is among the world's least developed, contributing only some two percent to world production. The South Asian people are pressing for peace and development in order to improve their livelihood. Regional cooperation is one of the routes through which they may attain goal'.[149] Similar sentiments were expressed by China's External Affairs Minister, Qian Qichen when he told Indian Foreign Minister, Narasimha Rao, 'China appreciates and supports South Asia Regional cooperation and hopes that the organisation will play an active role in peace, stability and development of the South

Asian region'.[150] This was a note worthy development in China's South Asian policy.

To sum it therefore, by 1991 China had registered a formidable presence in the South Asia. China began in 1963 from a position of weakness in South Asian, its only ally, Pakistan, being a state with limited capabilities and uncertain stability. Thus it adopted a multifaceted approach towards the region. In order to safeguard the precarious balance of power between Pakistan and prevent the emergence of an India controlled subcontinent, it supplied Pakistan with arms. It managed its alliance with Pakistan skillfully by broadening the base of the relationship to include not only the mutuality of strategic interests but also economic and development interests. China tried the same strategy and developed cordial relationship with other states in the region, i.e., Nepal, Bangladesh, Sri Lanka and Bhutan. From 1963 to 1979, China's stance towards the South Asian countries was primarily determined by its conflict with India. Therefore, Chinese encouragement of unfriendly and even hostile relations between India and the other countries in South Asia.

China was acting against India's security interest in the region. China was actively involved in destabilizing the security environment in the region. India, rightfully objected to China's high profile military role in the region. China's arms transfer to its archrival, Pakistan and other South Asian nationals concerned India. China continued to indulge as an intrusive power in the region. Thus, India perceived China's role in the South Asia as unfriendly.

From early eighties, there was subtle shift in China's South Asian policy. We can identify some elements of China's new policy in South Asia. Firstly, China desired to normalise its relationship with India. Secondly, China now encouraged bilateral settlement of outstanding problems between India and its neighbours. Third, China enthusiastically welcomed the process of regional cooperation in South Asia as a positive development. Fourthly, China decided to refrain from taking any stand on the internal political crises in any of the South Asian countries. However, the important point to note here is that China continued to cultivate India's neighbours in its quest for its long term interest to counteract India. China did not wish to downgrade its existing relationships with other South Asian countries and military ties with them continued unabatedly.
China continued to transfer nuclear weapons and missile manufacturing technologies to Pakistan.

If we review the evolution of China's policy towards South Asia, it is apparent that China's policy in South Asia was in a large measure determined its own relationship with India. It devised new means and subtle approaches with regard to South Asia to make Chinese presence felt in the region in the long term.

References

1. Quoted in P.K. Mishra, "China and South Asia", *in China Report* (New Delhi), Vol. 21, no. 5, 1985, p. 406.
2. Steven I. Levine, China and South Asia, *in Strategic Analysis* (New Delhi), Vol. 12, no. 10, January 1989.
3. See full text in R.K. Jain, *China-South Asia Relations 1947-1980,* Vol. II, (New Delhi, 1981), pp. 52-56.
4. Mohammed Ayub, "India as a Factor in Sino-Pakistani Relations", *International Studies* (New Delhi), Vol. 9, no. 3, January 1963, p. 292.
5. *Ibid.,* pp. 292-293.
6. Khalid Bin Sayeed, "Pakistan's Foreign Policy", *Asian Survey* (Berkeley), Vol. 4, March 1964, p. 749.
7. Bhabani Sen Gupta, *The Fulcrum of Asia* (New York, 1970), p. 179.
8. For details see, *China, India, Pakistan,* Pakistan Institute of International Affairs (Karachi, 1966), pp. 385-422.
9. Quoted in Bhabani Sen Gupta, n. 7, p. 180.
10. *Jawaharlal Nehru Selected Speeches,* Vol. IV, Publications Division, Government of India (New Delhi, 1964), p. 307.
11. Quoted in C. V. Ranganathan and Vinod C. Khanna, *India and China, The Way ahead After Mao's India War* (New Delhi, 2000) p. 138.
12. R. K. Jain, n. 3, p. 89.
13. *Ibid.,* pp. 92-94.
14. *Beijing Review* (Beijing,) no. 10, 5 March 1965, pp. 3-4.
15. *Ibid.,* no. 14, 2 April 1965, p. 5.
16. Quoted in T. Karki Hussain, *Sino-Indian Conflict and International Politics In the Indian Sub-continent*, 1962-66 (New Delhi), 1977, p. 73.
17. *Ibid.,* p. 70.
18. Beijing Review no. 37, 10 September, 1965, pp. 7-8.
19. Note of the Chinese Foreign Ministry, 8 September, 1965, White Paper XII, Ministry of External Affairs, New Delhi, p. 39.
20. Statesman, New Delhi, 14 September, 1965.
21. Quoted in Bhabani Sen Gupta, n. 7, p. 212.
22. For the text of the Chinese note, See Beijing Review, no. 39, 24 September, 1965.
23. Lok Sabha Debates, Vol. 46, 1965, col. 6334.
24. *Ibid.,* Col. 6570.
25. *Ibid.,* Vol. 47, 1965, Cols. 1893-94.
26. *Annual Report 1965-66*, Ministry of External Affairs, pp. 7-10.
27. *Annual Report 1969-70*, Ministry of Defence (Government of India), p. 1.
28. G.W. Choudhary, I*ndia, Pakistan, Bangladesh and The Major Powers: Politics of a Divided Sub Continent* (New York, 1975), p. 94.
29. *Beijing Review*, no. 47, 20 November 1970, pp. 8-9.

30. *Annual Report 1971-72*, Ministry of External Affairs, p. 23.
31. For China's Reaction to the Treaty see, S.K. Ghosh, The Indo-Soviet Treaty and China in *Journal of IDSA* (New Delhi), no. V, October, 1972, pp. 248-258.
32. *Beijing Review*, no. 46, 12 November 1971, p. 5.
33. *Annual Report 1971-72,* Ministry of External Affairs, pp. 28-29.
34. J.P. Jain, *China, Pakistan and Bangladesh* (New Delhi, 1974), pp. 165-67.
35. *Survey of Chinese Mainland Press* (Hong Kong, hereafter SCMP), 12 December 1971, no. 5042, p. 83.
36. *Beijing Review*, no. 49, 8 December, 1972, p. 11.
37. *Ibid.*
38. Quoted in J.P. Jain, *Nuclear India*, (New Delhi, 1974), Vol-II, pp. 339-40.
39. *Strategic Digest* (New Delhi) IV, no. 8, August 1974, p. 55.
40. *Times* (London), 15 December 1977.
41. *Beijing Review*, no. 27, 7 July 1978, p. 42.
42. *Times of India* (New Delhi), 10 July, 1978.
43. *Annual Report 1975-76*, Ministry of Defence, p. 3.
44. Quoted in C.V. Ranganathan and Vinod C. Khanna, n. 11, p. 139.
45. *Lok Sabha Debates*, Vol. 60, 1976, Col-166.
46. *FBIS, CHINA*-136, 13 July, 1980, p. C2.
47. *Annual Report 1981-82,* Ministry of Defence, p. 1.
48. *Beijing Review*, no. 24, 15 June 1981, p. 9.
49. *Ibid.*, no. 36, 6 August 1984, p. 8.
50. *China Daily* (Beijing) 2 May 1986.
51. Steven I. Levine, China and South Asia in *Strategic Analysis*, no. 10, XII, p. 1116.
52. *China Daily*, 16 September 1986.
53. *Lok Sabha Debates*, Vol. 8, 1985, Cols – 283-284.
54. Gargi Dutt and V. P. Dutt, *China After Mao* (New Delhi, 12990) n. 159, p. 409.
55. FBIS-CHI, 21 November 1989, p. 6.
56. Sujit Dutta, China and Pakistan, *China Report*, 30.2.1994, p. 138.
57. R. Bates Gill, Curbing Beijing's Arms Sales, *Orbis* (Philadelphia), Vol. 36, no. 3, Summer 1992, pp. 379-410.
58. Mushahid Hussain, Pakistan–China Defence Cooperation – An Enduring Relationship, *International Defence Review* (Surrey), no. 2, 1993, p. 110.
59. *Asian Recorder*, 24-31 December, 1989, p. 20934.
60. For details see, Aabha Dixit, Enduring Sino-Pak Relations: the Military Dimension, *Strategic Analysis*, 12(9), December, 1989. pp. 1067-1080.
61. For details see, R.R. Subramanian, *India, Pakistan and China* (New Delhi, 1989).
62. *FBIS – CHI*, 20 November, 1989, p. 9.
63. Lok Sabha Debates, Vol. 38, 1988, Cols-282-83.
64. *Ibid.*, Cols. 290-91.
65. Quoted in A.J. Chandy, "India, China and Pakistan", in Kanti Bajpai and

Amitabh Matoo, *The Peacock and The Dragon : India-China Relations in the 21st Century* (New Delhi, 2000), p. 301.
66. Quoted in M.L. Sondhi and Prakash Nanda, *Vajpayee's Foreign Policy : Daring the Irreversible* (New Delhi, 1999), p. 104.
67. *Asian Recorder*, 1964, p. 5874.
68. See A.S. Bhasin, *Documents on Nepal's Relations with India and China 1949-66* (New Delhi, 1970), pp. 251-54.
69. T.R. Ghoble, *China – Nepal Relations and India* (New Delhi, 1986), p.80.
70. A.S. Bhasin, *Nepal's Relations with India and China: Documents 1947-1992* (New Delhi, 1994), Vol. 1, p. 136.
71. Leo E Rose, *Nepal-Strategy for Survival* (Delhi, 1973), p. 273,
72. *Ibid.*
73. *Ibid.*, p.274.
74. T.R. Ghoble, n. 69, p. 54.
75. *Asian Recorder*, 1967, p. 7854.
76. *China Report*, September–October 1969, p. 24.
77. Quoted in T.R. Ghoble, n. 69, p. 58.
78. *Lok Sabha Debates*, 21 July 1969, Cols-230-40.
79. Xinhua, 27 February 1970.
80. *Patriot* (New Delhi), 7 June 1971.
81. Xinhua, 15 November 1972.
82. *Ibid.*, 23 June 1973.
83. *Beijing Review*, no.47, 22 November 1974, p. 17.
84. *Ibid.*, no.9, 28 February 1975, p. 4.
85. *People's Daily* (Beijing), 1 August 1975.
86. *Beijing Reivew*, no. 24, 11 June 1976. pp. 6-7.
87. Wang Hong Wei, "Sino-Nepal Relations in the 1980s", *Asian Survey*, Vol. xxv, no. 5, May 1985, p. 515.
88. Gargi Dutt and V.P. Dutt, n. 54, p. 405.
89. *Beijing Review*, no. 39, 28 September 1987, p.12.
90. Gargi Dutt and V.P. Dutt, n. 54, p. 406.
91. John W. Garver, "China and South Asia", *Annals of the American Academy* (Philadelphia), January 1992, p. 76.
92. *Lok Sabha Debates*, Vol. 3, 1985, Col-284.
93. The text of the 1950 treaty and letters is in R.K. Jha's *The Himalayan Kingdoms in Indian Foreign Policy* (Ranchi, 1986), pp. 347-50. The gist of the 1965 letters is presented in *Asian Recorder*, 27 August-2 September 1989, pp. 20740-42.
94. John W. Garver, n. 91. p. 77
95. Gargi Dutt and V.P. Dutt, n. 54, p. 407.
96. FBIS- CHI, 20 November, 1989, pp. 20-21.
97. *Ibid.*, 21 November, 1989, p. 12.
98. Ramakant, "Nepal's China Policy", *China Report,* no. 30, 2, 1994, p. 171.
99. *Link*, 24 June, 1990, p. 6.

100. Surjit Man Singh, China-Bhutan Relations, *China Report*, 30, 2 1994, p. 179.
101. *Beijing Review*, no. 46, 11 November 1966.
102. Surjit Man Singh, n. 100, p. 179.
103. Dorothy Woodman, *Himalayan Frontiers* (London, 1969), p. 314.
104. *Indian Express* (New Delhi), 18 June 1974.
105. *Ibid.*
106. Surjit Man Singh, n. 100, p. 179.
107. *Tribune* (Chandigarh), 5 November 1979.
108. *Sunday Standard*, 27 August 1979.
109. *Tribune*, 5 November 1979.
110. Tribune, 5 November, 1979.
111. Indian Express, 11 September, 1979.
112. Dong Ping, India's Special Relations with Bhutan, Beijing Review, No. 15, 12 April, 1982, p. 9.
113. *China Daily*, 12 April 1984.
114. *Ibid.,* 19 April 1984.
115. *Ibid.,* 21 April 1984.
116. *Ibid.,* 16 June, 1986.
117. Surjit Mansingh, n. 100, pp. 184-85.
118. *Ibid.*
119. V. Suryanarayan, "Sri Lanka's Policy Towards China", *China Report*, 30, 2, 1994, p. 206.
120. *News Review on China*, "Institute for Defence Studies and Analyses" (New Delhi), no. CH6/71, June 1971.
121. *Beijing Review*, no. 2 7, 7 July 1972, pp. 3-4.
122. See, "Sri Lanka: Roots of recent ethnic violence", in *Beijing Review*, no. 33, 15 August 1983, pp. 11-12, see also *China daily*, 29 July 1983.
123. *China Daily*, 18 November 1985.
124. *Beijing Review*, no. 12, 24 March 1986, p. 8.
125. S.D. Muni, *Pangs of Proximity: India and Sri Lanka's Ethnic Crisis* (New Delhi, 1993), p. 100.
126. V. Suryanarayan, n. 119, p. 212.
127. *S.D. Muni*, n. 125, p. 100.
128. For Chinese view point on this issue, see *Beijing Review*, no. 36, 7 September 1987, pp. 12-13.
129. Zhen Ru, Sri Lanka-Indian peace agreement and its influences, in (Materials on South and South East Asia) Chinese Academy of Social Sciences (Beijing), 1989, no. 28, p. 31.
130. For details see, Sujit Dutta, Chinese Military System, *Asian Strategic Review* (New Delhi), 1991-92, pp. 227-85.
131. R. Bates Gill, n. 57, pp. 379-410.
132. *Hindustan Times* (New Delhi), 1 September 1975.
133. *Beijing Review*, no. 9, 27 February 1976, p. 21.

134. See the text of treaty in India : Bilateral Treaties and Agreements, Vol. 9: 1976-77 (Government of India), pp. 285-89.
135. General Assembly Speech of Chiao Khan Hua, dated 5 October, 1976, Document No.229, in R.K. Jain (ed.), *China-South Asia Relations*, Vol. II (New Delhi, 1981), p. 262.
136. *Bangladesh Observer* (Dhaka), 3 September 1979.
137. Abu Taher S. Ahmed, "Bangladesh–China Relations: An Assessment", *BIISS Journal* (Dhaka) Vol. 13, no. 2, 1992, pp. 273-74.
138. *Bangladesh in International Affairs* (Dhaka), Vol. 1, no. 3, March 1978, p. 4.
139. Flow of External Resources into Bangladesh, "Economic Relations Division, Military of Finance, Government of Bangladesh", Dhaka, 24 December 1990, p. 58.
140. Abu Taher S. Ahmed, n. 137, p. 274.
141. *Bangladesh Observer*, 1 December 1978.
142. Anne Gilks and Gerald Segal, *China and the Arms Trade* (London, 1985), pp. 168-70.
143. Abu Taher S. Ahmed, n. 137, p. 280.
144. C.V. Ranganathan and Vinod C. Khanna, n. 11, p. 118.
145. *Annual Report 1982-83*, Ministry of External Affairs, p. 2.
146. *Times of India*, 11 August and 7 October 1987.
147. *Asian Recorder*, Vol. xxxvi, no. 37, 10-16 September, 1987.
148. *Lok Sabha Debates*, Vol. 38, 1988, Col. 378.
149. *Beijing Review,* No. 46, 15 November 1985, p. 11.
150. FBIS-CHI, No. 244, 20 December, 1988, p. 11.

5

The International Setting (1963-1991)

India-China relationship, although essentially bilateral in nature, has been compounded and even shaped greatly by external factors of regional and global settings. The previous chapter deals with the regional setting of India-China interaction. This chapter encapsulates the global setting and international aspects of India-China relations. India-China interaction, which is multidimensional, was shaped on the one hand, by the shifting nature of politics at the global level, and on the another hand, by the divergent interests and strategies of India and China, on many international issues. Further, the role of USA and USSR, the two superpowers and their relations in turn with the two concerned Asian Powers, also influenced. India-China interaction. Therefore, the international setting and aspects assumes importance in any comprehensive study of India-China relationship.

As far as international politics was concerned, the period beginning in 1963 was characterised by the west as one of détente, and by the Soviet Union as a relaxation of tension. For American leaders, 'détente' implied that neither state would challenge the *status quo* because such challenges tended to produce tension between the two superpowers. The world community had already witnessed the consequences of tension following Cuban missile crisis in October, 1962 and the need to avoid it in future.[1] Further, the Americans assumed that the Soviets would be willing to cooperate in the protection of the status quo in order to avoid tension in bilateral relations with the United States. For the Soviet leadership, relaxation of tensions like 'peaceful coexistence applied only to the relations between the two superpowers. The Soviets were not interested in preserving a global status quo. Certainly there was to be no truce in the ideological war.

For a decade, notwithstanding the differences both superpowers could design mutually acceptable norms for their own interactions. This trend, born during Cuban missile crisis, was central to world politics in this decade. It marked the end of the cold war, in which both the

Superpowers perceived each other as hostile and aggressive, pursued incompatible goals and manifested relatively high risk behaviours to protect their interests.[2] In 1963 both Superpowers took steps to reduce tensions. Firstly, in June 1963 there was 'Hot Line' treaty, by which a direct communications link between power centers in Washington and Moscow was established. Secondly and more importantly, in August 1963 a multilateral Test Ban Treaty was agreed upon, by which the Signatory powers including USA and USSR agreed not to test nuclear weapons in the atmosphere, outer space or under water.

The most important international event of 1963 was the open rift between Soviet Union and China, which had in fact brewing since late fifties but had been kept as a secret. There were many factors underlying the Sino-Soviet dispute.[3] It began with the 20th congress of the Communist Party of Soviet Union in 1956 and involved issues of ideology, revolution, international situation and Chinese interests. China was opposed to dialogue with the wanted state disturbed by the talks of 'peaceful coexistence' and more interested in revolution in Asia, Africa and Latin American. The Soviet Union refusal to provide China with a sample of an atomic bomb and technical data concerning its manufacture widened the rift between the two communist nations. India also figured as one of the factors underlying the rift. In 1963 during the exchange of polemics with the Soviet Union, the Chinese media wrote that 'one of the important differences of principle between the Soviet leaders and ourselves turns on the Sino-Indian boundary question.[4]

In early August 1963 the Soviet Union unfolded a powerful campaign against China. In a series of three articles Pravda publicly sided with India and denounced the Chinese leaders for exploiting the Cuban Crisis for aggression against India. It added that the fact has not escaped the attention of all countries that it was precisely when Cuba was threatened with terrible danger, when all peace loving people considered it their international duty to mobilize their forces to repel the threat of aggression against Cuba, the hostilities on the India – China border increased significantly.[5] In the opinion of Soviet Union, the Chinese attitude towards the Sino-Indian frontier issue had "nothing to do with ideology". It was purely nationalist in origin, and it had done "untold harm to the cause of socialism" quite apart from "encouraging the Indian reactionaries to exploit the border conflict and push India away from its nonaligned foreign policy and planned economy". Pravda also blamed the Chinese leaders for trying to destroy Soviet relations with India.

China rejected the Soviet charges that it had committed aggression against India. China denounced Pravda for allegedly serving as Nehru's "accomplice in evil deeds". Beijing described the Soviet stand on India-China crisis as "the first instance in history in which a socialist country, instead of condemning the armed provocations of the reactionaries of a capitalist country, condemned another fraternal socialist country when it was confronted with such armed provocations.[6] China continued to attempt to prove that Soviet policy towards India was wrong and protested loudly for betrayal of the socialist camp and for abandonment of proletarian internationalism.[7] China alleged that "the leadership of the C.P.S.U. and its press.

> Openly sided with Indian reactionaries, condemned China for its just stand on the Sino-Indian border conflict and defended the Nehru government. Two-thirds of Soviet economic aid to India have been given since the Indian reactionaries provoked the Sino-Indian border conflict. Even after large scale armed conflict on the Sino-Indian border began in the autumn of 1962, the leadership of the C.P.S.U. has continued to extend military aid to the Indian reactionaries.[8]

By now Soviet Support to India was evidently a major issue in Sino-Soviet rift. For the Chinese it was this particular action of Soviet Union which rankled most. China fully comprehended that the USSR's stand provided the Nehru government with a tremendous political lever. Hence, it understood Nehru's Statement that "Soviet neutrality in the India-China Conflict was of greater help to India than all the military aid which India received from the west".[9] China also noted that the Indian government had made it an important aspect of its foreign policy to exploit Sino-Soviet differences and to widen these further.

China was enraged by the fact that both the superpowers helped India and condemned China. As already mentioned USA under Kennedy administration adopted a friendly approach towards democratic India. Kennedy, it may be recalled, had perceived India as the key area in Asia and wanted it to win the political and economic race against China. Arthur M. Schlesinger recalls Kennedy's famous remark: "We want India to win the race with China... If China succeeds and India fails, the economic development, balance of power will shift against us".[10] The Kennedy administration responded promptly to the Chinese attack of 20th October, 1962. In a communiqué issued on 21 October, the State Department stated that the United States was "shocked at the violent and aggressive action of the Chinese communists against India. "It further stated that any Indian request" would be considered sympathetically.[11] Meanwhile, faced with the imminent collapse of its military in the north-east region, India was compelled to seek military equipments from the U.S.A. U.K. and U.S.S.R. On 26 October, India sent a general appeal for "Sympathy as well as support" to al governments. In making this appeal Prime Minister Nehru underscored the vital significance of the conflict between India and China. "this crisis is not only of India but of the world and will have far reaching consequences on the standards of international behaviour and on the peace of the world".[12] President Kennedy promptly sent an enthusiastic reply. The process of closer ties between India and USA was hastened by the Kennedy administration's recognition of the Indian position on the McMahon Line.[13] On 27 October, Ambassador Galbraith made the first official declaration about recognition of the McMahon Line: "the McMahon Line is an accepted international border and is sanctioned by modern usage. Accordingly, we regard it as the northern border of the NEFA area[14].

The United States started an emergency arms air-lift to India and for a week (in November1962) 10 U.S. jet fighters, airlifted on a round – the clock basis 60 plane loads of automatic weapons and ammunition to India from various stocks in the U.S. and Europe. [15]

When the conflict ceased on the Himalayan battleground, Kennedy faced the task of responding to Nehru's request for long term assistance to India. So as to effectively deter further Chinese attacks. A fact finding political-military mission headed by Auverill Harriman was sent to India.

However, During the next eleven months, i.e., until the end of the Kennedy administration, progress towards further U.S. arms aid to India was slow. 1963. In the meantime, a series of talks started between the United States and Britain regarding India's defence needs and other related matters. From April to May, 1963, two important Indian missions visited Washington. The first was a team of experts led by S. Boothalingam, Secretary, Ministry of Economic and Defence coordination and this was essentially a mission for procuring defence equipment and stores needed for the Army's overhaul.[16] In early June the President of India, Dr. S. Radhakrishnan, came to United States on a state visit. In a Joint Statement issued on 4 June, Presidents Kennedy and Radhakrishnan agreed that their two countries "Share a mutual defensive concern to thwart the designs of Chinese aggression against the sub content."[17] In the meeting between Kennedy – Macmillan in Brich Grove, Sussex, U.K., the two statesmen reaffirmed their policy of "continuing" help to India by providing further military aid to strengthen its defence against the threat of renewed Chinese attack.[18].

The Indian government was a bit disillusioned with the United States modest offer. Any systematic development of India's defence potential as envisaged under a five-year defence plan (1954-69) – in view of the Chinese threat – called for sizeable capital and technical input. An additional Indian concern was to ensure the continued progress of its economic development. Under these circumstances, India found Soviet Union quite understanding. The growing Sino-Soviet rift underlined India's vital importance to the Soviet policy makers. Therefore, the Indians found Soviet Union all set to favourably respond to their request. Be that as it may, the U.S.A. support to India boosted India's sagging morale at a crucial juncture. The support which India received from both the superpowers, U.S.A. and U.S.S.R. rankled China.

By the end of 1963, China found itself ranged against both the superpowers which for different reasons were aiming at isolating it and hence were eager to support India. The fact that India stood to gain out of the situation was provocative enough for China to began a counter – offensive on the diplomatic front. It therefore, spared no effort to criticise the Soviet action in propping up a regime which it described as having sold out to the west. China tried hard to link India with the US and the Soviet Union imagining that there was some kind of collusion against China.[19] With the support of the Soviet Union, India would be able to continue wearing "the cloak of non-alignment" and to use Soviet aid to cover up the fact that it was a protégé of the United States and with Soviet Support would be able to attack China.

The Soviet Union rebuked the Chinese leaders for asserting that the Nehru government was "imperialist" and "expansionist" and expressed doubt that in the light of such "false allegations" it was difficult to believe the Chinese wanted to resolve the border dispute peacefully. It also questioned "why the Colombo powers asked only China to withdraw and not India?"[20]

The Chinese response to the Soviets forms the most comprehensive indictment of the Soviet stand on Sino-Indian differences. The Chinese media contrasted what it described as Soviet partisanship with the Strict neutrality of the Afro-Asians. It declared that the stand and the policy of the Soviet leaders on the Sino-Indian boundary question amply proved that they no longer considered the "imperialists, headed by the U.S." and the reactionaries of all countries to be their enemy. "It is the Marxist Leninists.. China in particular who are their enemy.... They have openly declared their alliance with the Indian reactionaries. They probably think that by joining with all the scoundrels in the world in shrieking abuse, they can discredit and isolate China.[21] It followed that Sino-Soviet polemics on India-China conflict had become an important function of the intense antagonism which emerged as fundamental between the two communist powers. A détente with the west remained high on Soviet priority as was evident in its compromise on Cuba and the Signing of the partial test ban treaty of August 1963 and on Inner space in 1964.[22] The Soviet Union also founded it necessary to isolate China as it challenged the entire edifice of Soviet perspective and goal on international affairs. By the end of 1963, the contradictions between the two communist protagonists were taking precedence over other issues. China had become the principal adversary against which Soviet Union was sharpening its criticism. By this time, Sino-Soviet differences on their 4,500 miles long frontier in the Far East and Central Asia had become an additional factor in their mutual hostility.[23]

In view of what has been noted above, it inevitably followed that in the post – 1962 period, Soviet policies towards South Asia were formulated to off set Chinese influence and to restrain China from disturbing the status quo on the Sino-Indian border. Since the 1962 war had exposed India's military vulnerability, the Soviets effectively demonstrated the fact that they would not only watch over India's Security interests but also assist it substantially. Chine in turn deliberately contributed towards enlarging the scope of the cold war by getting further involved in South Asia, particularly on the Indo-Pak question and simultaneously, continued to maintain its political – diplomatic confrontation against India.

China claimed that "massive military aid" to India from the Soviet Union had opened a "new chapter of collaboration" between the Soviet Union and the United States to align India against China. The Chinese media widely quoted the statement of Indian Defence Minister, Chavan replying to members of parliament's stated Categorically that India could use the Soviet Migs and tanks 'against China'.[24]

The fall of Khruschev in October, 1964 delighted the Chinese leaders, who regarded the event as a "major victory" of their policy. The new Soviet leaders however, refused to make any concession on the frontier question and other fundamental issues. The Soviet stand on India hurt them the most. China felt slighted.

To the Chinese, India become the most vital issue in their relations with the Soviet Union, India was seen as having poisoned Sino-Soviet relations. This infuriated the Chinese to the point of irrational hatred. India, on its part, was concerned that when the world was moving towards a peaceful settlement of the grave problems and when the Soviet Union and the USA are striving to their utmost ability to put an end to the cold war, there should be this relapse into violence and aggression on the frontiers of India.[25] The gulf between Moscow and Beijing over India widened further. In May 1965, when Prime Minister Shastri visited

Moscow, China alleged that the "Soviet revisionist clique and the Indian reactionaries are bedfellows in opposing China . . . . now Khruschev's successors are pursuing Khruschev's line to form an anti-China alliance with Nehru's successors'. India's foreign policy of non-alignment and peaceful coexistence was another major target of Chinese criticism and condemnation. For China, the policy of non-alignment and peaceful coexistence stood in the way of their war like theory of uninterrupted struggle and confrontation with the "imperialists" and "the revisionists". The fact that India's foreign policy played some part in bringing about relaxation in the cold war and in the détente between the two power blocs was particularly disliked by China. During the year 1965-66 the Chinese tried hard to link India with the US and the Soviet Union imagining that there was some kind of collusion between these three powers against China.[26]

In the Indo-Pakistan conflict in the Rann of Kutch and subsequently over Kashmir in 1965, the Chinese sided with Pakistan. When the Soviet Union came up with an offer of good offices to end the conflict; China alleged, What the Soviet leaders intend to do is, in the name of good offices, to aid the Indian aggressors to force Pakistan to accept India's annexation of Kashmir as legitimate.[27] On 9 December, 1965, Soviet Media announced that Indian Primer Shastri and Pak President Ayub had agreed to the Soviet proposal to meet in Tashkent on 4 January, 1966. Despite the basic difference in the Indo-Pak approaches due to Soviet mediation, Shastri and Ayub reached an accord at the end of the week long secret confabulations. The Chinese Government was the only nation to have been displeased with the accord reached at Tashkent. China attacked the Tashkent talks as "a product of joint US-Soviet planning" and charged that the Soviet Union had "instigated and encouraged the Indian aggressor and brought crude pressures to bear on Pakistan". It was evident that the Chinese government considered the restoration of peace on the Indian subcontinent as a setback to their own plans and designs.[28] The Chinese charged that Soviet leaders had feigned neutrality in the Indo-Pak conflict but had in fact backed India at every step and that those "adding fuel to the flames" in the situation were precisely the Soviet leaders, in addition to the U.S. imperialists and they wanted to start another anti-China campaign on a global scale.[29] Prime Minister, Lal Bahadur Shastri repudiated the Chinese pretension to be a guardian of Asian countries and asserted that "no self respecting nation in Asia , large or small, strong or weak, will accept the dominance of the Chinese".[30]

China also alleged that India was toeing U.S.'s line on Vietnam.[31] China misunderstood India's constructive role as chairman of the

International control commission. When Indian Premier Mrs. Gandhi went to U.S.A. in 1966, the Chinese media stated that "each time an Indian Prime Minister goes to the USA there is the task of begging for help to keep the government's head above water.[32] China continued to blame Soviets and stated that "the Soviet revisionist clique spares no expense to rear anti-China hatchet men in Asia, the Indian reactionaries . . . . this clique has given the reactionary Indian Government nearly 900 million U.S. Dollars worth of military aid since 1962 This amount far exceeded the 340 million dollar military aid U.S. imperialism gave India over the same period".[33]

In the meantime, there were reports of Sino-Soviet border tension at the end of 1965, and again in the spring of 1966 Moscow renewed its defensive alliance with outer Mongolia and there were reports of substantial movement of Soviet troops into eastern outer Mongolia.[34] The net result of simmering tensions Sino-Soviet orders was the intensification of armed patrols by both sides. On 2 March, 1969, Soviet and Chinese forces fought a two-hour battle for control of Damansky island in the Ussuri River. During the months following the Ussuri clashes of March 1969, the Soviet union rapidly built up forces along and near the Chinese border and stated that unless Beijing agreed to hold formal talks on the territorial issue it might be subjected to invasion or the destruction of its nuclear installations,[35] In June 1969, the Soviet leader Brezhnev announced the Soviet project to promote the creation of a Collective Security System in Asia to erect barriers to the expansionist ambition of China in Asia.[36]

The Chinese reaction was predictably sharp.[37] They denounced the Soviet project as a new move on the part of the "Soviet revisionist leaders to rig up a military alliance against China."[38]

Subsequent Soviet Statements sought to counter the Chinese charges. Soviet Premier Kosygin said that the Soviet proposal was aimed at "uniting the peace-loving forces in Asia, not for war but as a "barrier" against aggressions. Nevertheless, he urged India, Pakistan and Afghanistan to join together to face "the new hegemonic forces in Asia".[39] India, it not may be noted here did not show any enthusiasm for the Soviet project. Still, China stated that "every one knows that the Soviet revisionist renegaude clique views the Indian reactionaries as important partners in its anti-China line up.... Thus, by the end of 1969, Sino-Soviet hostility had scaled new heights and India became an important factor in Sino-Soviet rift. The potential for war following the border incidents between the two communist giants would encourage momentous changes in the first half of the next decade.

II

The advent of the decade of the seventies witnessed shift from bipolar strategic balance to development of triangular diplomacy among the three countries, i.e.,+ U.S.A., U.S.S.R. – P.R.C. By now China had emerged as an Asian Power by virtue of its advance towards a viable nuclear force; followed by the historic decision in October, 1971 to admit People's Republic of China in the United Nations. Communist China now became a permanent member of the Security Council. Internally, China emerged from the chaotic days of cultural revolution and leadership in the hands of moderate Zhou En Lai, under the tutelage of Mao Zedong. The early 1970s marked the convergence of American and Chinese thinking about their major common problem, i.e., the Soviet Union. For Beijing, the Soviet Union became major threat and following U.S.A.'s decision to reduce its military role in South East Asia, Vietnam in particular, China no longer considered U.S. as major threat. The new administration in U.S. under Richard Nixon was disenchanted with the Vietnam war. American foreign policy took into account the continuing Sino-Soviet hostility and its inescapable impact on Soviet-American rivalry and détente. By developing a triangular relationship with China and the Soviet Union, the United States could derive considerable diplomatic leverage from the dispute between the two communist giants, even while refusing to take sides. In 1970 and 1971, U.S. took many steps to send positive signals to China and once China made up its mind, the movement towards a Sino-American détente gathered considerable momentum. Meanwhile the relations between India and the USSR accelerated in early seventies, leading to consolidation of ties between Delhi and Moscow. The three developments, i.e. China's split with the Soviet Union, conflict with India and rapprochement with the USA meant that India and the Soviet Union had acquired a new geo-strategic commonality of interest.

The impending thaw in Sino-American relations added to the alarm in India over the pro-Pakistan position of both the United States and China in the South Asian Crisis, raising fresh apprehensions of a possible Sino-American Pakistani axis against India. The U.S. Secretary of State Henry Kissinger warned the Indian government in July, 1971 that if war broke out in the Subcontinent, China might intervene. He further stated that if China attacked India this time, India should not expect the United States to provide military and other support, as it had done in 1962.[40]

South Asia witnessed escalation of Indo-Pakistani crisis over East Pakistan in 1971. Now, on the one hand, the triangular diplomacy contributed to the development of the crisis; and on the other, in turn was influenced by perceptions stemming from it."[41] In fact, Nixon and Kissinger's main consideration initially was the China connection within the framework of the emerging triangular diplomacy. In mid-July, 1971, Kissinger secretly visited China via Pakistan and a direct American-Chinese link was established. Sensing the approaching Sino-U.S. accord and having played the role of messenger between U.S. and China, Yahya Khan boasted in July that, in a war with India, Pakistan will not be alone"[42] On 17 July, 1971 it was announced that President Nixon would visit China before May 1972, and Dr. Henry Kissinger, who had been reported to be indisposed in Pakistan, was actually in Beijing conferring with Premier Zhou Enlai. U.S. tilt against India was adopted after the China connection was secured.

Indian and Soviet interests began to converge as the Soviet Union failed to resolve its disputes with China, and India failed to attract the benign attention of the Nixon administration of USA.[43] On 9 August 1971, Soviet Foreign Minister, Andrei A. Gromyko and Indian Foreign Minister, Swaran Singh Signed in New Delhi a Treaty of Peace, Friendship and Cooperation between the two countries.

The most significant section from the view point of India's interests was article IX"— in the event of either party being subjected to an attack or a threat thereof, the High Contracting Parties shall immediately enter into mutual consultations in order to remove any such threat and to take appropriate effective measures to ensure peace and the security of their countries".[44] From a Soviet viewpoint, the treaty was probably understood as a part of the planned network of bilateral treaties which would underpin Brezhnev's Asian Collective Security System, and which was designed to isolate China. India's interests were more pressing : to deter China and the United States from intervening to help Pakistan and to ensure Soviet diplomatic support, especially in the United Nations.

The Indo-Soviet Treaty followed the dramatic Sino-US rapprochement. Specifically, it was an insurance policy taken out in case of China's military intervention in the Bangladesh crisis.[45] China reacted strongly to Indo-Soviet treaty. The first Chinese comment on the treaty came on 25 September, 1971 when a member of a visiting Chinese trade delegation reportedly said that China "certainly does not regard the signing of the recent Indo-Soviet treaty as a friendly act so far as it is concerned". He also said that China was watching the "growing USSR-India collaboration against China".[46]

On its part, the Indian Government behaved with great restraint even in the face of grave provocations and stressed the need for better relations between India and China. In the Parliament many members underlined the need of fluidity vis-à-vis China. The External Affairs Minister of India, Shri Swaran Singh stated that "inspite of the hostile and bellicose statements made by China against us, we have deliberately refrained from being provoked in order not to increase tensions." In this connection, he also clarified that the Indo-Soviet treaty did not stand in the way of India's normalising of relations with China, and was not directed against China or any other country. The minister further stated:

> We cannot accept any conditions that the normalisation of relations with any country may deter us from developing friendship with any other country. The Soviet Union itself has been trying to normalise relations with china and would be happy to see the normalisation of relations between India and China as we would be happy to see normalisation of relations between China and the USSR.[47]

The Indo-Soviet Treaty also had ramifications for Sino-American relations with Pakistan. They coordinated their policy to encourage Pakistan to resolve the crisis in its own way. The U.S. endeavoured to frighten India by raising the threat of a Chinese invasion if India did not cease its aid to the dissidents in East Pakistan. This and other moves of the U.S. encouraged the Chinese to strike an aggressive posture towards India. A week after Kissinger's meeting with Zhou, China abandoned its cautious policy on East Pakistan. Chinese foreign minister, Ji Pengfei denounced the freedom struggle in East Pakistan as "unpatriotic" and accused India of "interference" in Pakistan's domestic affairs. Emboldened by Sino-U.S. support, Yahya Khan threatened on 6 November, 1971 that Indo-Pakistani relations had reached the "point of no return" and declared that the war was the only possibility between the two nations. The following day he assured his countrymen that in the event of an Indo-Pakistan war "China will intervene on behalf of Pakistan".[48]

In a statement, the Soviet Union, on its part, warned the Chinese against intervening in the conflict and said that in the event of (Chinese) interference the Soviet Union would not "remain in different to the developments taking place in direct proximity of the borders of U.S.S.R. and involving its security interests.[49] The Chinese accused Moscow of "instigating India to commit large scale aggression against Pakistan" and vociferously attacked the Indian expansionists for trying to "dismember" Pakistan and establish a "puppet state" in East Pakistan like the Japanese set up in Manchukuo. Reacting sharply to the Chinese criticism of the Soviet stand on the Indo-Pakistan conflict the Soviet Union denounced the Sino-American designs to prevent normalisation of conditions in the subcontinent and accused them of planning to establish a "Sino-American condominium" there.

From the beginning the American policy in this crisis was guided by the fact of Chinese connection. The U.S. position was influenced by the strong Chinese support for Pakistan. As the war proceeded, the U.S. took a firm stand in favour of the Sino-Pakistani position. Kissinger wrote that "we have to prevent India from attacking West Pakistan.[50] On 10 December, U.S. decided to send the U.S. Navy and the air craft carrier USS Enterprise along with 2000 combat ready marines, towards the Bay of Bengal. As a scholar has put it, this decision indicated the U.S. resolve to support China. The aim was to "demonstrate to China that we were a reliable country to deal with, and that we stand for a mutual friend".[51] The U.S. position was above all with an eye to its new relationship with China.

India however, achieved its main objective, the independence of East Pakistan and creation of Bangladesh, despite Chinese and American opposition. India continued to base its policy on its own interests. It found Soviet support but at the same time it was careful not to move too close to the Soviet Union.

China, however regarded India's victory over Pakistan as an increase of Soviet influence on China's Southern flank. Following developments in Bangladesh , China took a consistently hostile stand against India and supported the Pakistan Government vis-à-vis Bangladesh. Both inside and outside the United Nations, China violently criticised India. China regularly and consistently condemned India as having committed "aggression" on Pakistan with the help of Soviet "Social imperialism". [52] When the war came to an end, the Chinese began to seek ways of reducing the Soviet presence in the sub continent and welcomed the Shimla agreement of 1972 between India and Pakistan.

Following the new Sino-US rapprochement in 70's China leaned with U.S.A. against its current enemy U.S.S.R. As for the U.S., the new dialogue with China formally spelled the end of the containment policy of the 50's and 60's. China had finally won western acceptance and universal recognition of her vastly enhanced status in the emerging global balance of power although China still lacked sufficient economic and military resources to conduct a global diplomacy on the scale of either superpower. Nevertheless, China's enhanced diplomatic status, her ideological influence in the third world, and, above all, her geopolitical importance in Asia had forced the United States and the Soviet Union into a triangular relationship. Now, one of the primary aims of Mao's revolutionary diplomatic line was to take advantage of the interacting forces in the Moscow-Washington- Beijing triangle to weaken Soviet Union.

One of the most interesting characteristics of the triangle was that while each party was antagonistic to the other two, yet none of the three bilateral relationship, i.e. U.S.-U.S.S.R., U.S.S.R.-China, China-U.S. was exclusively antagonistic.[53] For China, the principal objective in playing the triangular game was to reduce Soviet-American Collusion to a minimum, mount opposition to the two super powers by highlighting such collusion, and contain Soviet expansionism by threatening collusion with the United States.

In China's perception, between, the two superpowers, the Soviet Union was clearly the more aggressive. The Soviet policy of détente was dismissed by the Maoist leadership as a propaganda exercise intended to conceal the imperialist ambitions of the Soviet revisionist leadership. China's conception of her own role in confronting this challenge was essentially two fold: to alert the world to the real nature of hegemonism and to mobilise a new united front capable of defeating it.[54] It was in order to pursue this struggle and form the broadest possible United front against Soviet Social- imperialism that China had moved towards détente with the United States.

The decision on full normalisation of relations between the United States and China from 1 January, 1979 was announced in Beijing by Premier Hua Guofeng on 16 December, 1978. The Joint Sino-U.S. Communique stipulated that the U.S. recognised the Government of the People's Republic of China as the sole legal Government of China and that within this context the U.S. would maintain cultural, commercial and other unofficial relations with the people of Taiwan. The U.S. also added that "acknowledges the Chinese position that there is but one China and Taiwan is a part of China". Both Countries reaffirmed the principles of the Shanghai Communique of 1972.[55] This relationship fitted in with Deng's policy of opening to the world. The core of this policy was the utilisation of the opportunities for trade with the west, accessibility to U.S. market and western technology for the modernisation of Chinese economic structure.[56]

As far as Sino-Indian relations were concerned, the Soviet factor remained as important as ever. The defeat of Mrs. I Gandhi in the 1977 general elections emboldened the Chinese to believe that Soviet - Indian relations were based on thin ice and it was possible to wreck this relationship by adopting a friendlier attitude with the new Janata regime in New Delhi. In a commentary Xinhua declared that "the outcome of the national election showed the unpopularity of the internal and external policies of the congress party government. With the support and connivance of Soviet social imperialism the Congress government pursued for years a policy of expansionism and thus isolated itself not only in South Asia but also in the whole world.. Only the Kremlin mouthpiece Tass described the internal and external policies of the Congress Party as "Progressive"... Soviet attempt to influence the Indian election is futile.[57] Moscow, however, reminded New Delhi that despite sweet words of "normalisation of relations with India", China remained a "serious menace" to the security of India. They warned that the Karakoram highway built by the Chinese a cross the Indian territory illegally occupied by Pakistan represented the "greatest danger" to India. "The road is constructed to serve China's military strategic aims" and "cannot but disquiet India".[58]

When India's External Affairs Minister A.B. Vajpayee visited to Soviet Union in September, 1978, he assured his hosts that his forthcoming visit to China would in no way affect Indo-Soviet friendship and that India had "her own experience with China and her eyes and ears are wide open". In February, 1979 when Vajpayee was in China, China invaded Vietnam. Much to the embarrassment of India, Deng Xiaoping stated that China was determined to teach a lesson to Vietnam and linked China's attack with earlier at lack of India in October, 1962. Vajpayee reacted by cutting short his trip to Beijing. After Vajpayee's visit to China, Soviet leader Leonid Brezhnev reportedly told Premier Morarji Desai: "Your Foreign Minister's visit to China was not well received by our public. I do not know how your people reacted to it but our people took it very ill.[59] The Soviet Union cautioned the Indian leadership against dangerous intention of China and advised not to trust China.

After wards Vietnam occupied centre stage of international politics. In 1978, Chinese living in Vietnam began to flee northward, claiming persecution by the Vietnamese government. Border incidents became common. The Indo-China Cauldron was boiling. The murderous policies of the Khmer Rouge and Pol Pot and the impending trouble in the peninsula were followed by the Soviet – Vietnam Treaty of Friendship and Mutual alliance. As a result China charged that Vietnam had become "the Cuba of the orient.[60] Meanwhile, relations between Vietnam and communist Cambodia (renamed Kampuchea) worsened. Historic animosities, persecution of Vietnamese in Kampuchea, and the Savagery of the Kampuchea government encouraged Vietnam to invade Kampuchea in December, 1978. China perceived that its legitimate zone of influence was being disturbed and it retaliated in February, 1979. China sent its troops into Vietnam to retaliate against Vietnamese border provocations, but in effect to punish Vietnam for sending its troops into Cambodia and toppling the Khmer Rouge regime and installing in its place a pro Chinese Government. The Soviet Union harshly condemned the Chinese attack as an unprecedented brazen bandit attack in which the Chinese rulers revealed fully to the world the perfidious, aggressive essence of the great-power policy pursued by them.[61]

On the Kampuchean issue, India and China differed widely. While Beijing Supported Khmer Rouge and Pol Pot regime, New Delhi Supported Heng Samrin regime. China perceived India's stand in Kampuchea was influenced by India's close relationship with the Soviet Union. The differences on Kampuchean issue affected India-China normalisation process for a while.

III

Sino-Soviet ties were, further worsened by developments in Afghanistan. In April, 1978, one such coup brought to power members of the two rival factions of the Afghan communist party and this was termed as the Saur revolution. The religious groups in Afghanistan did not accepted this turn of events and they began to resist the new regime. Rivalry among the communist factions produced another coup in 1979 and generated more instability. Therefore, in December, 1979 the Soviets decided to send their troops into Afghanistan. The Soviets claimed that the Afghan government had requested it. The Soviet leader Brezhnev pledged to withdraw the forces when stability returned and foreign interference in Afghanistan ended. President Carter of U.S.A. rejected the Soviet allegation of Western meddling and demanded an immediate Soviet withdrawal.

The Afghanistan issue put relations between the two superpowers on a new footing and a new cold war loomed on the horizon for the next decade. China's attitude towards Afghanistan changed significantly in the aftermath of the 1978 revolution. Even before the alleged Soviet invasion, the Afghan revolution was seen as part of the Soviet grand strategy, having global rather than purely regional implications.[62] With the Soviet invasion of Afghanistan in December 1979, the situation became critical. In China's perception - the Soviet Union was determined to become the dominant power in Asia and Beijing was alarmed. The massive Soviet military deployment on the Sino-Soviet border was in itself disturbing for China. There were reportedly some 48 Soviet divisions on the border and another 10 in Mongolia equipped with the most modern weaponry.

Afghanistan crisis signalled the return of the cold war between superpowers but this time the theatre changed from Europe to Asia. Though the global triangular diplomacy remained intact, but gradually there was subtle shift within it. These subtle changes no longer remained subtle over the next two years when China adopted "independent foreign policy." In 1982 China's foreign policy was transformed by objective changes in international situations and Chinese priority. In his report to the 12th National Congress of the Communist Party of China, the General Secretary of the party said the policy is based on "the five principles of peaceful co-existence" and establishing and developing normal, friendly relations with all the countries that treat China as an equal; strengthening unity and cooperation with other third world countries and friendly nations; and opposing hegeonism and maintaining world peace.[63] The essential feature of this new foreign policy was that China "will not attach itself to any big power or bloc of nations and will not submit itself to the pressure of any big power". The general principle was to oppose hegemonism and to promote peace.[64] China was noting and responding to other changes that were taking place in the international scene. The most important was the "decline of the Super powers", which was in the offing. Both the super powers were facing reverses.

In 1980, Moscow and Beijing traded charges and counter charges on Afghanistan. The Chinese called it blatant aggression while the Soviets accused China of having teamed up with the West to send counter - revolutionary gangs into Afghanistan. China announced in January 1980 its decision not to resume talks with the Soviets on improving relations because of what it called Soviet "invasion of Afghanistan".[65] The Soviet presence in Afghanistan also created major threats to the Security of China's close ally, Pakistan. Thus, Pakistan was assigned a crucial role: a frontline state, providing sanctuary on its territory for the Afghan Mujahideen. Such an operation was discussed by Chinese and American officials during Defence Secretary Harold Brown's January 1980 visit to Beijing. During those talks, China and U.S.A. agreed to cooperate in aiding Pakistan.[66] In terms of diplomatic support. China urged the U.S. to renew its lapsed security relation with Pakistan, and encouraged the U.S., Western Europe and Japan to provide economic assistance.[67]

In regard to Afghanistan, India called for a political settlement through negotiations among the parties concerned on the basis of withdrawal of foreign troops, stoppage of all forms of outside interference and the preservation of the independence. Sovereignty, territorial integrity and non aligned status of Afghanistan.[68]

Mrs. Indira Gandhi returned to power in January, 1980 and she was determined to reconsolidate India's bond with the Soviet Union which she believed the Janata government had weakened. Consequently, she hosted Soviet President Leonid Brezhnev's visit to India in December 1980. During President Brezhnev's visit, Mrs. Gandhi directly expressed India's 'opposition to all forms of outside interference in the internal affairs of other countries, whether through induction of regular troops or through infiltration.'[69] Soviet-Indian economic and military cooperation expanded substantially during 1980-84, with large new Soviet trade credits and supply of a wide range of advance military equipment. At the same time, however, Mrs. Gandhi was apprehensive of becoming tied too closely to Soviet Union. She was aware of the potential dangers posed to India's long term Security interests by Soviet troops entry into Afghanistan. These concerns led India to seek to diversify Indian diplomacy by expanding its ties with Western Europe and the United States.

Equally importantly, India wanted to improve relations with China and stressed its role in the non-aligned movement.[70] China, too was interested in improving relations with India after the developments in Afghanistan. China tried to facilitate normal relations with India by avoiding the Kampuchean issue where both nations were pursuing altogether different policies. India was one of the main supporters of Vietnam and Kampuchea at the United Nations and within the Non-Aligned Movement. The exception to this was China's Virulent criticism of India's recognition of the Heng Samrin regime in Kampuchea in July 1980. India's close friendship with the Soviet regime in Kampuchea led China to suspend Foreign Minister Huang Hua's long scheduled trip to India.[71] Despite China's ardent desire by that time to improve relations with India for the sake of lessening Soviet influence throughout the South Asian region, it took China ten months to swallow its anger over India's Indochinese policy and reschedule Huang Hua's India visit in June 1981. The Chinese termed India's move in Kampuchea "a foolish decision that completely discredits the Indian government internationally". It alleged that India's move was due to the stepped-up Soviet aid to India.

In the aftermath of Brezhnev's December, 1980 visit to India, China concluded that India had not yet capitulated to Soviets. It noted that "Brezhnev did not get everything he wanted .... He had not been able to alter India's stand on the Afghanistan issue, despite his going to India in person."[72] In June, 1981 Chinese foreign minister, Huang Hua arrived in India. In India, Huang Hua called for India and China to "seek common ground on major issues while preserving differences on minor ones," and noted that "the basic starting point for Chinese foreign policy is to oppose hegemonism." During Huang's 1981 visit the two sides agreed to begin discussions on the border issue and other bilateral exchanges.

Nevertheless, India was concerned over the re-emergence of Cold War Scenario in Asia. During a debate on Demand for Grants of Ministry of External Affairs for the year 1981-81, a congress member of Lok Sabha, Eduardo Faleiro stated:

> We are living in a region which has turned into one of the major theatres of super power fonfrontation. During the Nixon Kissinger era the strategy was to contain the USSR by allying with China. In recent times, it seems that the strategy has been revived. And it is in this context that the arming of Pakistan must be viewed. These arms are to be used against this country. [73]

Another member Mr. R. L. Bhatia stated:

> China has always been mocking at our philosophy of peace and non alignment. They have been directly or indirectly interfering in our affairs. So long as China believes in revolution as a way to freedom, and in aggression in the case of disagreement, there is no possibility of having normal relations with it .... If they are sincere, and if they want friendship with us sincerely, they must remove the impediments which stand in the way of a good friendship". [74]

The Soviet concern about the possibility of improvement in Sino-India relations was heightened by the visit of Huang Hua to India. The Soviet media devoted even greater space than usual to 'exposing' China's policy in Asia and China's threat to peace and security in the region.[75] China was denounced for its destabilising manoeuvres relating to India's internal situation, the border problem and other differences with India. A long article in New Times shortly after the first round of Simo-Indian talks enumerated China's various "anti-Indian" activities, like occupying Indian territory, arming Pakistan and supporting separatist insurgencies in India's north east. Clearly, China's intent, the article warned, was to weaken Soviet-Indian friendship.[76]

During Mrs. Gandhi's September 1982 visit to Soviet Union, the Soviet leaders warned her that China's ultimate aim was to dominate all of Asia and Brezhnev himself reminded her that the Soviet Union was threatened "from both east and west." Mrs. Gandhi assured Soviet leaders that India's efforts to improve relations with China would not be at the cost of its "trusted and tested friendship" with the Soviet Union.[77] At a Moscow news conference the Indian Prime Minister also said for the first time that she "would like Soviet troops to leave Afghanistan".[78] India, it was clear was following an independent approach in its relations with both China and the Soviet Union.

China significantly modified its relations with the superpowers. It scrapped its earlier talk of a united front (with the United States) against (Soviet) hegemonism, and began gradually to expand cooperative relations with the Soviet Union across a whole range of areas. It toned down its criticisms of Soviet foreign policies and began to balance criticism of Soviet moves with criticisms of American moves. Simultaneously, it reaffirmed China's membership in the Third world. Collectively these adjustments were known as China's "Independent Foreign Policy." As a result, by distancing itself somewhat from the U.S. and engineering a limited improvement in Sino-Soviet relations, China put itself in a better bargaining position with the U.S.[79]

An analyst of Chinese foreign policy believed that China's desire for better relations with India also played a role in its adoption of an "independent foreign policy" in 1982.[80] China saw a limited disengagement from the U.S.A. and limited rapprochement with the Soviet Union as a way of demonstrating to India that China was not pro-American and anti-Soviet. Therefore, improved Sino-Indian relations would not undermine India's relations with the Soviet Union. The same demonstration would also reduce Soviet opposition to closer Sino-Indian ties and discourage Soviet Union from using its influence to block Sino-Indian rapprochement.[81] China also stressed its opposition to imperialism, its struggle for development and its membership of the third world. Thus, China affirmed its fraternity with India and thereby, created an atmosphere conducive to Sino-Indian friendship.

As a result, both India and China agreed to discuss various international issues with the fourth round of Sino-Indian Official level talks in October, 1983. Both sides hoped that agreement on broad international issues would facilitate improvement of bilateral ties. Prior to departing for the fourth round of talks in 1983, the head of the Chinese delegation Hong Dafei told journalists that China and India shared common views on many international issues, such as safeguarding world peace, the North-South dialogue and South-South dialogue, so this time I will be glad to exchange my ideas with Indian friends."[82] This exchange of views o international issues continued through the next round of talks. After the sixth round of talks in November 1985, Indian external affairs minister, BaliRam Bhagat enumerated nuclear disarmament, South Africa and North-South relations as areas of agreement.[83] Commentary in influential Chinese media enumerated other international issues i.e. Israel's aggression and expansion, Namibia and the American invasion of Grenada on which India and China agreed, and stressed the two countries common commitment to non-alignment, development of the five principles of peaceful coexistence, and their common struggle against imperialism.[84]

By 1984, China began to emphasise its independent foreign policy and demonstrated it by strongly criticising USA on issues on which it said U.S. was pursuing hegemonist policies. Sino-U.S. relations were stabilised in the 1984 when Chinese Premier, Zhao Ziyang visited U.S. Zhao he underlined the economic dimension of the relationship and confessed that there were "still some difficulties in the current Sino-U.S. political relations."[85] Meanwhile, China's relations with USSR also improved China condoled the death of Brezhnev. Some progress in expanding relations took place in the wake of a week long visit of Soviet Vice-Foreign Minister, M. Kápitsa in September, 1983 During the 1983 U.N. General-Assembly Session, the Chinese foreign minister, Wu-Xueqian, reversed previous policy and announced his decision to meet the Soviet Foreign Minister, Andrei Gromyko. China took one step further towards restoring some balance in relations with the two big Powers with Wu declaring that "Sino-Soviet relations and Sino-U.S. relations are two different things and they cannot be linked together."[86] China was trying to nudge both super powers into offering more concessions to it. Relations between China and the USSR could still not stand comparison with its relations with USA, but the movement ahead was unmistakable. In 1984, the new Soviet President, Konstantin Chernenko reaffirmed his country's desire for better relations with China. China and the Soviet Union also concluded four new agreements, including the first long term trade pact after their rift.

Meanwhile, in India, Prime Minister Mrs. Gandhi was assassinated in October, 1984 and was succeeded by Rajiv Gandhi. Throughout 1985 there was a virtual explosion of optimistic statements from both sides. According to one Indian analyst, during 1985 New Delhi was optimistic about a possible breakthrough in Sino-Indian relations because of the post- 1982 thaw in Sino-Soviet relations and the greater distance between Beijing and Washington.[87] In mid 80's Indo-US relations were warming up. Prime Minister Rajiv Gandhi visited U.S. in June, 1985. The new Premier was tending to open up and widen his options, in terms of closer ties with western nations rather than depending largely on Soviet support. Rajiv's visit to the United States was successful, the Americans reduced the limits on technological exports, and Government of India agreed to improve conducive conditions for American business[88] As a result there was substantial changes in Indo-U.S. relations.

Shortly after Rajiv Gandhi's 1985 state visits to USSR in May and to USA in June, Chinese media noted the similarities between Indian and Chinese policy towards the superpowers in article in People's Daily (Renmin ribao) in August 1985. For the sake of achieving a stable international environment, the article noted, Rajiv Gandhi was pursuing a "two friend policy" of striving to develop friendly relations with the United States while maintaining such ties with the USSR. China was then attempting to do precisely the reverse, to develop friendly ties with the USSR while maintaining cordial ties with the United States. The article also noted Indian reluctance to cooperate with the Soviet Union against Chine: "India and the USSR have many common views on international issues. However, there are differences in some aspects. India did not respond to the Soviet proposal on holding a Pan-Asian peace and security conference" during Rajiv Gandhi's May 1985 visit to Moscow.[89] Thus, by improving relations with Moscow, the degree of convergence between Indian and Chinese policies had increased and facilitated improvements in Sino-Indian relations.

The Soviet response to the thaw in Indian-China relations in 1984-85 was more restrained than its earlier response. In contrast to the virulent criticisms during the 1978-79 and 1981-82 periods, Soviet propaganda in 1985 did not attack China's efforts to improve ties with India. Nor did it warn New Delhi of Beijing's evil schemes. The Soviets depicted a comprehensive United States- Pakistan alliance directed against all "progressive" countries in South Asia, including Soviet allied Afghanistan and India.[90] India was concerned over the reemergence of Cold War atmoshphere and threat posed to India's security by the inclusion of military equipments being acquired by Pakistan from the USA and China.[91] Only in late 1985 the Soviet Union accused China of arming Pakistan against India.

In 1985, Mikhail Gorbachev took over as General Secretary of the Communist Party of Soviet Union and began to take unprecedented new initiatives that in many ways were to change the face of the world.[92] Included in these initiatives was a serious new approach towards China. A month before his July 1986 Vladivostok speech, Gorbachev briefed Indian External Affairs Minister P. Shiv Shankar on "major Soviet foreign policy initiatives." Both leaders reportedly "voiced their mutual satisfaction" with Soviet-Indian "trust, friendship, and cooperation" and pledged to develop those bonds further. Even in his Validivostok speech Gorbachev praised India at some length, and before his bid to China, said "the friendly relations between the USSR and India have become a stabilising principle on an important scale".[93]

In his famous speech at Vladivostok on 28 July, 1986, Gorbachev sincerely proposed to improve relations with China. He made a series of offers to China to reverse the ideological as well as inter-state disputes which had marked their relationship.[94] He also offered China talks for the reduction of the military built up by the two countries on their borders. He also gave an obvious concession to China by agreeing to take midstream as the dividing line of the border between the two on the Ussuri river as the Chinese had been demanding.[95] Gorbachev's attempt was part of the general Soviet drive towards the relaxation of international tensions and an easing of the arms race. Vladivostok wa only a beginning; the full implications of the Soviet leader's new diplomacy was felt over the next three years. Both sides decided to move forward in developing relations. Another break through was the resumption of Sino-Soviet border talks suspended for the past nine years. The resumption of border talks symbolised that Sino-Soviet relations were on the mend.[96]

The first test of Soviet support for India under the new initiatives taken by Gorbachev for Sino-Soviet rapprochement came in the summer of 1986; when Chinese and Indian patrols in Sumdorong Chu valley of Arunachal Pradesh came within eyeball to eyeball range. This generated a border crisis which continued till spring 1987, with both sides stepping up their patrols in the disputed area, and moving substantial military forces in the region.[97] There was widespread concern about the possibility of a India-China conflict and India naturally looked towards Moscow for signals of support. USSR however, remained silent. The pressure on India increased further in October 1986 when American defence secretary, C. Weinberger visited India and delivered a message from Deng Xiaoping that either India stop "nibbling" at Chinese territory or face dire consequences. Weinberger then moved to Pakistan where he announced that the U.S. intended to supply Pakistan with AWACS aircraft, M1 Abrams tanks, and an improved version of the F-16.[98]

India was concerned over these developments. During a Lok Sabha debate on Demand for Grants of Ministry of External Affairs for the year 1987-88, a prominent member of opposition, Shri Syed Shahabuddin stated that "Our relations with China are also running into difficulties day-by-day, especially in the context of new posture that China has adopted.... My colleague here said about the nexus between China and Pakistan. I also feel that there is a gang-up between China, Pakistan and America.[99] Intevening in the debate Minister of External Afairs, Shri N.D. Tiwari stated that "we, as a matter of principle, are committed to resolving the border problems with China through peaceful means. But let China also reciprocate. We are amazed to see in this context that the activties of the

Chinese in the Sumdorong Chu valley have not been helpful"[100]

It was in these circumstances that Gorbachev visited India in November, 1987. Throughout his visit Gorbachev reiterated that improved Sino-Soviet ties would not be at the expense of Soviet relations with India. He said that "what we are doing to improving our relations with china will not weaken our relations with India."[101] The Soviet Union also extended generous economic and military assistance including MIG-29s to India. Notwithstanding this, Gorbachev refused to take India's side in its growing tension with China. During the press conference, he pleaded ignorance regarding the Sumdorong Chu incident and refused to take sides. Instead he called for better relations between the Soviet Union, China and India, So no one will have to choose sides."[102] He called for a political approach.[103]

In the meantime, the international politics witnessed dramatic changes. The superpowers increasingly resorted to resume dialogues to ease tense relations between themselves. President Reagan and Gorbachev held a summit at Reykjavic in Iceland in October, 1986. Though the summit had failed but it raised the hopes for achieving success in advancing the process of nuclear disarmament. Finally, both USA and USSR signed INF Treaty in December, 1987 to eliminate a particular class of all land based nuclear-missiles. This was the first time that Moscow and Washington agreed to reduce their nuclear arsenals instead of only limiting them.[104] Further, Afghan imbroglio which remained on important issue in US-USSR-PRC triangular relations throughout the eighties, was showing signs of being resolved. This led to the conclusion of the April, 1988 Geneva Accord on Afghanistan to which Pakistan, Afghanistan, the Soviet Union and the United States were the Signatory powers. The four instruments of the agreement called for the complete withdrawal of Soviet troops by 15 February 1989, the voluntary return of Afghan refugees under Safeguards and the restoration of Afghanistan's status as an independent, non-aligned nation. China welcomed the signing of the Geneva accord and termed it as a "positive development."[105] India welcomed the Geneva agreement and tried to help the process of reconciliation.

As the pace of Sino-Soviet rapprochement accelerated in 1988 the Soviet Union continued to encourage improvements in Sino-Indian relations. The linkage between Sino-Soviet-Indian relations was apparent during the build up to the Sino-Indian and Sino-Soviet summits of December 1988 and May, 1989. In October, 1988 the Chinese top leader, Deng Xiaoping publicly announced at the same time, his forthcoming meetings with Mikhail Gorbachev and Rajiv Gandhi.[106] In the next month, November 1988 Gorbachev made his second visit to India. This visit came just a month before Rajiv Gandhi's visit to China and two weeks before Chinese foreign minister, Qian Qichen arrived in Moscow to pave the way for Gorbachev's May 1989, summit with China. Relations with China was an important agenda of Gorbachev-Gandhi's meeting of November, 1988. It was widely believed that Gorbachev argued that China could no longer afford to be confrontational because of the demands of its modernisation programme, and that India, USSR and PRC should simultaneously strive to improve relations. He also reassured India that Moscow was not reordering its Asian priorities in Beijing's favour and at New Delhi's expense. To help convince his Indian hosts of this, Gorbachev signed four agreements further expanding bilateral cooperation. Among these was the largest credit yet supplied to India by the Soviet Union, $ 234 million for 20 years at 2.5 per cent annual interest.[107] The Chinese media commented on Gorbachev's efforts to nudge India towards better relations with China; Gorbachev and Gandhi reportedly devoted considerable time to discussion of Sino -Soviet and Sino-Indian relations. Gorbachev in his open speeches emphasised China's rule in Asian and world affairs and said that a good relationship among China, the Soviet Union and India is vital for the fate of Asia and World progress. "We're glad to see the signs of improved Indian-Chinese relations," he said, adding, "Our own relations with China are also increasingly encouraging."[108]

It was in this background that Indian Prime Minister, Rajiv Gandhi visited China in December, 1988. His historic visit was in large measure successful and gave an impetus to India-China relations. Thus, the Soviet nudge was an important factor in India-China Summit of December, 1988. India's decision to go ahead to normalise its relations with China was clearly in response to changing global scenario, which was marked by easing of relations among the nations and increasing friendly relations among the nations.

There was a marked improvement in the international climate in the year 1988 confrontation gave way to dialogue presaging a trend towards a saner, safer world. The emergence of détente between the Soviet Union and the U.S. which had resulted in the INF Agreement raised the expectation of further steps towards nuclear disarmament and peace. The emerging détente also set in motion the process of conflict resolution in different parts of the world.[109] During a Lok Sabha debate on Demand of Grants of Ministry of External Affairs for the year 1988-89, the Prime Minister, Shri Rajiv Gandhi said that:

> The world is changing very rapidly, especially international relations, in the last two or three years. New attitudes are

> developing, new ways of thinking are springing up and all this will pose new challenges to all countries in the world especially countries like India who play a significant role in international affairs. In such a situation, one cannot remain mired in the past. One must remain flexible.[110]

Therefore, the cumulative effect of the change in the direction of international politics on India-China relations was distinsctly positive. The relaxed atmosphere of international politics had a positive impact on India-China relations.

The Soviet leader, Mikhail Gorbachev visited China in May, 1989. China and the Soviet Union announced a new starting point for the normalisation of bilateral relations on the first day of Gorbachev's historic visit to Beijing.[111] China had already made a new theoretical assessment of the Soviet Union and had dropped its earlier view that the Soviet Union had degenerated into "Social imperialism". Both countries decided to reduce their armed forces on the Sino-Soviet border to a minimum. The joint communique underlined the Five Principles as constituting of the basis of their relationship. The Soviet Side favoured establishing "new political thinking" in international relation and the Chinese side in establishing a new international political order on the basis of the Five Principles of Peaceful coexistence.[112]

By the beginning of nineties, India and China shared perceptions of the emerging world order. In August, 1990 when Iraq attacked Kuwait, the invasion provoked Strong international reaction. The two superpowers jointly condemned the aggressor and demanded unconditional Iraqi withdrawal. The U.S.A. sent a formidable force in the Gulf region and UN adopted resolution to end aggression.[113] China in principle, opposed the involvement of foreign powers in regional conflicts. India and China were opposed to the use of force. But under the leadership of U.S.A., the western powers did use force and Iraq withdraw from Kuwait. After this both India and China were concerned at the growing assertiveness of USA in the face of declining importance of the USSR. The Chinese media noted that the world was becoming multipolar, with the two Super powers sharing more power with new emerging force such as Japan, Europe, India and Brazil. Neither Washington nor Moscow was able to unilaterally manipulate the world situation.[114]

India and China opined that a new world order should be democratic, multilateral, just and fair. In August, 1991 the USSR disintegrated into many new independent states with Russia emerging as most important successor state. With this, the socialist system in Soviet Union and nearby Eastern European nations came to an end. China and India, were caught unawares by this dramatic change in international politics. The international political landscape was fast changing and India as well as China were left with no option but to adjust accordingly.[115] With the disintegration of USSR as a nodal power centre, India lost a reliable friend in international political arena. China in consequence lost that importance it commanded in the strategic calculations of USA ever since seventies.

In December 1991, before his forthcoming visit to India, the Chinese Prime Minister, Li Peng said that the present world situation was far from stable and infact, had become even more turbulent. Li said the establishment of a new international world order was an important topic for discussion, which needs to be addressed immediately. He further stated that China and India could find common ground in this regard.

In the post Cold war era, China wanted a peaceful environment. China felt that what ever may have been the outcome of the cold war, it should acquaint itself with the new situation and consolidate its position. China's efforts to maintain peace and stability in Surrounding countries turned its attention to wards its dominant South Asian neighbour, India. According to a leading analyst, "China particularly focused its attention or seeking out neighbouring countries with whom it had some basic territorial difference and with whom it had to face a conflictual situation during the Cold War[116] India-China rapprochement in the 1990s was marked by growing mutual confidence and a spirit of cooperation and accommodation.

Cooperation was facilitated by a shared perception of the opportunities and challenges in the post cold war world. A peaceful environment was needed for a economic cooperation and development to tap the opportunities offered by globalisation. Both countries realised that "the challenge of the times is that economic struggle cannot be substituted by political struggles, nor won through tensions and confrontations. Since both countries are learning this lessor it becomes easier for them to turn away from conflict and tension".[117] Both were apprehensive of and wanted to resist US attempts to dominate the world order. Both looked forward to building greater economic co-operation and good relations in general with the Asia-Pacific nations. The volatile politics of the newly emergent Central Asian Republics posed an additional security threat to both these multiethnic and multi-religious countries.

In December, 1991 when the Chinese Prime Li Peng came to India, both countries emphasised on a world order which was equaitable and where there is no international oligarchy, obviously the reference was to USA. It was decided that officials of both countries should keep in touch with each other on international issues. In his speech under the auspices of the Indian Council of Cultural Relations, Li Peng said Indian and Chinese leadership shared many identical views.[118] He said while the old order had broken down, the new one was yet to take shape. Prime Minister, Narasimha Rao stated that :

> We meet at a time when the world situation is subject to rapid and fundamental transformations. It is a time when imaginative approaches are called from the international community to build a durable structure of peaceful and stable inter-state relations based on mutuality of interests and credible guarantees for the survival of mankind. We have to meet the challenges of terrorism, anarchy. Fissiparous tendencies and violence. We must replace conflict by dialogue and consensus. Together, India and china, must address the common problems that lie before us - the problems of population, environmental degradation and economic development. I believe that the demands of our times is for reconciliation, consensus and the cognizance that our own interests lie tin the reconciliation of the interests of all [119]

Under these circumstances, India and China stressed on substantially improved bilateral relations and underlined the need for stable situation around the borders. The bilateral relationship between India and China continued to be, influenced in a large measure by the emerging international political configuration in the post cold war world.

References

1. For details See, Graham Allison, *Essence of Decision* (Boston).
2. For details of the Cold War, See L. Gardner, *The Origins of the Cold War* (Waltham, 1970), J. Gaddis, *The United States and the Origins of the Cold War* (New York, 1972), V. Mostony, *Russia's Road to the Cold War* (New York, 1979).
3. For details See, Donald S. Zagoria, *The Sino-Soviet Conflict* (New York, 1962), William E. Griffith, *The Sino-Soviet Rift* (Cambridge, 1964), and Harold C. Hinton, *The Sino-Soviet Confrontation: Implications for the Future* (New York, 1976).
4. "The Truth about how the leaders of the C.P.S.U. have allied themselves with India against China", *Beijing Review (Beijing)* no. 45, 8 November) 1963, p. 19.
5. *Pravda* (Moscow)10 August, 1963.
6. *People's Daily (Beijing)* 27 February 1963.
7. For details see "The origin and Development of the differences between the leadership of the C.P.S.U. and ourselves", in *Beijing Review*, no. 37, 13 September 1963, pp. 6-20.

8. *Ibid.*, p. 18.
9. Quoted in T. Karki Hussain, *Sino-Indian Conflict and International Politics in the Indian Sub-Continent* (New Delhi, 1977), p. 155.
10. Quoted in Arthur M Schlesinger, *A Thousand Days : J.F. Kennedy in the White House* (Boston, 1965), p. 523.
11. Quoted in J.K. Galbraith, *Ambassador's Journal : A Personal Account of the Kennedy Years* (New York, 1969), pp. 378-79. See T. Soren Sen, *Kennedy* (New York, 1969), p.748.
12. See T. Soren Sen, *Kennedy* (New York, 1969), p.748.
13. *Ibid.*
14. J.K. Galbraith, n. 11, p. 386.
15. See K. Subrahmanyam, "U.S. Policy Towards India", *China Report* (New Delhi) January-April, 1972, particularly the Section on 'Military aid to India', pp. 43-44.
16. *Hindu* (Madras) 29 April 1963.
17. For text See, *Foreign Affairs Record* (Ministry of External Affairs, New Delhi), 1963, p. 438.
18. Department of State Bulletin, no. 49, 22 July 1963. p. 119.
19. *Annual Report 1965-66*, Government of India, Ministry of External Affairs, (New Delhi), p. 3.
20. *Pravda*, 9 September 1963.
21. *Beijing Review*, 8 November, 1963, p. 27.
22. Quoted in T. Karki Hussain, n.9, p. 157.
23. In March 1963, China brought out the question of unequal treaties of past and present between China and the Soviet Union. For details see, Dennis J. Doolin, *Territorial Claims in the Sino-Soviet Conflict: Documents and Analysis* (Stanford, 1965).
24. *Beijing Review* no. 41, 9 October 1964, p. 24.
25. *Chinese Threat*, (Publications Division, Ministry of Information and Broadcasting, Government. of India, New Delhi), 1963, p. 63.
26. *Annual Report 1965-66*, Ministry of External Affairs, p. 3.
27. People's Daily, 6 September 1969.
28. *Annual Report 1965-66*, Ministry of External Affairs, p. 10.
29. *Beijing Review*, no.39, 24 September 1965, pp. 14-15.
30. *Annual Report 1965-66*, Ministry of External Affairs, p. 7.
31. On the USA involvement in Vietnam, See George M. Kahin, Intervention : How America Became Involved in Vietnam (New York, 1986).
32. *Beijing Review*, no.15, 8 April 1966, p. 30.
33. *Ibid.*, no.20, 17 May 1968, p. 24.
34. Quoted in Harold C. Hinton, *China's Turbulent Quest* (New York, 1970), p. 133.
35. *Ibid.*, pp. 160-61.
36. *Pravda*, 9 June 1969.
37. Xinhua, 28 June 1969
38. *Ibid.*, 5 July 1969.

39. *Pravda*, 3 June 1969.
40. Quoted in Norman D. Palmer, *The United States and India* (Prager, 1984), p. 47.
41. Henry Kissinger, *White House Years* (Boston, 1979), p. 854.
42. Quoted in Bhabani Sen Gupta, "South Asia and the Great Powers", p. 227, in W. Griffith, ed., *The Great Power Triangles*, (Cambridge, 1985).
43. Surjit Mansingh, India's *Search for Power* (New Delhi, 1984), p. 142.
44. See the text of Treaty in *India: Bilateral Treaties and Agreements*, Vol. 7, 1971-73, Government of India (New Delhi, 1997), pp. 62-66.
45. Surjit Man Singh, n. 43, p. 88.
46. *Hindu*, 4 September 1971. For details See, S.K. Ghosh, The Indo – Soviet Treaty And China, *Journal of IDSA* (New Delhi), no. 5, October 1972, pp. 248-258.
47. *Lok Sabha Debates*, Vol. 14, 1972, Cols-216-17.
48. *Times of India* (New Delhi) 8 November 1971.
49. Tass (Moscow), 5 December 1971.
50. H. Kissinger, n. 41, p. 903.
51. Quoted in L. Lifaschultz, *Bangladesh: The Unfinished Revolution* (London, 1979) p. 156.
52. *Annual Report 1971-72*, Ministry of External Affairs, p. 24.
53. For the operation of the triangle See, M. Tatu, *The Great Power Triangle* (Paris, 1970).
54. *Beijing Review*, no. 49, 5 December 1975, p. 8.
55. *New York Times*, 22 December 1978.
56. For details see, Michael Yahuda, *Towards the End of Isolationism: China's Foreign Policy After Mao* (London, 1983).
57. *Xinhua* (Beijing), 24 March 1977.
58. *Pravda*, 23 April 1978.
59. Arun Gandhi, *The Morarji Papers* (New Delhi, 1983), p. 29.
60. *New York Times*, 9 November 1978.
61. Quoted in Gangi Dutta and V.P. Dutt, *China After Mao* (New Delhi, 1990), p. 279.
62. Turmoil in Afghanistan, in Foreign Broadcasting Information Service (hereafter FBIS), CHI-113, 18 June 1979, F/2.
63. For details see, Samuel S. Kim, ed, *Chinese Foreign Policy in the 1980s* (Colarado, 1984).
64. Gargi Dutt and V.P. Dutt, n. 61, p. 207.
65. *New York Times*, 20 January 1980.
66. FBIS - DRC (Daily Report China), 16 January 1980, p. 3.
67. FBIS-DRC, 23 January 1980, p. F2.
68. *Annual Report 1981-82*, Ministry of External Affairs, p. VI.
69. Quoted in Surjit Man Singh, n.43, p. 157.
70. Thomas W. Robinson, *The Soviet Union and Asia in 1981, Asian Survey* (Berkeley) Vol. 22, no.1, January 1982, pp. 25-26.
71. *Far Eastern Economic Review* (Hong Kong) 15 August 1980, pp. 14-15.

72. *Beijing Review*, no. 51, 22 December 1980, pp. 8-10.
73. *Lok Sabha Debates*, Vol. 15, 1981, Col. 309.
74. *Ibid.,* Col. 351.
75. S. Irodov, "Disappointed Hopes", *New Times* (Moscow), July 1981, p. 22.
76. A. Usvatov, "China – India: After the First Round of Talks", New Times, March 1982, pp. 30-31.
77. Quoted in Robert C. Horn, "The Soviet Union and Sino-Indian Relations", *Orbis,* (Philadelphia) *26* (4), Winter 1983, pp. 904-905.
78. Times of India (New Delhi), 11 September 1982.
79. For details see, C.L. Hamrin, "China Reassesses the Superpowers", *Pacific Affairs* (Vancouver), Vol. 56, no. 2, Summer 1983, pp. 209-231.
80. John W. Garver, The Indian Factor in Recent Sino-Soviet Relations,*China Quaterly*, (London), March 1991, pp. 55-85.
81. *Ibid.,* p. 71.
82. FBIS-DRC, 25 October 1983, pp. W2-3.
83. *Annual Report 1981-82*, Ministry of External Affairs, p. V-II.
84. FBIS-DRC, 5 August 1985, pp. F1-2.
85. *Beijing Review,* no. 28, 11 July, 1983, pp. 8-9.
86. Xinhua, 17 September 1983.
87. Manoranjan Mohanty, "Indian-Chinese Relations: A Positive Frame", *India Quarterly* (New Delhi), Vol. 61, no. 1, January-March 1985, pp. 17-22.
88. A Rahman, "US-India Cooperation Science and Technology", Quoted in A.P. Rana, ed, *Four Decades of Indo- U.S. Relations* (New Delhi, 1994), pp. 293-94.
89. FBIS-DRC, 31 August 1985, p. F1.
90. Ibid, Daily Report Soviet Union (hereafter DRSU), for 1985-86.
91. *Annual Report 1983-84*, Ministry of External Affairs, p. IV.
92. Zao Dian, "The Vladivostok Challenge", *Asian Defence Journal* (Kualalumpur) October 1986, p. 3.
93. FBIS-DRSU, 29 July, 1986, p. R12.
94. Quoted in C.V. Ranganathan and Vinod C. Khanna, *India and China. The way Ahead After,* "Mao's India War" (New Dehi, 2000), p. 88.
95. *New York Times*, 29 July 1986.
96. Xinhua, 8 February 1987.
97. *Far Eastern Economic Review*, 9 April 1987, pp. 38-40. Tension on the border and 7 May 1987, pp. 33-35.
98. *Ibid.,* 4 June 1987, pp. 42-43.
99. *Lok Sabha Debates*, Vol. 27, 1987, Col 438.
100. *Ibid.,* Col. 294.
101. *Beijing Review,* no. 48, 1 December, 1986, p. 10.
102. FBIS-DRSU, 2 December, 1986, pp. D29.
103. *Hindustan Times*, 10 December 1986.
104. *Beijing Review*, no. 51, 21 December 1987, pp. 10-12.
105. *Beijing Review*, no. 17, 25 April 1988, pp. 9-10.
106. FBIS-DRC, 14 October 1988, p. 1.

107. *Far Eastern Economic Review*, 1 December 1988, p. 38.
108. *Beijing Review*, no. 49, 5 December 1988, p. 12.
109. *Annual Report 1988-89*, Ministry of External Affairs, p. iii.
110. Lok Sabha Debates, Vol. 38, 1988, Col 471.
111. C.V. Ranganathan and Vinod C. Khanna, n. 94, p. 88.
112. See the text of Joint Communique in Beijing Review, no. 21, 29 May 1989, pp. 11-13.
113. *Ibid.*, n.35, 27 August 1990, p. 4.
114. *Ibid.*, no.2, 14 January 1991, p. 25.
115. For details see, M. Rasgotra and V. D. Chopra, eds, *India's Relation with Russia and China: New Phase* (New Delhi, 1997).
116. Quoted in Kanti Bajpai and Amitabh Mattoo, eds, *The Peacock and the Dragon: India-China Relations in the 21st Century* (New Delhi, 2000), p. 256.
117. V.P., Dutt, "India-China: Promise and Limitation", in *Indian Foreign Policy: Agenda for the Twenty-First Century* (New Delhi, 1999), Vol. 2, p. 235.
118. *Frontline* (Madras), 3 January 1992, p. 10.
119. *Selected Speeches of P.V. Narasimha Rao*, Vol. I, Publications Division, Government of India (New Delhi, 1992), p. 344.

6

Constructing Rapprochement (1992-1997)

The decade of 1990's in general and the aftermath of 1991 in particular were marked by the important developments in the bilateral relations between the Asian giants of India and China. After the historic summit following China visit of prime minister, Rajiv Gandhi in December 1988 and the return visit of Chinese Premier, Li Peng to India in December 1991; the post cold war period witnessed the construction of Sino-Indian rapprochement. After the disintegration of Soviet Union, both nations realized the urgency of stabilizing the borders and further improve bilateral relations in an uncertain world order, which was largely unipolar.

Survey of Literature and Analytical Framework

One broad school argues on the following line. John W. Garver in his masterpiece "Protracted Contest" highlights the geopolitical clash between the foreign and diplomatic policies of India and China. In the words of Garver, "This study isolates and analyses the conflictual clement of Republic of India People's Republic of China relations during the second half of the twentieth century." The author on the other hand partially agrees with the fact of geopolitical conflict but feels Garver over plays this point. Garver himself concedes in some ways when he writes "Relations between any two states cannot be reduced entirely to conflict. One can always find elements of policy cooperation as well." Another equally important aspect which author wants to argue is the fact that there has been protracted negotiations to resolve the enduring and vexed issues, which constitute the essentials of "geopolitical conflict". May be the western world in general and Garver in particular misses the point of protracted negotiation between the Asian giants and India's sincere attempts to resolve the conflictual elements of its multifaceted interaction with PRC.

Though Garver could not altogether deny the significance of diplomacy and in his own words describes about the fact that "the centrality of conflict does not lessen the importance of diplomacy ... in conflictual relations among states, diplomacy may regulate that rivalry and keep it from intensifying perhaps leading to war." Nevertheless, Garver while acknowledging the role and importance of diplomacy, cannot help emphasizing the point of geo-political conflict and summarizes the essence of Sino-Indian interactions by highlighting the fact that "at bottom lies a deep and wide conflict of interests and per captions." Equally important part of story is the fascinating account of first normalisation of relations and later on the unfolding of the process of Sino-Indian *rapprochement*. The construction of *rapprochement* edifice and initiation of step-by-step approach to tackle all outstanding issues including the vexed question of border is an good example of method of diplomacy pursued by two developing but mature powers. Undoubtedly the politics and tactics were simultaneously going on but these factors were not allowed to come in the way of rapprochement.

The point that author wishes to underline is the abovementioned situation of geo-political conflict is not unique but on the contrary quite common between the two powers, who share common areas of neighbourhood and more so in the case of great emerging powers like china and India. Furthermore, world history is replete with examples of geo-political conflicts between great emerging powers like England vs. Spain, France vs. England, France vs. Germany, between India and China etc. Thus, the geo-political conflict is at best one part of the story, the other part of continuous negotiations to resolve all issues is equally important.

On the another hand, there is a school of thought in India and its adherents are people like C.V. Ranganathan and Vinod C. Khanna, who in their seminal work. India and China the way ahead after "Mao's India war" correctly argue that "India-China relations are not an all-or-nothing proposition, but a mixed bag of issues with varying degrees of solvability." The work is undoubtedly a valuable "addition to forward-looking problem-solving debate in both countries on the contentious boundary question." The author feels that because of their diplomatic background in the last chapter entitled "The way Ahead" they are too optimistic in some ways. The author at the same time is in agreement when they seek to fashion good relation between themselves.

The point that author seeks to highlight is there has been a distinct historical experience in India's dealings with China, which in large measure is both complex and complicated. India, therefore has to be cautious on the one hand and draw appropriate lessons, on the another hand. Overall, a more confident India must craft its policy towards China in a more realistic and reciprocal framework. Furthermore, the simplistic assessments needs to be avoided like the argument that once boundary issue is resolved possibly all problems between these two Asian giants would disappear. However, author is broadly in agreement when these seasoned diplomats write "the future should not be allowed to be come hostage to the persistence of old memories however unpleasant." The author only suggests that Indian perspective should take note of China's vibrant strategic culture use of force, its grand strategy and people's liberation Army's role as an important and often one of the most crucial elements in the China's decision-making on matters concerning PRC's defence and even foreign policy. At the same time, China's policy of opening up and economic reforms which emphasise interdependence also needs to be taken note by Indian policy makers. Infact the Sino-Indian Relations exist at many levels and simply stated are complex in nature. The dual elements simultaneously exist : conflictual or competitive and cooperation or diplomatic negotiations. As both nations are port of developing world, though China is more developed therefore, the relationship between both Asian giants are unique. The bilateral relations are conditioned in large measure by global political configuration and the regional context.

In the beginning of 1990's the foreign policy objectives of both sides were rooted in the post cold war period.

China's Motivations

China in large measure saw two note worthy changes : first, the strategic level was marked by the disintegration of Soviet Union and the political plane, was marred by the Democracy movement of 1989. Second, it saw the unfolding of economic globalisation in a steady manner. These two important changes influenced Chinese foreign policy in many ways. From now onwards, internal stability was keyword for the domestic political order. Which was of foremost importance for the continuation of economic modernisation. Equally important, it brought a shift in Chinese strategic orientation concerning global power configuration. Immediately after the collapse of the cold war bipolar world order, the us emerged as the sole superpower. This largely compelled China to rethink on the alternative approach. It was in this backdrop that Deng Xiaoping formulated concept of the "New International Political and Economic Order."[1]

Defined simply new international political and economic order proposed :

(a) Mutual respect for sovereignty and territorial integrity, mutual non-aggression and non-interference in each other's internal affairs.

(b) Oppose hegemonism and power politics

(c) Sovereignty and equality among nations.

(d) Respect for the national conditions of the countries and seek common ground while reserving differences.

(e) Mutually beneficial cooperation and common development.

In short, because of above mentioned factors. China was pursuing a policy of engagement with India tempered with some sober thinking regarding India. China in cold war phase had already established strategic advantage over India and also in its neighbourhood. The Chinese thinking was largely motivated, in the words of a beating practitioner of Indian foreign policy, recognition of "the thawing of relations between Russia and China," China's concentration on internal modernisation, "emerging challenges to China's political and territorial cohesion," and an "incurrent of desiring peaceful and stable relations with all its neighbours."[2] Nevertheless, in its dealings with its, northern neighbour India adopted a cautious stance and the Government of India's image of China in some ways was mixed, as Dixit opined "I was clear in my mind."

India's Motivations

From India's viewpoint the initial years of 1990's were challenging particularly from the security dimension in backdrop of collapse of Soviet Union. The fact of demise of bipolar structure compelled India to seek more stable relations with China in an uncertain global setting. With the disintegration of the Soviet Union in 1991, India terrible lost a good friend and ally. According to an analyst. Soviet disintegration had manifold impact on Sino-Indian relations. First, an impediment in establishing friendly relations between both sides had been removed. Second, the fact that India lost a trusted friend, it became urgent necessity to further improve relations with China. Third, the Soviet disintegration had brought about loss of approximately 20 per cent of India's export market, thereby compelling India to look for new export market.[3] Furthermore, during the prime Ministership of P.V. Narasimha Rao (1991-1996) India witnessed unleashing of economic reforms designed to accelerate overall growth rate. The net effect of renewed pursuit of economic development meant that India would not pursue aggressive action to resolve its disputes with China.

Moreover, India also desired a peaceful international environment to further its economic growth and defence modernization. Like all the developing nations, India faced difficult economic reforms in the years ahead and therefore desired to pursue stable relations with China. Simultaneously, the political leadership was clear that the initiation of economic reforms meant overall rise of India until a decade, when it was assumed India's power would grow in a substantive way and this would enhance its bargaining position with China. In short, India's motivations in the beginning of 1990's to improve its relations with china were largely based on realistic considerations. As J.N. Dixit sums up succinctly, "that at most India and China could be friends whose relations would be based on practicality and convergence of mutual interests, tempered by appropriate reticence and objectivity about each other's interests. Security perceptions and economic requirements."[4] The improvement in bilateral relations was based first and foremost on shared national conditions. The factors evolving in post cold war period called for expanded political-economic ties rather than hostilities. At the diplomatic level. Since the decade of 80's, India and China started giving each other assurances of goodwill and agreed to work toward building a future oriented relationship. In short, the Asian giants were Constructing Rapprochement, which was in their mutual national interest.

Bilateral Political Interactions

One of the most important distinctive features of Sino-India rapprochement ever since historic visit of Indian Prime Minister, Rajiv Gandhi was the regular political interactions between the highest leadership, which imparted certain dynamism the bilateral relations. This positive trend continued unabated in the post cold war period as both sides realised its importance in building stable and cooperative relationship.

An important manifestation of intensified political interactions was the visit of the Indian president R.Venkataraman to China in May 1992. In his talks with the top leadership of China both nations expressed satisfaction at the working of the Joint Working Group, agreed to deepen economic cooperation and reiterated faith in the famous principles of peaceful coexistence. During the visit "emphasis was also laid on taking concrete steps to promote mutual Confidence Building Measures (CBMs)."[5] Yet, it was during the first Indian President's visit that China 'conducted nuclear test which generated Indian apprehensions in some ways.

Later on the year 1992 also witnessed direct contact between the defence establishments of both sides which heralded a new phase of confidence building measure. The Indian initiative of sending its Defence Minister Sharad Pawar to Beijing in July 1992 was a milestone in 'security building measures' between the two neighbours. The historic visit of Indian Defence Minister to China and subsequent talks with his Chinese counterpart alongwith other senior officials of the people's Liberation Army "laid the basis for greater stability and predictability, as far as the military situation along the frontiers of the two countries is concerned."[6] In course of talks, the Chinese hosts made "special efforts to impress upon Pawar the purely coincidental nature and timing of its ray nuclear tests."[7]

The visit of Prime Minister P.V. Narsimha Rao to China in September 1993 was a major step forward in consolidating the growing process of Sino-Indian rapprochement. The most noteworthy feature of the summit meeting between the premiers of both sides was the conclusion of the "Agreement on the Maintenance of Peace and Tranquility along the Line of Actual Control in the India-China border areas", which was signed in Beijing on September 7, 1993.[8] In the words of two seasoned Indian diplomats who specialize on China, the agreement "binds the two sides to a peaceful resolution of the boundary question through friendly consultations. It states that neither side shall use or threaten to use force against the other by any means.... The Agreement also provides for retaining military forces along the Line of Actual Control to a minimum level compatible with friendly and good neighbourly relations between the two countries."[9] The 1993 agreement was undoubtedly a significant development in the annals of bilateral relations between the two Asian giants. In the backdrop of Post Cold War world, it stabilized relations on the one hand and initiated numerous confidence building measures, on the other hand. The agreement in some ways was manifestation of China's good neighbourly policy and India's pursuance of pragmatic policy towards China.

The positive outcome of historic Agreement of 1993 was logical culmination of the new chapter of diplomatic negotiations that began in 1981, and further carried forward by the summits at highest political level since 1988. In the words of a well respected Chinese expert on India, "in September 1993, the former Prime Minister P.V. Narasimha Rao declared in Beijing that the India-China relations had reached a stage of maturity. He meant that the two countries would not allow their differences to hinder the development of their relations based on mutual benefit. I have always shared this view. Many Chinese scholars also felt encouraged to see the positive developments during that decade."[10] Later in November 1993, Chairman of CPPCC (Chinese People's Political Cosoltative Conference) Li Ruihuan visited India as part of ongoing exchange of high level political interactions and emphasized on good relations between two nations. In December 1993 as part of exchanges between the defence establishments of both sides, PLA Deputy Chief of the General Staff Lt. Gen. Xu Hauizi visited India.

The year 1994 witnessed the continuation of high level political and military exchanges. In July, the Chinese Vice Premier and Foreign Minister, Qian Qichen visited New Delhi and expressed satisfaction at the growing ties between both nations. In September, the Chinese Defence Minister Chi Haotian visited India.[11] Earlier in July, General B.C. Joshi became the first Indian Chief of Army Staff to visit China dn met with his Chinese counterpart and other senior PLA officers.[12] It was felt by both sides that exchanges at the level of services Chiefs will increase the knowledge and awareness of each other's capabilities and intentions.

Later in October India's Vice President and old China hand Shri K.R. Narayanan visited China and reviewed bilateral ties with top Chinese leadership. The year also marked fortieth anniversary of enunciation of principles of peaceful coexistence 'Panchsheel', which was celebrated by both nations. Both sides emphasised the principles as the basic tenet of their foreign policies.

By mid 1990's some tangible shifts in China's South Asia policy were discernible. According to an Indian analyst, "Some of the more noticeable examples of this shift : first, the PRC had been notably mild in its reactions to India's stand on the CTBT; secondly, China voted against Japan, in Support of India's bid for a non-permanent seat in the security council; and as mentioned earlier, its approach to the handling of territorial disputes was also different now, as witnessed in its stand on the Kashmir issue."[13] China urged India and Pakistan to solve all outstanding issues including Kashmir in peaceful way. China refrained from supporting Pakistan's line on Kashmir and called for a peaceful settlement of the dispute through calm and self-restrained bilateral negotiations between both sides and in the words of two diplomats this "shows a marked weakening of what has been described as China's 'verbal deterrent support' to Pakistan." In the year 1995 high level visits continued apace. In November, Chinese National People's Congress Chairman Qiao Shi visited India.

On November 28, 1996 the Chinese President Jiang Zemin come to

India alongwith high level delegation led by the Chinese Vice Premier and Foreign Minister, Minister for Foreign Trade and Economic Cooperation, Minster for Civil Affairs and the Chairman of the Tibet Autonomous Region's Government. Durirg his visit, another important step similar to 1993 Agreement was taken and both nations concluded "Agreement on confidence building measures in the Military Field along the Line of Actual Control in the India-China border Areas" which was signed by I.K. Gujral and Qian Qichen both Foreign Ministers of respective nations.[14] The preamble to the agreement mentions the five principles of peaceful coexistence and notes that "it serves the fundamental interests of the peoples of India and China to foster a long-term good neighbourly relations." President Jiang urged both sides to solve the boundary issue in a peaceful manner and said that India should approach the problem "in a forgiving and under standing manner so as to arrive at fair and reasonable solutions."[15] About the Agreement, Jiang said that it is a major step towards building mutual trust and setting the atmosphere for resolving the border problem.[16]

Commenting on the Jiang's visit and conclusion of the 1996 Agreement, One Indian Analyst summarised that "On the one hand, it was hailed as a virtual no-war pact, and on the other hand, there were many who pointed out that most of the features of this new agreement were included in the 1993 Agreement during Rao's visit. It has also been argued that the stipulation in Article One of the 1996 Agreement that "neither side shall use its military capability against the other side" refers only to the forces in the border areas. There was nothing in the nature of a breakthrough on the boundary question. Jiang's visit was more in the nature of sustaining India-China ties, which were on the upswing, but there was a palpable underlying reality, namely, that it was not a relationship between equals."[17] Whereas a Chinese analyst highlighted some of the notable CBMs between both sides, which included "Representatives of Border Guards of the two countries meet two times every year regularly; establishment of Hot-Line between Headquarters of command of Border Guards of the two countries; pre-notification of military maneuvers and troop movements in the India-China border area; and Exchange of visits between high ranking and mid-ranking officers of the armed forces of the two counteries."[18]

Overall, Jiang's visit was significant in political and economic level as both sides reiterated desire to further continue the process of rapprochement. Apart from ongoing efforts to resolve the border dispute, both nations emphasised on strengthening economic and trade relations and enhanced cooperation in Science and technology and other areas.

Meanwhile the high level military exchange continued apace. In 1996, Admiral V.S. Shekhawat became the first Indian Navy Chief to visit China. Later in October 1997, Gen. V.P. Malik the Vice Chief of the Army Staff visited Beijing.[19] Both sides in some ways concurred that these visits would give an impetus to the ongoing military confidence building and would result in the establishment of a regular communication channel between the two armed forces.

The net affect of regular political interactions and military exchanges were positive. Indeed till the year 1997 the bilateral relations registered upward momentum. Overall the pace of Sino-Indian relations witnessed certain dynamism and indeed brought about stable ties between these two important rising powers. However, in India there was "a palpable under lying reality, namely, that it was not a relationship between equals."

Efforts to Resolve Border Dispute

The India-China border covers a distance of approximately 4056 kilometers, which is divided into three sections : the western (2176 km), middle (554 km.) and eastern sector (1326 km.).[20] The *Western Sector* involves the boundary between India's Ladakh area of Jammu & Kashmir and Xinjiang and Tibet in China. According to the Chinese view, this sector begins from Karakoram Pass in the north down to the area in the south of the Ari district of Tibet, Ladakh and Himachal Pradesh.[21] India in this sector correctly argues that China occupies about 38,000 sq. km. of its territory, and this not includes the area ceded by Pakistan to china. It may be noted here that Pakistan illegally ceded 5180 sq. km. area in Pakistan Occupied Kashmir to China in 1963 border agreement.[22] The *Middle Sector* comprises of Indian state of undivided Uttar Pradesh and Himachal Pradesh and Ari district of Tibet in China. The disputed area in this sector covers about 2000 sq. km.[23] However, according to another viewpoint the area under actual dispute may be only 40-45 sq. km.[24] The *Eastern Sector* starts at the China-India-Bhutan border junctions and extends to the China-India-Myanmar border junctions. This sector consists of Indian state of Arunachal Pradesh and Chinese region of Tibet. The area under dispute in this sector is approximately 90,000 sq. km.[25] This sector involves the question of Indian claim of the Chinese recognition of McMahon Line (by Simla convention of 1914) and Chinese denial of the line and regarding it as an imperialist imposition.

The eastern sector according to Chinese viewpoint is "the most disputed area". According to them the Sixth Dalailama, Tsanyun Gyalto hailed from Monyul area. It consists of – Monyul, Loyul and Lower Tsayul in all three parts – "notch of the traditional customary boundary and south of the... McMohan line" covering a total of 90,000 sq. km. The Chinese side press their claim by stating that they exercised administrative and jurisdictional control over this area and that the dispute arose due to "colonialists... press (ing) northwards beyond the traditional customary boundary."[26]

The Cold War Phase

During the late cold war period between June 1981 and November 1987 eight round of official level talks were held to resolve the border issue, but no breakthrough was made. It was during Rajiv Gandhi's China in 1988 visit that both nations decided to set up a Joint working Group, which was to search a fair and reasonable solution to the border issue. The JWG was to be chaired by the Foreign secretary on the Indian side and the Vice Foreign Minister from the Chinese side. In some ways therefore, JWG was an advancement from the previous mechanism in that it enjoyed joint mandate. Furthermore, the JWG was also vested with the task of initiating CBMs designed to maintain peace and tranquility along the border areas.

India throughout the cold war period pursued reasonable and forward looking policy to resolve the vexed border issue. In the year 1990, India took another step forward to resolve its border dispute with China. At the second meeting of JWG in New Delhi the Indian side stated that it accepted there was a dispute over the border and proposed a set of interlocking principles that could be used sector by sector to come up with an entirely fresh alignment for the border. But India also made it clear that while this new point was open for discussion and negotiation, it also represented the limit of Indian flexibility. In other words the point put across was that while adjustments were possible, accommodations that would drastically alter the Line of Actual Control that now constitutes the border were not.[27] Earlier in the first meeting of JWG at Beijing from July 1st to 4th 1989, both sides agreed that military experts would work out measures to ensure "peace and tranquility" along the LAC.[28] The third meeting of JWG was held in Beijing on May 13, 1991 and no substantive development took place in the talks. Both sides explained "each other's positions and agreed to continue the process."[29]

In December 1991, when Chinese Li Peng visited India, he spoke about the need to resolve the border problem through mutual understanding and mutual accommodation. The Indian position was that mutual understanding and mutual settlement should not legitimize the gains of armed intervention and should be based on logistical and administrative considerations.[30] During Li's visit both nations expressed hope for the JWG to play some what more concrete role and agreed that it should discuss some specific measures for maintaining peace and tranquility along the border areas. Both sides also reached an understanding that they should regularize the meeting between frontier guards.[31] Premier Li said in order to find a solution to border issue it is important for us first, to have sincerity and then, also to have patience because this issue is rather complicated and is left over from history. The Chinese Premier's visit to India was concluded with the issue of the Sino-Indian Joint communique, which in some ways indicated mutual concerns about the Post-Soviet international situation.[32] The communique among other bilateral issue also suggested that 'the JWG should step up its work in search of the earliest possible solution to the border dispute.

The Post Cold War Period's Efforts

The period witnessed 'quickening pace' of ongoing negotiations because of urgency of stability in the border areas. Further, it saw initiation of effective Confidence Building Measures (CBMs) in the border areas. The fourth meeting of JWG was held in New Delhi from February 20-21, 1992 which included officials of Defence ministry from two nations for the first time. Both sides agreed to hold flag meetings between border personnel at Bumla in the eastern sector and at the Spanaggur Gap area in the western sector in June and October every year.[33] The officials proposed direct telephone links between local commanders. In addition, opinion about other CBMs, like prior notification of military exercises were also discussed. The fifth meeting took place in Beijing from October 27 to 29, 1992. During the meeting there was frank exchange of views on the border and both sides stated each other's positions.[34]

The sixth meeting of the JWG was held in New Delhi from June 25 to 30, 1993 and discussions "focused on mutual transparency on the location of military positions, prevention of air intrusion and redeployment of forces along the LAC. Furthermore, both sides also agreed to open one more border trade point at the Shipkila pass between Namgya in India's Himachal Pradesh and Jiuba in Tibet, in addition to the existing one at the Lipulekh pass opened in July 1992."[35]

In September, 1993 both nations concluded the Agreement on the maintenance of peace and Tranquility along the Line of Actual control, which comprises of nine articles. Article 1 declared that "the two dies are of the view that the India-China boundary questions shall be resolved through peaceful and friendly consultations." It further stated that "Pending ultimate solution of the boundary question, the two sides shall strictly respect and observe the LAC." It also provided for "where necessary, the two sides shall jointly check and determine the segments of the LAC where they have different views as to its alignment."

Article 2 stated that "each side will keep its military forces in the areas along the LAC to a minimum level compatible with the friendly and good neighbourly relations between the two countries." Regarding reduction of military personnel and principle of security it further declared that the two side agree to reduce their military forces along the LAC in conformity with the requirements of the principle of mutual and equal security to ceilings to be mutually agreed." Article 3 provided that "neither side will undertake specified levels of military exercises in mutually identified zones. Each side shall give the other prior notification of military exercises of specified levels near the LAC..."

Article 4 provides for meetings and consultations between the border defence personnel of the two countries to sort out problems. Article 5 declared prevention of air intrusions and restrictions on air exercises to be mutually agreed. Article 6 enunciated that references to the LAC in it do not prejudice each side's substantive position on the boundary question. Article 7 provided for commutations on effective verification measures and supervision of reduction of military forces to agreed levels. Article 8 provided for the establishment of the Expert Group consisting of diplomatic and military experts to help the JWC and settlement of differences.[36] In short, the important features of 1993 Agreement were : troop reduction, conflict avoidance as well as notification measures and composition of the Expert Group. The agreement was first concrete achievement of the JWF. In some circles the agreement on the LAC was considered as the, 'first step towards a final settlement' of the border dispute between both Asian giants.

The year 1994 witnessed the continuation of meetings and the establishment of the Expert Group resulted in fresh round of meetings. In February from 3rd to 6th to be prices the first meeting of the India-China Expert Group was held at New Delhi. The meeting discussed 'the scope of functions and powers, future tasks and modalities' to be followed. The second meeting of the Expert Group was held at Beijing on April 21 to

23rd and both sides agreed on the work regulations.[37] In some concrete manner both sides concurred that the mandate of the Group meeting is to include assisting the JWG in clarification of the LAC, redeployment of military forces along the LAC verification mechanisms and so on.[38] Later on 6th and 7th July the seventh round of JWG meeting was held at Beijing, in which the Peace and Tranquility Agreement of September 1993 got ratified. In addition-periodical meetings of local levels between border officials was also discussed.

At the third meeting of the Expert Group held in New Delhi from March 2nd to 4th 1995, the two sides agreed to establish two additional designated points for meetings between military personnel at Nathu La in the Sikkim-Tibet Sector and another point to be agreed in the middle sector.[39] From August 18th to 20th, the eighth meeting of the JWG was held at New Delhi and both sides agreed to pull back troops from four forward outposts, two on each side, located in Wangdong area in the eastern sector.[40] The troops of India and China here stood "face to face". Some 50-100 yards from each other and this was the sumdorong Chu Valley in Arunachal Pradesh, where military clash was reported in 1986-87. As such this development augured well in that a similar incident would not happen again. According to an Indian Analyst during this round of meeting eight "pockets of dispute" were identified, viz., "Trig Heights and Demchok in the Western Sector, Barahoti in the Middle Sector and Namka Chu, Sumdorong Chu, Chantze, Aspaphila and Longju in the eastern sector."[41]

The year 1996 marked another step forward towards CBMs, which would in the long term pave the way for resolution of the vexed border problem. The fourth round of Expert Group meeting was held in Beijing from February 7th to 9th and both sides discussed concrete measures to implement the 1993 CBMs Agreement. Furthermore, during the ninth round of JWG meeting held from October 16th to 18th in Beijing; both sides agreed to increase reciprocal visits by military officials with the rank of major general. Moreover, they agreed to establish two additional meeting places along the eastern sector (Bumla Dichu), and one in a mountain pass along the middle sector. (Lipulekh near Pithrogarh) for border personnel regular flag meetings to be held twice a year.[42]

More importantly 1996 witnessed the conclusion of the "Agreement on Confidence Building measures in the military field along the Line of Actual Control in the India-China border areas" during India's visit of Jiang Zerin, the first Chinese head of state. The agreement signed on 29th

November comprised of twelve articles.

Article I declared that "neither side shall use its military capability against the other side". Article II stated that "the two sides reiterate their determination to seek a fair, reasonable and mutually acceptable settlement of the boundary question". Article III went into specific details about reduction of military forces "within mutually agreed geographical Zones" along the LAC, the exchange of data on reduction of forces and categories of armaments, and decisions on ceilings on military forces and armaments to be kept by each side within these zones. The ceiling would be in consonance with the principle of "mutual and equal security". Article IV to VIII death with various CBMs designed to stabilize the border areas and exchange of information etc. Article IX provided for "in case a doubtful situations develops.. either side has the right to seek a clarification from the other side".

The declaration of article X was important. It recognised "the need for the two sides to arrive at a common understanding of the alignment of the LAC, and to speed up the process of clarification and confirmation of the line. Initially, the exercise would be to clarify the alignment in those segments where both sides have different perceptions. There is also a stipulation for the exchange of maps indicating respective perceptions of the entire alignment of the LAC as soon as possible." Article XI was equally important and stated that detailed implement measures required under Article I and Article X shall be decided through mutual consultations in the JWG on the boundary question. The India-China Diplomatic and Military Expert Group shall assist the JWG in devising implementation measures under the Agreement."[43]

The Agreement of 1996 was based on the foundation of Agreement of 1993 and was undoubtedly as significant development in the bilateral Sino-Indian relations. The Chinese President, Jiang Zemin termed the agreement as a factor that would further enhance peace and security and eventually create a sound climate for the resolution of the boundary question.[44] Two Indian Diplomats wrote that "a perusal of the two agreements, as a whole, would show that a comprehensive scheme of CBMs have been indicated. If implemented, the Agreements would go a long way to ensuring that each side is able to defend its side of the LAC in a non-provocative and non-violent manner."[44] A well respected Chinese Analyst Considered the treaty as a "no-war pact" between the two sides, on the ground that the 1996 CBMs Agreement removed the only dangerous or explosive element in the bilateral relationship."[45] In short, the 1996

Agreement was a step forward in further initiation of CBMs and generated stable ties between both nations.

The year 1997 saw the continuation of meetings. First, from 3rd to 5th March the fifth round of Expert Group meeting was held in New Delhi. Both sides discussed establishing an additional meeting site in the eastern sector and also rearrangement of meeting times.[46] Second, from 4th to 5th August the tenth round of JWG meeting was held in New Delhi. Agreements signed during the visit of Jiang Zemin in November 1996 was ratified. The two sides focused on implementing the 1993 and 1996 CBM agreements and pledged to continue dialogue on a mutually acceptable border.[47] There was no substantive progress during the meetings. According to an Indian analyst the main obstacle was that both sides were still unable to narrow their differences on troop reductions along the border.[48] Further because of domestic compulsions, the Government of RoI faced constraints in moving ahead without much Chinese support on the issue of border dispute. Recognizing this fact both sides pursued step by step approach.

Nonetheless, the positive factor of peaceful border was recognised by both nations. In the words of a Chinese Analyst, "with the signing of the LAC agreement, the legalistic and historical framework of the border claims has been thrown on the remotest back burner, or even behind the burner shelf. There is widespread support to the LAC agreement in both India and China, which will further strengthen the determination of Indian and Chinese leaders to boost the momentum for exploring a final solution."[49] The Agreements were seen as steps based on "rational politics and objective realities" in the course of the comprehensive border settlement.

However by the end of year 1997, some circles in India were not totally satisfied with the overall pace of negotiations to resolve border issue with China.

China by mid nineties had grown both in economic and military terms into a fast rising regional power with aspirations towards global power. As such being its neighbour India rightfully head anxiety about behaviour and intention of substantive rise of China as well its implications for India's security.

As two noted diplomats wrote that "it is a fact, however, that progress in their implementation has been rather slow."[50] Still India pursued the policy of continuation of talks and serious engagement. At the same time being a rising power itself India in its rightful search for power was also looking for building leverages with China. India perceived that leverages would enhance its position including acceleration of pace of negotiations to resolve border issue as well as better understanding of its security concerns by China. Therefore in India continued to pursue two pronged policy viz., engagement and building leverages with China. In this period the policy of engagement was the dominant trend on the part of India.

Growing Economic Cooperation

Economic Cooperation between both nations constituted an important component of first normalisation process and later on in the overall rapprochement process. After India-China war of 1962, both sides resumed trade in 1978. Earlier in pre 1962 phase, the 1954 bilateral Trade Agreement lapsed in 1962. In 1984, the two nations signed the most Favoured Nation Agreement, which boosted bilateral trade.[51] Furthermore, during the China visit of Rajiv Gandhi in December 1988 both nations agreed to establish Joint Group on Economic Relations and Trade, Science and Technology (JEG).[52] Since then trade ties between India and China have been expanding. The year 1991 saw signing of the memorandum between the Government of the Republic of India (here after RoI) and the Government of the People's Republic of China (here after PRC) on Resumption of Border Trade.

Table 1

Years	*Indian Imports in US $ million*	*Indian Exports in US $ million*	*Trade Balance*	*Trade Values*
1993	259.16	416.57	+154.41	675.73
1994	573.00	322.00	−251.00	894.00
1995	769.00	398.00	−367.00	1162.00
1996	689.54	719.16	+29.64	1406.00

Source: Cited in Keshav Mishra, Sino-Indian Relations in the Post Cold War Era. Indian Journal of Politics, 35, 1-2, 2001, p. 66.

The post cold war period saw an impressive growth in bilateral trade. But the total volume of bilateral trade constituted only a small fraction of each nation's share of international trade. In 1990 the volume of Sino-Indian trade was $ 200 million, which by 1992 reached to $ 339 million and by 1995 stood at $1.16 billion.[53] The overall volume rose more than five fold. India became China's largest trade partner in South Asia in this period.

In the year 1997 Indian imports were $ 933.1 (million) and exports were $ 897.3 (million). Therefore total trade value went up to $ 1.83 billion.[54]

Table 2

Year	*China as % Share of India's Exports to the World*	*China as % Share of India's Imports from the World*
1992	0.51	0.4
1993	1.41	1.21
1994	0.89	2.39
1995	0.93	2.35
1996	1.9	1.85
1997	1.94	2.72

Source: Cited in Charan Wadhva, India-China Economic Cooperation: Recent Trends (1990's) and Future Perspective (2025) (30) in a presentation collection for conference on India in 21st century : External Relations, Shanghai Institute for International Studies Publication, Shanghai, 2002, p. 209

The main items of Indian exports included mineral products, chemicals, vegetable oil, jewellery and semi precious stones, animal products and machinery. The main items of Indian imports were organic chemicals, electronics goods, mineral products like metal surgical coke, textile materials like silk, textile yarn, base metals, machinery and medical and surgical equipment. At the border trade mainly the essential commodities composed main items. There was huge potential for expansion of trade ties between India and China.

Further, both sides worked towards establishment of facilitory framework for boosting trade and economic cooperation, which included a maritime transport agreement, MOU on banking relations and an agreement on the avoidance of double transaction. From 1992 to 1997 many agreements protocols and MOUs were concluded to boost overall economic cooperation between India and China. In the year 1992 two protocols were signed between both sides. The first dealt with custom Regulation, Banking Arrangements and Related matters for Border Trade. The second was concerned with entry and exit procedures for Border Trade. The year also saw signing of Memorandum of understanding on cooperation in Agriculture between the ministry of Agriculture of RoI and the Ministry of Agriculture of PRC.[55]

The year 1993 first saw the protocol between the Government of RoI and PRC for extension of border trade across Shipkila Pass. Secondly in the year, both sides MOU between the Governments of RoI and PRC on cooperation in the field of geology and Mineral Resources. Later both nations also concluded Agreement on Environment Cooperation.[56] Further in 1994 both sides signed MOU on simplifying the visa procedures between RoI and PRC. Last but not least in the above mentioned phase, both sides concluded Agreement on maritime Transport. All these efforts boosted bilateral economic cooperation.

Joint Ventures

During the period under study both nations started setting up joint ventures to promote bilateral economic cooperation. Among Indian companies include drugs and pharmaceuticals companies, viz, Ranbaxy established a joint venture in Guangzhou, Dr. Reddy's Laboratories and Aurobindo Pharma in Datong in Shanxi. Orissa Industry Co. Ltd. has built a solely funded refractory materials plant in Dahun, Liaoning Province.[57] Orind set up a wholly owned factory in steel refractories at Dalian, and Essel Packaging also set up a wholly owned venture in Guangzhou.[58]

China's investment in India is in a variety of fields like telecommunication, metallurgical industries, transportation and electrical industry. In the year 1992, China Metallurgical Import and Export Company (CMIEC) and Indian Essar Corporation agreed to build a medium size steel industry with an annual production capacity of a million tons in the eastern state of Orissa. Again the same Chinese Company (CMIEC) and India's Usha Corporation agreed in June 1993 to construct two slag concrete plants. Further, Huawei Technologies set up R & D software centre in Bangalore. Other Chinese Companies in India in Clude, China National Machinery Import and Export Corporation (CNMIEC), China National Petroleum Corporation (CNPC) etc.[59]

Thus during the above mention period bilateral economic cooperation and trade ties had grown despite constraints. Among the constraints were following : first, there existed information gap which often inhibited businessmen to explore each other's markets. Second, there were high tariff and non-tariff barriers on selected products of export. Thirdly, the infrastructure which would serve the needs of the expansion of bilateral trade and investment were simply inadequate. Like till the period there was no direct air service between both nations, even banking services were found wanting and business to business contacts while growing were at low and erratic level.[60] Nonetheless, both sides were convinced about the potentiality to be tapped.

The economic cooperation was an important input to growing relationship between the two Asian giants and would further enhance bilateral ties.

Bilateral Collaboration in Science and Technology

The contacts in the sphere of science and Technology between RoI and PRC started with the exchange of visits of various scientific delegations, which were later followed by official level talks. In these meetings mutual views on joint interaction in science and technology were exchanged. As a result growing visits of scientific exchange happened in a number of areas, which included seismology and earthquake engineering, Chemistry of natural products, laser science and technology, plasma physics, astronomy and biotechnology.

It was during prime Minister, Rajiv Gandhi's China visit on 22 December 1988 that agreement on cooperation in the field of science and Technology was concluded between the Governments of RoI and PRC. Accordingly it was decided to convey a meeting of the joint committee on science and technology annually and to formulate bilateral exchange programmes in S & T.[62] Both sides concluded another agreement which was signed by Chinese Academy of Sciences and Indian National science Academy.[63] It was during the second meeting of the India-China subcommittee on S & T cooperation, which was held in Beijing in July 1991 that the priority areas of cooperation were identified. These included lasers, material science, remote sensing technology, aerospace, chemical-industry, agricultural and fisheries, electronics, biotechnology and pharmacy. Two Indian scientists wrote, "a number of joint collaborative proposals were identified in the above mentioned areas and recommended at the Third meeting of India-China sub-committee on S & T cooperation held in New Delhi in April 1993."[64]

Some of the significant Agreements signed between scientific agencies of both nations were :

1991 : MOU between the Ministry of Acro-space Industry of PRC and the Department of Space of RoI on cooperation in the peaceful Application of outer space sciences and Technology.

1992 : Move on Cooperation in Agriculture between the ministry of Agriculture of RoI and PRC.

1993 : MOU between Governments of RoI and PRC.

1995 : MOU between Ministry of Metallurgical Industry of the Government of PRC and ministry of Steel of the Government of RoI.[65]

There were other areas of cooperation which were being gradually widened in a bid to enhance bilateral interaction. Culture was also an important area of cooperation between both nations. In the year 1992, both sides signed a protocol between the ministry of Human Resource Development Department of Education, Government of India and the state Education commission of PRC on cooperation in the field of Education for the year 1992-1993. The year 1993 witnessed conclusion of agreement between the Ministry of Information and Broad casting of the RoI and the ministry of Radio, Film, Television of the PRC on Radio and Television Cooperation. Earlier in the year 1992 both sides signed memorandum of consultation in the field of social welfare.[66]

In the sphere of other areas of cooperation, both sides concluded MOU on cooperation in the field of Civil Services, Personnel Management and Public Administration between the Ministry of Personnel, Public Grievances and Pensions of the Government of the RoI and the Ministry of Personnel of the PRC in 1992. In the same year both sides also signed MOU between the office of the Comptroller and Auditor General, RoI and the Audit Administration, PRC. Later in the year 1996 both nations signed on agreement on cooperation for combating illicit trafficking in narcotic drugs and psychotropic substances and other crimes between the Governments of the RoI and PRC.

These steps were in the right direction and contributed in consolidation of bilateral relations. Overall, these concrete actions were helpful in strengthening of friendly bond between both nations. As both nations were part of developing nation states, therefore, they were learning from each other in terms of experience. As such it was positive development.

In the immediate aftermath of uncertain phase of post cold war world order, both India and China were compelled to construct rapprochement which was already gathering movementum in many ways since the decade of 80's and in more tangible manner particularly from the historic visit of India's Prime Minister Rajiv Gandhi in 1988. The high level political interaction contributed to enhanced understanding between both nations. As a result of the summit level talks of 1993 and 1996, the bilateral relations registered all round improvement. Another important development in the bilateral relations was the beginning of high level military exchanges which was designed to enhance mutual interactions between defence establishments of both nations. On the border issue, the Agreements of 1993 and 1996 were significant developments, whereby both nations agreed to ensure peace and tranquility on the LAC on one hand and moved ahead with CBMs on the other. It seems that both sides were following step-by-step approach to resolve the sensitive and complex issue of borders. Furthermore to broaden the base of bilateral relations, both nations moved forward in a more determined and nature manner to cooperate in the areas of economy, trade, science and technology and culture etc. The combination of all these developments in some ways constructed Sino-Indian Rapprochement by the year 1997.

However, the structure of rapprochement was slightly weak in that there was distrust between both nations. Equally important was the fact that the structure of rapprochement was tilted more in favour of China much to the determent of India's security. In India's strategic circles a notable trend emerged that Sino-Indian relations "was not a relationship between equals". Another noticeable trend shared in India was the slow pace of border negotiations and "progress in their implementation has been rather slow". In spite of all these drawbacks, India pursued the policy of engagement and acted as a mature nation in the interest of peace and stability.

References

1. See for details, Deng Xiaoping, Selected Works of Deng Xiaoping, Vol. III (English edition), Foreign Language Press, Beijing, 1994, p. 275.
2. J.N. Dixit, South Block Years : Memoirs of a Foreign Secretary, USB Publishers, New Delhi, 1996, pp. 231-32.
3. Ramesh Thakur, The Politics and Economics of India's Foreign Policy, Oxford University Press, Delhi, 1994, p. 84.
4. See n-2, p. 239.
5. Faisal O Al-Rfouch, Sino-Indian Relations : From Confrontation to Accommodation (1988-2001), China Report, Vol. 39, No. 1, 2003, pp. 28-9.
6. Sujit Dutta, "India-China Relations : The Post Cold War Phase" in V.D. Chopra and M.K. Rasgotra (eds). India's Relations with Russia and China, Gyan Publishing House, Delhi 1997, pp. 156-57.
7. Manoj Joshi, Coming closer : Sharad Pawar's China Visit, Frontline, 28 August 1992, pp. 37-9.
8. See the full text of Agreement in C.V. Ranganathan and Vinod C. Khanna, India and China – The Way Ahead-After "Mao's India War", Har Anand

Publications, New Delhi, 2000, Appendix-B, pp. 185-87.
9. *Ibid.*, p. 171.
10. Ye Zhengjia, "China-India Relations" in A Presentation Collection for Conference on India in 21st Century : External Relations, Shanghai Institute for International Studies Publication, Shanghai, 2002, pp. 172-73.
11. See n-6, p. 156.
12. Cited in Keshav Mishra, Sino-Indian Relations in the Post-Cold War Era, Indian Journal of Politics, Vol. 35, Nos. 1-2, 2001, p. 65.
13. Alka Acharya, "India-China Relations : An Overview" in Kanti Bajpai and Amitabh Mattoo (eds), The Peacock and the Dragon : India-China Relations in the 21st Century, Har Anand Publications, New Delhi, 2000, p. 187.
14. See the full text of Agreement in n-8, Appendix-C, pp. 188-95.
15. "Sino-Indian accord on border confidence building viewed" Zhongguo Xinwen she 29 November 1996 in Foreign Broadcasting Information service-China (here after FBIS-CHI) – 96-232, 3 December 1996.
16. *Hindustan Times*, 30 November, 1996.
17. See n-13, pp. 188-89.
18. Xia Liping, "China-Indian Security Relationship" in n-10, p. 107.
19. Cited in n-12, p. 65.
20. Cited in M.V. Rappai, India-China : Need for Border settlement, Indian Defence Review, 15,3, 2000, p. 127.
21. For details of the Chinese view see Wang Hongwei, Qimalayashan Quingjie : Zhongyin Guanxi Yanjiu (The Himalayas Sentiment : A study of Sino-Indian Relations), Zhongguo Zangxue Chubanshe, Beijing, 1998, pp. 157-59; and Zhao weiwen, Yin Zhong quanxi fengyunlu 1949-1999 (Record of story India-China Relations, 1949-1999) Shishi Chubanshe, Beijing, 2000 pp. 140-43, Cited in Srikanth Kondapalli, "India-China Border Perspectives" in n-10, p. 136.
22. Cited in n-20, p. 127.
23. "Sino-Indian boundary" China News Service 8 May 1986.
24. See n-20, p. 127.
25. *Ibid.*
26. Cited in Srikanth Kondapalli, "India-China Border Perspectives" in n-10, p. 138.
27. Manoj Joshi, Falling Hurdles, Frontline, 3 January, 1992, p. 11.
28. Waheguru Pal Singh Sidhu and Jing-dong yuan, Resolving The Sino-Indian Border Dispute, Asian Survey, 51, 2, 2001, p. 356.
29. *Ibid.*
30. Cited in n-12, p. 62.
31. Chinese Prime Minister Li Peng's Interview to Front Line, January 3, 1992, p. 121.
32. For the text of the communique see Renmin Ribao (People's Daily),

December 17, 1991, p.1.

33. Xinhua, February 21, 1992, in FBIS-CHI, February 24, 1992, pp. 19-20.
34. See n-28, p. 356.
35. Fang Tien-SZe, The Sino-Indian Border Talks Under the Joint Working Group, Issues and Studies, 38, 3, 2002, p. 158.
36. The complete text of the 1993 Agreement is also available at *www.fmprc.gov.cn/eng/23691.html.*
37. See n-35, p. 160.
38. FBIS-CHI, April 26, 1994, p. 22.
39. See n-35, p. 160.
40. *Ibid.*
41. Cited in Srikanth Kondapalli, "India-China Border Perspectives "in n-10, pp. 142-43.
42. See n-28, pp. 356-57.
43. The complete text of the 1996 Agreement is also available at *www.fmprc.gov.cn/eng/23690.html.*
44. The Hindu, 30 November, 1996.; See n-8, p. 173.
45. Wang Hongwei, Ximalayashan qingjie : Zhongy in guanxi yanjiu, Beijing, 1998, p. 376 cited in n-35, p. 163.
46. See n-35, p. 153.
47. See n-28, p. 356.
48. See Swaran Singh, Sino-Indian CBMs : Problems and Prospects, Strategic Analysis, 20, 4, pp. 543-59.
49. Liu Xuecheng, The Sino-Indian Border Dispute and Sino-Indian Relations. University Press of America, Lanham, 1994, pp. 177-78.
50. See n-8, p. 173.
51. Cited in Strategic Digest, 33, 5, May 2003, p. 377.
52. See n-12, p. 65.
53. See n-5, p. 36.
54. See n-51, p. 376.
55. *Ibid.*, p. 377.
56. *Ibid.*, p. 378.
57. Cited in BM Gupta and SM Dhawan, India's Collaboration with Republic of China in Science and Technology, China Report, 39, 2, 2003, pp. 200-01.
58. Shahul Hameed, India and China : The Economic Relationship, n-13, p. 212.
59. See n-57, p. 200.
60. Charan Wadhva, "India-China Economic Cooperation : Recent Trends (1990's) and Future-Perspective (2025)" in n-10, pp. 200-02.
61. See for details, International Linkages in Indian National Science Academy. Pursuit Promotion of science : The Indian Experience, Indian National

Science Academy, New Delhi, November 2001, pp. 370-78.
62. See n-61, pp. 370-78.
63. See n-57, p. 201.
64. *Ibid.*
65. See n-51, pp. 377-78.
66. *Ibid.*, p. 377.

7

The Brief Breakdown (1998)

A combination of factors at the international, regional and bilateral levels brought about brief breakdown in the process of Sino-Indian rapprochement in the year 1998. As has been mentioned earlier the structure of rapprochement was tilted from the very beginning in favour of China. India by 1998 was mature and rising power and because of perceived cumulative disadvantages vis-a-vis China, it wanted to balance the structure of rapprochement in some measure.

Rise of China

China, by this point of time emerged as a powerful power in terms of population, Industrialisation and overall modernisation, including of the armed forces. In the post cold war period. China concentrated on building a Comprehensive National Power (CNP). As the Chinese President Jiang Zemin stated, "the essence of the current international competition is a comprehensive competition in national strength based on economic, scientific and technological strengths".[1] Some of the Chinese analysts linked the ancient strategy of 'victory without war' with the concept of CNP.[2] In addition, China's nuclear weapons and missiles capability, its permanent membership in the United Nations Security Council and its closed and communist political system give it an important place in global order and more particular in Asia.

Inspite of pursuance of 'independent foreign policy of peace', China mainly perceived four major threats to its security in the post cold war period. The General Secretary of Communist Party, Jiang Zemin in his report to the 14th Party Congress in October 1992 Stated that in the post-cold war period the world would face on outbreak of ethnic, territorial and religious conflicts.[3] From the Chinese perceptions following four are threats: USA on the issue of Taiwan, Japan on the issue of Diaoyutai (Senkaku) islands, recent spurt in 'militarism' and the Japan – USA renewal of security treaty in 1997 which enhanced the role of Japanese forces in the Taiwan straits under 'certain circumstances', Vietnam on the issue of the border dispute and the Gulf of Tongking (South China Sea Islands) and, last but not least, India on the issue of the border.[4]

More specifically the Chinese National Defence University – Commissioned report identified following source of the conflict under which local war would be fought :

- Unresolved territorial disputes.
- Undecided disputed borders.
- Contradictions in the oceanic interests (of nations) becoming creasingly acute, and
- Taiwan's drift towards 'independence'.[5]

Therefore, India was viewed as one of the potential nations with which border conflict was possible. Apart from this fact, China's emergence as a rising power was a well recognised a global reality.[6]

The strategic circles of USA recognised that China will be its leading challenger in Asia. The fact was testified by the 1997 strategic Assessment published by the National Defense University : "Dealing with China as a rising power is the most compelling of all of the many challenges facing the United states and its regional allies."[7] The point that is being made is even superpower like US recognised the fact of rising China. As such its overall rising capabilities including military, particularly nuclear and missile build up, had security implications for its neighbourhood and India also happened to be one of the neighbours of China with which territorial dispute continued. Commenting on the rise of China an Indian analyst cautioned, "two factors make this agenda problematic and destabilizing : first, China's increasingly assertive nationalism with the PLA at the core of defining national identity and security goals, and second, China's deeply rooted real politic strategic culture and its repeated use of force in pursuit of the national interest.[8]

Furthermore, the Chinese leadership perceived conflict as a marked characteristic in human affairs. As the inheritors of strategic culture, violence is also an option before them. In the words of Alastair Iain Johnston : "The Chinese leadership believes that conflict is due largely to the rapacious role of the adversary, and that in this zero-sum context the application of violence is highly efficacious for dealing with the enemy. These assumptions generally translate into preference for offensive strategies followed by progressively less coercive ones, where accommodation is ranked last."[9]

China Threat

All of the factors mentioned above combined together contributed to the making o 'China Threat Theory.[10] Many analysts argued that with its economic development, China would increase its military strength and pursue an expansionist policy. The theory of China Threat was so pervasive that one of the important Chinese leader, Li Ruihuan, Chairman of the National Committee of the Chinese People's Political consultative Conference (CPPCC) stated that "the 'China threat' theory is concocted for the purpose of containing China's development, a move which will not be beneficial to China, nor accure to the security of Asia or the rest of the world."[11]

The official Chinese media pointed out that China is a developing country, its development level is very low, and its economic structure needs further upgrading. It further claimed that militarily, China pursues a defensive policy.... China's military expenditure remains at a very low level compatible with the needs of national security. The official media alleged that "the 'China threat' fallacy, on the other hand, is targeted at sowing discord between China and the other Asian-Pacific countries, especially at harming China's friendly relations with its neighbours. By creating tensions in the relations between China and other Asian nations, the west gets the benefit of selling arms to those countries."[12]

Notwithstanding Chinese media's denial of 'China Threat' theory the fact remained that the actual amount of China's defence spending increased.[13] Chinese overall political system generally lacked transparency and the military system was veiled in total secrecy. Further, with rapid help of Russian military complex Chinese military modernisation was underway at a rapid pace. An Indian analyst stated that "this has forced Asian states to adjust their Post-Cold War strategies, with China now the dominant focus of security concern."[14] Thus, at the international level the fact of Rise of China and partly 'China Threat' theory was well recognised fact.

China in South Asia

The net effect of Sino-Indian Rapproachement as perceived in New Delhi was the fact that China while continued to further improve its relations with the pre-eminent regional power. India but did not wish to downgrade its existing relationships with other South Asian Countries. In particular, Sino-Pakistan relationship continued to evolve into an autonomous relationship irrespective of India's grave security converns arising out of Sino-Pak enduring defence relations visible in the field of nuclear and missile cooperation. On the part of China, it makes perfect strategic sense to "build up" Pakistan not only to contain and neutralize Indian power, but also to tie India down in sub-continental concerns.[15] From the Chinese perspective, "to sacrifice Pakistan would be tantamount to conceding South Asia as India's Sphere of influence".

The Indian experience of Sino-Indian Rappraochement in the regional context till 1997 with its complexities has been appropriately summarised by a leading western analyst as : "yet India has also been compelled to acquiesce to a steady increase in Pakistan's military capabilities, with China playing a crucial role in the process. It is probably fair to conclude that, without China's large-scale, sustained, and comprehensive assistance, Pakistan's military capabilities would be far less potent and parless threatening to India than they are today. Nor has India succeded in weakening the core of the Sino-Pakistani entente. The mutual trust, familiarity, and parallel interests that constitute that core remain unchanged by Sino-Indian rapprochement. This constitutes a major constraint on India's freedom to act."[16]

Apart from Pakistan, China continued conventional arms transfers to Bangladesh, Nepal and Sri Lanka.[17] Furthermore, the growing defence ties between China and Myanmar aroused Indian apprehensions. One analysts termed this development : "just as China's support for Pakistan puts pressure on India to the west, so closer Chinese ties with Burma adds to India's strategic concerns in the east."[18] Among the bases and military assets built with the Chinese assistance are the naval base at Hainggyi Island and radar station at CoCo Islands, south west of the Burmese coast. The Chinese helped to construct five new ports and upgrade others along Burma's coast, from victoria point in the south to sittwe in Northern Arakan.[19] From China's point of view a military powerful Myanmar friendly with China meant that India was placed in an unfavourable security environment.

In short, the regional context was not simple as it seemed, on one hand, China pursued policy of improvement of relations with India. Simultaneously, it "amed at the strategic encirclement of India in order to marginalise India in Asia and tie it down to the Indian sub-continent."[20] Therefore, China in South Asia was pursuing policy of both engagement and balance of power.

Problems at the Bilateral Level

Inspite of Sino-Indian rapprochement, there were several underlying tensions in the bilateral relations. The difficulties were produced at broader level by the existence of two Asian nationalisms, two sets of strategic interests and different politico-strategic cultures.[21] The most concrete problem was the unresolved issue of border. China was yet to recognise Sikkim as part of India. Despite the continuation of border negotiations, India perceived that "progress in their implementation has been rather slow". Overall India also perceived that Sino-Indian relations" was not a relationship between equals". Therefore, in early 1998 an economically growing India felt more confident at a time when uncertainties of post cold war in a relative degree had settled and it looked for leverages against China to accelerate the pace of Sino-Indian rapproachement to its advantage. In the words of an analyst, "the loosening of the traditional alliance with Moscow, an uneasy relationship with the sole surviving superpower, the United States, economic restructuring. China's strategic encirclement of India through its military alliances with Pakistan and Myanmar, concerns about the rise of China as the second most important economic and military power in the world, and the fear of marginalisation in the post-cold war era, coupled with an inability to find a new and sound niche for itself as an effective and acceptable regional power in the international system, all forced India to rethink its approach to national security."[22] Therefore, due to developments at international, regional and bilateral levels, India was compelled to chart out new course towards China alongwith continuation of policy of engagement.

New Government in India

India's new government led by the Bharatiya Janata Party and its coalition allies, which came to office in March 1998 assigned priority to national security. In the new priority. "a firmer approach to dealing with China was central to this thrust". According to a western-expert of Sino-Indian relations, "the new approach implemented by Prime Minister Atal Behari Vajpayee's government shortly after taking power included four elements : more frank public expression of Indian concerns about China's activities in South Asia ; open establishment of India as a nuclear power possessing a minimal nuclear deterrent; a Marginally more assertive policy on the ultra-sensitive Tibet issue; and reaching an understanding with the United States regarding India's deteriorating security situation, including the threat posed by China."[23]

The present work however, is in agreement with first two elements and does not subscribe to the point about Tibet. It is the considered view that John Garver's assertion about India's more assertive policy on the ultra-sensitive Tibet issue" requires more substantive evidence and objectively there are none to prove the point. The point regarding India's reaching an understanding with the United States appears to be simplistic which in fact is not the case. In the initial stages, the US on the contrary pursued sanctions against India. At best due to sustained diplomatic negotiations with US, at a later stage due to effective representation of strong viewpoint of India, US was compelled to appreciate in some measure India's 'deteriorating security situation'. Therefore, argument of 'understanding with the USA' appears to be simplistic by the western analyst, which tries to depict the role of western nations in general and the USA in particular in a favourable way. From India's perspective this in fact is not the case.

The first important bilateral contact of the year 1998 was in April, when the chief of General staff of PLA, General Fu Quanyou visited India as part of exchange of high level military visits. It was for the first time that the chief of PLA was in India, as such it was important development.[24] General Fu told media persons that it was important for both sides to carry out gradual and early demarcation of the Line of Actual Control. In talks with the PLA chief, the ministry of defence, GOI raised the contentious issues of Sino-Pak missile and nuclear collaborations, wrong projection of the Chinese maps and the border disputes alongwith the issue of the LAC.[25] More specifically, India's defence minister George Fernandes in talks with PLA Chief of staff made clear India's concern and objections to China's transfer of missiles and missile technology to Pakistan. To this General Fu emphasised the Chinese viewpoint that relations among nations be based on the five principles of peaceful coexistence as a agreed by both sides. Finally, Prime Minister Vajpayee cleared India's position by stating that improvements in Sino-Indian relations "should be based on the recognition and respect for each other's concerns."[26] At the end of the talks, India and China committed themselves to peaceful resolution of bilateral disputes.[27]

Furthermore, another evidence of Indian new administration's more frank articulation of its concerns about China's activities in its neighbourhood came in early May, when the Defence Minister George Fernandes called China a "bigger potential threat" than Pakistan. He stated that a massive electronic surveillance establishment by Beijing in CoCo islands near Andaman and Nicobar islands was monitoring everything in India. He further stated that there were moves by China to convert the surveillance set up into a major naval base which would be a direct threat to us.[28] Fernandes reiterated that "China has provided Pakistan with both missile as well as nuclear know-how." He also stated that china has its nuclear weapons stockpiled in Tibet right along India's borders, where a lot of elongation of air fields is going on to station Russian made Sukhoi. Further on the eastern frontier with Myanmar, he said that Chinese have trained and equipped the Burmese army. Therefore, all these fact point out that the potential threat from China was greater than that from Pakistan.[29]

China on its part expressed utmost regret and resentment over the statement by the India's Defence Minister and stated that it has "seriously destroyed the good atmosphere of improved relations between the two countries." The Chinese Foreign Ministery spokesman, Zhu Bang Zao, termed Fernandes statement as absolutely ridiculous and unworthy of refutation. He described Fernandes "Criticism of China's relations with other countries" as absolutely fictititious and entirely baseless. The spokesman stated that "China does not constitute any threat to other countries" and it has no basis in facts, therefore, "the chinese side has to express extreme regret and indignation over this."[30] Thus, the Chinese side first signalled in a nuanced way the mild breakdown when its spokesman stated that Fernandes statement has "seriously destroyed" atmospherics of improved bilateral relations. India on its part continued to reiterate its faith in the dialogue mode and later on the Ministry of external affairs stated that New Delhi "remains committed to the process of dialogue for the development of a friendly, cooperative, good-neighbourly, mutually beneficial relationship with China, our largest neighbour."[31]

True to its vibrant democratic credentials India was divided even on Fernandes statement about China. The opposition parties and some security experts criticised Defence Minister's statement. The former Prime Minister, I.K. Gujral called him temperamentally an adventurist and accused him of arousing "the nations's Chauvinistic Zeal" on the China issue.[32] However, there were others who believed that the Defence Minister merely articulated the silent majority's views on Indian security environment.[33] All the facts that the minister stated were earlier published in the annual reports of the Defence Ministry in the 1990's. For instance the 1993-94 annual report mildly noted the "reported proliferation of missiles in our neighbourhood such as in Pakistan, Saudi Arabia and Iran". It further stated that "Pakistan has also reportedly acquired M-11 missiles from China."[34] The 1996-97 report pointedly stated : "China has supplied M-11 missiles to Pakistan and is aiding it with technology and manpower as well in the development of its indigenous missile programme."[35] The report made it clear in no uncertain terms "India's concerns regarding China's defence cooperation with Pakistan, its assistance to Pakistan's clandestine nuclear programme, and the sale of missiles and sophisticated weapons systems by it to Pakistan were conveyed to the Chinese side."[36] Therefore, the Minister's statement was culmination of what was written and Indian concerns were declared openly in the year 1998. The experts of this school of thought "called for increased attention to the instruments of Indian national power and far greater thought about how these instruments could be used effectively to serve Indian interests."[37] And one of the instruments was to acquire nuclear weapons.

India's Nuclear Tests

The most important elements of India's firm priority to national security was undoubtedly nuclear weapons. In all, on 11th and 13th May, 1998 India tesed five nuclear devices, including one hydrogen bomb and the tests brought about an end to ambiguity and uncertainty about India's nuclear posture. Commenting on India's rational for the nuclear tests in May 1998, two seasoned diplomat wrote : "Besides the security dimension, there was also the growing belief that India needed these weapons which were perceived as the new currency of power and prestige in international relations, a currency which China had acquired. The indefinite and unconditional extension of the NPT, legitimizing the nuclear hegemony of the five nuclear weapon states (who also happen to be the Five Permanent Members of the Security Council and whom we may call the P-5/N-5), including China, was seen as condemning India to a permanent position of strategic and status inferiority in relation to its neighbour. In short, whatever the role domestic politics may have played in the final decision, and whatever the views one may hold on the wisdom of the new Indian nuclear policy, there is no denying the fact that the China factor – made even more pressing by the Sino-Pak cooperation in this field – has been the most important ingredient in the chain of events which culminated in India's nuclear tests of 11 and 13 May, 1998."[38]

Further, in the words of a person who was closely associated with the tests, "In one short sentence, India's neighbourhood was getting a bit rowdy in the nuclear sense and the Government had no choice but to exercise the option for safeguarding national security interests."

The triangular dimension of India-China-Pakistan was important aspect in the overall regional context. As another leading analyst summed up : "Contrary to the common perception of an India-Pakistan nuclear contest, China was in fact the most important actor to induce India to exercise its nuclear option. India's nuclear and missile capabilities owe much to the dynamics of Sino-Indian rivalry. It is the adversarial nature of the Sino-Indian relationship which has driven the Indian and, in turn, Pakistani nuclear weapons programmes. Uncompromising attitudes and deep suspicion of each other's intentions have led to a situation where each has sought to negotiate only from a position of absolute strength. Contingent with this distrust have been feelings of mutual insecurity. India's defence policy has always been based on "keeping one step ahead of Pakistan and on a par with China".[40] In sum there were numerous reasons for India's decision to go nuclear and China was very important factor in overall Indian security calculus.

Explaining the rationale behind India's nuclear tests. Prime Minister A.B. Vajpayee wrote to the US president Bill Clinton and cited the "deteriorating security environment", he further wrote : "India had an overt nuclear weapon state on ours borders, a state which committed armed aggression against India in 1962... an atmosphere of distrust persists mainly due to the unresolved border problem... To add to the distress that country has materially helped another neighbour of ours to become a covert nuclear weapon state. At the hands of this bitter neighbour we have suffered three aggressions in the last fifty years."[41] A close perusal of Prime Minister's letter points out to the fact that it "did not explicitly name China, but the implications were clear. It dwelt first and longest on the threat from China. Sixty-eight words targeted China, compared to 48 addressing the Pakistani threat to India."[42] Thus, India in a nuanced way indicated to the US its rationale behind the nuclear tests of 1998.

China's Official Response to the Indian Nuke Tests

China strongly opposed the Indian nuclear tests. Though there exists scholarly opinion that China's initial response was "relatively measured" and "subdued". One can substantiate this argument by the statement of the spokesman, Ministry of Foreign Affairs on 12 May, 1998. The Spokesman, Zhu Bang Zao said : "The Chinese Government is seriously concerned about the nuclear tests conducted by India... India's conducting of nuclear tests runs against international trend and is determental to the peace and stability of the South Asian region."[43] Further, the official media like People's Daily reported : "India today conducted three underground nuclear tests in the Pokharan area of Rajasthan... Twenty-four years ago, in May 1974, India carried out its first nuclear explosion at the same location. According to reports, India's major opposition parties, the congress and the United Front, and other parties have expressed support for these nuclear tests. Strategists and security analysts are of the view that this was a concrete exercising of the nuclear option of the government, and that it stemmed from considerations of national security and national interests. According to media reports received here America and Pakistan have condemned India's nuclear tests."[44]

The report was matter of fact and quite fair. In fact, one western analyst of Sino-Indian relations wrote : "Beijing radio, however, explained the tests in terms of India's rejection of western pressures – an interpretation which implied approval of the tests."[45] The point that is being made here is notwithstanding initial Chinese response which may appear to be measured has to be taken as only one part of the story, which in large measure is simplistic. The issue should be judged in a holistic way, then only the larger picture will emerge.

On the whole, the complete picture makes it very clear the severity of Chinese strong opposition of India's nuclear tests. The official media commented after the nuclear tests : "In disregard of the strong opposition of the international community, the Indian government conducted two more nuclear tests on 13 may following the 11 may tests. The Chinese government is deeply shocked by this and thereby expresses its strong condemnation. This act of India is nothing but outrageous contempt for the common will of the international community for comprehensive ban on nuclear tests and a hard blow on the international effort to prevent nuclear proliferation. It will entail serious consequences to the peace and stability in South Asia and the world at large."[46]

Furthermore, the PLA's newspaper Liberation Army Daily (Jiefangjun Bao) reported : "Indian nuclear weapons programme originates from her idea to seek big power status. Much before Indian independence, congress leader Nehru said in his Discovery of India, 'India cannot continue to be a second rate country in the world as she is today. She has to prosper or perish. After independence, all successive governments inherited this idea and deemed it a strategic target to seek big power status, and then took to (its) nuclear weapons programme as a means to achieve this end... In march this year, after the BJP government came to power it changed the nuclear policy of earlier governments and clearly pointed out in its government agenda that 'it would re-examine India's nuclear policy and exercise the right to induct nuclear weapons'... Indian nuclear tests this time have shocked the world and all the governments and international organisations have issued statements condeming it... Now, with the combined efforts of international community, the process of nuclear disarmament in the world has gained momentum, the nuclear non-proliferation treaty is extended for ever and the CTBT has also been worked out. Under these circumstances, India conducting nuclear tests runs contrary to international trend and (is/prejudicial to regional and world peace and stability.[47] The strong anti-Indian reaction from the Chinese army's mouthpiece was not very surprising.

Continuing the anti-Indian tirade, the China Daily reported that "Most Chinese, who believe India's five underground nuclear tests have defied international efforts to prevent the proliferation of nuclear weapons, are greatly concerned and severely critical of India, a nationwide survey revealed yesterday. Eighty-nine per cent of the people surveyed strongly criticise India for the tests, and 80 per cent agree that the United Nations should place sanctions on India to forestall any further nuclear threat... More than 91 per cent people said they were shocked by India's unwise manner' in showcasing its military power through nuclear tests, and 80 per cent said they worry about the aftermath on China's national security. Seventy-eight per cent said they believed India's action has posed a threat to China...."[48] The nationwide survey was done by the social-survey Institute of China under the state-statistics Bureau and findings were based on telephonic interviews with 1,500 citizens at Beijing, Shanghai, Tianjin, Wuhan, Changsha, Guangzhou, Chongqing-Dalian, Harbin etc.

It seems that China was opposed to India's nuke tests well as projection of China threat to be the rationale behind the tests. In the words of two leading analysts, China's "reaction was identical to that of the rest of the P-5/N-5 fraternity, which has taken upon itself the guardianship of the non-proliferation regime represented by the NPT and the CTBT. But there are additional reasons which influence the specific Chinese perceptions. The Indian move, followed in quick succession by Pakistan, has undermined China's unique status as the only "legitimate" Asian nuclear weapon state."[49]

A close study of Chinese response makes it clear that it rejected India's assertion that direct Chinese threat and continuing nuclear and missile assistance to Pakistan were the main reasons for India's nuke tests. Moreover, at a broad level China's objective in Asia was to prevent rise of a peer competitor'. The competitive element in Sino-Indian relation was based on this fact. China was clear from the cold war period that India 'alone has the size, might, numbers and above all, the intention to match China'. Therefore, at one level China pursued balance of power in South Asia since early 60's. At the regional level, China was proliferator and transferred missiles, i.e., M-9, M-11, missiles know how and nuclear technologies and equipments.

In the aftermath of nuclear tests in South Asia, China got a good opportunity to project itself as a responsible global power safeguarding the international non-proliferation regime. At the bilateral plane, China continued in a nuanced way to deal with India in a level of hierarchy and showed no concern for India's security concern at this juncture. On the contrary, a commentary by the official news agency Xinhua, referred to the repeated smearing attacks on China by India. Unrelenting, it further carried forward verbal attacks against India by stating that Prime Minister's Vajpayee 'claim of the Chinese invasion of India in 1962 historically brooks no distortion'. The commentary raked up the border issue and claimed that India was occupying 90,000 sq. km. of Chinese territories between the traditional line in the eastern section of the borders and the illegal McMahon line.[50] The Chinese fresh attempts to rake up the border issue at a time when CBM's were underway following the agreements of 1993 and 1996 were unwarranted and totally uncalled for.

Following China's strong response and strident anti-Indian propaganda offensive, New Delhi was compelled to ask its ambassador, Vijay K. Nambiar to return to capital for urgent consultations. The GOI however, adopted policy of restraint and acted as a responsible power. The Principal Secretary to the Prime Minister, Mr. Brajesh Mishra told the media persons that India and China needed to go back into dialogue mode and India wants the best of relations with China.[51] Later, commenting on the statement Chinese Ministry of Foreign Affairs spokesman said that China had noted the remarks regarding India's willingness to improve relations with China. He stated, 'we hope that the Indian side will demonstrate Sincerity through concrete action.' The spokesman further added, 'China has always held that improving as well as developing Sino-Indian relations are in keeping with the mutual interest of both sides, and to this end, China has made persistent and unswerving efforts.'[52]

The comment aside, Chinese intense response to Indian nuclear tests was starkly noticeable. According to two China specialist Indian analysts, "visitors to China Spoke of the deeply hurt feelings in the Chinese political leadership, which had personally invested in better ties with India over the preceding few years and resented China being called a threat. Secondly, the fact that the Vajpayee letter was addressed to the American President was interpreted in China as being a deliberate attempt to build a nexus with anti-China lobbies in the USA."[53] There was another argument about China's strong reaction to Vajpayee's letter to President Clinton. According to a western analyst it can be understood at three levels. At one level, "it had to do with the fact that the letter, and similar if less authoritative comments by officials of the new Indian government, posed a direct challenge to Beijing's long-standing efforts to refute "the China threat theory..." It saw dissemination of information about various "threats" posed by China as preparation of public opinion for a new anti-China containment effort. Consequently, Beijing went to considerable lengths to damn and refute "the China threat theory" and its proponents. Vajpayee's letter to Clinton was as authoritative and powerful assertion of a "China threat" as could be imagined. At a second level Vajpayee's letter meant that India had begun to lay directly before the United States,.Indian concerns about China's relations with other countries of South Asia, From Beijing's perspective, China's relations with other countries were not the proper concern of India... For India to pressure to judge what was appropriate in Sino-Pakistan or (to go back to Fernandes' early May comments) Sino-Myanmar relations was, in fact, a manifestation of Indian hegemonism. In effect, India's leaders were soliciting American "understanding" for India's hegemonistic efforts in South Asia. At the deepest level, Vajpayee's letter implied an Indian – U.S. alignment based on a common understanding of a China threat. China, the letter asserted was a covert proliferator of nuclear weapon and missile technology. Pakistan, strongly backed by China, was sponsoring terrorism abroad. India needed substantially to increase its defence capabilities, by acquiring a nuclear deterrent, to deal with these threats. India's new government hoped that washington would show understanding of this. This was a profoundly dangerous development for Beijing..."[54] For China both the Scenarios nuclear India as well as nuclear India aligning with the USA ere dangerous developments. China was comfortable with the multipolar world but it wished Asia to be unipolar. Now, China was prepared to cooperate with the USA on South Asian non-proliferation issues.

China was at the forefront in ensuring tough line by the security council on India. China's role partly peaked because it was its 'turn to coordinate and chair' the UNSC meeting. China alongwith the USA called a meeting of the Foreign Ministers of the members of P-5 (UNSC) on 4th June that adopted a Joint communique 'pledging the Permanent Five to cooperate closely to secure Indian and Pakistani freezing of their nuclear weapons programmes, prevent the esclation of the arms race in South Asia, and strengthen the nuclear non-proliferation mechanism in that region'. On 6th June 1998, China alongwith other members of UNSC adopted Resolution 1172. The resolution *inter alia* condemned India and Pakistan's nuclear tests, "demanding that those countries refrain from further tests, and "calling upon' them "immediately to stop their nuclear weapons development programmes, to refrain from weaponization... cease development of ballistic missles capable of delivering nuclear weapons, and further production of fissile material for nuclear weapons."[55] Moreover, there were Chinese analysts, who recommended strong measures against India, arguing that a 'less than resolute response could prompt other potential threshold countries to follow suit'.[56]

China's pro-Pakistan tilt continued. Even before the UNSC resolution. China told the USA to adopt tough sanctions against India in the face of Pakistan's nuclear tests on 28th and 30th May and 'urged Washington to distinguish between India and Pakistan, and focus primarily on India as the initial transgressor'.[57] Further, the Chinese President told AFP chairman Jean Miot that "India originated the tense situation in the region" and therefore "the tensions in South Asia must be firmly blamed on India."[58] Though China on June 10, 1998, promulgated "Regulations on the control of the Export of Dual use Nuclear materials and Related Technology", designed to impose strict controls.[59] But a western analyst wrote, "Beijing also apparently broadened its covert assistance to Pakistan's Missile programme after May 1998. Shipments of Speciality steel, guidance systems, motors and technical assistance increased.[60] In mid June the Chinese President alleged that India was targetting China. India made it clear that its 'nuclear programme was only for the purpose of defence and in no way posed any threat to any of our neighbours including China'.[61]

China also threatened 'tilt towards Pakistan's position on the sensitive Kashmir issue'. On 6th June UNSC meeting, China's UN Representative Mr. Qin Huasun in Subtle way suggested Chinese 'return to a pro-Pakistan position such as had characterized Chinese policy prior to 1990'. He stated: "Pakistan and India should look for a solution (of the Kashmir issue) acceptable to both sides... In accordance with the principles of the relevant United Nations resolutions and the Simla Agreement (of 1972) and through peaceful negotiations."[62] As mentioned in the previous chapter, in the wake of Sino-Indian rapprochement and particularly in post-cold war period, China had 'moved away from endorsement of Pakistan's position on Kashmir'.

China also revived the term 'hegemony' and alleged India's pursuance of regional hegemony as part of media propaganda. In the words of an analyst, "Beijing's ressurection of the term "hegemony" for the 1998 propaganda offensive was significant... its resurrection in 1998 implied that China would. Once again, Oppose Indian policy in South Asia. "Hegemonism" is by definition unjust and must be opposed... Chinese commentary in the second half of 1998 explicitly named Bangladesh, Nepal, Sri Lanka and Pakistan as South Asian Countries concerned with India's new push for regional hegemony."[63] The negative trends of Chinese response was reminder of hostile period of India-China relations in the 1960's — when China carried out hostile propaganda against India on a range of issues – border, Kashmir India's hegemonic aspirations, etc.

Meeting of the Expert Group and Breakdown of Rapprochement

Despite the negative atmospherics, India continued the policy of engagement and went ahead with the sixth meeting of the Border expert group. The meeting was held at Beijing on June 8th and 9th 1998, and in the meeting due to India's nuclear tests no progress was made. After the expert meeting, the Indian Ambassador to China Mr. Vijay K. Nambiar said that the Indian side had sought "early progress" on the boundary issue.[64] In the words of Chinese Foreign Ministry Spokesman : "The Chinese side pointed out that the Indian leaders have recently made speeches slandering China, severely hurting the feelings of the Chinese people and destroying the good atmosphere of steady improvement in relations between the two countries. We strongly demand that the India immediately stop all the gratuitous attacks against China and take concrete steps to steer the bilateral relation on to the track of normality as early as possible. The two sides made no progress on the border issue."[65] The statement of spokesman suggested in a way the bilateral relations from China's viewpoint was certainly not normal.

India on the other hand, kept on trying to fix a date for the JWG meting throughout the second half of the year but China did not agree.[66] As on analyst wrote, "Beijing also suspended the Sino-Indian Joint Working (JWG) set up following Rajiv Gandhi's December 1988 visit to China and designed to discuss the border issue." Therefore, it could be safely stated that the joint mechanisms failed to materialise in 1998 and there was breakdown in the process of Sino-Indian rapprochement despite India's sincere efforts to continue with it. The summer of 1998 witnessed the lowest ebb of Sino-Indian bilateral relations after a long point of time. Indeed the developments proved the existence of misperceptions between both sides and also the limitations of Sino-India rapprochement. Infact, it also pointed out, partly the fact of continuity of competitive element in bilateral relations.

Chinese Experts Response

Mean while in China, the experts on India toed the government's line. According to Sun Shihai, Deputy Director of the Institute of Asian and

Pacific Studies of Chinese Academy of Social Sciences, taking "China threat theory" as the reason for its development of nuclear weapons, India was only trying to seek an excuse'. He wrote : 'The major purpose of India's nuclear testing was to make the international community recognise its status as a big country. After the cold war, India's international standing has declined, and many important international organisations and forums have yet to approve India's applications for membership. India also clearly requested to become a permanent member of the UN Security Council, but it has been foiled in its request. It was because of this that India tried to squeeze it self into the rank of big powers through nuclear testing and make the international community pay attention to it'. He further emphasised that 'China would never pose a threat to India'... Shihai held: 'India's nuclear testing has put the Pakistani Government under great pressure because its military and social circles have asked the Government to "adopt resolute measures". Last but not least he recommended that 'the international community should adopt a unified attitude to safe guard world peace and stability and should impose sanctions on India to force it to sign the NPT and the CTBT.'[67]

Another analyst. Ma Jiali of China-Institute of Contemporary International Relations, wrote : "India is developing a formidable force, which already ranks fourth in the world, and is continuing to modernise its conventional, missile and nuclear arsenals". He further wrote that due to India's potential and its predominance in South-Asia, it is a much sought after partner by great powers, particularly the USA, there by 'whetting' India's ambition for 'great-power' status.[68]

Former Chinese Ambassador to India, Cheng Ruisheng in an interview to China's military newspaper Liberation Army Daily (Jiefangjun Bao) said: "At the news conference on 19 March 1998, Premier Zhu Rongji extended his best wishes to the new Indian Prime Minister Vajpayee and the Indian people. However, Shortly after that, Vajpayee and his associates began attacking China repeatedly. This cannot be justified in any way. In my view, the main reason for this is that the Indian authorities, forseeing that India's nuclear tests would evoke strong condemnation in the international community had to find an excuse that could confuse world opinion to reduce the pressure from the international community. The "China threat theory", which still enjoys some support in the international community, came in handy as a "Shield". Viewed at a deeper level, this incident shows that a handful of people in India still harbour hostile sentiments toward China, despite the fact that the constant improvement of Sino-Indian relations over the years is moving gradually to eliminate the shadow of the

1962 Sino-Indian border conflict. Indian leaders are attempting to use the So-called "China threat theory" to foment nationalist sentiment among the people. So as to gain more support at home.'[69]

Therefore in academic as well as policy making circles of China, nobody tried to understand India's security concerns. During the first Semi-official discussion in December 1998 between scholars of both sides after Pokharan II tests, in a slight departure, a seasoned expert on India stated : "Although the Chinese side expressed understanding of India's need to carry out nuclear tests for its security needs, it could not understand why India thinks China's nuclear weapons are a threat to India, and felt that India should not have used China as the reason for its plans for realizing nuclear weapons."[70] Thus, there was not much difference between official and non-official Chinese response.

China-USA Joint Statement

Meanwhile during President Clinton's visit to China, both nations issued "Sino-US Presidential Joint statement on South Asia" on 27th June 1998.[71] On India's part the development was 'manifestation of U.S. alignment with China against India. In many ways it seemed that U.S. approved of 'China playing a larger role in South Asia'. The development undoubtedly caused resentment in New Delhi. By aligning with the USA, on one hand, Beijing believed "it could nip in the bud any Indian hopes of emerging as a challenger over the long term to China's primacy in Asia." The U.S. on the other hand perceived. "Beijing's new stance on non-proliferation is a welcome sign of the political will to punish nations like India who gate crash into the exclusive nuclear club."[72] It appears that 'Beijing made, or at leat attempted to make, U.S. handling of the South Asian nuclear situation a test of U.S. "Sincerity" towards China'. It seems that U.S. on this issue come up to China's expectation much to the discomfort of India. But India in the summer of 1998 was confident and as quoted in India Today." What is emerging is a more self-centred India that is single-minded in its pursuit of national interests, rather than on abstract universal goals."[73] In sum, China even in its diplomacy with the USA pressurised India and thereby created difficult international situation against it.

Continuation of China's Hostile Approach

On 9th July 1998 India offered to China an agreement for no-first-use of nuclear weapons, China bluntly told New Delhi to give up its nuclear weapons programme and sign the NPT and CTBT.[74] One Chinese analyst conceded the point, a 'nofirst use' between New Delhi and Beijing could help in establishing nuclear stability but Chinese acceptance would be 'tantamount to acknowledging India's nuclear weapon state status.'[75] China preferred to deal with India on this issue in hierarchic manner. Earlier in the months of May-June, according to an Indian analyst, the reported cases of Chinese transgressions across the LAC was highest.[76] The Chinese Ambassador Zhou Gang told the press persons of Indian newspapers : "The cause of and responsibility for the current situation concerning Sino-Indian relations are known to all. It is the Chinese side that has been victimised. The Chinese side sincerely hopes that the above mentioned abnormal situation should be reseversed as early as possible. But it is not upto the Chinese side, it is upto the doer to undo the knot."[77] The Ambassador further stated : "we have noticed the Indian side's intention to improve its relations with China. We pay heed not only to what one says, but also to what one does." In the opinion of an analyst, "for the next nine months insistence that India "untie the knot" its words had created in Sino-Indian relations was a key Chinese theme."[78] The same theme was repeated by Ambassador Zhou Gang on 20 October 1998 in New Delhi in the conference of Indian Association of International Affairs.[79]

The cumulative effect of Chinese response casted a negative spell over the Sino-Indian rapprochement. China reacted strongly and cancelled the scheduled November Joint working group meeting in Beijing.[80] Commenting on the Chinese displeasure and anger, an Indian analyst wrote : "This decision, which clearly contravened a clearcut understanding regarding a mechanism set up at the Prime Ministrial level, was not politic to say the least."[81] Undoubtedly, Indian nuclear tests in May 1998 and subsequent strong Chinese response both caused 'major setback' in bilateral relations. It appears that the events relating to nuclear tests in May contributed to the beginning of animosity, 'the roots of suspicion' uncovered both deep regional as well as bilateral concerns, i.e. India-China-Pakistan triangle, border disputes, the Tibet issue and now the nuclear issue. In short, there was brief breakdown of Sino-Indian rapprochement in the year 1998.

In fact throughout the year, New Delhi showed its willingness to continue the policy of engagement and meetings of various bilateral mechanisms. Despite refusal from Chinese side, India made 'consistent overtures' and 'conciliatory statements' to assuage perceived Chinese ruffled feelings in a bid to reduce bilateral tensions; though at times New Delhi's signals may 'have not always been consistent.' The Prime Minister Vajpayee in a concrete statement to Parliament in September 1998, emphasised 'the fundamental Indian desire to have friendly relations with China' and 'a satisfactory solution to the border dispute through negotiation'.[82] Another step taken in September was to instruct diplomats to 'avoid any mention of China in their dealings with the other four permanent Five powers'.[83] Furthermore, the statement in October 1998 by the Chief of the Indo-Tibetan Border Police that the Chinese were amassing troops along the LAC was also 'termed as inaccurate' by the government of India.[84] Carrying this further forward, in October, Brajesh Mishra, Principal secretary to Prime Minister stated that India did not see China as an "enemy" and that it would like to 'solve all problems through substantive dialogue.'[85]

However, in the words of a leading western analyst on the subject, "these conciliatory portions of Mishra's statement were offset by a statement that the Indian government "would welcome" negotiations between the Dalai Lama and the Chinese government. Shortly before the statement Vajpayee had met the Dalai Lama – as most Indian Prime Ministers had done at one time or another during their periods in office. Beijing condemned this meeting as interference in China's domestic politics and violation of China's pledge not to allow the Dalai Lama to engage in "anti-China" activities in India."[86] Viewed from Indian perspective, on the whole till the end of the year, none of Indian 'overtures seemed to make any difference'. Therefore, notwithstanding India's initiatives, the fact of breakdown of rapprochement was a reality.

Finally in December 1998, when Mr. Jaswant Singh was appointed as India's new Foreign Minister, the Chinese counterpart, Tang Jiaxuan sent a congratulatory message to him. Jaswant Singh stated that China should help India "untie the knot" through frequent consultations'.[87] Thus, atleast by the year end both sides showed willingness in some ways to restart engagement policy.

It may be mentioned here that despite brief breakdown of Sino-Indian rapprochement the slow and steady progress in bilateral trade was registered in year 1998. The bilateral trade in 1998 reached US $ 1.92 billion. However, the trade balance was in favour of China by US $ 110.89 million.[88] Further, one of the largest Chinese corporation, China National Chemicals Import and Export Corporation decided to expand its business with India.[89] In short, the prospects of enhanced economic Cooperation existed inspite of tense relations. But the overall point remains that trade can only thrive in an overall relaxed atmosphere, which surely was missing in 1998. The negative developments of 1998 brought about chill which froze the bilateral relations. To conclude in short, therefore the year 1998 witnessed brief breakdown of the Sino-Indian Rapprochement.

References

1. Cited in C Uday Bhaskar, Role of China in the Emerging world order, Strategic Analysis, 16, 1', April 1993, p. 5.
2. This phrase simply means, Under Certain military pressures, one can coordinate a political and diplomatic offensive to psychologically disintegrate the enemy forces and subdue them. See for details, Tiejun Zhang, Chinese Strategic Culture : Traditional and Present Features, Comparative – Strategy, 21, 2, 2002, pp. 73-90.
3. See for Jiang Zamin's Report to the 14th Party Congress, Beijing Review, Vol. 35, No. 43, 26 October, p. 26.
4. See for details David Shambaugh, The In security of Security : The PLA's Evolving-Doctrine and Threat Perceptions Towards 2000, Journal of Northeast Asian Studies, Vol. XIII, No. 1 Spring 1994, pp. 3-25. Also, Yan Xuetong, Security Strategies Change with the Times, China Daily, 28 October, 1996.
5. Liu Gongji and Luo Haixi (eds), Guofang Lilun (Theory of National Defence), NDU Publications, Beijing, 1996, p. 94.
6. See for details David Shambaugh, Containment or Engagement of China ? Calculating Beijing's Responses, International Security, Vol. 21, No. 2. Fall 1996, pp. 180-209. Also Shambaugh, Growing strong : China's Challenge to Asian Security. Survival, 36, 2, Summer 1994, pp. 43-59. Ross H. Munro, The Asian-Interior : China's Waxing Sphere of Influence, Orbis, 38, 4, Fall 1994, pp. 585-605.
7. Strategic Assessment 1997 : Flashpoints and Force structure, National Defense University, Washington, 1997, p. 45.
8. Sujit Dutta, "China's Emerging Power and Military Role : Implications for South Asia" in Jonathan D. Pollack and Richard H. Yang (eds), In China's Shadow : Regional Perspectives on Chinese Foreign Policy and Military Development, National Security Research Division, Rand, 1998, p. 94.
9. Alastair Iain Johnston, Cultural Realism : Strategic Culture and Grand Strategy in Chinese History, Princeton University Press, New Jersey, 1995, p. 249.
10. One analyst viewed the emergence of Chinese hegemony in Southeast, South and Central Asia. See for details Ross H. Munro, The Asian Interior : China's Waxing Sphere of Influence, Orbis, 38, 4, Fall 1994, pp. 585-605.
11. Cited in Beijing Review, February 4, p. 11.
12. Ren Xin, 'China Threat' Theory Untenable, Beijing Review, February 4, pp. 10-11.
13. *Ibid.*, p. 11.
14. See No. 8, p. 93.
15. Quoted in A.J. Chandy, "India, China and Pakistan", in Kanti Bajpai and Amitabh Mattoo (eds), The Peacock and The Dragon : India-China Relations in the 21st Century, Har Anand Publications, New Delhi, 2000, p. 301.

16. John W. Graver, Protracted Contest : Sino-Indian Rivalry in the Twentieth Century, Oxford University Press, New Delhi, 2001, p. 242.
17. Surjit Man Singh, An Overview of India-China Relations, Indian Defence Review, April 1993, p. 75.
18. Cited in Keshav Mishra, Sino-Indian Relations in the Post-Cold War Era, Indian Journal of Politics, 35, 1-2, 2001, p. 68.
19. Cited in J. Mohan Malik, "Burma's Role in Regional-Security – Pawn or Pivot" ? In Robert I. Rotberg ed, Burma Prospects for a Democratic Future, Brookings Institutional Press, Washington, 1998, p. 113.
20. Col. Gurmeet Kanwal, China's Strategic – Encirclement of India, Indian Defence Review, Vol. 15, 3, July 2000, p. 13.
21. Sujit Dutta, "India and the Emerging Global Order in Jasjit Singh ed., Asian Security in the 21st Century, Institute for Defence Studies and Analyses, New Delhi, 1999, p. 51.
22. J. Mohan Malik, India Goes Nuclear : Rationale, Benefits, Costs and Implications, Contemporary Southeast Asia, Vol. 20, 2, August 1998, p. 193.
23. John W. Garver, The Restoration of Sino-Indian Comity following India's Nuclear Tests, China Quarterly, No. 168, December 2001, p. 866.
24. Frontline, May 22, 1998, p. 30.
25. *Times of India*, April 28, 1998.
26. *Hindu*, april 28, 1998.
27. See No. 25.
28. "China is threat Number One." Times of India, May 4, 1998.
29. *Ibid.,* See also John Burns, "India's New Defence Chief Sees Chinese Military Threat," New York Times, May 5, 1998, A. 6.
30. See for details, Foreign Ministry News Briefings, Beijing Review, May 25, 1998, p.7.
31. *Times of India*, May 7, 1998.
32. *Ibid.*
33. See for details, *India Today*, May 18, 1998, p. 24.
34. Ministry of Defence, Government of India, Annual Report, 1993-94, pp. 2-3.
35. Ministry of Defence, GOI, Annual Report, 1996-97, p. 2.
36. *Ibid.*, p. 6.
37. See No. 16, p. 388.
38. C.V. Ranganathan and Vinod C. Khanna, India and China : The Way Ahead After "Mao's India War", Har Anand Publications, New Delhi, 2000, p. 149.
39. Director, I DSA and Project Coordinator of nuclear tests of 1998, K. Santhanam, "Some Major Changes in Southern Asia and Their Likely Impact on India's Future Foreign Policy" in A Presentation Collection for Conference on India in 21st Century : External Relations, SIIS Publication, Shanghai, 2002, p. 6.
40. See n. 22, p. 193. See also Sujit Dutta, India's Evolving Relations with China, Strategic Analysis, July 1995, p. 483.

41. See the text of letter to President Bill Clinton, New York Times, 13 May, 1998, p. A-12.
42. See n. 23, p. 868.
43. Xinhua, 13 May 1998, Cited in Foreign Broad Casting Information Service, Daily Report, China (hereafter FBIS-CHI), no. 98-133.
44. People's Daily Report by Li Wenyun, 12 May 1998. Cited in China Report, 35, 2, 1999, p. 218.
45. See n. 23, p. 867.
46. China's Statement on India's Nuclear Tests, in Beijing Review, June 1, 1998, p. 7.
47. Liberation Army Daily Report, 14 May 1998. Cited in China Report, 35, 2, 1999, pp. 219-20.
48. China Daily Report by Jiang Jin Gen, 16 May 1998, Cited in China Report, 35, 2, 1999, p. 220.
49. See n. 38, p. 149.
50. Cited in n. 18, p. 70.
51. *Ibid.*
52. Statement by Chinese Ministry of Foreign Affairs Spokesman, 21 May 1998, Cited in China Report, 35, 2, 1999, p. 221.
53. See n. 38, p. 152.
54. See n. 23, pp. 869-70.
55. UN document S/RES/1172, 6 June 1998. See www.un.org/docs/scres/1998/sres1172.htm.
56. See for details, Zuo Yunhua, Chinese Perspectives on the South Asian Nuclear Tests, Working Paper, Stanford University Press, Stanford, 1999.
57. See n. 23, p. 871.
58. Cited in Xinhua, 3 June 1998, FBIS-CHI-98-154.
59. See n. 38, p. 153.
60. See n. 23, p. 874.
61. Hindu, June 15, 1998.
62. Cited in n. 23, p. 873.
63. *Ibid.*, pp. 873-74.
64. Cited in Xia Liping, "China-Indian Security Relationship : Retrospects and Prospects" in a Presentation collection for conference on India in 21st Century: External Relations, SIIS Publication, Shanghai, 2002, p. 108.
65. Foreign Ministry news briefings, in Beijing Review, June 29, 1998, p. 22.
66. See n. 23, p. 872.
67. Wen Wei Po interview of Sun Shihai, 26 May 1998, cited in China Report, 35, 2, 1999, pp. 221-23.
68. Ma Jiali, 'India's Elevating Strategic Position', Helping Yu Fazhan (Peace and Development), n. 4. 2000, pp. 20-23, cited in Faisal O-Al-Refouh, 'Sino-Indian Relations : From Confrontation to Accommodation (1988-2001) in China Report 39, 1, 2003, p. 30.
69. Liberation Army Daily interview of Cheng Ruisheng, 27 May 1998, cited in China Report, 35, 2, 1999, pp. 223-24.

70. Wang Hongwei, "Tancheng Duihua, Shi Yi Zeng Xin" (Frank Dialogue, Dispelling Doubts, Increasing Trust"), Nanya Yanjiu (South Asia Research), no. 1, 1999, pp. 14-17. Cited in n. 23, p. 869.
71. See the text of "Sino-U.S. Presidential Joint Statement on South Asia," 27 June 1998, in Beijing Review, July 20, 1998, p. 17.
72. "India Blasts China-U.S. Summit Call on South Asia", Reuters, 28 June 1998. See www.R11998063001623.html.
73. Raj Chengappa and Manoj Joshi, "Hawkish India" India Today, 1 June 1998, p. 10.
76. Cited in Srikanth Kondapalli, "India-China Border Perspectives" in See n. 64, pp. 146-47.
77. See the text of Chinese Ambassador Zhou-Gang's Joint Interview to Four Indian News Papers, 17 July 1998 cited in China Report, 35, 2, 1999, pp. 230-33.
78. See n. 23, p. 871.
79. Cited in *Ibid.*
80. Cited in W.P.S. Sidhu and Jing-Dong Yuan, "Resolving the Sino-Indian Border Dispute" in Asian Survey, 40, 2, Mar/Apr. 2001, p. 358.
81. Alka Acharya, "India-China Relations : An overview in Kanti Bajpai & Amitabh Mattoo, eds, The Peacock and the Dragon : India-China Relations in the 21st century, Har Anand Publications, New Delhi, 2000, p. 194.
82. Cited in Ibid, p. 193.
83. Cited in See n. 23, p. 879.
84. Cited in See n. 81, p. 193.
85. Cited in Economic Times, 29 October, 1998.
86. See n. 23, p. 880.
87. *Ibid.*
88. See for details, India-China Trade in 1998. Changhai-India Business, Shanghai, 3, 4, April 1999, p. 8.
89. See, China's No. 1 Firm to Open Shop in India, Economic Times, 3 October, 1998.

8

Reconstructing Rapprochement (1999-Present Phase)

The process of Sino-Indian rapprochement was irreversible and inspite of brief breakdown, the existence of diverse driving forces at bilateral regional and global levels brought about the reconstruction of the edifice. As such, gradually from the year 1999 both sides restored the process of rapprochement and began the policy of engagement in a more substantive and meaningful way. In other words, both nations were reconstructing Rapprochement in the changed context of nuclear India.

India was always in favour of engagement of China, an important neighbour which loomed large over India's security environment. All India did in 1998 by Pokharan II nuclear tests was it brought nuclear asymmetry with China to an end. Thereby, the perceived tilt in favour of China was balanced to the comfort of India. India at the official level outlined a friendly framework for Sino-Indian relations and stated : "we seek a relationship in which both sides are responsive to each other's concerns. We remain committed to the process of dialogue to resolve outstanding differences and to the development of friendly, cooperative, good neighbourly and mutually beneficial relationship with China.[1]

A more responsive China, which wanted to put past behind and on its part, the Chinese Ambassador to India, Zhou Gang stated : "It is inevitable that there exist some concerns between the two big neighbours. As long as both sides proceed from the overall interests of the bilateral friendly relations and handle these concerns on the basis of mutual trust, with a positive, flexible and pragmatic approach and in a truth-seeking and forward-looking spirit, the differences will be narrowed gradually and problems resolved involved instead of coming in the way of the normal developed of bilateral relations."[2] These official statements made it clear that both sides desired to move ahead with the process of rapprochement.

Among other factors, in the words of an expert. "The increased Indo-U.S. understanding that had emerged out of the Jaswant Singh strobe Talbott talks by the end of 1998 was a significant factor pushing Beijing to begin repairing Sino-Indian relations in early 1999."[3] Be that as it may be, one point emerged indisputably that India displayed nature diplomacy in allying international misgivings against its Pokharan II tests. As a result, India successfully engaged the major powers and resumed high-level political visits. For example, Prime Minister A.B. Vajpayee visited France in September 1998, which was followed by first meeting of the Indo-French Strategic Dialogue in October 1998. The Prime Minister of Russia, Y. Primakov visited India in December 1998, and earlier in September, the President K.R. Narayanan visited Germany. The Principal Secretary to Prime Minister and national security advisor, Brajesh Mishra visited London and Paris in June 1998 and January 1999. Equally important, the India-Japan Foreign office consultation was carried out in January 1999.[5] It was in this backdrop that China decided to 'moderate its positions on India'.

The Track II level contacts involving analysts, academicians also played an important role in pushing forward the bilateral relations. In this context, the visit of Cheng Ruisheng, the former Chinese ambassador to India alongwith a delegation in early 1999 was significant. During his New Delhi visit, he alongwith current Ambassador, Zhou Gang met with the Indian President, K.R. Narayanan, an old China hand. The Indian President stated that China did not constitute a threat to India or vice versa and emphasised on the need for cooperation between both sides. In the words of an expert, "Narayanan's words sufficed for Beijing to begin the process of Un-thawing relations with New Delhi."[6] Later in February, 1999 the officials of both nations held bilateral meeting at Director-General level.[7] The Chinese Foreign Minister, Tang Jiaxuan termed it "useful discussions held in Beijing not long ago" and announced that shortly the Joing working group would meet.[8] Consequently, the 11th round of the JWG meeting was held on April 26th and 27th 1999 at Beijing.[9] This was the first high level India-China contact after the Pokharan-II tests of May, 1998. As such, the meeting of JWG in 1999 symbolised the resumption of Sino-Indian rapprochement.

Resumption of Political Interactions

As a result of reciprocal keenness the process of Sino-Indian rapprochement started gathering momentum. One of the fundamental elements in the process of rapprochement was the political interactions at high level. The year 1999 marked the beginning of Reconstruction of Sino-Indian Rapprochement. Therefore, to impart dynamism in someways, the Indian Foreign Minister, Jaswant Singh visited Beijing in June, 1999. The visit was a part of India's Initiative to improve relations with China and specifically a measure to 'untie the knot'.

China on its part by agreeing to receive Jaswant Singh signalled its intent to reengage India. In this context, an analyst identified three broad factors which prompted Beijing to pursue re-engagement with one of its important neighbours. In his words, "China seemed to take note of India's big power diplomacy' in the past year that enabled New Delhi to over come the post Pokharan international isolation. Beijing was reluctant to lag behind in this respect and hence had to bring itself upto expedite its move of re-engaging New Delhi. Second, India's burgeoning economic growth and advances in information technology hold vast potential for China, which the latter did not want to lose. Finally, the Changing international situation, and the downward trend in Sino-US relations, also prompted China to review its approach towards India."[10] Further, Jaswant Singh visited China at the time of Kargil conflict between India and Pakistan.

Therefore, the Kargil factor also pushed China to re-engage India. Indeed, in the words of a western analyst, "The mini-war between India and Pakistan at Kargil in the spring of 1999 added urgency to both Chinese and Indian desires to repair their strained relations... In the first instance, tense Sino-Indian relations would reduce the ability of China to work with the United States as a "Strategic partner" in upholding "peace and stability" in South Asia... A more remote but even greater danger for Beijing was that, as India and Pakistan slid toward war, China might end up supporting Pakistan alone... yet to provide such assistance to Pakistan in the Context of already sour China-India relations could have a seriously adverse impact on India's alignment vis-à-vis the United States. Beijing needed to demonstrate quickly to both New Delhi and Washington that it was part of the solution and not part of the problem in South Asia."[11]

The visit of Indian Foreign Minister was significant on two counts. First, it was after eight years that the foreign minister was visiting Beijing. Secondly and more importantly, this was the first visit by a high level political dignitary to China Since the Pokharan II nuclear tests. China from now, recognised the fact that the bilateral relations were back on even keel and the negative developments of 1998 were things of the past. The point was underlined by the statement of Chinese foreign minister, Tang Jiaxuan who stated : "Sino-Indian relations have entered a process of improvement and Singh's visit to China is an important step in this process. The prerequisite for the development of Sino-Indian relations should be that both countries do not consider each other a threat... We are pleased to see that China and India have reached a consensus in this regard."[12]

Jaswant Singh concurred with his Chinese counterpart's statement and reiterated the point that : "The Indian government does not think China is a threat to India. The Indian government's basis policy is to develop good-neighbourly relations of friendship with China."[13] As a result of visit of Indian Foreign Minister, both sides agreed to hold 'security dialogue' and to give clarification of the Line of Actual Control.[14] Therefore, Jaswant Singh's Beijing visit was successful both in terms of substance and symbolism. The Indian side, appreciated the importance of India-China security dialogue. Infact, one security analyst saw the development "breakthrough and an acceptance by China to discuss each other's security concerns including the nuclear question... India must take this opportunity to tell the Chinese clearly that its nuclear and missile assistance programme with Pakistan is of grave concern to India. China cannot eat its cake and have it too."[15]

Commenting on this positive development, an eminent expert observed that "The initiation of the security dialogue with China was a fruit of the BJP government's handling of China Policy... Issues under discussion, let along disagreements, had not been made public or focused by association with a specific high-level interaction in Sino-Indian relations. Some issues of concern to India, China had refused to discuss. Beijing's response to India's broaching of nuclear issues, for instance, had been that since India was not a nuclear weapon state under the NPT regime, China had nothing to discuss with India in this regard... With the initiation of a separate, fairly high profile, and regular security dialogue, India secured Chinese agreement at least to listen and respond to Indian concerns. It also established a mechanism for focusing public attention on whatever disagreements might emerge."[16]

Further, the foreign ministers of both sides again met in July 1999 on the sidelines of ASEAN Regional Forum meeting in Singapore and exchanged views on bilateral and international issues. During the talks, both sides agreed to send a joint expedition to. Everest in 2000 to mark fiftieth year of the establishment of mutual diplomatic relations. Moreover, India and China agreed that both nations work out modalities of new 'security dialogue' and intensify joint cooperation in regional and international forums.[17] Later in October, 1999 the Indian President reiterated in the Parliament that India would seek to improve its relations with China.[18] Thus, by 1999 both nations were reconstructing in away the edifice of rapprochement. Even a noted Chinese analyst accepted the fact and viewed it from the Chinese perspective, "Afterwards, the Indian President and Foreign Minister expressed their willingness to improve and better relations with China on different occasions, clarifying many in correct statements. Under the joint effort of both governments, the current Sino-Indian relations began to move out of the shadows and return to a healthy orbit."[19]

During the first round of security dialogue in March 2000, India sought Chinese understanding for its nuclear weapons programme. But China on the contrary, asked India to renounce its nuclear weapons programme and abide by the UN Security Council Resolution 1172.[20]

India rejected Chinese plea for implementation of Security Council Resolution and reiterated that every nation has a right to determine its own security requirements.[21] More importantly, India took up the issue of Chinese assistance to Pakistan's nuclear and missile programme. The Indian officials conveyed to their Chinese counterpart that this had an adverse impact on regional stability to which we have been obliged to respond in a 'responsible and restrained' manner.[22] As was the usual practice, China replied that its relations with Pakistan were normal relations between two states and were not directed against India.[23] Thus, the first meeting could not produce any concrete results. Yet, the fact that in the meeting security specific issues were raised was a notable development in Sino-Indian bilateral relations. Viewed in the longterm of bilateral relations, to expect concrete result in one or two meetings was unrealistic as well. As such, this development of security dialogue symbolised the continuation of Sino-Indian rapprochement.

Another positive development at the bilateral level was the China visit of Indian President, K.R. Narayanan in May-June, 2000. The President met the top Chinese leadership and sincerely conveyed India's determination to improve relations with China. Underlining the significance of K.R. Narayanan's China visit, an expert observed : "This was the first visit by a highest-level leader since the May 1998 test and reciprocated Jiang Zemin's 1996 visit to India. During Narayanan's visit China did not raise the issue of India's nuclear weapons programme-but neither did it give any sign of relaxing its demand for full implementation of Resolution 1172."[24] Thus, the visit symbolised the continuation of beneficial political interactions at the highest political level.

Furthermore, the visit of Chinese Foreign Minister, Tang Jiaxuan to

New Delhi in July 2000 was another step forward in the ongoing exchanges at political level designed to further improve Sino-Indian rapprochement. The Chinese foreign minister conferred with his Indian counterpart on a number of issues. Which included the 'boundary, nuclear issues, U.N. reforms, cross-border terrorism, and Chinese help to Pakistan's missile and nuclear programmes.'[25] In the words of an eminent expert, the visit of Tang Jiaxuan was 'the final step towards restored India-China comity'.[26]

It seems in this phase, China on its part, demonstrated equal enthusiasm in reengagement with India. Earlier in July, 1999 the Chinese spokesperson of Foreign Ministry, Zhang Qiyue stated : "India is a major neighbour of China and to develop good neighbourly, friendly and cooperative ties with India is one of China's basic national policies."[27] Similarly, in January 2001, Li Peng, one of the important leaders outlined some 'basic tenets' of China's policy towards India, which included "a political commitment at the top in Beijing to intensify the relationship, expansion of economic cooperation, enhancing mutual understanding by addressing outstanding issues such as the border dispute, and an assurance that China stood for peace and stability in the subcontinent."[28]

In January 2001, Li Peng, Chairman of the Chinese National People's Congress (NPC) standing committee visited India and exchanged views on important bilateral and global issues with the Indian political leadership. Li Peng emphasised the point that "developing good-neighbourly and friendly relations with India is our permanent guideline as well as the important content of China's foreign policy of peripheral peace."[29] China also expressed its willingness to cooperate with all the countries, including India to fight terrorism.[30] However, on cross border terrorism emanating from Pakistan, the Chinese side was not forthcoming. Overall, Li Peng's nine-day goodwill visit to India was a major step forward in Sino-Indian rapprochement. The visit was first by 'a top-level Chinese visitor since the May 1998 tests, and the first since Jiang Zemin's 1996 visit'.

During Li Peng's visit, an expert has raised the point of a confident India, "on the last day of li's visit, tested the intermediate range missile Agni II with a range of 2000 kilometers and capable of reaching southern China."[31] To substantiate the point, the expert cited one New Delhi based newspaper's report that the timing of the test "was not a mere coincidence" but "makes it clear that India would like to deal with Beijing on a one-to-one basis and not from a position of disadvantage."[32] The paper noted the fact that China had tested a nuclear weapon during Beijing visit of the Indian President R. Venkataraman in May, 1992 and observed : "The message, if there is one in the [Agni II] test's timing, is that India's nuclear and missile programmes are here to stay and that this country will deal with China on the basis of equality."[33] There is some truism in the expert's assertion.

Later in February 2001, the second round of security dialogue was held. India again conveyed its concern to China over Beijing's supply of nuclear and missile technology to Pakistan.[34] As was the usual Chinese reply, it again stated that Sino-Pakistan relations was not aimed against India. Nevertheless, India made it clear that the supply of weapons of mass destruction to Pakistan was directed against it notwithstanding the Chinese denial. As such, it rightly perceived the acts of Chinese proliferation as destabilizing the strategic equilibrium of South Asia and determental to India's security.

The year 2002 witnessed the continuation of mutual interaction at the highest political level. In January, 2002 China's Prime Minister, Zhu Rongji visited India. It was after ten years that a Chinese Premier visited New Delhi and returned the visit of India's Prime Minister, Narasimha Rao in September, 1993. As such, the visit was significant and showed the positive outcome of continuation of political interactions at the high level. The Chinese Premier expressed confidence that his visit would help in promoting mutual trust and cooperation between the two countries and "inject new vitality" for a sound development of the Sino-Indian constructive partnership in the new century.[35] The highlight of Zhu Rongji's visit in the words of an analyst was that "a major emphasis was laid on providing a boost to economic ties between the two countries and bilateral cooperation on counter-terrorism. Premier Zhu had offered to share intelligence with India on the developments in the northeast, and Jammu Kashmir. On its part, India expressed its readiness to appraise the Chinese with information about the ughyur insurgency in the Xinjiang province of China."[36] Therefore, in the wake of 9/11 and ongoing cross border terrorism and in overall way to contain the menaane of terrorism, both nations decided to hold regular dialogue on the matter. Despite this development, China was yet to condemn Pakistan's role in fomenting cross border terrorism in India. On balance, the decision to hold bilateral dialogue on terrorism was a positive development.

During his visit, Premier Zhu put forward five-point proposal to develop bilateral relations :

- Maintaining high-level mutual visits, and exchanges in different fields,

- Strengthening mutual-beneficial cooperation in economic and trade fields,
- Improving the exchanges and cooperation in scientific and technological fields,
- Promoting regional economic cooperation, and
- Properly resolving problems in the bilateral relations.[37]

During Chinese Premier's visit, China and India concluded six agreements dealing with economic cooperation, tourism, peaceful development of outer space, water conservancy, science and culture. Besides, China announced to open a regular flight between Beijing and New Delhi from March, 1999.[38] Further, Premier Zhu met with the top Indian leadership and exchanged views on bilateral, regional and international issues. He stated that there is more consensus than division, more interest than friction, and problems between the two nations can be solved through consultation. Agreeing with his Chinese counterpart, the Indian Prime Minister said China does not pose any threat to India, nor does India believe that china regards India as a threat. The President, K.R. Narayan and Foreign Minister, Jaswant Singh shared the same view and said that the existing problems between the two nations should not hinder the development of India-China ties.[39] On relations between India and Pakistan, the Chinese Premier repeated China's position on the issue, noting that as a friendly neighbour of both countries, China sincerely hopes both sides can resolve their disputes through consultation and other peaceful methods.

The Chinese Premier, Zhu Rongji visited Mumbai and Bangalore, which was a clear signal of China's eagerness to step up bilateral trade and economic cooperation with India. At Bangalore, he praised the development of India's information technology (IT) and said "your achievements have made us, your friendly neighbour, very proud."[40] To boost bilateral economic cooperation, he instantly approved India's IT giant, Infosys-plan to open a branch in Shanghai. Zhu further-proposed that India and China work together to promote each other in the Information Technology Sector and "make progress together".[41] In short, the visit of Zhu Rongji was a major step forward in the reconstruction of Sino-Indian Rapprochement. In the words of the Chinese Foreign Ministry Spokesman, Sun Yuxi, "the visit has enhanced the friendship between China and India, increased bilateral understanding and trust, and promoted exchange and cooperation in wide ranging fields."[42] He further added that both sides have much more common interests than differences and any disputes between them will not affect the normal development of bilateral ties and finally, they should resort to friendly consultation to resolve such disputes.[43]

In India, the political analysts termed the Chinese Premier's visit to India a success and advanced bilateral relations between both sides.[44] However, Some security analysts urged India to take up security issues and sounded cautions note as well. For instance, one analyst wrote first that, "The state of Jammu and Kashmir is an integral part of India as Tibet is an integral part of China, therefore, there is no question of any negotiation on this issue." He further observed that "only points of discussion on this vital question of India's sovereignty is the recovery of the areas occupied by Pakistan and the territory illegally ceded by it to China in 1963."[45] The analyst wrote the above mentioned issue in the context of raising with China the genuine concerns against cross-border terrorism as well as states sponsoring terrorism' with the Chinese Premier. The second aspect was that of 'strategic nuclear weapons'. Therefore, the analyst wrote that "The help extended by China to Pakistan in acquiring nukes is well-known... On the basis of this reality Indian leadership must ask the Chinese side to not only desist from giving further help to Pakistan but also to ensure the safety of existing nuclear warheads and prevent them from falling into the wrong hands-the jihadis."[46] Thus the writing was reminder of the fact that in its anxiety to improve relations with China, India must not forget take up China's role in the region quite seriously. The aspect of security continue to be important issue between both sides. As such, the matter cannot be denied and must be dealt within a business like manner for durable mutual trust only then the rapprochement would be successful. Therefore, a lot more still remained to be done for prolonged peace and stability between both sides. Yet the progress achieved by Zhu Rongji's visit must be given its due success. Therefore, the visit of Chinese Premier, Zhu Rongji was an important step forward in further improving the bilateral relations between both sides.

In March, 2002 the Foreign Minister, Jaswant Singh visited China to further continue the growing political interactions at high level. An important daily newspaper of India, summed up the development in this way: "The inaugural flight of China Eastern Airlines between New Delhi and Beijing that Mr. Singh takes tonight reflects a new and pragmatic phase in the relations between the two Asian giants. That it has taken so long to have a direct air link between the two capitals underscores the kind of political rigidity that had delayed normal bilateral ties."[47] Earlier, China on its part stated before Jaswant Singh's visit that it wanted 'stable' relations with India. It, therefore, hoped that the beginning of direct flights between Beijing and New Delhi would act as a bond between the peoples of the two neighbours. The Chinese Foreign Ministry spokeswoman, Zhang Qiyue stated : "The Chinese Government attaches great importance to the long term, stable friendly relations and good-neighbourly cooperation with India," and Jaswant Singh's visit would be of "great importance in promoting friendly cooperation."[48]

Jaswant Singh held discussions with his Chinese counterpart, Tang Jiaxuan, Premier, Zhu Rongji and Vice Premier, Qian Qichen. It is important to note that Qian is incharge of Foreign Affairs in the Chinese Communist Party's (CPC) Polit Bureau. The Indian Foreign Minister also discussed matters of mutual interest with Dai Bingguo, head of the International Liaison Bureau of the CPC. The engagement with the Party leadership was significant in that the communist party happened to be important pillar of decision-making even in the foreign policy sphere. Jaswant Singh described the talks with the Chinese leadership in Beijing as "productive and substantive".[49] As a result of the visit, both nations agreed to complete the delineation of the Line of Actual control (LAC) within a reasonable time-frame and the decision to hold the first ever official talks between the both sides on ways to combat terrorism.[50] The developments reflected the broadening of political agenda between the both nations. Indeed, after his interactions with the Chinese Premier, the Indian Foreign Minister said that a framework had been put in place for a comprehensive dialogue on all issues. He further added that there were encouraging pointers of a qualitative change talking place in bilateral relations.[51]

The Indian Foreign Minister had one public engagement in the shape of an interaction with the academic community at Shanghai Institute for International Studies, Shanghai. He stated that the only possible future for Sino-Indian relations was a positive one. In the words of Jaswant Singh, "We will have our differences... As ancient civilizations, we must have the ability to engage, to move forward despite differences, and out of the overhangs of history. Our responsibility is to the two countries and to humanity... you asked about military relations. Yes, we can have them."[52] The positive point of Jaswant Singh's visit to China was that both sides laid a framework for a comprehensive engagement and concluded "productive and substantive" talks.

Later in April, 2002 the first meeting of India-China mechanism on counter-terrorism was held in New Delhi.[53] During the meeting, the two sides shared respective national experiences and exchanged views on strengthening cooperation in countering terrorism within the framework of U.N. In the words of an Indian analyst, "progress in India-China coming together on this issue had been so slow precisely because this issue was bound to project China's "all weather" friend Pakistan in different light."[54] Still, both sides termed the first meeting as useful in that it enhanced mutual understanding on the issue.

Furthermore, the meeting between Chinese President Jiang Zemin and Indian Prime Minister, A.B. Vajpayee in June, 2002 on the side lines of summit on building Confidence and Cooperation in Asia (CICA) at Almaty, Kazakhstan symbolised continuity of political interactions at the highest level.[55] During the meeting, Jiang Zemin recalled with pleasure his friendly visit to India in 1996. Prime Minister, Vajpayee said he is looking forward to visiting China and exchanging in depth views with Chinese leaders on further development of bilateral relations. On the issue of ongoing tension in South Asia, the Chinese President said that peace benefits both sides, while fighting hurts both and further added that China's consistent position is to promote peace.[56]

Despite the events of 9/11 and ongoing war against terrorism, China was specifically yet to condemn role of its 'all weather friend', Pakistan in fomenting cross border terrorism against India. Nonetheless, the fact of meetings at the highest level highlighted the usefulness of political interactions between the both sides.

In November, 2002 the 16th congress of communist Party of China was held and the fourth generation of leadership assumed the responsibility of party and nation building. The leadership was predominantly technocratic and drew up a blueprint for China's development in the new century. The Report presented by the General secretary, Jiang Zemin. Stated that "no matter how the international situation changes, we will, as always, pursue the independent foreign policy of peace". The report reiterated the theme of peace and Development as the corner stones of Chinese foreign policy. In the foreword section of the report it was stated that "A developing China needs a peaceful international environment and a favourable climate in its periphery".[57] In the wake of 9/11, war against terrorism and American presence in China's Periphery coupled with new leadership in China compelled it to renew policy of re-engagement with India after 2002 in a more substantive way.

In January, 2003 the Speaker of Indian parliament, Lok Sabha Mr. Manohar Joshi visited China as part of high level contacts. Among other important leaders, the speaker met with the Chinese President, Jiang Zemin who briefed him on the 16th Congress of CPC.[58] The President added that China needs a peaceful international environment and favourable surrounding environment in order to reach the targets set at congress. Thus, in the backdrop of 16th party congress and current complicated but changing international situation, compelled both nations to further improve their bilateral relations.

Further, in April 2003 the Defence Minister, George Fernandes visited China and it was after eleven years that an Indian defence minister visited Beijing. He met with the new leadership, which included his Chinese counterpart, Gen. Cao Gangchuan, foreign minister Li Zhaoxing and Premier, Wen Jiabao. During his meeting with the Defence Minister, the Premier noted that the two countries have had a friendly relationship for 99.9 per cent of their mutual interface and that only 0.1 per cent was unpleasant – an oblique reference to the negative events of 1962 and 1998.[59] Mr. Fernandes also met with Jiang Zemin, Chairman of CMC and exchanges views on bilateral and international issues. The visit symbolized continuation of amicable high level political contact between the two Asian giants. The visit also laid background for up coming visit of the Indian Prime Minister.

Later, on May 31, 2003 the Chinese President Hu Jintao met with the Indian Prime Minister, A.B. Vajpayee on the sidelines of celebrations marking the 300th anniversary of St. Petersburg, Russia. Hu stated : "To further develop good neighborly and friendly relations and realized common prosperity is the Common wish of the two peoples and the trend of times. The new central leadership in China attaches great importance to relations with India and would like to work with India to greatly strengthen cooperation in all areas and bring bilateral constructive and cooperative partnership to a new level."[60] Prime Minister said he was happy to see the healthy development of India-China relations in recent years. He further added that he was looking forward to visiting China. Thus, the meting at St. Petersburg set the stage for Prime Minister's upcoming summit in Beijing.

Meanwhile the second meeting of India-China dialogue on counter terrorism was held in Beijing on 13th June, 2003. Both sides exchanged view son the international and regional counter terrorism situation, bilateral cooperation on counter terrorism, role of the United Nations in combating global terrorism and enhancing counter terrorism capabilities in overall way.[61] Both sides also took the opportunity to discuss in a general way upcoming visit of the Indian Prime Minister to promote bilateral relations.

India Debates Dealing with China

True to its rich traditions of debates and discussions in a Democracy, the foreign policy analysts wrote in newspapers about India's policy in the context of Prime Minister's upcoming visit to Beijing. For instance, one hardliner argued that 'China is seeking to exploit Vajpayee's yearning for a successful visit'. In the words of the analyst, "In the nearly 54 years since the communists seized power in Beijing, no nation has undermined India's interests more than China. The Chinese Communist Party and its institutions, particularly the PLA, remain implacably antagonistic towards India. Without the collapse of the anachronistic Chinese political system, it is unlikely that China would become a benign neighbour of India."[62] Another analyst criticized the writing of the hardliner and termed his article 'a tirade against China'. In the opinion of the former diplomat analyst, "china seems to be keen on friendship with India. Both of us can gain a lot by cooperation... The present visit offers an opportunity and a challenge particularly to Atal Behari Vajpayee to prove his leadership. Leadership implies vision and guts."[63]

A renowned expert argued that 'a new relationship between the Asian giants could contribute towards a less forbidding international situation'. In his words, "it is time now for a full détente with China that would include the resolution of the border dispute."[64] Another well known columnist wrote that "It's good diplomacy to have strong ties with Beijing. It's even better economics". He concluded, "It is enough if we see the Vajpayee visit in realistic terms. A steady-state relationship, kept lubricated with high-level exchanges, does both sides good without affecting either negatively."[65]

An academician specialising on China's Defence capability wrote that "On a bigger span we are stabilising India-China relations. Explicit war challenges and threats won't happen between us now. We are in a transitional period. As of today, we are neither friends nor enemies. We are neither allies nor rivals."[66] A well known defence analyst, wrote earlier in the context of the Indian Defence Minister's visit to China that "India and China have serious security problems to resolve... At a strategic level, Beijing's growing clout in the Indian periphery is seen as part of China's containment strategy". Referring to the challenging task of managing bilateral relations, he further wrote : "The challenge for India and China will be reflected in the manner in which they can build upon their shared interests political, economic and societal and build a base on which they can manage their respective anxieties about the other."[67] Therefore, by an large their was unanimity about the desirability of serious engagement with China, an important neighbour of India.

However, a confident India displayed 'stunning candour' regarding China's military might, particularly in respect of its nuclear forces, and the threat posed to Indian security. The Ministry of Defence (MoD) in its annual report for 2002-03 pointed out that the asymmetry of nuclear forces is "pronouncedly in favour of China." The report highlighted the fundamental determinants of India's security planning and observed that "the Indian armed forces have a two front obligation, which require them to safeguard the security of our borders with Pakistan as well as with China." In the wake of nuclear tests of 1998, India was guarded in expressing apprehensions about china. The report further stated that "China's close defence relationship with Pakistan takes a particular edge in view of the latter's known belligerence and hostility to India and its acquisition of nuclear assets."[68] In short, India due to its economic growth, foreign reserve and evolving strategic culture in the backdrop of Pokharan-II tests felt confident in dealing with China in a more assertive way.

Before leaving for Beijing the Prime Minister, on the part of India. Summarised his views about the current development and future of Sino-Indian relations in an interview to Chinese news agency, Xinhua on 21st June and stated : "In recent years, our two countries have launched a process of diversification of bilateral relations. We have successfully developed mutually beneficial bilateral cooperation, while simultaneously addressing our differences. Our dialogue now addresses not only the various areas in which we can improve bilateral cooperation, but also international issues such as terrorism, security, environment, sustainable development and multilateral economic regimes. Our trade relations are developing in a healthy manner. Exchanges are growing in culture, education, science and technology, media and tourism."[69] In sum, the Prime Minister's statement was forward looking and matter of fact as well. It pointed out the broadening of cooperation and addressing of differences designed to improve bilateral relations in a meaningful manner.

The Indian Prime Minister, A.B. Vajpayee visited Beijing, Luoyang and Shanghai from June 22 to 27, 2003. The visit was important one in that it was the first by an Indian Prime Minister in 10 years. Already, Vajpayee hand sent the right signals to Beijing through statement to the Chinese media. On June 23, he had first extensive talks with his Chinese counterpart, Wen Jiabao on bilateral issues and regional and international situation. A total of 10 agreements and a Declaration on Principles for Relations and Comprehensive Cooperation between the Republic of India and the People's Republic of China were signed on June 23.[70] The Joint Declaration was the first of its kind between India and China.[71] The Indian Prime Minister met with the Chinese President, Hu Jintao, who stated that "in order to achieve the goals set forth in the declaration, China and India should increase exchanges, strengthen mutual trust and establish a concrete foundation for the long-term development of bilateral relation so as to carry on the good neighbourly friendship between China and India from generation to generation."[72] The Prime Minister also met with the Chairman of CMC, Jiang Zemin. As of now, Jiang was the link between the previous "generation" and present fourth generation Chinese leadership. He was a 'key interlocutor during Vajpayee's diplomatic endeavour'. Jiang welcomed signing of the Joint Declaration and noted 'consensus on developing bilateral ties during Vajpayee's ongoing China visit'. He added that "he hoped the two sides would continue to settle existing issues through consultation on an equal booting, mutual understanding and accommodation".[73] He also expressed his confidence about the future of China-Indian relations.

The Chinese leadership are well known for choice of words in their diplomacy. Therefore, the use of word 'equal footing' was a new development. At this moment, it is difficult to state whether this symbolized some concession to India as there was a perception in India that China deals with it in a level of hierarchy ? Or this meant nuclearised India is in the same league therefore, India give some concession to China in the border dispute. Nonetheless, the introduction of the word 'equal footing', by Jiang Zemin must be noted with some significance.

The Indian Prime Minister took this opportunity to reach out to younger generation Chinese students and gave a speech at the prestigious Beijing University, Beijing. There, he stated that 'I would like to dwell on frequent description of "rivalry" between India and China'. Vajpayee stated that "we need to clearly understand the difference between healthy competition and divisive rivalry... We should focus on the simple truth that there is no objective reason for discord between us, and neither of us is a threat to the other. These simple but profound, principles should form the bedrock of the future India-China partnership."[74] Thus, the Prime Minister put the bilateral relation in a proper perspective and urged to carefully differentiate between competition in a positive way and rivalry in negative sense.

Similarly in an effort to reach out to the citizens of India, the Chinese Premier granted interview with the Indian correspondents. He was asked to elaborate on China's foreign policy towards its neighbours. Wen Jiabao stated that "the advancement of the modernization drive, the fulfillment of the reunification of the motherland and the preservation of world peace and promotion of common development are the three main tasks of China in the new century. China, therefore, needs a long-term, stable, peaceful international environment, especially a good neighbourhood environment, and is willing to make efforts in this regard."[75] thus, the Chinese Premier underlined the motivations of China to seek peaceful neighbourhood policy. It is in this backdrop that Chinese efforts to improve relations with India should be placed at a broader neighbourhood level.

Overall, the visit of Indian Prime Minister was hailed as a success by both nations. While the China Daily summed up the latest dialogue as "a handshake across the Himalayas", the Prime Minster Vajpayee said in Shanghai that his visit has "transformed the quality of the bilateral relationship". In the words of a leading Indian scholar on China, the Prime Ministers of both nations made this possible because they "took bold decisions on the two principal differences that have bedevilled the bilateral relationship – the territorial issue and the lack of trust that surrounded growing shared interests and strategic commonalities."[76]

At the political level, Prime Minister Vajpayee's visit to China resulted in 'four significant outcomes'. In the words of the editor of an Indian news magazine, "The first is the Joint Declaration itself. The second is the nomination of special representatives who will try and workout a framework for a boundary settlement from an overarching political perspective... while the work of experts and officials is important, politics holds the key to a boundary settlement in both India and China... Thirdly, on the question of Tibet, there seems to be a newly nuanced Indian official position. It is that India recognizes that "the Tibet Autonomous Region is part of the territory of the People's Republic of China"... Fourthly, India can take satisfaction from the official Chinese movement towards a recognition of Sikkim as an integral part of India... This movement has come in the agreement on expanding border trade through Sikkim."[77] In Short, Prime Minister Vajpayee's Visit in terms of concrete success was in the same league as Rajiv Gandhi's visit of 1988 and Narasimha Rao in 1993. Therefore, the political input was the crucial factor in transforming the bilateral ties and gave impetus to Sino-Indian rapprochement.

Resumption of Defence Relations

During the current period, establishment of direct contact between the defence establishment of both nations, symbolized the maturing of rapprochement. In May, 2000, the Indian military delegation consisting of members from National Defence College, New Delhi, Indian Military Academy, Dehradun and College of Combat; Mhow visited China under the leadership of Màjor General P.R. Ranjen of NDC. Major General Renjen stated that "Our meeting showed the eagerness of both sides to accelerate the normalization process of military-to-military relations."[78] Welcoming the delegation, Chinese side stated : "contacts between the Chinese and Indian military establishments would enhance mutual trust and understanding between the two neighbours,."[79] In August, 2000 the PLA delegation led by the Vice President of Academy of Military Sciences, Lieutenant General Tian Shugen visited India.[80] These visits symbolized the beginning of military exchanges suspended after Pokharan tests in 1998. Subsequently, in September 2000 two Indian naval ships visited the Chinese port city of Shanghai. The Indian flotilla was led by Vice Admiral Pasricha, who also called on Navy Chief of PLA, Admiral Shi Yun Sheng in Beijing.[81]

Later in April 2001 the Indian military delegation led by Lieutenant General HRS Kalkat, GOC, Eastern Command of Indian Army visited China. The delegation held discussions with PLA military officials, in particular with General Fu Quanyou and emphasized on the fact that both sides should resolve their existing problems with 'mutual understanding, mutual concession and mutual adjustment.[82] In may, the Chief of Staff of Indian Air Force, Air Chief Marshal A.Y. Tipnis visited China. The Indian Air Force on its part stated that "It is primarily a goodwill visit and an opportunity to strengthen bilateral military relations."[83] Further in May, two Chinese naval Ships – Harbin, a Luhu class destroyer, and Tailing, a fuquing class replenishmentship visited Mumbai in a goodwill mission.[84]

The China visit of Indian Defence Minister, Mr. George Fernandes in April, 2003 was an important milestone in the growing defence relations between both sides. The visit was after an 11 year gap and first since Pokharan-II tests.[85] He had substantive discussions with his Chinese counterpart and chairman of the central military commission, Jiang Zemin. As such, it was a notable development in bilateral military relations. Underlining the importance of visit, a noted defence analyst wrote : "The visit acquired considerable salience given the persona of Mr. Fernandes, his cabinet rank, and the centrality of China in the Indian security calculus... the image of an Indian defence minister inspecting a guard of honour in Beijing has a certain symbolism associated with it."[86] Another notable aspect of the Indian Defence Minister's visit to China was his effort to reachout to the 'PLA Scholar Warriors' in the shape of a speech at the National Defence University. Beijing George Fernandes urged both sides to strengthen bilateral relations and stated : "As two large developing nations we have convergences that span issues such as energy security and environmental degradation... I believe we can rise to this challenge if there is a conviction about the manner in which we are committed to nurturing this mutuality. To may mind it extends from the political to economic, military and societal matters. We in India are keen to take forward the relationship with China in a spirit of equality and in a manner that accommodates both our interests even while respecting each other's sensitivities."[87] He called for greater interaction between two defence establishments and further stated that "In the military area, our interaction remains modest... It is an ironic reality that we both have greater military to military contact with other nations than we do with each other. I hope that we can evolve a framework whereby there will be much greater contact, confidence building and cooperation between our two armed forces in a mutually acceptable manner and thus raise our friendliness to a higher level."[88] The minister's speech was positive and forward looking.

In 2003 after Vajpayee's China visit, the India Navy announced that the first even joint exercises with the PLA-Navy were being planned later this year. The exercise will be in the form of search and rescue operations in the India's east coast[90]. The point should be noted that the PLA has an important say in issues relation to the border issue. As such, the resumption of dialogue with the defence establishment is a welcome development. The former Chinese President, Jiang Zemin continues to be the Chairman of the Central Military Commission and wields considerable count. Therefore, both the Defence Minister and Prime Minister of India called on him in course of their China visit. In short, the resumption of defence relations and high level military exchanges between both sides, enabled the armed forces to enhance mutual trust and cooperation. Furthermore, in June 2003 following the conclusion of joint declaration, both sides agreed on the need to broaden and deepen defence exchanges, which will help enhance and deepen the mutual understanding and trust between the two armed forces. In short, the fact being mentioned in joint declaration was an important development. As such, this process gave an impetus to the overall process of Sino-Indian Rapprochement.

Renewed Efforts to Resolve India-China Border Issue

In the period, renewed efforts to resolve the vexed border issue continued apace. The Joint working Group mechanism resumed in April 1999 and consequently, the eleventh round of meeting was held at Beijing.

It should be remembered that the eleventh meeting was originally scheduled for November, 1998 but was cancelled by China due to India's nuclear tests and overall temporary breakdown of rapprochement.[91] The eleventh meeting was chaired by the Indian Foreign secretary, K. Raghunath and Chinese Vice Foreign Minister, Yang Wenchang. Both sides discussed the development of "friendly, good neighbourly relations" and expanded understanding on issues of mutual concern.[92] As this was the first meeting of the JWG after Pokharan II tests, India assured the Chinese side that it did not regarded China as a security threat. In the meeting both sides decided to further expand ties in other fields and opined that there was considerable scope for developing bilateral relations in economic, commercial and other fields.[93] Further, both sides agreed that India and China have to play important role in "Shaping the emerging new world order." Thus, this round of talks was confined to improve the general tenor of relations rather than discuss the border issue.

India's assertive policy vis-à-vis China seemed to yield some success when the Indian Foreign Minister, Jaswant Singh visited China in June, 1999, the Chinese side agreed to give clarification in the JWG of China's interpretation of the precise location of the Line of Actual Control along the border.[94] Later in November, 1999 the seventh meeting of India-China Expert group was held in New Delhi. In the meeting both sides reiterated their commitment to maintain peace and tranquility as envisaged by the agreements of 1993 and 1996.[95] Though no concrete progress was registered still the fact that China considered the meeting as forward movement was notable and signified the continuity of efforts to resolve the issue.[96]

Later, on April 28 and 29, 2000 the twelfth meeting of the JWG was held in New Delhi. The Indian side was led by Foreign secretary Lalit Man Singh and Chinese side by the Vice Foreign Minister, Yang Wenchang and they discussed the border issue and the President Narayanan's upcoming visit to Beijing.[97] Adopting a "forward looking" approach, both sides agreed to exchange maps as a further step towards working on the identification of the LAC,[98] Thus, both sides agreed to conduct "maps exercise", which basically meant exchange and comparison of their respective maps on the LAC and was step forward in 'identification of the line'. Accordingly, both sides close the middle sector as the first section to determine, as it was less disputable in comparison to the other two sectors of border.[99] The discussion also included clarification of the LAC and CBMs between the militaries.[100] After the JWG meeting, it seems that India has 'stepped up its efforts to find an early resolution' of the intractable border issue. In April 2000, the Foreign Minister Jaswant Singh conveyed to the members of Chinese delegation of the JWG that India strongly desires "result oriented negotiations".[101] Again during President K.R. Narayanan's China visit, it repeated its position that border issue is left over by history, Narayanan correctly stated that 'inherited problems' needed to be resolved and "must not be left over for history."[102]

As a result of India's stepped up efforts to find resolution of the border issue, China in some ways agreed to 'quicken the pace of the negotiations'. As the Indian sources pointed out, the first ever exchange of maps took place only after the Indian Foreign Minister, Jaswant Singh wrote to his Chinese counterpart and urged him to expendite the process of clarification and confirmation of the LAC.[103] In the words of an analyst, "However, this does not imply any shift in China's management of the border problem."[104]

It was during the eighth round of India-China Expert meeting held on November 13th and 14th, 2000 in Beijing that both sides for the first time exchanged maps on the 545 km long middle sector of the India-China border.[105] On the one hand, this process continued but China on the other hand also continued to emphasis the need for "patience and right conditions" to settle the vexed India-China border issue. For example while visiting India in January 2001, the chairman of standing committee of the National People's Congress, Li Peng stated that "in the spirit of mutual understanding and mutual accommodation, this issue can be resolved. Of course, given its complexity, it requires patience and right conditions for its settlement."[106]

Later, on June 28 and 29th, 2001 the ninth meeting of expert group was held in New Delhi. During the meeting, the delegations of both sides reviewed the other side's maps and exchanged views about differences.[107] During the thirteenth round of meeting of the Joint Working Group held on July 31 – August 1, 2001 at Beijing, the Indian side headed by the Foreign Secretary, Chokila Iyer reviewed with the Chinese Vice Minister of Foreign Affairs and rest of Chinese side the work of the Expert group on clarification of the LAC in the middle sector and recorded their individual perceptions on the maps. It was reported that there was a convergence of views on the LAC alignment along the large portions of the middle sector.[108]

Furthermore, on December 17 and 18th the tenth round of meeting of India-China expert group was held in Beijing. Both sides continued to exchange opinions on clarifying and confirming the middle sector alignment.[109]

The year 2002 witnessed two round of meetings of the expert group. First, on March 5th, the eleventh meeting was held in New Delhi. Both sides exchanged opinions on clarifying and confirming the LAC alignment, establishing more CBI's and general improvement of overall relationship.[110] Later, in April 2002 during China visit of the Indian Foreign Minister Jaswant Singh, both nations agreed to complete the delineation of the Line of Actual Control (LAC) within a reasonable time-frame. Jaswant Singh stated that the accelerated schedule for talks on the LAC "is something India has not been able to achieve for the last fifty years."[111] At Beijing, the Indian Foreign Minister also announced that maps relating to the western sector would be exchanged in June. Both nations hope to conclude the process of clarification of the western sector by the end of this year. Maps relating to the eastern sector will be exchanged early next year.[112] In the words of Minister, once the exchange of maps is complete, there will be "very little scope for confusion" and the process of delineation will begin. This development, according to Jaswant Singh, will help both sides reach a settlement of the dispute.[113]

In course of as interaction with the Chinese academic community at the Shanghai Institute for International Studies, the Foreign Minister was asked whether it was possible to resolve the boundary dispute. The Minister said, "it can and must be resolved. The shadows of the past should not be allowed to affect the future" of bilateral relations. It would be "a crime against our people and humanity if we allowed it to happen." He added that both the Governments were addressing the issues relating to the boundary in a "purposeful manner and will continue to do so in the future."[114] The Minister's statement underlined more keeness on the part of India to resolve the border issue in the face of China's insistence on patience to resolve the issue.

Later on June 17th, 2002 the twelfth meeting of India-China Expert Group was held in Beijing. Both sides exchanged views on the building up of trust and implementation of the CBMs, but did not exchange western Sector maps as planned.[115] Commenting on the ongoing round of meetings to resolve the border issue, one analyst wrote that "Given the current tempo of the talks, however, the clarification of the entire LAC will not be a short-term process; there will be no quick reaching of a final settlement about the alignment of the entire border. Moreover, China's reluctance to set a time frame to clarify and confirm the LAC may result in a delay of the border resolution."[116]

The China visit of Prime Minister A.B. Vajpayee in June 2003 witnessed notable developments designed to eventual resolution of the vexed border issue. Underlining the complex nature of the issue, an eminent Indian analyst wrote : "That now leaves only the territorial problem to be resolved, and makes it more manageable even though it is perhaps the most complex of all the territorial problems the world has known. It is not just a matter of adjusting rival claims and delimiting and defining the territorial limits of two neighbouring states. Instead, it is a tangled knot of the tangible and the intangible, of the 'real' and the 'notional."[117] Both nations agreed to the nomination of special Representatives who will try and work out a framework for a boundary settlement from an overarching political perspective. The Prime Minister after he returned stated that the boundary issue will be taken up soon on "the basis of the principles discussed which are to be followed for an eventual settlement". He elaborated, the exploration will be for a boundary settlement "from the political perspective of the overall bilateral relationship."[118] In the words of an analyst the conduct of this exploration has been entrusted to special Representatives who presumably share the political perspectives and have the full confidence of their Prime Ministers : Brajesh Mishra, National Security Adviser, and Dai Pinguo, the senior most Vice Minister in the Chinese Ministry of Foreign Affairs, reputed to have been hand-picked by former Chinese President Jiang Zemin."[119] With this development, coupled with the vexed question of maps showing the Line of Actual control involving both nations, China reckons that the issue has been put on the fast track.

Further, according to the Joint Declaration, India and China exchanged views on the boundary question and "expounded" their respective positions. Both sides reiterated their readiness to seek a fair, reasonable and mutually acceptable solution through consultations on an equal footing. Moreover, "the two sides agreed that pending an ultimate solution, they should work together to maintain peace and tranquility in the border areas, and reiterated their commitment to continue implementation of the agreements signed for this purpose, including the clarification of the Line of Actual control."[120]

In the opinion of a news columnist, "The phrase "equal footing" used in the Declaration (it was a formulation that was put forward first by Premier Wen Jiabao) could indicate that Beijing will negotiate on the basis of "give and take" as has been done with regard to Tibet and Sikkim... New Delhi and Beijing are aware that history has stood still after the 1962 conflict in the matter of resolving the border dispute. Aksaichin, the territory ceded by Pakistan to China in the early 1960's and Arunachal Pradesh, remain the bone of contention. Clearly, Mishra and Dai have a tough task on their hands."[121] Though the fact of complex nature of the border issue is indisputable but the step-by-step approach pursued by both sides in a forward looking manner would go a long way in eventually resolving the issue. In the words of an eminent expert, "with the adoption of a political approach to the problem, it has become easier to surmount this obstacle."[122]

China's recognition of Sikkim as an integral part of India in an indirect way by the agreement on expanding border trade through "Changgu of Sikkim state" was a positive development.[123] As an editor wrote, "India can take satisfaction from the official Chinese movement towards a recognition of Sikkim as an integral part of India... This movement has come in the agreement on expanding border trade through Sikkim."[124] From the side of China, two of their leading experts on the issue, Wang Hongwei and Ma Jiali pointed to the flexibility of China on the issue. According to them, "the first step might have already been taken to wards an eventual recognition of Sikkim as a part of Indian territory."[125] According to an Indian analyst, China's tacit recognition of Sikkim as an Indian state, "Prime Minister Vajpayee has now returned to Jawaharlal Nehru's formulations of 1954 and 1958, which described Tibet Region as a part of China, but used the more restricted territorial term created by the PRC – Tibet Autonomous Region." The analyst further wrote that by doing so, "Vajpayee had to retract the advances that Prime Minister Rajiv Gandhi in 1988 and then Narasimha Rao in 1991 had made in India's diplomatic posture on Tibet. The 1988/1991 formulation described "Tibet as an autonomous part of China". This had two implications : One, the use of the term Tibet meant the whole of the pre-1950 territorial configurations and not the much smaller Tibet Autonomous Region created by the People's Republic of China (PRC) and which merged large chunks of the Tibetan region into adjacent Chinese provinces such as Sichuan; two, it clarified India's support for Tibetan autonomy within China."[126] In India, at the other end of spectrum, another analyst argued : "The temptation to drow parallels with 1954 notwithstanding, the question is whether India is in any position to change the strategic equations vis-à-vis China over Tibet. No government since 1954 has ever voiced any inclinations in the matter."[127]

Be that as it may be, the Foreign Minister Yashwant Sinha described the accords reached by both sides as a "win-win" situation for both countries. Asked on the agreement on border trade meant a tacit admission by China over India's claims on Sikkim, the Minister said, "you can read the language for yourself. I do not know why there should be any doubt about any thing."[128] Asked if there was any confusion on the Indian position on Tibet, the minister said, "I would say there is no change in India's position and it continues to be consistent with the past positions we have taken."[129] On the decision to up grade talks on the border issue with the appointment of special political representatives, the minister described the step as a "very big development."[130]

Notwithstanding the optimism generated by Minister's remarks the complex issue of border reared up again and caused embarassment to the Indian government. On June 26, a 10-man Indian party were on a "routine mission" 14 km inside the Line of Actual control in Subhan Sari district in Arunachal Pradesh, when they were detained, disarmed and interrogated. They were finally released near the Yume Bridge across the Yume Chu river, three Kilometers deeper inside the LAC.[131] The Indian government admitted that the Chinese army Crossed the LAC and stated that the Chinese side "did not appear to have adhered" to the provisions of 1996 agreement. The Minister of Foreign Affairs said, "This is an area where there are differences in the perception of the LAC between the two sides." He observed that such isolated incidents could occur sporadically and definition of the LAC was underway.[132]

China on the other hand alleged that Indian troops had crossed into their side. The Spokesman of Chinese foreign ministry, Kong Quan stated that "we have noted the relevant report. China does not recognise the so-called Arunachal Pradesh mentioned by the Indian newspaper report." He further added that "After investigation, the reality is that India crossed the eastern part of the Sino-Indian line of actual control (LAC)."[133] Indian position on Chinese intrusion was that it on the one hand would be taken up through established mechanisms, and on the another hand, take steps to ensure the episode like this is not repeated and send a strong message. It was reported that the Cabinet Committee on Security (CCS) discussed measures to evolve a comprehensive border management plan which included better training, sophisticated arms and modern radar cover and telecommunication facilities along the India-China border.[134] A confident India in post Pokharan phase wanted to send clear message to Beijing that it is prepared to negotiate but not from position of weakness any more. The President of India on the eve of Independence day's message to countrymen mentioned the China visit of Prime Minister Vajpayee and indicated that it had paved the way for the resolution of certain outstanding issues.[135] The above mentioned border incursion was not a isolated case. In the words of an analyst, "Due to the fuzzy nature of the LAC, several transgressions of the line occurred over the last four decades, heightening tensions in both camps."[136]

Notwithstanding the Chinese incursion the overall point of CBMs, exchange of maps, seeking clarification on each other's position and finally the appointment of special representatives "to explore from the political perspective of the overall bilateral relationship the framework of a boundary settlement," are reflection of advancement in the eventual step towards resolution of the issue. Another step need to be noted which is, differences on the LAC have been identified. In the east they are, broadly, the areas around the Namka Chu, Chenju, Tulang La, Asaphila, Longju and Che Dong. It is Bara Hoti plus four other areas in the middle sector. In the west it is Trig Heights, near the Karakoram Pass, Chushul, Kongka Pass, Pangong Lake and Demchok in the South, traversed by the Indus and three others.[137]

In the post cold war period, the JWG and the Expert Group are important mechanisms, "the JWG has generated remarkable results in initiating the CBM's it's achievement on the alignment of the LAC has been limited."[138] Even the time frame on clarification of the Western Sector by 2002 and the Eastern Sector by about 2003 seems to have not been accomplished. Nonetheless, during Vajpayee's visit the adoption of political approach is a forward looking step. In the interest of both nations, the unilateral assertions and periodic transgressions should be avoided, otherwise this could upset the positive step-by-step approach to resolve the border issue. Indeed, efforts to resolve the complicated issue of border is going to be long, tortuous phase and full of bumps. Therefore, in the words of a retired foreign secretary, "Patience is a virtue that India must work on, especially when it comes to dealing with China."[139] Finally, it seems that in post Pokharan phase, India is more confident and handling the sensitive issue in a mature way. Although much is still desired to improve its overall border management.

Bilateral Economic Cooperation

The fact of growing economic cooperation and increasing trade ties have already been mentioned in earlier chapters as well. In the period, from 2002 when the direct flight started between India and China another step was taken forward to enhance economic cooperation between both nations.

Table 1. India-China Trade (1999-2001)

(US $ million)

Period	*Indian Imports*	*Indian Exports*	*Trade Balance*	*Trade Volume*
1999	1161.9	825.8	(–) 336.1	1,993.7
Growth	14.3	(–)8.8		3.4%
2000	1569.46	1350.41	(–) 219.05	2,914.22
Growth	34.3	63.9%		46.6%
2001	1896.3	1699.9	(–)196.4	3596.2
Growth	21.5	25.6		23.4

Source: Strategic Digest, 33.5, May 2003, p. 376.

Further, it was reported that bilateral trade was to the tune of $ 5 billion during the year 2002.[140] During his visit to India in January 2002, the Chinese Premier, Zhu Rongji exported to raise the level of bilateral trade to a level of $ 10 billion in the next few years. However, the overall trade balance is in favour of China. In the words of an analyst, "Cost competitive and technologically superior Chinese products are making waves in the Indian market and consumers are attracted towards them. The Indian industry is overawed by the invasion of Chinese products and consumers fascination for them. The Indian industry is faced with competition from Chinese products over a wide spectrum, ranging from capital goods to drugs, from yarn to batteries."[141]

Gradually the trend of Chinese sweeping the Indian market subsided and India was confident in enhancing trade ties with China. As one journalist specializing in trade affairs wrote, "A year ago, the dragon threatened to sweep us off our feet... A full year after, India is bound to see the dragon in different light : less of a threat and more of an opportunity... India's exports to China grew by a record of 96 per cent. Chinese exports to India too grew, but at a relatively moderate 38 per cent."[142] The other positive indicators were, the two-way trade turnover during April – February 2003-04 increased to $ 4200.4 million from $ 2954.3 million during April – February 2001-02. Though the balance of trade is still in favour of China, yet India has been able to considerably bridge the gap during 2002-03.[143] Equally importantly, Indian exports are not just raw materials and minerals, but manufactured items. But the threat of Chinese suppliers dumping their goods in India exists very much. According to the specialist journalist, "This is reflected in the anti-dumping action initiated by India in 2002-03. Of the 30 cases of anti-dumping action initiated, Chinese suppliers were involved in as many as 14 products, like caustic soda, float glass, raw silk, Vitamin-E among others."[144] Notwithstanding, these minor issues the big picture of trade ties continues to be encouraging.

Joint Ventures

The pattern of establishing joint ventures continued during the period. In the year 1999, Konka and Haier, two well Known Chinese Consumer durable companies, set up joint ventures in India. NIIT, a leading computer education company has set up 100 centres in 25 Chinese provinces and Aptech has more than 45 centres. Recently, Satyam Computer Services have set up a software development center in Shanghai. Orissa Industry Co. Ltd has constructed a refractory material plant in Dahun, Liaoning Province.[145] The process is continuing in an encouraging way.

Many steps were taken to promote economic cooperation between both sides. In this context, in August 1999, a "Kunming Initiative" was a notable development. An attempt was made to promote a growth quadrangle between India, China, Myanmar and Bangladesh and it was resolved to establish a forum for regional economic cooperation between four nations. It provided forum for active interaction among academics, governments and leaders of business and industry.[146] As such, it was positive step to strengthen regional economic cooperation in relatively backward areas of these four nations.

Further, after a gap of five years, the India-China JEG on Economic Relations and Trade met in February 2000 at Beijing. The Indian delegation was led by the commerce and Industry Minister, Murasoli Maran who also met with the Chinese Minister of Foreign Trade and Economic Cooperation (MOFTEC), Mr. Shi Guang Sheng and discussed ways to promote economic cooperation.[147] Later, both sides signed an agreement on February 22, which provided for India's support to China's entry into the World Trade Organisation (WTO) and for boosting bilateral trade.[148] The Chinese Minister stated that China appreciated India's Support on Beijing's entry into the WTO and added that this would provide further impetus to bilateral trade ties. Moreover, to further enhance bilateral trade, India put forward a list of about 180 export commodities, mainly agricultural products for granting lower tariffs.[149] From now onwards, both sides emphasized on enhancing bilateral economic ties during high level visit and Premier Zhu Rongji's India visit in no uncertain terms, underlined the point.[150] During Zhu's visit, business contracts worth more than $ 100 million were signed.[151]

The economic cooperation was further strengthened during Vajpayee's visit to China in 2003. He was accompanied by a strong contingent of business delegation which comprised from CII, FICCI and ASSOCHAM. During his visit, China announced to set up a $ 500 million corpus for investments in India. Further, both sides set a trade target of $ 10 billion by 2005.[152] To boost trade ties CII's office was set up in shanghai during the Prime Minister's visit and FICCI already has a functional office in Beijing.[153] Both the organisations recognized that huge trade potential exists. In Beijing, Prime Minister Vajpayee addressed a Seminar organised by the China council for promotion of International Trade, the CII and the FICCI, he said : "This has helped to further narrow our differences and to accelerate our cooperation." On trade ties with China he added : "Our bilateral trade has been growing rapidly. Though it is from a relatively narrow base, the recent annual growth rate of 30 percent in our bilateral trade is quite significant."[154] The Chinese Commerce Minister, Lu Fuayuan said that "From a strategic perspective, the two countries needed to accelerate trade in both "width and depth".[155] Moreover, the decision to open border trade route via Sikkim added a new chapter. Because of the proximity between both nations, $ 2.5 billion trade was already happening illegally every year.[156]

Even in the Joint Declaration the fact of continued expansion and intensification of bilateral economic cooperation was mentioned. Both nations decided to set up a Joint Study Group to draw up a programme of the development of India-China trade and economic cooperation. Further, both sides agreed to enhance cooperation at the world Trade organisation in the broader interest of developing countries apart from mutual benefit.[157]

After Vajpayee returned from China, India offered tariff concessions on 106 items imported from China and Beijing will reciprocate on 152 items. The tariff concessions offered by China would help India boost export of major products like chemicals, leather, textiles and diamonds.[158] This was under the Bangkok agreement of ESCAP.

Thus during the period economic ties assumed special place in overall bilateral relations. In the long-term, growing economic relations would help in the creating of overall conducive atmosphere to resolve all outstanding issues between both nations. As such, gradually the trade ties were being seen from "strategic perspective". In short, the economic dimension assumed the depth of "strategic perspective" and would gradually give some leverage to India, these developments were indeed notable. At the same time, the prevalent problems like the language barrier, tough market access, few banking Channels, unclear policy framework, arduous registrations process and lack of information still existed.[159] Notwithstanding these problems, the larger picture in mid to long-term was quite positive.

Mutual Cooperation in Science and Technology

This area was a component of overall process of the rapprochement and contributed in enhancing mutual understanding between both nations. Some of the important agreements concluded in the period were :

2000 : Memorandum of understanding signed during the 6th Joint Economic Group Meeting in Beijing on February 21-22, 2000 on cooperation in the field of steel between India and China.

2000 : In July, MOU on cooperation in the field of Information technology.

2002 : In January, MOU on the Application of phytosanitary measures between the Ministry of Agriculture of the Republic of India (RoI) and the state General Administration of the People's Republic of China (PRC) for Quality Supervision and Inspection and Quarantine (AQSIQ).

2002 : In January, MOU between ISRO and the China National Space Administration on cooperation in the peaceful use of outer space.

2002 : In January, MOU between Department of Science and Technology of RoI and the States' Administration of Foreign Experts Affairs of PRC on Exchange of Personnel between India and China.

2002 : In January, MOU between Department of Science and Technology of RoI and the Chinese Academy of Sciences of the PRC on cooperation in Science and Technology.

2002 : In January, MOU between the Ministry of Water Resources of India and Ministry of Water Resources of China upon provision of hydrological information of the Yalu Zangbu / Brahmputra river in flood season by China to India.[160]

Many agreements in the field were concluded during the Chinese Premier Zhu Rongji's India visit in January, 2002. These agreements and MOUs further strengthened the bilateral cooperation, and both sides agreed to undertake joint research projects, and organise seminars on a regular basis.[161] Further, the exchange visits of Scientific teams materialsed in a number of areas, including seismology and earthquake engineering, chemistry of natural products, laser science and technology, plasma physics, astronomy, and biotechnology.[162] During the last meeting of India-China sub-committee on S & T cooperation held in New Delhi on 8 February 2002, the new areas of bilateral cooperation were identified, which included traditional medicine, awareness programme on intellectual property rights, incubator parks in S & T, public understanding of S & T for rural and social development.[163] Apart from cooperation in government level, non-governmental projects on technology gathered momentum. Indians evinced Keen interest in China's antimalarial medicine, mini-tractor manufacture technology, mushroom cultivation, comprehensive use of flyash, laser medical equipment and paper making using agricultural waste. On the Chinese side, a number of Indian technologies were being utilized, particularly in the area of information technology.[164]

Moreover, both sides agreed to cooperate on preserving the environment and ensuring sustainable development alongwith coordinate positions on climate change, biodiversity and other issues in relevant multilateral for a. In 2003, the joint declaration also mentioned promotion of exchanges in Science and Technology and bilateral cooperation in agriculture, dairy, food processing, health and other sectors.[165]

Equally importantly there were other areas of bilateral cooperation and gradually these areas were being broadened to lay strong foundation for the comprehensive cooperation between both nations. In September, 2000 both sides concluded MOU on cooperation in the field of labour especially in Employment Services, Vocational Training and Social Security. To promote mutual tourism in January 2002, both nations signed agreement on cooperation in the field of tourism.[166] Further, the introduction of direct air service from March 2002 would further promote tourism between both sides. China also granted to India status of favoured tourist destination. In 2003, the joint declaration also comphasised the point that historical and cultural links between India and China will be strengthened, *inter alia,* through the promotion of exchanges in culture, education, youth, media and people to people relations. They also agreed to set up cultural centers in each other's capitals and facilitate their establishment.[167] In short, all these areas of bilateral cooperation symbolized the reconstruction of the Sino-Indian Rapprochement. Overall, these concrete actions and vision formulation to some extent helped in moving towards meaningful comprehensive cooperation between India and China. As such, these processes imparted certain dynamism to the emerging bilateral relations.

Thus, in the wake of brief breakdown of bilateral relations following the Pokharan II nuclear tests of India in 1998 and the resultant severe reaction of China, from the year 1999 both sides started to reconstruct the edifice of Sino-Indian Rapprochement. Pursuing a more assertive policy, India succeeded in moderate degree by bringing about co-relation of forces in its favour vis-à-vis China in that the clarification of maps in LAC as well as security dialogue to address India's security concerns were started from 1999. China in this period was slightly more responsive to overall India's concerns at a broad level and showed equal keenness in imparting dynamism to bilateral cooperation. As a result, by 2003 both nations succeeded in moving ahead towards reconstructing Sino-Indian Rapprochement in more meaningful way. Nonetheless, this positive development does not indicate that irritants no more exist, in fact, they are very much present.

As one analyst correctly wrote : "undoubtedly, the pace of Sino-Indian relations has recorded an upward trend in the post-Pokharan II period. Both India and China have shown readiness to consolidate their friendly relations by resolving outstanding issues through peaceful negotiations. Ticklish issues like the border dispute, the question of Tibet, India's misapprehensions about China's missile and nuclear assistance to Pakistan, China's perceptions about India's defence potential and its growing relationship with great powers, etc., entail the potential of bedeviling the ongoing process of entente cordiale between India and China."[168]

At the political level, as a result of Prime Ministerial summits of 2002 and 2003, the bilateral relations registered upward trend. The political input helped in the transformation of quality of bilateral relations. In particular, Prime Minister A.B. Vajpayee's China visit was successful and in the same league as erstwhile Prime Ministerial visit of Rajiv Gandhi in 1988 and Narasimha Rao in 1993. Similarly, the resumption of defence relations and high level defence exchanges enabled the armed forces to enhance mutual trust and understanding.

On the border issue, apart from maintenance of peace and tranquility, initiation of CBMs, the process of exchange of maps and seeking clarifications on each other's position continued. Furthermore, with the appointment of special representatives on border issue another step forward has been taken. It seems that the adoption of political approach would go a long way in resolution of the problem. Still, the incident of border incursion on the part of China was a negative episode. Despite step-by-step approach, the impression persists in India that China for obvious reasons does not desires to resolve the border issue in a time frame approach. Therefore, in a Slight manner China's dealings with India Smacks off a level of hierarchy despite the Pokharan II nuclear test and economic development of India. Nonetheless, the positive advancement and China's willingness to resolve the border issue in a forward looking and problem resolving manner needs to be acknowledged. It seems this slight change on the part of China to some extent was guided by India's assertive policy towards China. But going by China's strategic culture, importance of state sovereignty and territorial integrity, India has to be well prepared and careful. The political leadership of India, should integrate state craft, real politik dictates, economic strength into a fine-tuned diplomatic culture and coupled with evolving strategic culture deal with China and resolve the border issue.

Thus, by 2003 other aspect s of bilateral cooperation including economic and trade ties, culture, tourism and Science and Technology broadened the base of bilateral relationship and strengthened the overall structure of Sino-Indian Rapprochement. Moreover, the encouraging sign of economic cooperation and growing trade relationship need to be underlined. Finally, the adoption of declaration on principles for relations and comprehensive cooperation between India and China marked the reconstruction of Sino-Indian Rapprochement in a more balanced way. But it remains to be seen as to how this is effectively translated into reality.

References

1. Annual Report, 1998-99, Ministry of External Affairs, Government of India, p. 31.
2. Cited in C.V. Ranganathan and Vinod C. Khanna, India and China : The Way Ahead-After : Mao's India War; Har Anand Publications, New Delhi, 2000, p. 175.
3. John W. Garver, "the Restoration of Sino-Indian Comity following India's

Nuclear Tests," China Quarterly, 168, December 2001, p. 580.

4. Cited in Fang Tien-Sze, "The Sino-Indian Border Talks Under the Joint Working Group," Issues and Studies, 38, 3, September, 2002, pp. 167-168.
5. *Ibid.*, p. 168.
6. See n. 3.
7. Cited in W.P.S. Sidhu and Jing-dong Yuan, "Resolving The Sino-Indian Border dispute," Asian Survey, 41, 2, March 2001, p. 358.
8. See n. 3.
9. See n. 7.
10. Faisal O Al-Afouh, "Sino-Indian Relations : From Confrontation to Accommodation (1988-2001)," China Report, 39, 1, 2003, p. 32.
11. See n. 3, pp. 880-81.
12. Xinhua, 14 June 1999 in FBIS-CHI-1999-0614.
13. Cited in n. 3, p. 883.
14. Hindu, June 15, 1999.
15. See for details, Maj. Gen (retd.) Ashok Mehta, "Putting the Past Behind," in http://www.rediff.com, dt. 21-6-99.
16. See n. 3, p. 884.
17. Cited in Xia Liping, "China-India security Relationship : Retrospects and Prospects" in A presentation collection for conference on India in 21st century : External Relations, SIIS Publications, Shanghai, 2002, pp. 108-09.
18. Cited in *Ibid.*, p. 109.
19. Ma Jiali, "China and India – Striving Towards a Constructive, Cooperative Partnership," Indian Defence Review, 15, 4, October 2000, p. 25.
20. SWB, FE/3784, March 9, 2000, G/2.
21. *Ibid.*, FE/3785, March 10, 2000, A/3.
22. *Ibid.*, A/4.
23. Cited in n. 3, p. 885.
24. *Ibid.*
25. Cited in *Ibid.*, p. 886.
26. *Ibid.*, p. 885
27. See for details, Beijing Review, 42, 27, 5 July, 1999, p. 15.
28. Cited in n. 10, p. 32.
29. People's Daily, January 14, 2001.
30. See for details, John Cherian, "Li Peng in India" Frontline, 18, 3, 3 February 2001, p. 127.
31. See n. 3, p. 886.
32. Pioneer 18 and 19 January 2001, in FBIS-CHI-2001-0118 and FBIS-CHI-2001-0119.
33. Cited in n. 3, p. 887.
34. SWB, FE/4067, February 10, 2001, A/2.

35. News from China, 14, 2, January 15, 2002, Embassy of People's Republic of China, New Delhi, p.2.
36. See n. 10, p. 33.
37. Wenhui Daily, 15 January, 2002.
38. Cited in n. 35, p. 8.
39. *Ibid.*
40. *Ibid.*, pp. 6-7.
41. *Ibid.*, p. 7.
42. *Ibid.*, p. 8.
43. *Ibid.*
44. See for details, V.V. Paranjpe, "Agenda of Hope," *Hindustan Times*, 14 January, 2002, Bhabani Sen Gupta "the Importance of Zhu Rongji's Visit," Pioneer, 15 January, 2002 and K.K. Katyal, "The Zhu Visit," Hindu, 28 January, 2002.
45. See M.V. Rappai, "Time for Some Hard Talk," Pioneer, 13 January, 2002.
46. *Ibid.*
47. C. Raja Mohan, "Jaswant Singh Heads East," Hindu, 29 March, 2002.
48. http://www.fmprc.gov.cn.dt 28th March, 2002.
49. Cited in John Cherian, "India and China : Some Positive Movement," Frontline, April 26, 2002, p. 48.
50. *Ibid.*
51. *Ibid.*, p. 49.
52. See the text of Minister's Address and Q & A's transcript, Shanghai, April 1, 2002 in http://meadev.nic.in/speeches/campc-siis.htm
53. "Chinese, Indian Officials Meet on Countering Terrorism," http://english.peopledaily.com.cn/200204/24/eng20020424_94599.html.
54. Dr. Swaran Singh, "United States' War on Terrorism and its Impact on India-China Ties", in n. 17, p. 123.
55. See http://fmprc.gov-cn/eng/30809.html dt 5-6-2002.
56. *Ibid.*
57. See the Full text of Jiang Zemin's Report at 16th Party Congress on November 8, 2002 available in http://www.fmprc.gov-cn/eng/37815.html.
58. See http://fmprc.gov-cn/eng/40334.html.
59. C. Uday Baskar, "Small Leap Forward", *Times of India*, May 13, 2003.
60. See http://fmprc.gov-cn/eng dt. 31-5-03.
61. See http://fmprc.gov-cn/eng/51023.html.
62. See for details, Brahma Chellaney, "Beware the dragon's designs," *Hindustan Times*, June 8, 2003.
63. V.V. Paranjpe, "Climb over the Wall," *Hindustan Times*, June 17, 2003.
64. V.P. Dutt, "It's time for détente with China" *Hindustan Times*, June 22, 2003.

65. Anand K. Sahay, "Taste of China", *Hindustan Times*, June 23, 2003.
66. Dr. Sri Kanth Kondapalli, "India-China : Neither friends nor enemies," http://www.rediff.com dt 19.6.03.
67. See for details n. 59.
68. Cited in, "China a threat : MOD report," *Hindustan Times*, May 31, 2003.
69. http://www.meadev.nic.in/govt/int xinhua.new.htm dt. 21-6-03.
70. See for details, Amit Baruah, "Taking a New Road," Frontline, July 18, 2003, pp. 4-12.
71. See the full text in Hindu, June 25, 2003 and http://www.meadev.nic.in/foreign/ind-china.htm, and http://www.fmprc.gov-cn dt. 24-6-03.
72. http://www.fmprc.gov-cn/eng/51768.html.
73. Ibid/51775.html.
74. See the text of Prime Minister's Speech at Peking University, 23 June, 2003 in http://www.meadev.nic.in/speeches/pmpeking Unvi.htm.
75. http://www.fmprc.gov-cn/eng/51620.html.
76. Mira Sinha Bhattacharjea, "A new Phase," Frontline, July 18, 2003, p. 12.
77. N. Ram, "Towards a Cooperative Partnership, Frontline, July 18, 2003, pp. 8-9.
78. SWB/FE/3849, May 25, 2000, G/2.
79. *Ibid.*, G/1.
80. SWB/FE/3919, August 8, 2000, G/1.
81. SWB/FE/3952, September 22, 2000, G/1.
82. Cited in n. 10, p. 33.
83. *Times of India*, May 19, 2001.
84. *Hindustan Times*, May 23, 2001.
85. See for details, n. 59.
86. *Ibid.*
87. See the text of speech by Shri George Fernandes at the National Defence University, Beijing, April 22, 2003, Strategic Digest, 33, 5, May 2003, pp. 364-65.
88. *Ibid.*, p. 365.
89. On the Chinese Perspective of military-to-military relations, See for details, Fan Zhenjiang, "China and India – Military to Military Relations," Indian Defence Review, 15, 4, October 2000, pp. 19-22.
90. Cited in John Cherian, "Right Signals, positive Moves,: Frontline, July 18, 2003, p. 18. See also, "India, China to Chart New Course with naval exercise," Hindustan Times, June 28, 2003.
91. Cited in W.P.S. Sidhu and Jing-dong Yuan, "Resolving the Sino-Indian Border Dispute," Asian Survey, 41, 2, March 2001, p. 356.
92. Cited in Sri Kanth Kondapalli, "India-China Border Perspectives," in n. 17, p. 143.
93. Cited in n. 4, p. 168.

94. Cited in n. 3, p. 883.
95. Cited in n. 4, p. 153.
96. Hindu, November 29, 1999.
97. See n. 92.
98. See n. 4, p. 152.
99. Annual Report 2000-2001, Ministry of External Affairs, GOI, p. 28.
100. See n. 91.
101. Hindu, April 30, 2000.
102. *Ibid.*, May 30, 2000.
103. "Summary of Press Briefing by the Official Spokesperson" June 22, 2001, Ministry of External Affairs, GOI, available in http://meadev.nic.in/news/20010622.htm.
104. See n. 4, p. 175.
105. Hindu, November 25, 2000.
106. SWB, FE/4038, January 8, 2001, G/1.
107. Hindu, June 30, 2001.
108. *Ibid.*, August 13, 2001.
109. See n. 4, p. 153.
110. *Ibid.*
111. Cited in John Cherian, "India and China : Some Positive Movement," Frontline, April 26, 2002, p. 48.
112. *Ibid.*
113. *Ibid.*
114. Cited in C-Raja Mohan, "Border dispute with China can be resolved," Hindu, April 2, 2002.
115. See n. 4, p. 153.
116. *Ibid.*, p. 171.
117. See n. 76, p. 13.
118. *Ibid.*, p. 14.
119. *Ibid.*
120. See the full text of the Joint Declaration n. 71.
121. Amit Baruah, "Taking a New Road," July 18, 2003, p. 10.
122. See n. 76, p. 14.
123. See the text of declaration on border trade in Hindu, June 25, 2003.
124. See n. 77, p. 9.
125. See n. 76, p. 16.
126. Sujit Dutta, "India's Gain on Sikkim Comes at a price," *Sahara Times*, July 5, 2003.
127. Alka Acharya, "Fences, Fancies and Inferences," *Hindustan Times*, June 29, 2003.
128. Cited in PTI, "India, China both gainers, says Sinha, *Hindustan Times*, June 26, 2003.
129. *Ibid.*
130. *Ibid.*

131. Sudhi Ranjan Sen, "As PM visited China, its army visited Arunachal," *Hindustan Times*, July 24, 2003.
132. Cited in, "Intrusion Violates agreement : India," *Hindustan Times*, July 26, 2003.
133. See the statement http://ww.fmprc.gov.cn dt. 25-7-2003.
134. S.R. Sen, "China Intrusion to dominate CCS meet," *Hindustan Times*, August 15, 2003.
135. Jay Raina, "Build nation, not Shrines," *Hindustan Times*, August 15, 2003.
136. See for details of border transgressions, n. 92, pp. 146-48.
137. Cited in A.G. Noorani, "Fall of the map," *Hindustan Times*, July 8, 2003.
138. See n. 4, p. 183.
139. S.K. Singh, "Slow cranes flying," *Hindustan Times*, July 9, 2003.
140. See, "Boosting Trade," *Hindustan Times*, June 28, 2003.
141. See n. 10, p. 37.
142. Priya Ranjan Dash, "Dragon is no threat, exports to China double, "*Times of India*, May 27, 2003.
143. *Ibid.*
144. *Ibid.*
145. Cited in, China Report, 39, 2, 2003, pp. 200-01.
146. Cited in Gulshan Sachdeva, "India-China Economic Cooperation in a Growth Quadrangle"? in Kanti Bajpai and Amitabh Mattoo, eds, The Peacock and the Dragon : India-China Relations in the 21st Century, Har Anand Publications, New Delhi, 2000, p. 223.
147. Cited in "Strengthening India-China Trade" World Focus, 224, February 2000, p. 24.
148. Cited in "India, China Sign Pact on WTO," *Ibid.*
149. *Ibid.*
150. See for details, Wang Hongwei, "Sino-Indian economic and scientific cooperation promising," Beijing Review, 7 March 2002, pp. 7-9. See also, n. 35, pp. 3-11.
151. See n. 111, p. 48.
152. See n. 90, p. 17.
153. Cited in Sheela Bhatt, "A business boost for Sino-Indian ties," in http://www.rediff.com dt. 21-6-03.
154. Cited in Amit Baruah, "Quality of ties with China has Changed, says Vajpayee," *Hindu*, June 25, 2003.
155. *Ibid.*
156. Times News Network, "Sikkim trade route to herald new era," *Times of India*, June 25, 2003.
157. Cited in the text of Joint Declaration, see the full text in n. 71.
158. Cited in K.A. Badrinath, "India, China set to cut import duties,"

Hindustan Times, June 28, 2003.

159. Cited in n. 153.

160. Cited in, “Agreements/MOUs between India and China,” strategic digest, 33, 5, May 2003, p. 378.

161. Cited in B.M. Gupta and SM Dhawan,” India’s collaboration with People’s Republic of China in Science and Technology,” China Report, 39, 2, 2003, p. 202.

162. *Ibid.*, p. 201.

163. *Ibid.*

164. See for details n. 150, pp. 10-11.

165. See no. 71.

166. See no. 160.

167. See no. 71.

168. See no. 10, p. 34.

9

The Regional Context

Situated at the geo-political centres of Central Asia and West Asia on one hand to East Asia and South East Asia on the other, South Asia occupies an important geo-strategic position. The Regional Context of Sino-Indian interaction in cold war period meant South Asia, but in the post cold war period, it has been increasingly seen as Southern Asia. As an Indian analyst wrote," South Asia is defined as the region that stretches from Iran and Afghanistan in the South West to Myanmar in South-East and the Indian ocean .... The principal country in the region is India. India's strategic reach and geopolitical weight; its pivotal location straddling the busy sea lanes of the Indian-Ocean in the South, East, and West Asia on its flanks, and China, Central Asia and Russia on the north; gives meaning and makes sense to South. Asia... Myanmar, Bangladesh on one side and Afghanistan, Pakistan and Iran on the other, or Nepal and Bhutan in the north and Sri Lanka or Maldives in the South have very limited strategic linkages. However, they all be come an integral-part of South Asia as a region because India binds and links each of them into a unit."[1]

Geopolitical Conflict

It is precisely in this region that India and China interacted at many levels. In the Cold war period, from the year 1949 to be precise, as PRC took over Tibet since then, China became 'an integral part of the Southern Asian geopolitical and strategic environment'. As a leading proponent of School of Geopolitical School of thought described : "Sharp conflict between national policies erupted over Tibet in 1949 as the Chinese People's Liberation Army (PLA) was preparing to occupy that region. Conflicting policies over Tibet contributed substantially to war in 1962 and have plagued Sino-Indian relations ever since. Disagreements over Tibet are linked to others dealing with the entire Himalayan region. From 1949 through 1999 India and China have viewed the Status of Nepal, Bhutan, and Sikkim very differently. India has insisted on establishing a special relation with those regions, one that guarantees India's Security interests regarding China. Beijing, on the other hand, has insisted on establishing on its right to conduct the full range of regular state-to-state relations with those entities and has viewed Indian assertions to the contrary as acts of hegemonism. In the mid-1950's China reached a strategic understanding with Pakistan founded on their convergent interests vis-a-vis India. Successive Chinese and Pakistan regimes have maintained and deepened this strategic entente, much to India's dismay."[2]

Carrying forward the argument of 'dominance of Geopolitical Conflict' in Sino-Indian relations, John W. Garver further wrote : "Across the Indian Ocean and South Asian region, India watches warily as China expands its military and political roles, fearing that it is sliding into a state of "strategic encirclement" by China. Fundamental uncertainty is introduced into the Sino-Indian relationship by an unresolved territorial dispute, with China claiming virtually an entire Indian state and India claiming a strategically important western route into Tibet. That territorial dispute triggered a month-long intense war in 1962... Since 1962 the territorial dispute has slid several times into tense confrontation. The resolution of the territorial dispute also touches on the security of India's northeastern states and that of China's Tibet."[3] Without further minutely debating into Garver's assertions, the point which is being made here is that partly the element of geopolitical conflict is true secondly, there is wide gap between India and China on regional issues, which acts as a hindrance in the rapprochement.

The Optimists

The other School of thought led by C.V. Ranganathan, Vinod C. Khanna, who in a more optimistic way argue that 'India-China relations are not an all-or-nothing proposition, but a mixed bag of issues with varying degrees of solvability.' The assertion in some ways is true but in overall analysis the school depicts China as a benign power, which appears to be rather simplistic. Ranganathan and Khanna argue that "For obvious reasons, India has watched China's relations with other South Asian Countries with very keen interest. In the worst period of India-China relations, in the 1960's and early 1970's, China seemed to go out of its way to build linkages with India's neighbours to fit them into a larger anti-Indian design.

Over the last two decades, there has been, from India's point of view, a gradual change for the better. Sino-Pak relations, however, continue to be a source of great concern to India...."[4] Aside from overall optimistic note, the seasoned diplomats concede the point about anti-Indian designs of China during the cold war period. In the post cold war period, they point about China facing a 'dilemma. Ranganathan and Khanna wrote, "On the one hand, it has to be very careful in responding to any Pakistani request for further assistance in the nuclear weapon and missile fields because of the American pressure, its own international treat, commitments, its interest in stable Sino-Indian relations and its own security concerns. On the other hand, it would not like to see the nuclear power balance in the sub-continent tilt to heavily in India's favour."[5] Apart from the benign depiction of China, the optimist school of thought does have shades of pragmatism as well.

As such, willy-nilly the authors point out the pursuance of balance of power against India in post cold war phase. In the chapter entitled, "The special case of Pakistan" the authors conclude in a careful and cautions way that "In the meanwhile, unless there is a very significant reduction in China's military collaboration with Pakistan, Particularly in nuclear and missile fields, there will continue to be a widespread perception in India that China pursues a deliberate anti-Indian strategy in its relationship with Pakistan. Many in India will continue to argue that China's objective is to constrain India by a threat of a two front war and by locking it within South Asia so that it cannot emerge as a rival to China on the wider regional and global stage."[6] Indeed, the authors discern the element of competitiveness between the two important nation states at regional as well as global level. On balance, this school of thought on the whole appears to be optimistic while they are aware of the complexities of regional dimension of India-China multifaceted interactions.

Cold War Period

From 1949 to 1991, China traversed a long way in steady manner and registered a robust influence in South Asia. China began in the early sixties from a position of weakness in the region, its evolving close relationship with Pakistan was a nation with limited capabilities and politically unstable. The political leadership of China adopted the policy of real politic on one hand and appeared as reasonable power before the smaller South Asian nations, on the other hand. In order to safeguard the precarious balance of power between Pakistan and prevent the emergence of an India controlled sub-continent, China gradually developed close defence relations with Pakistan-China carefully nurtured its alliance with Pakistan and skillfully broadened the base of relations which included not only the mutuality of strategic interests but also economic and development interests. Nevertheless, the visibility of strategic culture and translating into reality by building roads, penetrating into the region, giving political support to regimes etc, pointed unmistakably towards integrated and long term planning by China.

China adopted the same tactics and developed close and cordial relationship with other smaller states of South Asia, i.e., Nepal, Bhutan, Bangladesh and Sri Lanka. In the cold war period, China's policy towards the region was primarily determined by the state of its relations with India. As from the late 1950's China's relations with Indian begin to deteriorate, China encouraged unfriendly and even hostile relations between India and the other nations of South Asia. As a result of the hostile policy, China clearly acted against India's security interest in the region.

The South Asian dimension proved an important factor in Sino-Indian interaction. The conflicting perceptions of India and China towards South Asia generated tension and further aggravated the overall relationship. China, perceived itself as a part of the region because of geographical contiguity, historical linkages and common heredity with the Mongoloid group of people in the region. Further, China Shares borders with Afghanistan, Pakistan, India, Nepal, Bhutan and Myanmar. Indeed, the South Asian nations hold the key to stability and security of its two trouble-turned Autonomous Regions of Tibet and Xinjiang. As a result of all these facts, China Considered it natural to get involved in the intra-regional affairs of the region. Moreover, China's interest in the region stemmed from the perception of its security threat and status as well as regional and global roles.

Notwithstanding the continuity of conflicting perceptions between both sides, from early 1980's a nuanced shift in China's South Asian policy was discernible. The important constituting elements were following: firstly, China desired to normalise its relationship with India and took initiatives in this regard. Second, China now encouraged bilateral settlement of the outstanding problems between India and its neighbours. Third, China enthusiastically welcomed the process of regional cooperation in the region as a positive development. Last but not least, China decided to retrain from taking any stand on the internal political crises in any of the South Asian nations.

However, the important point to note here is that China continued to cultivate. India's neighbours in its quest for long-term interest to balance India. China did not wish to downgrade its existing relationships with other South Asian nations and defence relations with them continued unabatedly. It continued to transfer missiles, missile technologies and nuclear weapons technology. In the later phase of cold war period, Sino-Pakistan relationship continued to evolve into an autonomous relationship irrespective of India's grave security concerns arising out of Sino-Pak enduring defence relations in particular in weapons of Mass-Destruction. The Indian security analysts, maintained that there was Sino-Pakistani nexus against India, which sought to cap Indian power and influence in the region. The reasoning is that China has supported Pakistan in its core national interests and helped make the latter a formidable military power only to check a potential Indian challenge to Chinese preponderance in Asia. Taken to its logical conclusion, such a line of thinking tends to argue that, as China wants to assert its presence more in the Northeast and Southeast Asian regions, it makes perfect strategic sense to "build up" Pakistan not only to contain and neutralize Indian power, but also to tie India down in sub-continental concerns.[7] Nonetheless, by mid 1980's the political leadership of China were learning to manage the ambiguous complexities of international relations without making unduly restrictive choices or becoming identified with one side or other side. In this context, Chinese leaders however, emphasised that the gradual amelioration of Sino-India relations would not take place at the expense of China's existing relationship in South Asia. A western analyst looks at the Regional context of Sino-Indian interaction and terms as 'the delinking of Sino-Indian Rapprochement and Sino-Pakistani Relations'. He wrote : "Several broad policies served Beijing's interest in sustaining its entente with Pakistan while engineering rapprochement with India. The most important of these was covert assistance to Pakistan's nuclear weapons program. Another Chinese policy designed to handle these contradictory PRC interests was to persuade India to delink Sino-Pakistan and Sino-Indian relations.... Improvements in Sino-Indian relations should not be held hostage to intractable issues like the border dispute or Sino-Pakistan relations."[8] Be that as it may be, one thing is for sure that despite Chinese attempts 'to persuade India to delink Sino-Pakistan and Sino-Indian relations', India never agreed. There was no way India could ever agree to such Chinese attempt.

The Triangular Relationship

Another framework of summarising the regional context is the argument of 'India-China-Pakistan as a strategic Triangle'. In the words of an Indian expert of International Relations, "a triangular strategic relationship implies the following : first, that the three countries are more or less independent actors free to take their own decisions (actor autonomy); second, that each state is constantly aware that its behaviour towards any one state in the triangle has implications for the other (interdependence); third, that at any given time, there is a tendency for two of the countries to gang-up against the third (alliance-formation); and finally, that all three expect the mutually-influencing relationship to endure for sometime (protractedness). Actor autonomy, interdependence of decision-making, alliance-formation, and protractedness-all these mark the India-China-Pakistan relationship."[9]

Further elaborating the triangular relationship, the expert wrote : "Historically, India, China and Pakistan have constituted a nuclear strategic triangle. Since China's first nuclear test in 1964, Indian thinking about nuclear issues has been strongly influenced by Beijing's decision to become a nuclear weapon state. As India's nuclear programme grew, and after 1974 when India first tested a nuclear device, Pakistan has tied its nuclear choices to India's ... Pakistan turned to China for nuclear assistance... This link has been maintained for a quarter of a century and has ramified into the area of missile cooperation. The Pakistan-China nuclear link has, in turn, intensified India's desire for nuclear weapons. The Indian government suggested in May 1998 that its decision to test five nuclear devices was related to the continuing cooperation between Pakistan and China on nuclear and missile related techonologies."[10]

However, the limitation of triangular relations becomes apparent because 'only India has publicly acknowledged and indeed insisted on the linkages between India, China and Pakistan'. Pointing out this aspect, the expert wrote : "China refuses to admit that its nuclear weapons programme has had any effect on the South Asian decisions. In particular, it denies that India's decision to become a nuclear weapon power is related to China's weapon programme or to China's nuclear links with Pakistan. Pakistan also rejects the notion that India has any serious anxieties about Chinese nuclearisation, even though Islamabad links its own nuclear program to India's."[11] Limitations aside, the framework is useful only for comprehending Sino-Pak relations, which only is one set of the overall regional context.

China's Perception of the Region in Post Cold War Period

China's perception of the region could be seen in terms of change and continuity. In this backdrop, an analyst wrote : "In his first meeting with kissinger in July 1971, Zhou described the South Asian subcontinent as a prime area of "turmoil under heaven" and this remains the case thirty years later with the ongoing war on terrorism and the India-Pakistan nuclear stand off."[12] The description of South Asia as an area of "turmoil under heaven" is significant and goes down to suggest China's perception of instability in South Asia, which stems from overall importance of stability in China's scheme of priority. Though in 1960's and even in early 1970's

China politically and economically was far from stable. But when it came to the region like South Asia, China preferred to perceive from the prism of level of hierarchy, which partly may be the product of middle kingdom complex.

A Chinese Scholar observed : "Indian attitude towards its neighbours is like that of a hegemony and it uses force to solve disputes with its neighbours, which affects external relations of this region. India fought four wars with Pakistan, India and Bangladesh also had military clashes. In Sri Lanka, it sent IPKF and interfered in Sri Lanka affairs. India annexed Sikkim. India frequently pressurizes Nepal in the matter of providing support for the transport of imported and export goods.

India did not support the 1971 Sri Lankan proposal to make Indian ocean a Zone of peace and the 1975 Nepalese proposal to make Nepal a Zone of peace... In the matter of problems of South Asia, China has common understanding with many South Asian countries and China's relations with them are rather good..."[13]

Another study by a western scholar pointed out : "Few if any of China's strategic thinkers seem to hold warm or positive views of India for China's future."[14] In the post cold war period, India's Socio-economic indexes were manifestation of a developing country on the move, in particular economic reforms were yielding reasonably good results. But in large measure, the Chinese leadership and analysts were 'Skeptical'.

In the words of another analyst, "Chinese leaders and officials in the early twenty-first century remain as contemptuous of India's socioeconomic achievements and as dismissive of New Delhi's claims of being "the world's largest democracy" as were Mao and Zhou in the 1960's and 1970's... Much like Zhou, his successors are uncomfortable with India's "great power dreams" (daguomeng), especially the ultra-nationalist view of India's history propounded by the BJP-led nationalist forces. There exists in the Chinese mind a deep distrust of India-with the converse also holding true... They believe that India's rise is not in China's interests because acceptance of South Asia as India's sphere of influence would undermine China's role and stature as the preeminent power in Asia."[15]

It was in this context that China continued to pursue balance of power in the region but in a nuanced way. However, the military relations with other South Asian nations, especially with Pakistan remain unaltered.

Commenting on China's Regional posture in the period, an Indian analyst wrote : "As neighbouring states, each is affected — some positively and some negatively – by China's military power, posture, strategic thinking, and evolving role. China thus shapes in a major way the regional balance of power and security environment. Only India has common borders with a greater number of states in the region than China. Beijing has over the years also developed some of its closest external relationships in the region built on defense and intelligence ties, military transfers, and political support. Unlike China's ties in East Asia where they are essentially economic, its South Asian ties are primarily politico-military in content."[16] Thus, the Chinese in a nuanced way continued to cultivate India's neighbouring nations and defence relations was important means to serve China's national interest in the region. The official line of China, as articulated by the foreign ministry was that "China is willing to maintain and develop friendly relations with India, Pakistan, and all countries in South Asia on the basis of the Five Principles of peaceful coexistence."[17]

Sino-Pak Relations in Post Cold War Period

The salience of Sino-Pak relations did not diminish despite the end of cold war, the disintegration of Soviet Union and improvement in Sino-Indian relations. China's motives in maintaining close relations with Pakistan are to balance India by building up Pakistan, gaining access to Pakistan's US supplied advanced conventional weapons system and cultivating an Islamic state. In the words of an Indian analyst, "China's attempt to use Islam as a political tool was a dangerous policy to enhance its image in the third world and Islamic world. At times it also presented itself as a defender of Islam or even as an honorary Muslim state by Championing the cause of Palestine and supporting Islamic holy war in Afghan resistance during 1980's. In 1987, China told visiting Chairman of ICO that one billion Chinese and one billion Muslims could be a great force against any sort of hegemonism."[18] A Chinese Scholar looked at Pakistan as an alternative centre of Islamic civilization and therefore a nucleus country of Islamic civilization. He even tried to explain nuclear tests conducted by India and Pakistan in 1998 and Kashmir issue as a conflict between two civilizations, viz., Islamic and Hindu civilizations.[19]

Apart from Islamic factors and others, Sino-Pak entente primarily emerged to balance India. As an analyst wrote about the regional context, "for Beijing sustaining a strong Pakistan independent of Indian domination and linked militarily to China is a fundamental element of maintaining a position of strength vis-a-vis India. If India were able to uncouple China and Pakistan, subordinate Pakistan, or destroy its military – potential, India would be able to concentrate its forces against China... In other words, a prudent Chinese policy would sustain Pakistan against India."[20] In this context, a Chinese work assumes importance in that 'the study said, under certain circumstances India's leaders might decide on war with China. The main precondition for such a war would be to improve India's relations with Pakistan so that India could avoid a two-front war'.[21]

Furthermore, China wanted to maintain a tested relationship with Pakistan as a Shining example of cooperation between the two developing nations. In many ways, China noted the changes in the post cold war period. At the international level with the disintegration of Soviet Union, the bipolar world came to an end. As a result, in South Asia USA showed less interest. By this time, U.S. had already imposed Sanctions on Pakistan under the presser amendment. Therefore, for Pakistan establishing further close relationship with China became more urgent.

The 14th congress of Communist Party of China held in 1992 in its political report noted the fact that 'the bipolar pattern has ended'. But at the same time the report recognised that 'the formation of a new political pattern will be protracted and complex'. Moreover, the worry some and unstable features as well as contradiction of emerging international power politics made the party anxious. The report further stated that "there are still all kinds of contradictions in the world, ethnic disturbances, territorial disagreements and religious disputes have occurred in many countries and have even developed into bloody conflicts and regional wars".[22] The above mentioned conditions were there in South Asia as well in general and Pakistan in particular.

Political Aspects

Sino-Pak relations were defined as an 'all weather friendship'. Both sides emphasised the point that the Sino-Pak bilateral relationship have become a model for nations with different social systems to develop their relations. Before going into details a point needs to be mentioned. According to an Indian analyst during early 1960's when China's relations with India deteriorated, relations between China and Pakistan began to develop. While the border negotiations between China and Pakistan was underway on January 1962, the Chinese government asked from Pakistani government for a written understanding (Shumian Liangjie) on relationship with China vis-a-vis its membership of two military organisations (SEATO and CENTO) and clarifications on earlier assurances/guarantees (baozheng). On March 19, 1962 the then Pakistani Ambassador to China brought along all the previous written clarifications (Shumian dengqing) provided by his government.[23] As Pakistan was USA's military ally, therefore the alliance constituted a security threat to China. The master of real politic that the Chinese political leadership were, as such only after written explanations (Shumian Jieshi) from the government of Pakistan that the obstacles could be removed and Sino-Pak relations evolved smoothly. Pakistan was dissatisfied with its alliance with the US at that point of time, as it was not dependable due to pursuance of the policy of paying importance to India and thereby slighting Pakistan (Zhongyin qingba). Thus with one concrete action by China, it met its strategic objective in the South Asia.

Features of Political Aspects

It is pertinent to underline the important features of political aspects of bilateral relations. First, Pakistan regarded development of its relations with China as 'cornerstone of its foreign policy'. China's response to the internal developments in Pakistan was testimony to the fact that friendly relations with Pakistan would not be affected by change in nature of regime or change of personalities. Secondly, there was a tradition of frequent exchange of high level visits during which the leadership shared their views on bilateral, regional and international issues.[24] Further, during the visits and interactions both sides expressed mutual support on critical issues like Pakistan on 'One China Policy', against separatist tendencies in Tibet and Xinjiang and China on broad issue like sovereignty and territorial integrity of Pakistan, Kashmir at a broad level.

In the words of an Indian analyst, "Before the conclusion of Sino-Pak border agreement in 1963, the Prime Minister of the two countries exchanged visits only once in 1956. However, after 1963 the bilateral visits have been more regular and helped to deepen the cooperation between the two governments. Visit pattern (See Table No. 1) shows that Pakistan leaders visited China more frequently than the Chinese leaders. Moreover, the Pakistani leaders on resumption of office paid first foreign visit to China. Also, whenever Pakistan was confronted with crisis the higher leadership visited Beijing to consult with the Chinese leadership."[25]

Furthermore, China noted the common approach of South Asian nations to concentrate on economic development in particular reforms programme in post cold war period. Almost all of the regional countries began to emphasis on the competition for overall national strengths on the basis of developing the economy. At the same time, China commented positively about the preeminent regional power, India's efforts to improve its relations with most of its south Asian neighbours. However, China underlined 'the Indo-Pak contradiction as the major contradiction' in the region and the intensification of the Kashmir issue.[26]

Table 1

Visits to Pakistan	*Visits to China*
President Yang Shangkun Oct 1991	P.M. Nawaz Sharif — Oct. 1992
CPPCC Chairman Li Ruihuan Dec. 1993	P.M. Benazir Bhutto — Dec. 1993
NPC Chairman Qiaoshi Nov. 1995	President Farooq Leghari — Dec. 1994
President Jiang Zemin Dec. 1996	P.M. Benazir Bhutto — Sept. 1995
NPC Chairman Li Peng April 1999	President Farooq Leghari — April 1997
Premier Zhu Rongji May 2001	P.M. Nawazsharif — Feb. 1998
	P.M. Nawazsharif — June 1999
	Chief Executive General Pervez Musharraf — Jan. 2000.
	President P. Musharraf — Dec. 2001
	President P. Musharraf — Jan. 2002
	P.M. Zafarullah Khan — Mar. 2003

Source: Ministry of Foreign Affairs, Pakistan http://www.forisb.org/pak_china.html and Ministry of Foreign Affairs, PRC http://www.fmprc.cn.in/eng/9408.html.

Throughout the post cold war phase, Pakistan continued to seek the help of China on Kashmir issue. China on the other hand, continued to advise Pakistan to resolve the issue through dialogue. A western analyst on Sino-Indian relations has shown evolution of the China position on Kashmir in the tabular method :

Table 2

Nov. 16, 1989 Li Peng TV interview in Pakistan	Should "resolve on the basis of the five principles of peaceful coexistence and through friendly consultations."
Feb. 15, 1990 Li Peng to Akhund	Should "act in accord with relevant UN resolutions and accords reached by both countries, and resolve the dispute on the basis of friendly consultations."
Feb. 20, 1990 Qin Tiwei to Bhutto	Should "solve the Kashmir issue in accordance with the relevant United

	Nations resolutions and agreements between the two countries."
March 23, 1990 Qian-Qichen in New Delhi	Should "resolve problems through mutual peaceful consultations on the basis of the Five Principles of Peaceful coexistence." The Kashmir issue " has been discussed by the United Nation."
April 18, 1990 MFA-Spokesman	Should "Seek a peaceful solution through negotiations."
May 8, 1990 Li Peng to Nusrat Bhutto	Should "Seek a peaceful solution through mutual consultation."
May 24, 1990 MFA Spokesman	Should "work to ease tension through dialogue."
December 15, 1991 Li Peng during India visit	"As for disputes between India and Pakistan, we hope the two countries will settle them properly through negotiations... and will not resort to force."

Source: John W. Garver, Protracted Contest, New Delhi, 2001, p. 230.

In the year 1994, Pakistan in fact sent a special envoy to China, who met with the Chinese Foreign Minister, Qian Qichen. The special envoy stated that Pakistan intended to move a resolution in Human Rights commission in Geneva.[27] When Pakistan tabled resolution on human rights violation in Kashmir at Geneva, China advised Pakistan not to move the resolution.[28] China did not support the move partly because it feared US intervention on the pretext of human rights issue in its internal affairs, particularly on Tibet. Commenting on China's policy on Kashmir in post cold war phase, the observation of a western analyst is noteworthy on the level of China's deterrent support of Pakistan he wrote : "In this area too, China distanced itself from Pakistan during the process of Sino-Indian rapprochement. By deterrent Support I mean threats, explicit or implicit, that China might enter a military conflict on the side of Pakistan. Such support was an important component of the Sino-Pakistani relation during the 1960's, 1970's and 1980's."[29] Thus, this subtle shift in China's policy on Kashmir was noted in India much to the chagrin of Pakistan.

In the post cold war period, Chinese foreign policy was largely motivated by its domestic agenda. China aimed at the maintenance of stability in its neighbourhood for concentrating on development and modernization. It was in this background that Chinese President Jiang Zemin visited India in November 1996 to further consolidate bilateral ties with India. During his India visit both Asian giants concluded Agreement on Confidence Building Measures in the military field along the Line of Actual Control in the India-China border areas. Commenting on this important development, the spokesman of foreign ministry of Pakistan said that the Sino-Indian border agreement was not a source of concern for Pakistan. He said Pakistan understood China's policy of freezing its disputes with India. He further added that, "we have a historical relationship with China which has transcended political changes in both countries and we have full trust and there is complete understanding."[30] An important daily of Pakistan wrote that "for all the atmosphere of amity that has emerged at the New Delhi meeting, the fact remains that China and India are also strategic, military and economic rivals in the region and beyond."[31] Therefore, it underlined the point that Sino-Pakistan Salience for India remained intact.

President Jiang Zemin's Pakistan Visit of 1996

During his visit of Pakistan, Jiang Zemin emphasised on developing the relations in the future in consonance with the emerging economic realities and evolving global political configuration. The visiting Chinese President stated that China was ready to join hands with South Asian Countries in building a good-neighbourly relationship that is long-term, stable and oriented towards the 21st century. Accordingly Jiang proposed several steps such as, broadening exchanges including direct contacts and dialogue between top leaders handing down the friendly relations from generation to generation, promoting-mutual benefit and common development, properly handling existing disputes in the spirit of seeking common grounds while setting aside differences and finally, working together towards a better future through unity and cooperation.

The Chinese President in his address to the Pakistan senate on 2nd December 1996, made the most important point : "we should look at the differences or disputes from a long perspective, seeking a just and reasonable settlement through consultations while bearing in mind the large picture. If certain issues cannot be resolved for the time being, they may be shelved temporarily so that they will not affect the normal state-to-state relations."[32] In fact, China urged Pakistan quite clearly to set aside Kashmir issue and enter into dialogue with India on various CBMs. In the words of Indian experts, "The speech delivered by him (Jiang Zemin) to the Pakistani senate on December 2 was seen as hinting at the end of a special-relationship with Pakistan. The primary focus of the talk was China's relations not with Pakistan but with South Asia as a whole. There appeared to be – from the Pakistani perspective – a disconcerting equation of India and Pakistan. The Pakistani senators could not have relished Jiang's advice 'If certain issues cannot be resolved for the time being, they may be shelved temporarily...' This appeared to apply to Indo-Pak relations, and by implication to Kashmir, a formula which China had succeeded in getting India to accept as far as the Sino-Indian border question was concerned."[33] Furthermore, the media in Pakistan also noted China's modification of pro-Pakistan position on the sensitive Kashmir question. From now onwards, in a way China was not concerned with the escalation of the Kashmir issue since it viewed the issue as strictly 'bilateral'.[34] The Chinese stand on Kashmir was severely criticized by Pakistani media. An important daily wrote : "the fact of the matter is that China has given a free hand to India to play at its will in Kashmir ignoring the right of the Kashmiri people to self determination."[35] Thus, on Kashmir issue the Chinese position shifted and it was 'closer to the Indian stand than that of Pakistan'.

In the post cold war period, China pursued tight rope balance between the two states of the South Asia. It apparently avoided to get bogged down in South Asian politics. China at all costs preferred stability in the region. Firstly, it was concerned with unfolding political uncertainty in Afghanistan and its implications on nearby Xinjiang Autonomous region. Secondly, China was concentrating on building comprehensive national power, where economic modernization was the top priority of the nation. Last but not least, stability in South Asia an important geo-strategic unit of periphery was in China's overall interest at this point of time.[36] However, Pakistan turned down the suggestion of its time tested ally China on this matter. Being the creator and supporter of extremist groups, which took the concrete shape of Taliban, Pakistan simply could not back track from the course it once charted.

Instability in Xinjiang Autonomous Region

The Xinjiang Autonomous Region, Strategically important for China has been instable primarily because of separatist tendencies amongst the uighurs. In the post cold war period, the Islamic independence movement, in particular East Turkestan organisation started resorting to terrorism for realising their aim of establishing East Turkestan in XAR. As such, China was concerned about the growing influence of Taliban and its Pakistan's linkage.[37] The extremists of 'East Turkestan Islamic Movement' received training in Afghanistan as well as Pakistan and on return set up secret cells in Xingjiang to carryout terrorist activities. To meet the challenges of instability. China adopted numerous tactics. Among them an important step was China as well as Russia and three other Central Asian Republics institutionalised the 'Shanghai five partnerships' (later on Shanghai Cooperation Organisation) to meet the Challenges of separatism, extremism and splittism in the region, preserve stability and promote inter state cooperation.[38]

According to an estimate the terrorists provoked more than 200 violent incidents in Xinjiang from 1990 to 2001, which resulted in 170 deaths and 500 injuries. The separatist elements were reported to have links with Taliban, Chechen militants and even Osama Bin Laden etc. It also came to light that about 1000 'East Turkestan' terrorists were trained in Afghanistan.[39] China was well aware of Pakistan's relationship with Taliban. It, therefore, expected from its 'all weather friend'. Pakistan to help China in stopping financial support, training and over all support to uighur separatists. China on its part, also warned Pakistan that uighur Muslim militants were being trained in Afghanistan and madrasas of Pakistan. In fact in year 1997, China sent a list of 12 Uighur extremists wanted in China to Pakistan. Pakistan promptly set them back and six of them were later hanged.[40]

China also established contacts with Taliban through Pakistan. It was reported that a Chinese diplomat visited Kandahar on December 12th, 2000 to discuss the UN sanctions. The visit was in response to a plea by Taliban to China in backdrop of US, Russia move to enforce more strict UN sanctions against Taliban. The three member delegation was led by Chinese ambassador to Pakistan, Lushulin.[41] China was also reported to have paid several million dollars for access to USA's cruise unexploded missiles left over from its attack on Osama Laden's bases in Afghanistan.[42] Thus, China pursued many tactics in dealing with instability in Xinjiang, which influenced its policy in Some ways with Pakistan as well.

Post 1998 Developments

In May 1998, when India conducted nuclear tests, the spokesman of Chinese foreign affairs ministry stated that China is 'deeply shocked by this and expresses its strong condemnation. Before conducting reactive nuke tests after India's test, the Pakistani foreign secretary, Shamshad Ahmed visited Beijing and discussed the developments with Chinese Foreign Minister, Tang Jiaxuan. It was reported that Pakistan took Chinese into confidence before its chagtai tests.[43] China continued its Pro-Pakistan slant and it only expressed its 'deep regret' over Islamabad's nuke tests. China, further helped, its 'all weather friend' in containing international censure of Pakistan.[44] Moreover, China in a veiled threat to India indicated that it could change its 'neutral' stand on Kashmir issue, if the situation warrants in near future.[45]

As the Kargil Conflict escalated in May-June 1999, the Pakistani leadership expected Chinese help. China stated that both South Asian nations should "settle their divergence through peaceful dialogues in a frank and patient spirity". China also urged India to "exercise restraint and relax the current tense situation".[46] But the state controlled Chinese media took pro-Pakistan position. For instance a news daily wrote : "The current situation began on 26 May 1999 when India launched air raids ... India claimed that the operations were aimed at clearing out mujahedeen who had infiltrated into Indian territory. Pakistan urged India to observe restraint... India, however, continued with operations... India had also refused Pakistan's offer of talks to alleviate tension. In May 1998, after both countries conducted nuclear tests, India claimed that it would use force to recover territory in Kashmir. Pakistan had stated that it would use any means necessary to protect its national security. All of this brings Kashmir to the brink of a nuclear crisis."[47]

The Chinese Army's mouthpiece stated : "since the five successive nuclear tests conducted in May last year, more so since April this year, Indian armed forces have been exposing their powerful weapons one by one... All these large-scale advanced weapons development in such a short time undoubtedly indicate to the world India's dream of becoming a military super power... Since the eighties India started pursuing a policy of 'regional deterrence', and a military strategy aimed at seeking a military strength and consolidating on the gains, containing China and deterring Pakistan, Controlling weak and small neighbours, and intercepting big power penetration outside the region and thereby clearing hurdles in its path towards becoming a world power."[48] The media coverage was distinctly pro-Pakistan.

The Chinese response to the visits of Pakistan's foreign minister Sartaz Aziz and Prime Minister in June was simply not encouraging. In fact, Premier Sharif's China visit was cut short from the originally scheduled six days to just two. Further, Chinese President told Sharif of China's hope "that Pakistan and India, out of the fundamental interest of both peoples, will ease tensions between them at an early date." Another top leader, Li Peng stated much to Chagrin of Pakistan that "China always holds that the nuclear and missile rivalry in the region and the tensions in Kashmir are not in the interests of the local people."[49]

Later China advised Pakistan to observe the Line of Control and withdrawal of the Pakistani intruders from Kargil. The spokes-person of the Chinese Foreign Ministry on July 1, 1999 expressed hope that "both India and Pakistan can earnestly respect the LoC in Kashmir." China was concerned over security and stability over its south-western borders. It clearly desired therefore, to avoid taking sides in India-Pakistan conflict. At broader global level, China also apprehended that conflict between its neighbours could enhance America influence in the region. Nonetheless, during Pak's foreign minister visit to Beijing, China re affirmed its commitment to the "Sovereignty and territorial integrity" of Pakistan.[50]

According to John W. Garver, "China assured Aziz of China's deep and abiding interest in and support for the sovereignty, territorial integrity, independence and security of Pakistan. But these statements of support were not publicly announced during Aziz's visit." As such, China on its part, Signaled to Pakistan a shift but in a subtle way.

Commenting on China's reactions to the Kargil conflict two Indian analysts wrote : "Beijing seems to have made a special effort to appear as even-handed as possible. This could not have been of much comfort to Pakistan. When, despite the Kargil conflict, the Chinese persevered with their invitation to the Indian Foreign Minister, Jaswant Singh, to visit China, the Pakistani Foreign Minister, Sartaj Aziz, rushed off for a one day "working visit" to Beijing on June 11, 1999, on the eve of his visit to Delhi... If Sartal Aziz had hoped that he would be able to proceed to Delhi with his diplomatic hand strengthened by a more favourable Chinese position, he must have been disappointed. The Chinese leadership was not willing to extend any public support to Pakistan or to criticize India even by insinuation, or mention UN or any other kind of international intervention."[51]

In the final analysis, Pakistan was disappointed by China's stance on Kashmir in general and Kargil conflict in particular. But the issue of Kashmir is only one of the driving forces of Sino-Pak relations. The fact that Chinese were still committed to the "Sovereignty and territorial integrity" was no mean achievement. Moreover, the close military relationship between the armed forces of both sides continued apace. As a western analyst appropriately summed up Pakistani perception of China in the regional context : "They (Pakistani official and specialists) Saw China as a reliable friend that, unlike the United states, could be counted on in emergencies. Subtleties of language were less important to them than underlying perceptions and purposes, and against these, they were confident, would lead China to continue to support Pakistan against India. They understood Beijing's need to mince words for the sake of placating India but remained confident that when push came to shove, China would be there."[52] Bilaterally, therefore, Sino-Pak relations are still strong and serve national interest of both countries.

Sino-Pak Economic Relations

The bilateral economic relations evolved in the backdrop of political and strategic relationship between both nations. One of the primary objectives of China was to strengthen its mutual relations based on sound economic underpinning, which would nurture, sustain and consolidate the political relations. Thus, the long-term goal was to develop Pakistan as a strong state with viable economic infrastructure. Accordingly, a joint committee on economic, trade and scientific and Technical cooperation was established under an agreement signed in October 1982, after the economic, trade and technical cooperation agreement of February 1965.

The annual volume of bilateral trade is around on billion U.S. dollars (see Table 3).

Table 3. China's Trade with Pakistan

(Million US Dollars)

Year	*Value*	*Exports*	*Imports*	*Balance*
1993	848.63	752.22	96.41	655.81
1994	768.00	606.00	162.00	444.00
1995	1010.80	786.68	223.12	564.56
1996	963.75	621.48	342.27	279.21
1997	1067.00	688.00	379.00	309.00
1998	913.00	524.00	389.00	135.00
1999	971.00	581.00	390.00	191.00
2000	1162.00	670.00	492.00	178.00

Source: Ministry of Foreign Affairs of PRC http://www.fmprc.gov.cm/eng/4408.html.

China's exports to Pakistan basically consist of manufactured engineering and consumer items. Important among them are like machinery and equipment, textile machinery, electrical items, electronics, steel products, pig iron, chemicals, pharmaceutical products, telecommunication applications and fertilizers etc. The imports from Pakistan comprised of raw cotton, leather goods, textile fabrics, chromium ores and concentrates, fish, sugar, petroleum products etc.

As is evident from the table that Pakistan has been facing deficit in the balance of trade with China. As such Pakistan has time and again asked China to correct trade imbalance. However, considering the price and quality Chinese goods are more favourable. Another problem is Pakistan lacks large infrastructure base to produce items at large scale to sustain export oriented demands. The Joint committee on economic cooperation was an institutionalised arrangement and provided for regular consultation to promote bilateral cooperation.

The 11th session of the joint committee was held in Beijing in May 2000. The committee during the meeting discussed Chinese assistance in rehabilitation of Pakistani railways, construction of Gwadar deep seaport, expansion of Pakistani Steel mills and saindak copper complex etc. Final agreements on these projects were concluded during the Pakistan visit of Chinese premier, Zhu Rongji in May 2001. The committee covered discussion to expand cooperation in tele-communication, agriculture, information-technology, urban planning and transportation, oil and gas, small/medium size hydropower plants and other infrastructure developmental projects.[53]

Both sides also established Border Trade organisation which held 16th annual meeting in June 2000 to expand the scope of border trade, its volume. The organisation is expected to play important role in near future in promoting western China Development as well as trade with Central Asian Republics. To impart dynamism in overall economic cooperation, both sides agreed to establish a Business council in 1999 between the Federation of Pakistan Chamber of Commerce & Industry and China Council for the Promotion of International Trade. The Business Council is aimed at enhancing Commercial exchanges, trade and joint ventures and facilitating the resolution of Commercial disputes between trading partners from the two sides.[54] The two government have signed a series of agreements covering promotion of trade and investment, transfer of technology and avoidance of double taxation. Further, in the post cold war period after the emergence of Central Asian Republics both sides are working on several transit routes and one such route is through the Karakoram highways that links Pakistan, China, Kyrgyzstan and Kazathstan. In November 1998 the four nations namely Pakistan, China, Kazakhstan and Kyrgyzstan signed an agreement on "traffic in transit to further promote the existing trade relations through roads from Almaty to Karachi by using the Karakoram highway."[55]

Economic assistance from China constitutes an important aspect of bilateral economic relations. China provided loans to Pakistan on favourable terms with the option of repayments made in the form of locally produced goods. Between 1990-95 loan of $ 218.90 million were extended to Pakistan. And from years 1995 to 1999, loan of $ 80 million were extended to Pakistan. (See Table No. 4) Moreover in 1998, China

Table 4. Economic Assistance from China

(Million US $)

Period	*Grants*	*Loans/Credits*	*Total*
1960-65	60.00	—	60.00
1965-70	46.40	—	46.40
1970-75	—	217.40	217.40
1975-80	—	15.40	15.40
1980-85	—	60.50	60.50
1985-90	—	224.60	224.60
1990-95	—	218.50	218.50
1995-99	12.00	80.00	92.00
Total	118.40	816.40	934.80

Source: Federation of Pakistan Chambers of Commerce and Industry.

extended a medium term loan of $ 150 million as part of a balance of payment support to Pakistan. There has been a shift in Chinese government's economic assistance policy in the period of modernization. Instead of offering interest free loans, now China preferred interest subsidized preferential loans and commercial loans. The last interest free loan document was signed in 1993.[56] Thus, China in reforms period was giving up the tradition of interest free loans and recorded to market principle.

These and previous loans have been used to set up projects in the four provinces including two textile mills in the North West Frontier Province, two Sugar Mills in Sindh and a copper mine in Saindak.[57]

Among the prime example of Sino-Pak economic relations are projects like Heavy-Mechanical complex in Taxila capable of producing machines that would make cement. Sugar, textiles, road building equipment and railway engines. Recently, China has offered special facilities to develop garment and leather industry. It agreed to invest in Pakistan's textile sector by supplying machinery and technological Know-how.

For the purpose, China on its part agreed to provide soft loan of $ 25 million.[58] In the year 2000 both nations signed six memorandum of understanding in the fields of economic and technical cooperation. Similarly in 2001. Pakistan received $ 1.5 billion package of bank deposits and investment from its 'all weather friend'.[59]

The Sino-Pak bilateral economic ties were component of comprehensive relations between both sides. China made it clear that "the Chinese government as always, would continue to take part in Pakistan's economic building, by extending as much economic and technological assistance as possible and also by promoting and encouraging the Chinese companies to invest more and more in Pakistan's economic and trade sectors."[60] In short, Sino-Pak economic relations should not be seen in terms of trade figures and amount of economic assistance. Viewed from Pakistani perspective, Chinese economic support is a part of the overall support to Pakistan.

China-Pakistan Defence Relations

The Sino-Pak defence relations was the most important element of their overall bilateral relationship. The genesis of defence relations goes back to Sino-Indian Conflict of 1962. As early as mid 1960's, the then Indian Foreign Minister. Mr. Swaran Singh stated that China-Pak collusion: "Beginning as a marriage of convenience it was nourished by a common hatred for India and seems to have now become an integral part of the foreign policies of China and Pakistan... We have in our preparation and in our attitude keep always this in mind and all our future actions will have to be carefully taken, keeping this dual danger always before us."[61]

Gradually from mid-1960's onwards, China emerged as the major arms supplier to Pakistan. In the year 1966. Pakistan on the occasion of its national day military parade, displayed at capital city a number of T-59 tanks and MIG-19 fighter planes which it received from China. After 1965, Pakistan received large quantities of military supplier for its army as well as air force from China. Some of the important items included complete equipment for two of its infantry division, about 350 tanks, 120 MIG air crafts, large number artillery pieces, vehicles, spares for tanks and aircraft etc.[62]

Commenting on military aspect of Sino-Pak bilateral relations, a western analyst observed : "Large-scale and sustained assistance to Pakistan's military development has been one of the most important dimensions of the Sino-Pakistani entente. It was unaffected by the Sino-Indian rapprochement... China has been, alongwith the United states, Pakistan's major supplier of military equipment. Of Pakistan's two major suppliers, China has been far more understanding of Pakistan's perspectives. Twice when the United States suspended arms aid to Pakistan – in 1965 and in 1990 – China stepped in to met Pakistan's needs."[63] China transferred weapons for army, navy and air force. (see appendix)

Characteristics of Mutual Defence Cooperation

- China supplied defence equipments continuously unlike the western countries who frequently cut off supplies.
- China helped in the development of modern weapons systems.
- Further, the terms on which it supplied equipment encouraged self reliance as well as indigenisation efforts. Moreover, it provided supply of spare parts, established local production and ancillaries facilities and granted license production etc.
- Financially for Pakistan the Chinese weapon systems were comparatively reasonable and at times credits were made available by China. In cold war period it was available at friendship level costs.
- China supplied weapons of Mass Destruction which included nuclear weapons Know-how, missile and missile technology.
- Overall, the military relationship with China was quite suitable for Pakistan, as it would keep agreements secret and away from the international press.[64]

Defence Cooperation

In the post cold war period, China remained Pakistan's principle supplier of all modernized weapons including conventional, WMD etc. In the period, close Sino-Pak military relations continued apace. In fact, in August 1992 in course of the visit of Pakistan chairman of the Joint

Chiefs of Staff Committee, General Shamim Alam Khan, the Chinese military officials assured the visiting General that "Sino-Pak relations will not be affected by Changes in the international situation."[65] By and large, China on its part followed the assurance.

Earlier during cold war phase, two Heavy Rebuild factories at Taxila and Margala were established between 1971 and 1979 with technological and financial assistance from China. Similarly, other defence industrial centres which came into being later with Chinese assistance included Heavy Mechanical complex at Taxila, Pakistan aeronautical complex at Kamra, Light Air Craft Manufacturing Factory, Pakistan Machine Tool Factory and the Karachi Shipping and Engineering Works.[66] Further, in 1989 both Countries concluded a MOU covering a ten year period for stepping up joint procurement and R & D in defence industries.[67]

Among the important joint projects were following :

Main Battle Tank 2000 (Al-Khalid)

In 1988, it was decided that Pakistan would manufacture new MBTs and build heavy industries – at Taxila – with the Chinese assistance in order to carry out its indigenous programme. The project was approved by Pakistan's Defence committee of the cabinet and subsequently contract with China North Industries Corporation (NORINCO) was concluded in May 1990.[68]

Pakistan pursued a four-phased approach :

- Upgrade the existing T-59 MBT.
- Assembling/manufacture of T-69 II MBT.
- Co-production and manufacture of the T-85 MBT.
- Production of the MBT 2000 with 45 per cent taken from existing vehicles (10 per cent of T-59, 15 per cent T-69II and 20 per cent T-85) and 55 per cent new components. It is expected that 65-70 per cent of key components will be manufactured in Pakistan, 20-25 per cent will be supplied by China and rest will come from other nations.[69]

As mentioned earlier the Heavy-Industries at Taxila built with Chinese assistance – earlier known as Heavy Rebuild Factory – is located 36 km. west of Islamabad. By the end of December 1990, a protocol was concluded with China which included the establishment of the following factories : Hull Fabrication Factory, Turret Manufacturing Factory, Gun Barrel-Manufacturing Factory and Flexible Machining Centre.[70] These facilities have successfully undertaken manufacture of Chinese T-69 II and T-85II AP MBTs. In many respects the MBT 2000 Seems to be identical to the Chinese NORINCO T-90II MBT. As a result of step by step approach, the Pakistan army has placed a contract for the first batch of 15 vehicles, while it is entering production at the Heavy Industries Taxila.[71]

Karakoram 8

K-8 is basic jet trainer/light attack jet which was developed by Nanchang Aircraft Manufacturing Company, Jiangxi and later on decided to be co-developed with Pakistan at Pakistan Aeronautical Complex (PAC), Kamra.[72] As mentioned above, the PAC was established with Chinese assistance at Kamra about 75 km from Islamabad.

K-8E

The K-8E aircraft is a new jet trainer developed by China under Sino-Pak ventures. The aircraft is an upgraded version of K-8 which is designed for training and also for armament operation training.[73]

FC-1

China's fighter aircraft programme launched in 1991 following cancellation of the USA participation in development of Chengdu Super-7. A letter of intent for the joint development by China and Pakistan was concluded in February 1998, which was followed by signature of joint development and production agreement in June 1999. The FC-1 is seen as a potential replacement for shenyang J-6, Chengdu J-7, Nanchang Q-5 (Fantan) etc.

Gwadar Port

Gwadar Port which has strategic significance is being constructed by Chinese assistance. The construction is being undertaken by China's Harbin Engineering Company (CHEC). China agreed to extend US $ 200 million financial package for the first phase which included $ 50 million grant, $ 50 million soft loan, and $ 100 million investment for construction of the port.[74] Furthermore, the Chinese delegation led by Wu Bangguo, Vice Premier was there during the laying of foundation stone of Gwadar port.[75] While the Chinese, on the one hand, highlighted the economic dimensions of the Gwadar port project, the Pakistani viewpoint, on the another hand, was strategic, as articulated by no less a person than President Musharraf himself, who said : "As and when needed the Chinese navy would be in Gwadar to give a befitting reply to anyone."[76] It was also reported that China asked Pakistan for independent control over certain facilities at Gwadar port in lieu of its assistance to develop it.[77] To be precise, China demanded berthing facilities at Gwadar and ormara and listening posts on the Mekran Coast of Baluchistan to intercept the communications of the US military bases in the Gulf region. In this context, the reported statement of General Musharraf assumes significance, who stated: "God willing, the construction of project will be an antidote against the American poison being Spread in this region."[78]

Moreover, Chinese government has also offered funds and technical assistance for construction of the Mekran coastal highway from Karachi to Gwadar and from there further north to link Pakistan with Afghanistan and Central Asian Republics via Heart. Thus, in near future, Gwadar would be the shortest and most viable access to warm waters to Chinese industries located in the undeveloped western region of China via Karakoram highways, the Indus highway and proposed linkages. It is also being reported that Gwadar may be a forward base of China to monitor the USA's naval activities in the strategically important Persian Gulf region. This strategic move of China will enable it to reach the Gulf region at a time when USA has based its troops in China's neighbourhood including Pakistan, Afghanistan and CAR's as a part of war against Terrorism. Therefore, in some ways the Chinese presence at Gwadar would not only be a direct challenge to India but also to American power in the region.[79]

In short, Sino-Pak joint projects were quite robust. In the words of a renowned western expert, "Pakistan remained the largest recipient of Chinese military assistance".

Chinese Assistance for Weapons of Mass Destruction

China assisted Pakistani these crucial sphere in order to make Pakistan as counter weight to India in South Asia. Without the Chinese assistance, Pakistan's nuclear weapons and missile programmes would probably have been impossible. Clearly, China was a proliferator in South Asia and Contributed in some ways in unleashing strategic instability in this part of the world. From India's perspective, China supplied WMD to Pakistan for 'the revisionist agenda'.

The supply of ballistic missiles and related technology by China to Pakistan originated in the late 1980's. The contract for sale of M-11 missiles was reportedly signed in 1988 and supply began in 1991 in contravention of the guidelines and parameters of the MTCR. Commenting on this aspect, a well known western analyst wrote : "China also supplied critical assistance to Pakistan's efforts to develop missiles capable of delivering nuclear war-heads. In early 1988 Beijing and Islamabad Secretly concluded an agreement to cooperate in Pakistan's acquisition of M-11 ballistic missiles... Under the 1988 agreement China agreed to train Pakistanis in the operation of M-11, transfer necessary equipment and technology to Pakistan, transfer thirty or so complete M-11s, and build a factory in Pakistan for indigenous production of the missiles."[80] However, in the opinion of the analyst, "the motivations underlying China's assistance to Pakistan's ballistic missile program were complex".

The missile factory built with Chinese assistance at Fatehjang, some 50 km South-West of Islamabad, came to be known as the National Defence complex. The complex is manned by specialists from all related missiles and nuclear developmental organisations in Pakistan and supported by some Chinese technicians who work on missile guidance and solid fuel production. Later on it came to be known that China Precision Machinery Import.-Export Corporation (CPMIEC) provided Pakistan with M-11 missiles and related equipments like gyroscopes, accelerometers and on board computers.[81] The shaheen missile programme was initiated in 1995 and was given to the national Defence Complex. Despite Several imposition of USA Sanctions, i.e., 1991, 1993, 1998 and 2001 against China, latter continued to transfer different types of missiles and missile technology to Pakistan.[82]

Similarly with respect to Pakistan's nuclear weapons programme, China in a significant way supported its 'all weather friend'. In the year 1989 and 1990, two mini research reactors sold by China's National Energy Corporation became operational in Pakistan.[83] The Chinese assistance in nuclear sphere continued in post cold war period. In the year 1992, both sides ratified an agreement for the supply of 300 MW light water nuclear reactor using enriched uranium whose construction was completed by the end of year 1998 at Chasma.[84] Further in 1995, a US intelligence report revealed the sale of 5000 specially designed 'ring magnets' to A.Q. Khan Research Laboratories at Kahuta, which was unsafe guarded nuclear laboratory by China Nuclear Energy Industry Corporation.[85]

In the year 1996, US Arms Control and Disarmament Agency report stated that "since China's accession to the NPT, it appears that China may have continued to assist Pakistan's unsafe-guarded nuclear programme and may have continued contacts with elements associated with Pakistan's nuclear weapons related programme."[86] In March, 1996 Pakistan reported that it has completed work on a research reactor at Khushab, another facility outside of IAEA safeguards Pakistan claimed that the plutonium production reactor in 'indigenous', China was believed to have provided assistance in its construction.[87] In July, 1997 CIA report called China "the most significant supplier of weapons of mass destruction related goods and technology to foreign countries" from July to December, 1996.[88]

Later in the year 1997, China agreed to USA's demand for implementing new export controls over nuclear technology, materials and equipment and reportedly gave assurances about such transfers to Pakistan as well.[89] After the Indian and Pakistani nuclear tests, China signed the P-5 joint communique of June 4th 1998 and pledged to cooperate closely to prevent a nuclear and missile arms race.[90] Notwithstanding Chinese pledge, it was reported that Chinese assistance to Pak's nuclear and missile programme continues. At the regional level this trend was noted : "China has, in past, assisted Pakistan to develop its nuclear and missile capabilities. Despite denials by China, there are continuing reports of the transfer of missile parts and components technology to Pakistan in the year 2001."[91]

Inspite of the reports China kept on denying the fact of any assistance to Pakistan. For instance, the Chinese foreign ministry stated : "the allegation that China has assisted Pakistan in its long-range missile programme is totally groundless and relevant reports are out of ulterior motives. China has always abided by the joint communique of foreign ministers of the five permanent members of the UN Security council issued in June 98 nuclear tests in South Asia and also the UN resolution No. 1172."[92] Many analysts discerned the Chinese pattern of deception and denial on this practice.[93] Indeed, the fact of proliferation was pointed out by other assessments as well, i.e., that China continues to provide "significant assistance" to Pakistan's ballistic missile programme.[94] The fact of Chinese assistance to Pakistan's WMD programme is indicative of China's commitment to Pakistan's Security and is guided by its strategic consideration in the region.

Commenting on China's transfers of WMD weapons to Pakistan one Indian analyst wrote : "A collusion between New Delhi's most probable adversaries is sure to divide Indian attention, as well as keep its political military decision-makers off balance. Chinese help in crucial weapons related technologies have allowed Pakistan to leapfrog the knotty details in design and production of advanced defence engineering. What surprises, however is China's continued adherence to its nuclear and missile technology supply contracts with Pakistan even in the face of explicit threats of sanctions and world wide condemnation."[95] Clearly, the transfer of weapons of mass destruction to Pakistan was directed against India. India rightfully perceived the act of Chinese proliferation as destabilizing the strategic equilibrium of South Asia and detrimental to India's Security. In March 2000, during the first round of Security dialogue, India "strongly conveyed" to China its concerns over China's assistance to Pakistan's nuclear and missile programmes. India on its part, believed, this created an "adverse impact" on regional stability in South Asia.

Afterwards, during the second round of India-China security dialogue in February 2001, India, again conveyed its concern to China over Beijing's supply of nuclear and missile technology to Pakistan.[96] China replied that its relations with Pakistan were normal relations and were not directed against India.

Reverse Engineering

From cold war phase, Pakistan had access to advanced western military technologies and arms, whereas China was isolated. As a result, Pakistan was window of opportunity to China for the western military hardware, machineries and technologies. With the use of reverse engineering, China was able to achieve important developments in technology. As one analyst observed, "China's remarkable concern for Pakistan may have yet another source. A relationship with Pakistan ensures China access to high technologies which are in Pakistani custody owing to the latter's position in the western alliance system during the cold war years."[97]

The trend of reverse engineering continued in the post cold war period as well. The then leader of opposition, Pakistan, Mr. Nawaz Sharrif in a speech at People's Institute of Foreign Affairs. Beijing in May 1996 acknowledged the fact of reverse engineering.[98] Indeed, J. Gaffney, joint director, centre for security policy in a testimony to the subcommittee on International Economic Policy and Trade of the House of Commons on International Relations on June 24, 1998 suggested security of Chinese involvement in reverse engineering of stinger missile and selling of such advanced shoulder fired surface to Air missiles to the countries that sponsor terrorism and others who may use such weapons to shoot down civil airlines and other planes.[99] It was reported that Pakistan transferred US manufactured F-16 to China for reverse engineering. The Chinese designed fighter jet J-10 was culmination of this process.[100] Furthermore, in December 1998 it was also reported that Pakistan arranged a meeting between the Chinese delegation and Taliban leadership at Kandahar after USA's cruise missile attack against the camps of Osama Bin Laden in August 1998 and got permission to take away an unexploded missile. Later, a Chinese delegation visited Afghanistan in April 1999 to take away the missile.[101] Thus, the dimension of reverse technology was on important aspect of Sino-Pak defence relations.

Sino-Pak Military Exchanges

The bilateral military exchange was an important component of overall defence cooperation commenting on the military exchanges between China and Pakistan, a leading expert wrote, "The frequency of high level military exchanges is a good, if rough, indicator of the intensity of Sino-Pakistan military cooperation. These exchanges were associated with new or ongoing cooperation and were essential for mutual familiarization that is at the Core of effective military cooperation."[102]

The high level military exchanges continued in the post cold war period and the details are given below in Table Nos. 5, 6, and 7.

The exchange of military delegations at service level consolidated the bonds of friendship and provided opportunity to discuss "matters of mutual interest", i.e., regional, international security issues. In addition the bilateral issue of military modernisation, sales of weapons, training etc were taken up in course of visits. Further, the two defence establishments continued to seek support at crucial juncture like the Kargil conflict. In May 1999, Pakistan's Chairman of the Joint Staff Committee and Army chief of Staff. Gen. Pervez Musharraf Visited Beijing. He met the PLA Chief of General Staff Fu Quanyou, who stated that Sino-Pakistan friendship would never change no matter how the world situation or domestic situation might change. Fu further stated : "The military ties between China and Pakistan are a vital part of the bilateral relation between the two countries and an important part of the Sino-Pakistan comprehensive cooperative partnership."[103] However, the PLA chief displayed level of maturity and" expressed the hope that all relevant countries in South Asia would resolve their divergences and problems through patient and candid dialogues."

Table 5. Navy Delegation

Month/ Year	*Visitors to China*	*Visitors from China*
May 1993	Chief of Staff of Navy, Adm. Saeed M. Khan	
Nov. 1997		Vice Adm. Shiyun Sheng, Commander PLA Navy
Aug. 1999	Navy's Air Division Chief Marshal Pervaiz Mehdi.	
May 2000	Chief of Staff of Navy, Adm. Abdul Aziz Mirza	
Nov. 2000		Deputy Chief, PLA Navy Yang Huaqing

Source: Relevant Volumes of SWB, POT, Pakistan Series.

Table 6. Air Force Delegation

Month/ Year	*Visitors to China*	*Visitors from China*
May 1992	Pakistan Air Force delegation	
May 1993		PLA Air Force Chief Lt. Gen. Cao Shaung Ming
April 1995	Chief of Air Staff Muhammad Abbas Khattak	
Nov. 1996	PAF delegation	
Aug. 1999	Chief of Air staff Pervaiz Mehdi Qureshi	
Feb. 2001	Chief of Air staff Mushraf Ali Mir	

Source: Relevant volumes of SWB, POT, Pakistan Series.

A well known western expert wrote : "Fu's endorsement of "dialogue" was equivalent to implicit rejection of Pakistan's efforts to internationalize the Kashmir issue through its precipitation of the confrontation over Kargil... Beijing rejected Islamabad's effort to internationalize the Kashmir issue, but paired this with continuing Chinese support for Pakistan's military capabilities, Inspite of Indian objections and Inspite of the small scale war underway between Pakistan and India."[104] Thus, in post cold war period even the Chinese defence establishment clearly hinted to Pakistan that it would not support outbreak of India-Pak conflict but assured Pakistan of its continuous support for Pakistan's 'military capabilities'.

The most important segment of military exchange was the army.

Table 7. Sino-Pakistan Army Delegation

Year Month	*Visitors to China*	*Visitors from China*
August 1992	Chairman joint chief of staff committee, Gen. Shamim Alam Khan	
November 1992	Commander of Air Defence Force of Army Lt. Gen Nazar Hussain	
April 1995		Deputy Director of Bureau of Military Equipment, Col. Rem Zhenqian
July 1996	Chief of Army Staff. Gen. Jehangir Karamat	
August – September 1998	Chief of Army Staff Gen. Jehangir Karamat	
May 1999	Chief of Army Staff Gen. Pervez Musharraf	
June 1999		General Armament Dept. Political Commisar, Lt. Gen. Li Jinai
August 2000		Vice Minister, Costind Zhang Weimin
November 2000		Nanjing Military Region, Political Commissar, Gen. Fang Zuqi
April 2001		PLA Chief of General staff, Gen. Fu Quanyou
January 2002	Chairman Joint Chief of Staff Gen. Muhammad Aziz Khan	
March 2002		PLA Deputy Chief Gen. Xiong Guang Kai.

Source: Relevant Volumes of SWB, POT, Pakistan Series.

All the three tables mentioned above prove the point that high level exchange of military delegations in three services was continuous and existence of strategic relations between China and Pakistan. Further, the two countries held first Defence and Security talk in March 2002.[105] It is important to note that PLA deputy chief and military intelligence Chief General Xiong Guangkai was in Islamabad in March 2002. Later on, the Deputy Chief of General staff Xiong Guangkai and the Director of Pakistan Joint Staff. Lt. Gen. Syed Pervez Shahid concluded an memorandum of Understanding in the same year at Beijing, which provided for a joint institution for regular and annual talks between the armed forces of both sides. Both nations felt that only through the process of institutionalization Pakistan could get rid of enhanced US influence in the post 9/11 world.[106]

Therefore, even after 9/11 the Sino-Pak defence relations continued to be special and cordial. The fact of special relations was mentioned in 2002 by Gen. Zhang Wannian, Vice Chairman of China's Central Military Commission in meeting with General Muhammad Aziz Khan Chairman of Pakistan's Joint Chiefs of the staff committee and was quoted as telling Khan : "For many years the militaries of our two nations have maintained exchanges and cooperation at the highest and all levels and in every field. This fully embodies the all-weather friendship our national maintain."[107] In short, China played a crucial role in enhancing Pakistan's overall military capability as well as modernization. The all round bilateral defence relations were robust in nature. An Indian expert wrote : "Nonetheless, its defense and strategic ties with Islamabad remain an important element of its strategic posture in the region. The transfer of M-11 missiles in 1991 and nuclear know-how and materials such as ring magnets for uranium enrichment indicates China's abiding interest in keeping alive the Pakistan card against India."[108]

Thus, in the regional context maintenance of military relations with Pakistan served China's strategic interest in the region. As one western expert observed : "China also views military relations between itself and South Asian countries as legitimate relations well within the purview of the Five Principles of Peaceful coexistence. To New Delhi, they constitute unacceptable threats to Indian Security. Because of these continuing fundamental tensions and rivalries, China's entente Cordiale with Pakistan remains important to Beijing."[109]

Further, since the mid 1990's China in some ways was concerned over the Shift in the overall balance of power in South Asia with the gradual rise of India coupled with the growing US-India relations and the talk of "India as a counter weight to China" in USA's policy circles. To add to China's discomfort the trend was happening at a time when Pakistan gradually descended into the ranks of failed states.[110]

Post 9/11 Developments in Sino-Pak Relations

The impact of the terrorist attacks in New York on September 11 was tremendous. Some experts argue that the attacks pushed us into a new phase of Contemporary history. South Asia entered a new period after 9/11 and became an important site of the anti-terrorism war. Initially, China was comfortable in view of prominence of Pakistan in U.S.A.'s war against terrorism. Moreover, China was concerned over the growing US-India ties in particular defence relations. In some ways, therefore, immediately after 9/11 China was comfortable with Pakistan's growing ties with US.

As a South Asian analyst of Chinese National Defence University wrote that in view of 9/11, under the new circumstances, "the United States, considering its own security interests, readjusted its policies towards South Asian countries and started paying more attention to the important role of Pakistan in the anti-terrorism war, therefore arousing the vigilance and jealously of India."[111] He also praised General Musharraf for his "clear-cut attitude towards fighting against international terrorism." In fact, it seems that China hoped that Sino-US-Pak triangular cooperation in the aftermath of 9/11 will materialise as happened in 1970's and again in 1980's after the Soviet's intervention in Afghanistan. And the growing triangular cooperation in some ways would wean USA away from India.

The fact of growing engagement between US and India had caused concern in China has already been discussed above. Many China's noted South Asia specialists expressed concern over the U.S. sale of arms to India which "enables it to become the first country to have close military relations with the world's two big powers – the U.S. and Russia."[112] China condemned terrorism on the one hand but its condemnation of Pak sponsored terrorism was opaque. China noted the situation in South Asia after 9/11, the continued tension between India-Pakistan, which further deteriorated after the anti-terrorism war. In China's perception. India intended to use the opportunity of the international anti-terrorism struggle to press Pakistan to stop once and for all "cross-border terrorism".

China faced difficult situation in the region. At a broad level, the Sino-Pak relations in future would be subjected to growing Pak-US relations. In fact the US military base in Pakistan which was being US in its war against terrorism caused concern to China coupled with USA's base in central Asian republics. Further, the growing US influence was also not encouraging for China's overall interest. At the same time, China wanted stability in its surrounding areas. Therefore, China surely did not relish outbreak of India-Pakistan conflict. To a large extent, despite 9/11 close ties between China-Pakistan continued.

According to one analyst J. Mohan Malik, "China's initial optimism that new Sino-US-Pak triangular cooperation in the aftermath of September 11 will wean Washington away from New Delhi turned out to be wishful thinking as the Bush administration officials went out of their way to assure India that USA's intensifying alliance with Pakistan would not come at India's expense".[113] Be that as it may be, China noted both trends after 9/11 as observed by one Chinese diplomat, "Before September 11", the United states was more inclined towards India between India and Pakistan and exerted pressure on Pakistan in various ways. However, President Musharraf made a major policy decision in Pakistan's strategy after "September 11" and agreed to cooperate with the United States in the anti-terrorism war, with Pakistan be coming again an ally of the United States... At the same time, relations between the United States and India saw continuous improvement, with new development in their military cooperation."[114]

Thus, inspite of 9/11 the 'all weather friendship' continued between China and Pakistan. During tension with India in the wake of 13th December, 2001 Indian Parliament attacks, General Musharraf visited China twice in December 2001 and January 2002. China supplied military hardwares and jets even in the face of Indo-Pak military standoff.[115] In short, the fruitful cooperation between two countries continued. After the 16th Party congress, Pakistan's prime Minister Mir Zafarullah Khan Jamali was the first noted leader from South Asia to visit and discuss with the new Chinese leadership in March 2003. During Jamali's visit, Jiang Zemin the Chairman of China's CMC welcomed Jamali and said Pakistan is one of the south Asian nations that have the closest relations with China. He further stated that China will adhere to the principle of "friendship and partnership with neighbours" set forth in the 16th CPC National Congress so as to develop friendly exchanges and cooperation with neighbouring countries. Jiang underlined the fact that China regards Pakistan as an earnest and reliable friend and brother.[116] Jamali was the first head of government to be received by the new Chinese leaders i.e., President Hu Jintao and Prime Minister Wen Jiabao. Jamali and Wen presided over the signing ceremony of four agreements, including one on economic and technical cooperation.[117]

Thus, China desired peace and stability in South Asia, which was vital to the security and economic development of China. But in a nuanced way Pro-Pakistan tilt was discernible, in particular in Liberation Army Daily etc. In the period, at one level, it was argued that "China's development of relations with either India or Pakistan is not directed against any third country and will not be detrimental to the interest of any third country."[118] But the extremely close Sino-Pak military relations underscored the continuity of the "India factor" in Sino-Pak 'all weather relationship'.

India's security environment was adversely affected by the evolution of Sino-Pak politico-strategic relationship. China's continued defence relations with Pakistan was central to India's strategic concern. Sino-Pak close relations to large extent increased inimical attitude of Pakistan towards India and gave Pakistan some sort of confidence, which became one of the factors in continuation of Indo-Pak conflictual relations. Thus, the long-term prospects of close Sino-Pak relations seem positive. The Sino-Pak entente cordiale in the last five decades has survived many changes. Pakistan on its part needs military assistance from China. China's need for support from Pakistan in its internal problems in Xinjiang Autonomous Region is an important factor. Moreover, China still has unresolved border problem with India. The evolving Indo-US relations coupled with growing national power of India in military and economic sphere has aroused Chinese apprehension. All these factors combine for a harmonious Sino-Pak relationship. Thus, the regional context of India-China multifaceted interaction at one level, would continue to be marked by the competitive element.

The point was conceded by the optimists as well, who portrayed benign image of China but observed : "there will continue to be a widespread perception in India that China pursues a deliberate anti-Indian strategy in its relationship with Pakistan. Many in India will continue to argue that China's objective is to constrain India by a threat of a two front war and by locking it within South Asia so that it cannot emerge as a rival to China on the wider regional and global stage."[119] Therefore, close Sino-Pak relations in particular military relations perpetuated hostile image of China in India. In short, at the regional level Sino-Pak relations was based on "strategic perspective on India" notwithstanding the Chinese subtle articulations and formulations.

Sino-Bangladesh Relations

In China's perception, Bangladesh was an important power in South Asia. Geo-strategically, Chinese proximity is evident as " between the north west corner of Bangladesh and the Southern most point of Tibet's Chumbivalley " lies India's Siliguri Corridor. Furthermore, "as China looks at the possibilities of a naval presence in the Indian ocean, the long Bangladesh coasts line along the Bay of Bengal could be an area of interest to it."[120]

The post cold was period in Bangladesh coincided with end of military rule and inauguration of democracy. It appears that both political parties, i.e., Awami league and the B N P agreed on the fact that maintenance of close relation; with china will be salient feature of its foreign policy. The head of successive governments in Bangladesh visited Beijing and met the political leadership to further strengthen and expand the bilateral relations. Sheikh Hasina of Awami league visited China first as the opposition leader in 1993 and later as Prime Minister in 1996.[121] It is important to note that after assuming the post of Prime Minister. China was the first country which she visited.[122] From Bangladesh viewpoint maintenance of good relations with China was partly to diversify its foreign relations. Geographically. Bangladesh shares its borders with India from threes sides. Therefore, geo-politically, cultural as well as economic gravitational pull of India was the dominant trend in Bangladesh's perception. Relations with China provided a good opportunity to Bangladesh to offset perceived India's dominance. China happily expanded relations with a small South Asian nation in the neighbourhood of India.

However, in post cold war period, China was not interested in fanning conflictual relations in the region. Though Begum Khaleda Zia of BNP did sought Chinese assistance in addressing grievances against India particularly on the water issue. But China carefully distanced itself from taking sides in the regional issues and called for bilateral approach. Further, during this period regime security was not the consideration in maintenance of relations with China. By this point of time, Bangladesh reverted back to democratic form of governance. This point was underlined by China as well during the Chinese Premier Zhu Rongji's Bangladesh visit. Zhu stated that China seeks to maintain friendly relations with countries, not with regimes.

From Chinese side, its foreign minister visited Dacca in 1994. The visit of Chinese Premier Zhu Rongji in January 2002 was important as this was first visit of head of Chinese government after a gap of 13 years. He reassured the Bangladeshi side of its friendship and commitment to continue as a development partner of Bangladesh.[123]

Economic Relations

Gradually, China emerged as partner in various developmental activities of Bangladesh. China provided assistance in forms of grants and loans on low interest. Apart from building core infrastructure like roads, bridges, China provided help in more concrete way in areas like telecommunications, cement plants and agrarian sector, etc.[124] Of equal importance was the conclusion of bilateral agreement in February 2000 to set up study on the construction of 100 MW hydro power plants on Matamuhuri and Sangu rivers. Further, areas on potential cooperation also included river training, dredging, flood control, irrigation, flood forecasting etc.[125] In short, China surely became developmental partner of Bangladesh. The fact became clear again during China visit of Begum Khaleda Zia in December, 2002, when bilateral agreements were concluded. Accordingly, China agreed to provide a grant of 7.25 million US $ for construction of the sixth Sino-Bangladesh Friendship bridge over the Dhaleshwari river.[126] China also agreed to grant Bangladesh an additional soft loan of approximately 6.4 million US $.

As far as trade ties are concerned, there has been rise in bilateral trade but trade balance has always been in flavour of China. (See Table No. 8) Despite Chinese assurances to address the issue nothing concrete has happened. During 1996-97, trade figures show that Bangladesh's exports to China was 55.5 million US $, while its imports were worth 446 million US $. Thus, the trade gap was whopping 390.5 millions US $ for Bangladesh.[127] Bangladesh main items of imports from China were manufactured goods like machinery, electrical equipments. Vehicles, aircraft and associated transport equipment, textile and textile products, plastic, rubber and mineral products. Bangladesh's exports include raw jute, jute yarn, frozen fish, Shrimps and leather. In the economic sphere, as far as bilateral tráde was concerned China enjoyed trade surplus. Though, China helped Bangladesh in development of its infrastructure.

Table 8. Bangladesh's Trade with China

(Million US $)

Year	*Total Trade*	*Total Trade with China*	*Share of Trade with China*
1993	6292	210	3.34%
1994	7234	311	4.30%
1995	9625	619	6.43%
1996	10232	660	6.45%
1997	10491	680	6.48%
1998	11192	575	5.14%
1999	12872	542	4.21%

Source: IMF, Direction of Trade Statistics Yearbook, 2000.

Sino-Bangladesh Military Relations

In the regional context, it is military relations which assumes importance. The foundation of Chinese military relation with Bangladesh was laid during the Presidency of General Zia-ur-Rahman. Among the motivating factors that shaped the relationship after the assassination of Mujibur Rehman in August 1975 was the supply of military spare parts to Bangladesh. Chinese weapons specifically suited Bangladesh's defence force. For as part of Pakistani defence force, they were more accustomed and trained to the Chinese brand of weapons than that of any other brands. The inflow of Chinese military aid took place in two forms : weapons and military advisors. China built arms and ammunition factory in Joydevpur and also took over Bangladesh's Soviet built MIGs.[128] Later on China Supplied F-6 fighter planes and for the army it supplied T-59 MBT.

Chinese-Bangladesh naval Cooperation began in 1980's with the transfer of Chinese warships. In the year 1980, China transferred fast attack craft. By 1995, Bangladesh received in all 26 fast attack grafts, a Romeo-class submarine, Six coastal patrol crafts, four large patrol crafts and a total of 36 Chinese made Ships.[129] In addition, it got hai Ying 2 L Ship-to-ship missile launcher as well as missile (for arms acquisition from China see appendix)

During the period of post cold war, bilateral military exchanges continued apace. (For details see Table 9) In November 1996, when Bangladesh's Air Force Chief of Staff, Jamaluddin visited China, he met with the defence minister and Vice Chairman of CMC-Chi Haotian. The Chinese Defence minister welcomed the furthering of exchanges and underlined the point that "cooperation in various areas is beneficial not only to the two peoples, but to regional peace and stability and development as well". Later in August 2000 when the visiting PLA delegation met with the foreign minister, Abduls Samad Azad, and praised the friendly cooperative relationship between both sides in the military field. He further stated that "Military cooperation between the two countries will develop more broadly and more deply."[130] The PLA delegation also held talks with Bangladesh's Chief of Army Staff, Jamaluddin Ahmed.

Later and more specifically, when Chi Haotian met the visiting Bangladesh Chief of Staff of Army, he said China is an "all weather" friend of Bangladesh. The Chinese Defence Minister further stated that both China and Bangladesh "Strongly Condemned hegemonism and power politics."[131] The use of words 'hegemonism' and 'power politics' was undeniably aimed at India. Earlier, in September 1996 the Chinese Defence

Table 9. Sino-Bangladesh Military Delegation

Year	*Visitors to China*	*Visitors from China*
1991	Army Chief of Staff Navy Chief of Staff	PLA deputy chief of general staff
1992	Commanding officer of capital area, Air Chief of Staff	
1993	Chief of Staff	PLA Air Force Chief of Staff
1994		PLA Chengdu Military Region commander
1995	Chief of Staff	PLA Chief of General Logistics Dept.
1996	Air Force Chief of Staff, Army Chief of Staff, Navy Chief of Staff	PLA Deputy Chief General Staff Department
1997		Lanzhou Military Region Commander
1998		PLA Deputy Director of General Political Department
2000	Chief of Naval Staff	Vice President of PLA Military Academy of Sciences

Source: SWB & POT, Bangladesh series, relevant volumes and John W. Garver, Protracted contest, New Delhi, 2001, p. 299.

minister visited Bangladesh to convey China's desire for continued military cooperation' in the wake of Change of government at Dhaka. He stated that Beijing attached 'great importance' to relations with Bangladesh, seeing them as playing an "active role in maintaining regional peace and stability."[132] The use of words regional peace and stability in a subtle way underlined the point that Chinese maintenance of military relations with India's small neighbouring states is necessary for the region. It can safely be concluded that China cultivated Bangladesh as a countervailing power in the region.

In this context during Prime Minister, Begum Khaleda Zia's visit to China in 2002 assumed importance. Immediately before her visit, the spokesperson of Chinese foreign ministry stated : "Bangladesh is a country of significance in South Asia. China-Bangladesh are friendly and close neighbours. A sound momentum of all-directional development has taken shape in the friendly cooperation between the two sides are helpful in maintaining regional peace and stability as well as promoting development of the region."[133] During Bangladesh's Prime Minister visit to Beijing in December, 2002 both sides concluded defence cooperation agreement. The pact was an effort to institutionalise the existing piecemeal agreements to enhance cooperation in training, maintenance and some areas of production.[134] With the conclusion of this agreement, China became the first country to have a broad based defence cooperation with Bangladesh. Bangladesh on its part, stated that the defence agreement was not a security treaty targeted against any third country but an umbrella agreement under which China would help Bangladesh modernise its defence sector.[135]

Nonetheless, the bilateral defence agreement in the regional context was an important development. Therefore, India took note of this regional development. In the words of J.N. Dixit, veteran diplomat Bangladesh's "close relationship with China has been... of particular importance to Bangladesh in the subcontinental and the Asian regional context. Linkages with China and Pakistan are of strategic and security interest from Bangladesh's perspective."[136] However, a confident India did not respond to growing Sino- Bangladesh military relations in alarming way. Be that as it may be, one western expert aptly summed up "stated plainly, the Sino-Bangladeshi military relation was useful to both because it created a balance of power favourable to constraining India."[137] Therefore, the fact of regional dimension at a broad level was relevant even in Sino-Bangladesh relations.

Sino-Sri Lanka Relations

Even in post cold war period, the bilateral relations between China and Sri Lanka continued to develop. From China's perspective, cordial relations with a country like Sri Lanka, strategically located in the Indian Ocean, would be extremely useful in their future activities in the overall region.

In the regional context, China-Sri Lanka military relations were significant. Though there was not much exchange of military delegations. However, China's arms transfer continued but on commercial terms. In the words of two diplomats, "Every now and then some Indian analyst expresses deep concern at the "profound" implications of these transfers for India's security. In most cases, according to reliable reports, Sri Lanka went to China or Pakistan or any other party only when India regretted its inability or unwillingness to be the supplier. Further, the nature of the arms supplied is as required for dealing with domestic insurgencies. They pose no threat to India."[138]

Thus, Sri Lanka was wracked by internal ethnic strife in the period. As such, apart from arms transfer, there was nothing worrying aspect about its dealings with China. Nonetheless, in future due to its geo-strategic significance "India has to monitor the kind of linkages which China may seek to establish as it strives to become a major naval presence in the Indian Ocean." The point was underlined by a renowned western expert who observed "China's relations with Bangladesh and with Sri Lanka are especially sensitive in the context of the evolving Sino-Indian naval presence".[139] Thereby, the situation warrants India to be careful as well as vigilant on China's military relations with its smaller neighbours.

Sino-Myanmar Relations

Myanmar's geopolitical location is unique as it lies at the tri-junction of the South, East and Southeast Asian regions. It shares land borders with both India and China. In China's perception, Myanmar is an important neighbours. It offers opening to the sea for South-western part of China, which occupies strategic location for access to the Bay of Bengal on one side and the Malacca strait on the other. Moreover, for the economic development of landlocked Yunnan province, Myanmar's position is important.

China's relations with Myanmar began to gather momentum after the military junta in the name of State Law and Order Restoration Council (SLORC) came to power in the year 1988. Gradually but surely military ties were cultivated as Myanmar faced isolation from the western nations led by USA. Similarly, China faced western condemnation for the Tiananmen massacre. As such, theré was convergence of national interests between both sides. From now onwards, China gave strong political support to SLORC, which needed support badly.

Military Relations

The growth of Sino-Myanmar military relations was an important development in the post cold war period. First, in October 1989, Myanmar signed arms procurement agreement with China and purchased extensively for its army and airforce.[140] Gradually, Myanmarese army's strength increased by 50 per cent between the period 1988 and 1992.[141] Further, Myanmar concluded another agreement with China in 1994 and procured armoured vehicles, missiles, helicopters and patrol boats.[142]

In all, Myanmar added 192 fighter aircrafts and transport (excluding fighter trainer), alongwith a good number of PL-2 air-to-air missiles. In its quest to modernize army it inducted 100 type 69-II MBT. Further, for navy

Myanmar procured as many as 34 patrol crafts. (For Chinese transfer of arms see appendix)

The exchange of mutual military delegations was frequent. (See Table 10).

Table 10. Sino-Myanmar Military Delegation

Year	*Visitors to China*	*Visitors from China*
1991		PLA Deputy Chief of General Staff Leads PLA delegation
1994		Commander of Chengdu Military Region
1995		SLORC Chairman and army commander SLORC Vice Chairman and Deputy Commander of Defence
1997	Air Force Delegation	PLA Lanzhou Military Region Commander
1998	Air Force Delegation headed by Com-in-Chief	
2001		PLA's two delegations
2002	SLORC Chairman	PLA-Navy officer delegation

Source: SWB, Relevant Volumes & John W. Garver, Protracted Contest, New Delhi, 2001, p. 264.

Chinese defence establishment strongly supported relations with Myanmar. In 1996, during Beijing visit of SLORC'S vice chairman Maung Aye, the Vice Chairman of CMC, Zhang wannian stated that "the ongoing visit would strengthen the military relations between the two nations."[143] Moreover, the PLA trained Myanmar's defence forces in the operation and maintenance of the Chinese transferred weapon systems. Thus, China trained large number of its defence for as.[144] It was also reported that Myanmar was interested in producing weapons in joint cooperation with China for its own defence and for export.[145]

China also continued to support rule of military in Myanmar. In the year 1996, the then premier Li Peng told a visiting delegation from Myanmar that "China upholds that all countries should be treated equally, irrespective of being big or small, rich or poor, powerful or weak. China opposes any interference in internal affairs of other countries or hegemonism."[146]

Among the bases and military assets built with the Chinese assistance were the naval base at Hainggyi Island and radar station at CoCo Islands, Southwest of the Burmese coast. Further, the Chinese helped to construct five new ports and upgrade others along Burma's coast, from Victoria point in the south to sittwe in the Northern Arakan.[147] More recently in late 2002, it was revealed that Burma is expanding with Chinese support its naval facilities on Great CoCo Island, the site of major signals intelligence facility situated near strategically important Andaman and Nicobar islands.[148] These bases and military assets have obvious security implications for India.

Moreover, in year 2002 it was reported that five warships ordered from China arrived at the Tenessarim naval base in mergui. A joint Burma-China naval exercise was on the anvil at a location between Mali and Kunthi islands. The experts stated that the warships could be a part of the more than 1 billion US $ weapons deal which the ruling SPDC made with China in the last year.[149] The fact suggests continuation of close bilateral military relations.

Furthermore, a high ranking PLA officer, General Zhao Nanqi said that China would extend its naval operations further than the South and East China seas to check attempts by India to "dominate" the Indian Ocean and other regional waters. General Nanqi further stated that "this is something which we cannot accept... We are not prepared to let the Indian Ocean become India's Ocean."[150] Thus, the close Sino-Myanmar military relations in post cold war period was a security concern for India. China's in roads into Myanmar from India's viewpoint was serious encroachment into India's sphere of influence.

The point was conceded by the optimists as well and renowned diplomats observed, "India has a legitimate concern about the electronic surveillance facilities set up by the Chinese in CoCo Islands. The Myanmar government insists that they have not offered the Chinese any military facility on their soil. They admit that the equipment is Chinese but claim that it is operated by the Burmese themselves... But Indian analysts believe that the facilities are too elaborate to be intended merely for Myanmar's own use. And the visits by Chinese technicians are too frequent to be exclusively for installation and maintenance purposes."[151] Another Indian assessment concluded that "From an India security perspective, China's post-1988 strategic ties and military relations with the military-dominated power structure in Myanmar has potential strategic implications almost as serious as Beijing's ties with Pakistan. It allows China to have two major allies on the two wings of India while it straddles the northern borders. China, Pakistan, and Myanmar together cover the bulk of India's land borders, and Beijing also has forged close naval ties with these states."[152]

Clearly, from China's point of view a military powerful Myanmar friendly with China, meant that India was placed in an unfavourable military situation. Another important Chinese objective was its overall naval aspiration to be in the Indian Ocean. As a renowned western analyst pointed out the fact that "Sri Lanka or Bangladesh would serve the PLAN for less well than Myanmar as a base for operations in the IOR. Both Sri Lanka and Bangladesh would be vulnerable to an Indian economic blockade... Both are too distant from China... Myanmar is equidistant from China and India, with overland transportation with China being somewhat easier than with India."[153]

The above mentioned scenario is the worse case assumption. Despite close Sino-Myanmar military relations, of late some positive developments have taken. India-Myanmar relations have also improved and Myanmar has joined ASEAN in its attempt diversify foreign relations. Further, the economic dimension of China-Myanmar relations have to be noted as well as the Kunmin initiative of China to develop economically the entire region and participation of the neighbouring nations. Nonetheless, the evolving military relations between China and Myanmar adversely affected India's Security environment, prompting it to be vigilant and careful.

One important Indian foreign policy analyst commenting on China's Regional posture makes an interesting point. He has identified three groups of regional states. In his words, "The first group comprises the states that have close, friendly ties with China and that welcome the growth of China's overall power and role : Pakistan, Iran, Bangladesh, Myanmar and Sri Lanka. These countries currently see China as an ally in their effort to enhance their political space, and to ensure a steady, and more affordable supply of military weapons and technology not available elsewhere... They don not have border disputes with China, nor are they affected adversely by its military power."[154]

He adds that "a second group comprises land-locked Nepal and Bhutan which have close security relations with Indian but which would be directly affected by a dominant or a hostile China, by migrations from China as a result of political turmoil in Tibet, and by a deterioration in Sino-Indian relations... China has tried to expand its ties with both countries and in the past even sought to undermine India's special relations with them."[155]

In the opinion of analyst, "India falls in the third category. The dominant power in the region with an independent foreign policy, India has had a troubled relationship with China over territorial and other issues such as Tibet, conflicting world views and strategic postures during the cold war, and over Chinese policies considered hostile by New Delhi."[156] He further added that "with the exception of Pakistan, most regional states have at times had strained relations with China." The observations underscored the point that in the regional context, China's overall role would be perceived differently. This fact, in near future would continue to pose challenges to India's security environments.

China-Nepal Relation in Post Cold War Period

Nepal is land locked between two giants : China on the South and India on the North. With the PLA's march into Tibet the buffer between China and India disappeared. From the Chinese perspective. Nepal's geo-strategic location became extremely important due to its vulnerabilities and sensitivities in the Tibetan Autonomous Region. The Chinese presence in Tibet caused adverse security implications for India. Nepal established its diplomatic relations with China in the year 1955, only after India and China signed agreement over Tibet in 1954. In the cold war period, China tried to wean Nepal away from India's influence. China's main objective vis-a-vis Nepal was to support the monarchy, provide economic assistance, build strategic roads and reduce Nepal's overall dependence on India. It also supported King Birendra's proposal of converting Nepal into a "Zone of Peace'.

More importantly, in March 1988, the North China Industrial Corporation (NORINCO) agreed to sell come 20 million US $ worth of light arms, ammunitions, and anti-aircraft guns to Nepal.[157] From China's perspective, military relations were part of normal state-to-state relations. Beijing argued that "a sovereign independent country such as Nepal has the right to acquire such materials as it deems necessary for its defense, and China has the right to sell such materials. Moreover, the materials sold to Nepal could not in any way be construed as constituting a threat to India."[158] India, on the other hand, viewed this as a serious development and as an effort by China to alter the military status quo in Nepal. After all, legally Nepal was obliged by the terms of the 1950 Indo-Nepali Treaty of Peace and Friendship. The letter exchanged at the time of the treaty and a further set of letters exchanged in 1965 provided for purchase of arms only from India or from third countries only with India's permission.[159]

China in the wake of improvement of relations with India from 1988 onwards reassured its friends in South Asia that 'better Sino-Indian relations would not reduce China's ties with them'. Thus, during his Nepal's visit in November 1989, Chinese Premier Li Peng stated : "It has always been China's steadfast policy to develop good neighbourly and friendly relations with every country in South Asia. No matter what happens in the international situation, China will always support Nepal and other South Asian countries in their efforts to safeguard independence and sovereignty."[160] Thus, China made it clear that it would be involved in South Asia.

In the post cold war period, India factor loomed large over Chinese consideration but it was argued in a nuanced way. Moreover, China wanted to Strengthen Security of its Tibetan Autonomous Region. To ease pressure on the Kodari Highway, it was decided to Speed up Syabrubensi Rasuwagadi (135 km. northwest of Kathmandu) highway project. The highway would link Nepal with Tibet's Kerung.[161] In 1999, the Chinese government allocated 670 million rupees for the some. Earlier, in August 2000 during the Nepalese foreign minister's Chakra Prasad Bastolla's visit to China, the latter agreed to open two more road links – Mustang Lizhi road and Kimathangka – Dingri road.[162] The Chinese Vice Chairman of CMC, Hu Jintao met with the visiting Nepalese foreign minister and stated that "China has always held that all countries, big or small, rich or poor, strong or weak, are equal numbers of world community endowed with right to choose their own course of development compatible to their specific situations."[163] Thus, in a subtle but sure way the reference point in the statement was aimed at India.

From mid 1990's, China decided to accelerate economic development in its western region. The western region was inhabited by majority of China's minorities and constituted turbulent area. After the recent by concluded 16th party congress, China has allotted 90 billion US $ for the Western Area Development Programme. In this context, the Chinese leadership emphasised the point that this would "create more favourable conditions and opportunities for cooperation between Nepal and Tibet Autonomous Region."[164]

Among the high level visits from Chinese side in post cold war period was the visit of President Jiang Zemin in December 1996. During his visit, leaders of both sides agreed to establish 'a good-neighbourly partnership of generation-to-generation friendship in the 21st century'. To broaden interaction at the political level, the friendly interactions between the government organisations, parliaments and political parties of both nations continued apace. Further, in 1996 regular diplomatic consulting mechanism was set up between the two Foreign Ministries, since then consultations were held annually and both sides could exchange views on bilateral relations and matters of common concern.[165] In February, 2001 the then King Birendra paid a state visit to China and in May, 2001 Chinese Premier, Zhu Rongji paid an official friendly visit to Nepal. More recently in July, 2002 the new King Gyanendra visited China as part of Maintaining good relations with Beijing.[166]

In the wake of emergence of Maoist insurgency, China supported government's initiative to restore order and stability and offered support on its part. In fact, the Chinese Ambassador to Nepal conceded the fact that Maoist insurgency has so far not caused "any sense of insecurity on our side," but took exception to the misuse of name of China's great leader Mao, on the one hand and Condemned the Maoists insurgents in Nepal as terrorists, on the otherhand.[167] At the political front, with the new dispensation in Kathmandu after October 4, 2002 dismissal of parliamentary government and November 26, imposition of emergency, China announced its firm support to measures taken by the king to restore national peace and stability.[168]

In the economic sphere, Chinese companies participated in developmental work like road, power station, telecommunication, irrigation etc. in Nepal. During the year 2000, the Chinese construction companies achieved six projects through international bidding and in 2001, the Chinese companies secured five projects. By the end of February, 2002 in Nepal there were in all 19 Chinese Construction companies, about 360 technicians and total 10 projects under construction.[169] Besides, there are a number of Nepal-China joint venture projects as well. Further, during King's visit to Beijing in 2002, both sides agreed to enhance economic cooperation. Accordingly, China granted Rs. 780 million for infrastructure building, promote border trade, tourism development and setting up of consulate in Shanghai.[170]

As far as trade ties are concerned China enjoyed huge trade surplus with Nepal. For instance in the year 1996 Nepal's total exports to China was 188.18 US $. Whereas imports from China was 5,52,92,447 US $. The trend persists in border trade as well. More recently, Nepal's total exports of Rs. 1.1 million to any imports from China of Rs. 4,130 million in year 1998-99, similarly exports of Rs. 2.1 million and imports worth Rs. 0,430 million in year 1999/2000 and finally exports of Rs. 2.1 million and imports worth Rs. 7,730 million underlines the fact of huge trade gap, which adversely affects Nepal's economy.[171] Despite Chinese assurances to balance trade and creation of governmental mechanisms nothing concrete has emerged.

Sino-Nepal Military Relations

The exchange of mutual military delegations continued during the post cold war period. In November 1996, Chief of Staff of Royal Nepal Army, Lt. General Dharmapalbar Singh Thapa visited China. During his visit he met with the Defence Minister of China, Chi Haotian, who emphasised that China wants to develop cooperative ties with all countries "especially its neighbours, on the basis of five principles of peaceful coexistence." He further stated that "China needs a peaceful international environment in order to concentrate itself on economic development." Lt. Gen. Thapa was the first Nepalese army Chief to visit China, as such this was an important development.

In the year 2000, the chief of Staff, PLA General Fu Quan you visited Nepal with a delegation.[172] King Birendra welcomed the Chinese military delegation and told General Fu that he hoped the military ties between Nepal and China will be further strengthened in the future. Further, in 2001 the Defence Minister and Vice-Chairman of CMC, Chi Haotian visited Kathmandu and stated that "Sino-Nepalese friendship in the new century not only serves the fundamental interest of the two peoples, but also contributes to peace and stability in the region."[173] Therefore, the Chinese military leadership perceived that for peace and stability in the region, military relationship is important. Thus, in a nuanced manner China signalled the India factor. But to assuage the security concerns of India, the Defence Minister of Nepal, Mahesh Acharya stated that "No arms purchases will be discussed and no agreements will be signed during the visit."[174] moreover, in the wake of emergence of the Maoist insurgents, China began to train the Nepalese army as well.[175]

In the post 9/11 US war against terrorism, America assistance to Nepal increased. Due to Crucial geo-strategic location of Nepal in context of Tibet issue, China took up the issue and conveyed concern on interference of outside powers. In the words of China's Ambassador to Nepal : "Some countries are utilizing this situation as an excuse to provide assistance which could be used to intervene in the internal affairs of Nepal."[176] In fact, the developments after 9/11 in Nepal was cause of concern for India as well. In short, the overall military relations between China and Nepal was growing. The exchange of military delegations at high level continued apace. During the post cold war period, China did not based openly its relations with Nepal on the premise of anti-Indianism but in a subtle way the regime support and some Chinese statements in nuanced manner pointed out the existence of broad regional context of bilateral Sino-Nepal relations. As such, in the regional context the presence of India factor was a constant variable and added comfort level of Nepal.

China-Bhutan Relations in the Post Cold War Period

Bhutan is located in the eastern Himalayas, it shares borders with India in the South, east and west and by the Tibetan Autonomous Region of China in the worth. Bhutan has special foreign policy links with India.

As of now, Bhutan does not have any diplomatic ties with China. Bhutan shares some 470 km border with China. Its borders with China is undermarcated and still remains to be resolved. Therefore, Bhutan-China relation revolves around the resolution of the border disputes.

As for the Chinese motivations, in the words of a leading western analyst, "It is worth reiterating that China's objective is not to bring Bhutan into its own sphere of influence or to establish some sort of Chinese special or security relation with Bhutan. It is enough, rather, to bring about the dissolution of India's special relation with Bhutan, slowly and cautiously."[177] In part, China met its objective during cold war period, as the Sino-Bhutan direct bilateral talks started from 1984. It is true that India did not participate in the talks, yet Bhutan kept GOI informed about talks with the Chinese.[178]

In the post cold war period, exchange of visits at various levels between the both sides have significantly increased. In all, seven round of talks were held till 1990. As a result of bilateral talks, the disputed borders narrowed down to 269 sq. kms. in three areas of north-west Bhutan.[179] In the year 1996, Chinese incursions were reported.[180] To allay Bhutanese fears and misgivings, China proposed agreement to maintain peace and tranquility in China-Bhutan border areas. Both nations concluded an agreement to maintain peace and Tranquility on Bhutan-China border in 1998 during the 12th round of bilateral border talks. This was the first agreement between the both nations. As such, it was an important development in bilateral relations. According to article 1, China stated that" (it) reiterates its position to fully respect the independence, Sovereignty and territorial integrity of Bhutan." Article 3 *inter alia* stated that both sides agree "to maintain status quo on the boundary as before March 1959. They will also refrain from taking any unilateral action to change the status quo of the boundary."[181]

In July, 2001 the Bhutanese foreign secretary visited Beijing alongwith a delegation. The Bhutanese delegation met with the Chinese foreign minister and discussed border and other issues of mutual interest. The Chinese government assured Bhutan that it treats all nations equally irrespective of difference in their size, strength or wealth. The king informed the National Assembly of Bhutan in July, 2001 that bilateral border talks with China under discussion were in three sectors, i.e., Doglam, Sinchulumba and Dramana areas.[183]

Further, in July 2002, the Bhutanese Foreign Minister told the National Assembly that China claimed to have documentary evidence of ownership of the disputed tracts of land. Bhutan on its part, urged China to be generous with a small neighbour. China stated that" as a nation which shared its borders with 25 other countries they could not afford to be generous with one particular neighbour."[184] Thus, it became clear that resolution of border problem is not going to be quite easy task.

Till the year 2002, in all sixteenth round of Sino-Bhutanese border talks were held. In fact, Bhutan's Foreign Minister, Lyonpo Jigme Yoser Thinley visited Beijing for the 16th border talks. He also met with the Chinese Premier, Zhu Rongji at Zhongnanhai.[185] The Bhutanese Foreign Minister also visited Tibet and added that he was impressed by the great changes taking place in Tibet. He further stated : "I appreciate China's efforts in the restoration and protection of religious sites."[186] The Tibet factor would be a determinant in the evolving bilateral relations. By and large, Bhutan has treaded cautiously on this count and not provoked China.

Thus, in the above mentioned period the bilateral relations between both sides have grown. China and Bhutan concluded first agreement to maintain peace and tranquility in the disputed borders. To sum up, therefore, in the words of two experts, "Looking ahead one would expect gradual but moderate increase in relations between China and Bhutan."[187]

In the strategically important Himalayan region, China tried to reduce India's influence in particular India's special relations with Nepal and Bhutan. In the post cold war period, due to improved Sino-Indian relations there was no alarming development in the Himalayan region from Chinese activities. Nonetheless, at a broad level, in the words of a Western expert, "yet Beijing denounces this as unacceptable hegemonism. Having consolidated its hold over Tibet, China now seeks to erode India's special position in the Himalayas. This, in any case, is the Indian perspective."[188] In the Himalayan region, the conflicting perspective was present between China and India.

As such, in South Asia India watched the substantial growth of China's relations with other nations. In India, opinion varied broadly about China's linkages with India's smaller neighbours and Pakistan. For instance, Col. Gurmeet kanwal wrote : "China's continuing nuclear and missile collusion and defence cooperation with Pakistan, its support to the military regime in Myanmar and increasing activities in the Bay of Bengal... its relentless efforts to increase its influence in Nepal, Bhutan and Bangladesh, are all pointers to a carefully orchestrated plan aimed at the strategic encirclement of India."[189] While another foreign policy analyst concedes the relaxed atmosphere but underlines the 'latent sources of political diplomatic friction' and cautions presence of instable factors in China's regional linkages which flow from : first, "unsettled border problems with India and Bhutan." Second, "The continuing political and ethnic tensions in Tibet... the consequent concern that separatism could lead to future regional tensions with united states, and India." Third and equally importantly, "China's military ties and destabilizing arms transfers to Pakistan, Iran, and military ruled Myanmar... and deploy naval power, which would touch off suspicions and tensions with the U.S., India, and Indonesia. Lastly as well as more importantly, "China's military build up... especially its naval and air power, and modernization of its strategic weapons. This could engender growing concern about the rise of a hegemonic, militarily assertive China."[190] On the other side of spectrum, the optimists argued that "To keep arguing that China seeks to confine India into a South Asian strait jacket misses a fundamental point. Whether or not India becomes a global actor depends on India alone... It is not a status anybody-not even China – can deny India... If in years ahead India fails to promote its interests on a regional or global level this will be due to its domestic and diplomatic failures. Any Chinese role in this will be marginal."[191]

Be that as it may be, one point is for sure that the regional context of Sino-Indian interactions does have to some degree competitive element as well. In particular, China's military relations with Pakistan and Myanmar concerns India's security environment adversely. It appears that in post 9/11 world, maintenance of peace and security in South Asia is in the overall interest of China. But its 'all weather friendship' with Pakistan and long-term national interest compels China to pursue linkages with other South Asian nations. In the final analysis, China viewed military relations with South Asian nations a legitimate relations, but for India, they constitute threat to Indian security environment. As such, there was serious difference between India and China on the regional dimension.

References

1. Sujit Dutta, "China's Emerging Power and Military Role : Implications for South Asia" in Jonathan D. Pollack and Richard H. Yang, eds., In China's Shadow : Regional Perspectives on Chinese Foreign Policy and Military Development, National Security Research Division, Rand, 1998, p. 99.
2. John W. Garver, Protracted Contest : Sino-Indian Rivalry in the Twentieth Century, Oxford University Press, New Delhi, 2001, p. 5.
3. *Ibid.,* pp. 2-5.
4. C.V. Ranganathan and Vinod C. Khanna, India and China : The Way Ahead After "Mao's India War", Har Anand Publications, New Delhi, 2000, p. 108.
5. *Ibid.,* p. 147.
6. *Ibid.,* pp. 147-48.
7. A.J. Chandy, "India, China and Pakistan", in Kanti Bajpai and Amitabh Matto (eds), The Peacock and The Dragon : India-China Relations in the 21st Century, Har Anand Publications, New Delhi 2000, p. 301.
8. See n. 2, p. 218.
9. Kanti P. Bajpai, "Managing a Strategic Triangle : India, China and Pakistan: in P. Saha Devan, ed., Conflict and Peace Making in South Asia, Lancer's Books, New Delhi, 2001, pp. 81-82.
10. *Ibid.*, pp. 84-85.
11. *Ibid.,* p. 85. See for further details on Pakistan China Cooperation, articles and documents in Peace Initiatives, Omnibus Issue (Guest Editor, Swaran Singh), "Sino-Pakistani Strategic Cooperation", Vol. V, Nos. III-IV, May-December 1999.
12. J. Mohan Malik, "Zhou, Mao, and Nixon's 1972 Conversations on India", Issues and Studies, 38, 3, September 2002, p. 186.
13. Xie Yixian (ed.), Diplomatic History of China 1949-79 (Zhong guo Waijiaoshi), Henan People's Publishing Agency, Zheng Zhou, 1996, p. 260.
14. Andrew Scobell, 'Cult of Defense' and 'Great Power Dreams' : The Influence of Strategic Culture on China's Relationship with India," in South Asia in 2020 : Future Strategic Balances and Alliances, ed. Michael R. Chambers, Strategic Studies Institute, U.S. Army War College, November 2002, p. 342.
15. See n. 12, pp. 215-16. See also for details, Shao Zhiyong, "India's big Power Dream," Beijing Review, April 12, 2001, p. 10. Michael Pillsbury, "Japan and India : Dangerous Democracies," in China Debates the Future Security Environment.
16. See n. 1, p. 99.

17. FBIS-CHI, December 16, 1991, pp. 18-20.
18. U.D. Bhat Koti, Sino-Pakistan Relations : A Chinese Perspective, Unpublished Seminar Paper, IDSA, 2002, p. 10.
19. See for details, He Daolong, "South Asian Policy Options of China", Nanya Yanjiu Jikan (South Asian Studies Quarterly), 3/2001, pp. 15-12. Cited in n. 18.
20. See n. 2, p. 241.
21. Fan Ming Xing, "Qian tan Yindu de dui Hua Zhanlue," (India's Strategy toward China) cited in *Ibid.*
22. FBIS-CHI-196, Octobers 8, 1992, p. 15. See the text of full report pp. 1-20.
23. Bei Monong, Zhou En Lai and New China's Foreign Policy (Zhou En Lai Yu Xin Zhongguo Waijiao), CCP Central Party School Publishing Agency, Beijing, 2002, p. 469.
24. Keshav Mishra, China-Pakistan Relations in the Post Cold War Era, Unpublished Seminar Paper, IDSA, 2002, p. 7.
25. See n. 18, p. 16.
26. See for recent Chinese views on South Asian Security Situation, Du You Kang, "South Asian Security and its impact on China", China Report, 37, 2, 2001, pp. 141-163.
27. FBIS-CHI-94, February 17, 1994, p. 16.
28. Public Opinion Trends (here after POT), Pakistan Series, 12 March, 1994, p. 581.
29. See n. 2, pp. 231-232.
30. POT, 3 December, 1996, p. 2845.
31. See for detailed account on Pakistan's Comments on Sino-Indian Agreement of 1996, POT, 4 December, 1996, pp. 2848-2850.
32. See the full text of Jiang Zemin's Speech, in Summary of World Broadcasts (hereafter SWB), FE/2786, 4 December 1996, pp. A-4 to A-6.
33. See n. 4, pp. 143-44.
34. An important Pakistani Daily Muslim on 24-11-1996 reported that 'with over emphasis on economic interdependence the Indians have in fact forced China to rationalize the new choices and to slowly distance them from Pakistan'. See for details, POT, 29 November, 1996.
35. The Muslim, 9 December 1996, cited in POT, 13 December, 1996, pp. 2946-47.
36. See for details of Chinese viewpoint, Cheng Rui Sheng, "China and South Asia in the 21st Century", in Muchkund Dubey and Nancy Jetly, eds, South Asia and Its Eastern Neighbours : Building a Relationship in the 21st Century, New Delhi, 1999, pp. 115-127.

37. M. Ehsan Ahrari, "China, Pakistan and the Taliban Syndrome", Asian Survey, 40, 4, July/August 2000, pp. 658-71.
38. See for the text of Declaration of Shanghai Cooperation Organisation, in FBIS-CHI-0615, June 15, 2001.
39. Anti Terror Research Centre, "A few Observations on Terrorism and Anti-terror Struggle", International Strategic Studies, CIISS, 4th Issue, 2002, pp. 21-22.
40. For Eastern Economic Review (hereafter FEER), June 25, 1998, p. 13.
41. FBIS-CHI-2000-2112, December 12, 2000.
42. Cited in n. 18, p. 20.
43. *Ibid.*, p. 21.
44. FEER, June 11, 1998, p. 22.
45. Zhongli, "Sino-Indian Relations After Indian Nuclear Tests", South Asian Studies Quarterly (Nanya Yanjiu Jikan, Sichuan Daxue Nanya Yanjiu Suo), 1/2001, pp. 44-45.
46. Cited in S. Kondapalli, "China's Response to the kargil Incident", Strategic Analysis, 23, 6, 1999, p. 1040.
47. Guang Ming Daily, 9 June 1999, Cited in Documents Section, Chinese Media Coverage of the Kargil Conflict, China Report, 35, 4, 1999, p. 529.
48. Liberation Army Daily Report by Li Yanan, 12 June 1999, cited in *Ibid*, pp. 530-31.
49. China Daily, 30 June, 1999.
50. Xinhua, 11 June 1999, FBIS-0CHI-1999, 0611, Also cited in Maqbool Ahmad Batty, Sino-Pakistan Friendship : An enduring bond, in Dawan, 1 October 1999. See for further details, Rifaat Hussain, "China's Kargil stance in perspective", The News International Pakistan, 27 June, 1999.
51. See n. 4, p. 145.
52. See n. 2, p. 234.
53. See for details in website of Ministry of Foreign Affairs, Pakistan, Pakistan-China Relation : http://www.forisb.
54. Beijing Review, September 12, 1999, p. 5.
55. Cited in Pakistan Horizon, 52, 1, January 1999, p. 72.
56. Cited in Shaheen Akhtar, "Pak-China Economic Relations", Regional Studies, 19, 3, Summer 2001, p. 47.
57. FBIS-CHI-194, October 6, 1992, p. 7.
58. Cited in S.A. Rizvi, "Chinese assistance for Pakistan", Pakistan and Gulf Economist, 20, 49, December 2001, p. 28.
59. Cited in Pakistan and Gulf Economist, 20, 48, p. 5.
60. Zhang Chengli, "China-Pakistan Relations and situation in South Asia", Pakistan Horizon, 49, 3, July 1996, p. 13.
61. Lok Sabha Debates, Vol. 47, 1969, Cols-1983-84.

62. Annual Report, 1969-70, Ministry of Defence, Government of India, p. 1.
63. See n. 2, p. 234.
64. See for details, http://www.subcontinent.com/sapra/bulletin/96.
65. Cited in Pakistan Horizon, 45, 4, October 1992, p. 70.
66. See n. 7. pp. 314-15.
67. *Ibid.*, p. 315.
68. Christopher Foss, ed., Jane's Armour and Artillery, 2001-2002, Jane's Publications Group, London, p. 70.
69. *Ibid.*
70. Cited in Aabha Dixit, Defence Production in Pakistan, Asian Strategic Review, 1991-92, p. 294.
71. See n. 68, p. 71.
72. Paul Jackson, Jane's All the World's Aircraft, 2001-2002, Jane's Publications Group, London, pp. 60-72.
73. SWB, FEW/0644, 14 June 2000, WG/13.
74. POT, Pakistan Series, January 1, 2002, p. 17. For details of agreement see POT, March 18, 2002, p. 1158.
75. POT, Pakistan Series, march 27, 2002, p. 1319.
76. Cited in G. Partha Sarathy, "The Gowing Sino-Pakistan Nexus," in The Tribune, May 23, 2001.
77. http://www.rediff.com/news/2002/jan/07China.htm.
78. FBIS-CHI-2002-0314, March 13, 2002.
79. See for details, Business Record, April 22, 2000, and The Dawn, July 29, 2001 and March 23, 2002.
80. See n. 2, pp. 236-37.
81. See for details http://www.fas.org/nuke/guide/pakistan/facility/fatehjung.htm.
82. Cited in Jane's Intelligence Review, April 2002, p. 47.
83. Cited in John W. Garver, "Sino-Indian Rapprochment and the Sino-Pakistan Entente", Political Science Quanterly, 3, 2, p. 335.
84. See n. 7, p. 318.
85. Cited in Chintamani Mahapatra, "American Approach to Sino-Pakistan Nuclear and Missile cooperation", Strategic Analysis, 21, 10, January 1998, p. 1412.
86. http://dosfan.bib.uic.edu/acda/reports/complian.htm.
87. http://www.ceip.org/programs/npp/chinafact/sheet72400.htm.
88. See *Ibid.*
89. See n. 85, p. 1407.

90. See for the copy of appended texts in After the Tests : US Policy Toward India and Pakistan, Brookings Institute and the Council on Foreign Relations, Washington, 1998, pp. 54-55.
91. Annual Report, 2001-02, Ministry of Defence, Government of India, p. 3.
92. Xinhua 4th July, cited in SWB, FE/3885, July 6, 2000, G/8.
93. See for details, Alexander L. Chopan, "Chinese Denial and deception : Theory and Practice, Issues and Studies, 37, 3, 2001, pp. 32-67.
94. Cited in Jane's Intelligence Review, May 2002, p. 43.
95. Seen 7, p. 327.
96. SWB, FE/4067, February 10, 2001, A/2.
97. See n. 7, p. 327.
98. Cited in Pakistan Horizon, 49, 3, July 1996, p. 164.
99. Cited in See n. 18, p. 13.
100. *Ibid.*
101. Hooman Peimani, Nuclear Proliferation in the Indian Subcontinent, Praeger Publishers, Westport, 2000, p. 117.
102. See n. 2, p. 237.
103. Xinhua, 25 May 1999, in FBIS-CHI-1999-0526.
104. John W. Garver, "The Restoration of Sino-Indian Comity following India's Nuclear Tests," China Quarterly, 168, December 2001, p. 882.
105. Cited in China's National Defense in 2002, See http://www.english.people.com.cn/ndpaper2002/ndf.htm. December 9, 2002.
106. 19 November 2002. FBIS-CHI-2002-1119.
107. Cited in Agence France Presse, January 16, 2002.
108. See n. 1, p. 100.
109. John w. Garver, "China and South Asia", The Annals of the American Academy, 519, January 1992, p. 67.
110. People's Daily, April 30, 2001.
111. Wang Baofu, "No Winner in Indian-Pakistani Conflicts" in Beijing Review, February 28, 2002, p. 13.
112. Rong Ying, "Can India become a Military Power" in Beijing Review, February 28, 2002, pp. 14-15.
113. Washington Times, March 19, 2002.
114. Cheng Ruisheng, "The Situation In South Asia After "September 11" and China's Policy, Foreign Affairs journal, 68, June 2003, pp. 37-38.
115. The advance weapons included aircraft F-8, anti-aircraft missiles, tanks, Ly-60N ground to air, medium-to-low range all weather missile system etc. See for details FBIS-NES-2001-1026, October 26, 2001.
116. www.fmprc.gov.cn.25-3-03.

117. See for details, *Ibid.*
118. See n. 114, p. 39.
119. See n. 4, pp. 147-48.
120. *Ibid.*, p. 118.
121. See for details, POT, Bangladesh Series, November 1993.
122. See for details of PM's visit to China, POT. Bangladesh series, September 1996.
123. Bangladesh observer, January 12, 2002.
124. A MOV to modernise telecommunications was concluded in May 1997. See for details POTm Bangladesh Series, May 1997. Further, China will help in setting gthree cement plants, See for details POT, Bangladesh Series, July 1999.
125. See for details, POT, Bangladesh Series, February, 2000.
126. Daily Star, 26 December, 2002.
127. Financial Express, 26 December, 2002.
128. Abu Taher S. Ahmed, Bangladesh-China Relations : An Assessment, BIISS Journal, 13, 2, 1992, p. 265.
129. See n. 2, p. 297.
130. SWB, Part 3 Asia Pacific, FE/3923, August 19, 2000, A/2.
131. Xinhua in SWB, FE/2766, November 11, 1996, C/I.
132. See n. 2, p. 299.
133. http://www.fmprc.gov.cn. Foreign Ministry Spokesperson's Press Conference on December 12, 2002.
134. China Report, 39, 2, 2003, p. 301.
135. Daily Star, 29 December, 2002.
136. See for details, J.N. Dixit, Liberation and Beyond : Indo-Bangladesh Relations, Konark Publishers, New Delhi, 1999, pp. 270-83.
137. See n. 2, p. 299.
138. See n. 4, p. 123.
139. See n. 2, p. 296.
140. See n. 2, p. 265.
141. Cited in J. Mohan Malik, "Burma's Role in Regional Security-Pawn or Pivot" ? in Robert I. Rotberg, ed., Burma Prospects for a Democratic-Future, Brookings Institutional Press, Washington, 1998, p. 111.
142. See n. 2, p. 265.
143. Xinhua cited in SWB, FE/2752, October 25, 1996, G/3.
144. See n. 2, p. 265.
145. SWB, FE/2200, January 13, 1995, B/5.
146. SWB, FE/2754, October 28, 1996, G/3.
147. See n. 141, p. 113.

148. China Report, 39, 2, 2003, p. 301.
149. BBC Monitoring Global Newsline, Asia-Pacific Political 9-2-2002.
150. See n. 141, p. 116.
151. See n. 4, p. 134.
152. See n. 1, p. 100.
153. See n. 2, pp. 309-10.
154. See n. 1, p. 100.
155. *Ibid.,* pp. 100-01.
156. *Ibid.,* p. 101.
157. See for details, n. 2, pp. 151-54.
158. See n. 109, p. 76.
159. The text of 1950 treaty and subsequent letters in R.K. Jha, The Himalayan Kingdom in Indian Foreign Policy (Ranchi, 1986), pp. 347-56. The gist of the 1965 letters is presented in Asian Recorder, 27 August – 2 September 1989, pp. 20740-42.
160. FBIS-CHI, November 20, 1989.
161. SWB, FEW/0664, November 1, 2000, WA/6.
162. *Ibid.*.
163. *Ibid.*
164. SWB FE/3930, August 28, 2000, G/1.
165. See website of Chinese embassy in Nepal, http://www.chinaembassy.nepal.org.
166. See for details Keshab Paudel, "Royal visit to China : Building Good Neighbourly Relations," Spotlight, July 19, 2002, pp. 16-20.
167. See for interview, Spotlight, July 5, 2002, pp. 22-23.
168. http://www.chinaembassy.nepal.org.
169. *Ibid.*
170. See n. 166.
171. Overseas Trade Statistics, Trade Promotion Centre, Kathmandu, 2002.
172. SWB, FE/3814, April 13, 2000, A/3.
173. SWB, FE/4077, February 22, 2001, G/2.
174. SWB, FE/4078, February 23, 2001, A/3.
175. *Ibid.*
176. See no. 167, p. 23.
177. See n. 2, p. 185.
178. Surjit Man Singh, "China-Bhutan Relations", China Report, 30, 2, 1994, pp. 184-85.
179. Cited in n. 4, p. 116.
180. *Ibid.*

181. See the text in Kuensel on line, Bhutan.
182. Kuen sel online, Bhutan.
183. *Ibid.*
184. Cited in *Ibid.*,
185. See n. 134.
186. Peoples Daily, October 22, 2002.
187. See n. 4, p. 117.
188. See n. 2, p. 186.
189. Col. Gurmeet Kanwal, "China's Strategic Encirclement of India", Indian Defence Review, 15, 3, July 2000, p. 200.
190. See n. 1, p. 103.
191. See n. 4, p. 161.

10

The Evolving Global Setting

The point has been mentioned that the Sino-Indian relationship is essentially bilateral in nature, but the relationship has also been shaped and conditioned by the evolving global setting. As such this chapter encapsulates the evolving global setting and international aspects of the India-China interaction. The India-China interaction, which is multidimensional and multi-layered, is conditioned on the one hand, by the evolving nature of politics at the global level, and on the another hand, by both the convergent and divergent interests and strategies of both nations. Furthermore, the role of USA, only superpower in the post cold war and other major powers, i.e., Russia and their relations with both nations, also influenced the India-China interaction. Therefore, the evolving global setting and international aspects assumes importance in the comprehensive study of India-China interaction.

In the post cold war period, multipolar was the key word for the Chinese foreign policy analysts. The collapse of the bipolar pattern in the cold war period was followed by a multi-polarization trend. One Chinese analyst termed the evolution of multi-polarization trend by the style of "one superpower and multiple powers."[1] Nonetheless, China accepted reality that from the comprehensive national power perspective, the USA is the only superpower in the world. The analyst categorized in terms of military force, the USA and Russia are the leaders. Economically, the US, Japan and the European Union are the three giants, with East Asia (excluding Japan) as the fourth pole. Politically, there are five major forces-the US, EU, Japan, Russia and China. Lastly, the analyst wrote : "Maybe, some regional powers will appear at the transition from a bipolar world to the multipolar one."[2] Thus, the Chinese analysts emphasized the point on multipolar world.

Another important development in the post cold war period was the Chinese foreign policy increasingly became more pragmatic and realistic. As the overall emphasis was on comprehensive national power, therefore, the political leadership realized the necessity of shedding the ideological baggage. In the words of a Chinese analyst, "all Chinese authors now agree that diplomacy constrained by ideology or by the façade of communist internationalism had not upheld Chinese national interests and they argue for distinguishing between ideological fantasy and China's real economic and political interests."[3] After a careful survey of China's diplomatic practice spanning the period of late 1980s and including the Gulf War of 1991, an expert concluded that the Chinese government followed a maxi/mini principle in the conduct of multilateral diplomacy – maximizing China's rights and interests and minimizing China's responsibility and normative costs. He described it as "an unprincipled quest to make the best of all possible worlds."[4] Be that as it may be one fact which stands out is, China was guided by the idea of national interest.

An analyst has attributed four reasons which brought about Chinese shift in attitude. In the words of analyst they are following : "First, the criticisms and humiliation brought about by the Tiananmen incident left the conservative Chinese communists with no alternative but to adopt a realistic and sterner attitude vis-à-vis the west. Secondly, the collapse of the Soviet Union provided an opportunity for China to fill the power vacuum thus created, and for this a real politik orientation was needed. Third, the awesome right of the US in the field of military technology was visible during the Gulf war which compelled the Chinese leaders to think in terms of the modernization of its armed forces, more nuclear testing and development of long range missiles. Fourth, its ambition to embark on the path of economic modernization reversed its erstwhile dislike of capitalism and encouraged an interest in aid, trade, capital and technology."[5]

Moreover, in the post cold war period, China began to emphasise on the multilateral cooperative mechanism. In a subtle way, China was apprehensive of US intentions in the Asia-pacific region. Viewed from Chinese national interest perspective, the multipolar rather than the unipolar world order suited China. As one Chinese analyst summed up, "[US hegemony] is no longer permissible, as was the case during the cold war era when powerful and rich countries ruled the world. The emergence of the multipolar pattern – an unavoidable trend in the post cold war history – is replacing the old system."[6] Therefore, partly to counter unipolar world order and partly to promote its national interest, China discarded its initial reluctance to join multilateral institutions. China joined the Asia-Pacific Economic Community (APEC) and the Asian Regional Forum (ARF), which it felt would on the one hand enhance its economic growth and security and on the another hand prevent disputes from degenerating to open hostilities. In short, to build its comprehensive national power, the political leadership emphasized on multilateral cooperation for security and economic matters, and desired maintenance of peace along its borders and in neighbouring nations.

It was in this background that China in post cold war period sought to improve its relations with India, its dominant South Asian neighbour. China's policy of maintaining good neighbourly relations with India followed from its conscious strategy of seeking peaceful environment in its surrounding areas. As a Chinese analyst wrote : "China particularly focused its attention on seeking out neighbouring countries with whom it had some basic territorial difference and with whom it had some basic territorial difference and with whom it had to face a conflictual situation during the cold war." Already from late cold war period, India-China relations were improving and Prime Minister Rajiv Gandhi's China visit in 1988 generated mutual trust and goodwill. The bilateral relations between both nations was marked by mutual confidence and spirit of cooperation.

Following the uncertainties created by the collapse of bipolar world, both India and China had a shared perception of the opportunities and challenges in the post cold war world. India in early 1990's embarked on the liberalization of its economy. Therefore, both nations desired a peaceful environment for economic development and also tap the opportunities offered by globalisation. Simultaneously, both nations were developing nations, as such on variety of issues like environment, human rights and search for autonomy in the world over, there was convergence of ideas and interests. Both sides realised that "the challenge of the times is that economic struggle cannot be substituted by political struggles, nor won through tensions and confrontations. Since both countries are learning this lesson it becomes easier for them to turn away from conflict and tension."[7] China on its part, stepped up the emphasis on improved relations with neighbouring states engaging in constructive dialogue about border disputes, normalizing state-to-state relations, and working to manage "problems left over from history." India on its part, in the wake of collapse of the USSR, wanted to enhance its security and expand its diplomatic maneuverability in the global system by stabilizing its relations with China. Therefore, the CBMs Agreement of 1993 and 1996 between India and China were beneficial for stable ties between both nations.

China's Relations with the Major Powers

The salient features of China's foreign policy in post cold war period was to :

- develop friendship with every surrounding country
- balance strategic relations with major world powers
- in particular, make efforts to stabilize the volatile Sino-America relationship.

China on the one hand, was apprehensive of unipolar world order, but on the another hand, was realistiç enough to engage with the USA in the post cold war period. As one Chinese analyst summed up. "No matter what changes have taken place in the world framework and the power balance, countries of the world need to join hands to build a new world order and develop effective systems to guarantee peace and stability in the world."[8] The leadership of China recognized the fact that USA will be indispensable power, consequently for stabilizing global and Asia-Pacific situations, China will have to deal with it. Further, the growing trade relations compelled both nations to pursue policy of engagement. At the bilateral plane, USA was the largest market for Chinese consumer goods, while China was a huge market for US agricultural products and high-tech products.

In short, Chinese leadership on its part sought to improve Sino-US relations and emphasized on the development of cooperative and constructive relations between both sides on the basis of equality and mutual benefits by advocating the principle of seeking common ground while reserving differences.[9] China's growing power, arms build up and military modernization concerned USA. A noted foreign policy expert wrote : "The Soviet-American relationship defined the previous half-century; Sino-American ties are likely to define the next."[10] Thus, for USA pursuing a policy of comprehensive engagement with China became an urgent necessity. Similarly, China's general policy towards the US was formulated as "increase trust, reduce trouble, develop cooperation and avoid confrontation."[11] Notwithstanding the intent on the part of both nations to improve bilateral relations, the presence of problems casted shadows over the emerging Sino-US relations. As one analyst wrote : "In the US, China was accused mainly of a poor human rights record, violations of intellectual property rights, not allowing US exports to enter Chinese markets, the sale of arms, and using US technology to enhance its military power. China alleged that US defence policy was oriented towards hegemony. Beijing was apprehensive of the US security alliance with Japan, criticized it for arms sales to Taiwan and called it a greater arms proliferator than Beijing."[12]

The first Clinton Administration (1993-96) was by and large conciliatory towards China inspite of controversies with it. According to U.S. News and World Report, the general tendency of Clinton's foreign policy was to strike a balance between moral rhetoric and geopolitical reality. It emphasized "diplomacy over force, small steps over grand gestures, prudence over boldness and domestic policy over geopolitics."[13] Though there was no exchange of visits at high levels but overall relations registered upward momentum. In may 1994, President Clinton decided to renew China's Most Favoured Nation (MFN) status and delinked it with human rights records. This step put an end to the ritual of annual renewal of China's MFN status. In the meanwhile developments in 1995-96, when China adopted 'an aggressive and strident stance' over Taiwan and test fired missiles were negative in nature and triggered a debate in US on how to deal with an aggressive China.

In the words of two seasoned diplomats specialising on China, "By 1996, it would be no exaggeration to state that a cold war atmosphere was driving intellectuals in both societies to extreme pronouncements. One manifestation in China of this was a book entitled China can say no... In another work, called megatrend China, by leading Chinese political scientists and military scholars, USA was portrayed as actively seeking war with China to split it and destroy it... Mirror image writings also abounded in USA, painting China in the worst possible light."[14] Broadly, two trends emerged in American policy circles. On the one hand, one group believed that China would grow into a rival of the USA, on the another hand, to the second group, China appeared less adversarial and they believed US should seek its partnership to bring about peace and stability in Asia.

After a period of twists and turns, during second term of President Clinton, Sino-US relations began to improve. In US, both President Clinton and secretary of state warren Christopher made policy statements, stressing the importance of relationship and promising to strengthen "constructive engagement "with China. During the fourth Informal Leadership Meeting of the Asia-Pacific Economic Cooperation in Manila in November, 1996, President Jiang Zemin met with President Clinton. Both leaders exchanged views on a series of issues concerning Sino-US relations in depth and reached some common understanding. They also reached a consensus on an exchange of visits by the heads of state in 1997 and 1998.[15] In the words of two experts on China, "In early 1997, in the first state of the Union Message of his second term, President Clinton sounded more positive about China than at any time in his first four years. In several other speeches he outlined American interests in "engaging" rather than "containing" China, in promoting a strategic relationship, fostering cooperation, not conflict. In a wide arc extending from Korea to South East Asia, including South Asia, Central and West Asia, USA needed China's cooperation. China's help was necessary in keeping weapons of mass destruction and other sophisticated weapons from proliferating."[16]

During Jiang Zemin's US visit in October 1997, the issue of non proliferation in South Asia was included in overall edifice of "constructive strategic partnership" between US and China. According to the Joint Presidential statement issued during Jiang's Visit, the two nations had "great potential for cooperation in maintaining global and regional peace and stability." South Asia was identified as one of the several areas.[17] This development was perceived in India as going against its overall security interest. In the words of an analyst, "In Indian eyes the October 1997 Sino-US joint statement suggested that, under the wing of the United States, China might play a larger security role in South Asia. "These nebulous Indian fears became far more concrete when India saw Washington aligning with Beijing after the May 1998 tests."[18] Gradually after the 1997 Summit, China was being seen from part of nuclear non proliferation problem to part of the solution. China promised US "not to assist any un safeguarded nuclear facilities in Pakistan, promised to cut off nuclear cooperation with Iran, and not to sell anti-ship cruise missiles." Furthermore, in June 1998, US President Bill Clinton visited Beijing. There he defended 'American values' and advised the Chinese people to cross over to the 'right side of history'.

During Clinton's visit to China, both nations issued on 27 June a "Sino-US Presidential Joint Statement on South Asia". In the words of an expert, "India would come to see this as an egregious manifestation of US alignment with China against India."[19] According to the joint statement, in the wake of nuclear tests by India and Pakistan, China and the United States had "Shared interests in a peaceful and Stable South Asia". Both nations therefore agreed "to work closely together... to prevent an accelerating nuclear and missile arms race in South Asia." The common goal of China and the United States was Indian and Pakistani accession to the NPT "as it stands, without any modification." China and the United States recognised the "responsibilities" of each other in South Asia and pledged "to contribute actively to the maintenance of peace, stability and security in the region."[20] The two nations expressed their joint commitment "to assist where possible India and Pakistan resolve peacefully the difficult and long-standing differences between them, including the issue of Kashmir."[21]

As a result of Clinton's visit to China, Sino-US relations saw enhanced cooperation. The two important visits was summed up by two Chinese analysts, "it (Jiang's visit) has eventually put a continual roller coaster relationship on an orbit of relative stability. President Bill Clinton's China visit served to flesh out the nascent consensus."[22] China on its part, was satisfied about the out come of Joint statement on South Asia in that it did not refer to 'China's long history of covert assistance to Pakistan's nuclear and missile programmes'. It is quite possible that China wanted 'unipolar' Asia, therefore, Jiang mentioned to his US counterpart that the nuclear arms race in South Asia had created sudden tension in the region. "These problems, if not promptly and properly settled, will cast a shadow over the future of the mankind in the next century."[23] The Chinese President further added : "In the new historical conditions, China and the US shared extensive common interests and shouldered unshirkable common responsibilities on major issues concerning peace and development in the Asia-pacific region and the world at large."[24] Seen from India's viewpoint, the evolving Sino-US close relations on matters affecting South Asia was described by the two experts : "the common positions evolved by China and USA condemning the tests, calling for a roll-back of Indian and Pakistani nuclear weapon programmes, and demanding that both subscribe to the NPT and CTBT were seen by some analysts in India as symbolizing a growing Sino-US condominium to evolve a new hierarchical international order to the determent of India's interests."[25] Apart from South Asia matters, on balance it could be safely stated that Sino-US relations in the post cold war period were based on 'a convergence and divergence of views and interests on various international and regional issues'.

As one analyst put this, "Their views were similar in terms of building a peaceful international order for greater economic cooperation and the need for nuclear non-proliferation. Their views differed whenever Washington's strategic goals clashed with China's national aspirations… Both realised the strategic importance of their bilateral relations for international relations in the coming century. While the US anticipated the rise of China as the second most powerful country, China felt that the US would be its real politik and not ideological adversary in the years to come."[26] Despite stability of Sino-US ties, there are many unresolved problems in the relationship.

China and Russia

In the post cold war period, there was no ideological confrontation between the two nations. From the mid 1980's onwards, in the wake of Gorbachev's assumption of power the bilateral relations registered upward momentum. As one analyst wrote : "The formation of a strategic partnership with Russia set the pattern for China's preferred approach to bilateral relations with great powers. Boris Yeltsin's initial state visit to China in December 1992 had laid the groundwork for improving Sino-Russian ties in the post-Soviet era and resulted in the September 1994 joint announcement during Jiang Zemin's return visit that China and Russia were establishing a "constructive partnership."[27]

In the post-cold war period, Russia on the one hand was a declining power, China on the another hand was an emerging major power. Still, Russia's military-industrial complex were technologically quite advanced. It was during his first visit to China in 1992, Russian President Yeltsin offered to sell fighter aircraft to China. China desired military modernization and it accepted Russian offer. Later on, apart from the fighter aircrafts, China also purchased wide range of Russian missiles, submarines and destroyers worth billion of dollars'[28] The Russian arms deliveries to China gradually became a significant component of Russian-Chinese trade relations. According to an estimate, China bought arms from Russia to the tune of $ 1.5 – 2 billion annually.[29]

Gradually, the good-neighbourly and friendly relationship between China and Russia made remarkable progress in 1996. In April, Russian President Yeltsin paid second visit to China and together with his Chinese counterpart Jiang Zemin, signed the third Sino-Russian joint Statement and announced their "resolve to develop a strategic partnership of equality, mutual confidence and mutual coordination toward the 21st century."[30] This was followed by China, Russia, Kazakhstan, Kyrghystan and Tazikistan signing in Shanghai the Agreement on confidence building in the Military Field in Border Areas. Subsequently, during President Jiang Zemin's Moscow visit in April 1997, both sides signed another joint statement, entitled concerning Global multipolarization and the Building of a New International order. In April 1997, both nations and three other central Asian Republics also concluded an agreement on mutual reduction of military forces in the border regions.[31] The declaration on the construction of a multipolar world was an important development. Both nations were concerned about the US domination of the global affairs. If Russia was anxious about NATO's eastward expansion, China was equally concerned about enhanced US-Japan security alliance. Moreover, the brazen way in which the US-led NATO, by passed the UN Security Council, bombed Yugoslavia into submission during the Kosovo crisis in some measure brought Russia and China closer. Yet, there was some limits to shared anti-US feelings as was pointed out by an analyst : "More importantly, an anti-American alliance would entail steep opportunity costs for both Russia and China as it would jeopardize their vital interest in continued modernization that depends on integration with an international economic system in which the US and its allies remained the key players."[32]

The point need to be underlined is that despite the existence of shared global security concerns, in particular 'unchecked American Superpower', there are problems in Sino-Russian bilateral relations. Firstly, the economic relations are not moving ahead because of Russia's economic crisis. At one stage, both nations set the target for two-way trade at $ 20 billion by the turn of the century. But, trade volume remained in the $ 5-6 billion range.[33] Secondly, as the analysts put it, "There continues to be much Russian concern about the "peaceful invasion" of the Russian Far East by the Chinese. There are deep seated racial fears of the "yellow peril" : a nightmare of huge hordes of Chinese pouring into the under-populated and neighbouring Siberian territories."[34] Notwithstanding the existence of problems, both sides continued to look ahead. From the Chinese perspective, Russian help in overall military modernization was extremely important factor in promotion of the relationship. In this context, two experts wrote : "China has not only become Russia's largest buyer of arms but also the largest foreign employer of Russian scientists and technicians. With 4000 of them now contributing their valuable skills to China's military modernization. General Zhang Wannian, Vice Chairman of the powerful Central Military Commission of China, paid a 10 day visit to Russia in the summer of 1999, and the Xinhua news agency said his talks in Moscow had been "a major step" toward the establishment of Sino-Russian strategic cooperative partnership."[35] Further, steps were being taken to advance economic cooperation in a bid to consolidate bilateral relations. During the Moscow visit of Premier Zhu Rongji in February 1999, both sides concluded some eleven agreements.[36] Gradually, energy security emerged as China's priority and with Russia, China undertook feasibility studies for the pipelines from eastern part of Siberia to Northeast China. In short, in the post cold war period the relationship between China and Russia became extremely close, consequently it was termed as 'strategic cooperative partnership'.

India's Relations with the Major Powers

The post cold war period, offered a Changed context to India to Shape its relations with the major powers. Gradually, with the end of cold war the external elements which inhibited the development of India-US relations were consigned to the background. A confident India, gradually veered towards realism, guided no more by idealism but to promote its national interests. Therefore, India realized the fact that US is the sole superpower with strong economy and the most powerful military machine in the world. India's vital national interests will be served by upgrading the relations with it, from cordial to most cordial.[37]

As one Indian analyst mentioned the fact which estranged the two democracies was the close relations between India and USSR. In its early stage of nation building, India led by Pt. Nehru treaded the path of "democratic socialism", established close relations with USSR, which understood India's security needs and got its military equipment mostly from it. USA was particularly irked when both nations concluded the Treaty of Peace, Friendship and cooperation in 1971. In the words of analyst, "Although Washington showed uneasimic step indicating its closeness with New Delhi, it was the 1971 treaty that became a principal yardstick which determined the US perception of India for the next two decades."[38] Furthermore, the US-Pakístan relations became one of the main sources of conflict between the US and India. In the post cold war period, US slowly but steadily promoted its relations with India at times even at the cost of ignoring Pakistan, since Pakistan's significance diluted in US's strategy after the disintegration of USSR. Moreover, on the crucial issue of Kashmir, during his visit to India in November 1991, the US Deputy-Secretary of State confirmed that America favoured the resolution of the Kashmir issue bilaterally between India and Pakistan in accordance with the Simla Agreement.[39] India was therefore, satisfied with the subtle US's shift in overall positive attitude towards it.

One Chinese analyst has attributed following motivations on the part of India to promote relations with US : "First, the goal of India's leaders was to make India as a world power since its independence. However, India's role and influence in the international affairs was reduced after the cold war. In the process of multi-polarization, India was eager to get a favourable place. So India hoped to develop closer relations with the US after it lost the support of USSR, to achieve its target of world power. Second, India hoped to get America's support and approval in settling the dispute over Kashmir and dominating South Asia. Third, India's economic reform needed a lot of capital, technology and market, and the US was the main source of what India needed (The US was already India's largest trade partner, foreign investor and supplier of advanced technology). India hoped to strengthen economic relations with America to achieve its economic takeoff. Fourth, with the end of the bipolar era, India's foreign policy driven by its own interest was tending towards confluence with the US interests. For example, both of them were concerned with the issues of international terrorism, religious extremism, drug traffic, etc."[40]

As a result of high level political visits, the bilateral Indo-US relations began to move from estrangement to 'strategic dialogue'. From US perspective. India was being projected in a more correct manner. For example, just before Bill Clinton's assumption of office in 1993, Carnegic Endowment, an important think-tank released a report entitled 'India and America after the cold war', which recommended the US administration to assign more priority to India as the world's largest democracy and as 'a potential partner' in efforts to resolve global disputes.[41] Thus, in initial phase of post cold war period, both India and U.S. stated about 'cooperative contact' and 'strategic cooperation'. Prime Minister Nara Simha Rao visited US in May, 1994 to strengthen Indo-US relations. The visit yielded positive results in that both nations narrowed their political differences. Equally important, both nations displayed intent to establish a 'new-partnership.' Further, to consolidate tie both nations agreed to enhance economic relations. Having initiated economic liberalisation and reforms programme, Narasimha Rao urged the US business community for more investments in India and stated : "I have come to here personally to invite you to invest in India and be honored partners in India's development."[42] The visit was a step forward in overall advancement of Indo-US relations. According to an Indian analyst : "Clinton's foreign policy, influenced by commercial interests, preferred China to India . China was at a relatively more advanced stage of economic liberalisation and development. China's huge market, excellent infrastructure facilities, business-friendly environment and trading networks sustained by a large number of over seas Chinese looked more suitable for US investments than India which was in the initial stages of liberalization and behind China in creating suitable institutions and a political consensus behind the reforms... In the decade of the 1990s, China won more concessions from the US than did India... In matters of nuclear non-proliferation and missile development also, China got greater weight age as Beijing joined the US-led non-proliferation regime."[43]

During Second term of President Clinton administration, new dynamism was injected to further improve Indo-US relations. India's BJP led coalition government under Prime Minister A.B. Vajpayee wanted to establish close relations with the USA, the sole superpower in the global political landscape.

But Indo-US relations witnessed down turn following India's nuclear tests in May, 1998. The US President, Bill Clinton stated that he was "deeply disturbed by the tests" and further added that "this action by India not only threatens the stability of the region, it directly challenges the firm international consensus to stop the proliferation of weapons of mass destruction."[44] Further, an independent US Tast-Force suggested that the nuclear tests had made South Asia and the world more dangerous. They had increased the chances of nuclear weapons being used "in case of a conflict between the two countries (India and Pakistan)."[45] Moreover, the USA imposed sanctions on India under the Glenn Amendment of the US Nuclear Proliferation and Prevention Act, 1994. The P-5 nations also adopted a Joint communiqué 'pledging the Permanent Five to Cooperate closely to secure Indian and Pakistani freezing of their nuclear weapons programmes, prevent the escalation of the arms race in South Asia, and strengthen the nuclear non-proliferation mechanism in that region'. Later on similar objectives the UNSC passed Resolution No. 1172.

According to an eminent western expert on Sino-Indian relations. "Following India's nuclear tests, China and India maneuvered to secure greater US support. Beijing's objective was to toughen the US reaction against India and ease American sanctions against Pakistan. India attempted to win US "understanding" of Indian nuclear expansion by stressing China's role in assisting Pakistan's nuclear and missile programmes."[46] The expert further added : "The initial US response to the South Asian nuclear crisis was guided by non-proliferation concerns and a desire for better relations with China an orientation which gave US policy a distinctly pro-China cast. Within months, however, the US dropped its alignment with China against India, and began moving towards a more strictly neutral position."[47]

After the tests, to discuss the issue of nuclear non-proliferation the US Deputy Secretary of State, Strobe Talbott Initiated dialogue with India's Jaswant Singh from July to November 1998. US had already noted strong negative Indian response to the June 1998 US-China statement on South Asia. In particular, India was strongly opposed to 'US endorsement of China playing a larger role in South Asia' because it was concerned about

Chinese proliferation activities in the region. As an expert pointed out in the wake of talks between Talbott and Singh, "Washington also showed a degree of understanding for Indian actions... It did considerably dilute the original content of Sino-US cooperation so as no to alienate India... In short, the United States began to balance between India and China, with both countries attempting to influence US policy towards the other and deeply fearful of an alignment of the other with the United States against itself."[48] Be that as it may be, one thing was sure that due to nature Indian diplomacy, the US realized the fact that relations with India must be improved. India had already declared moratorium on the nuclear tests and in South Asia, India and Pakistan initiated the Foreign secretaries level dialogue and summit diplomacy. In November 1998, President Clinton decided to use the Brownback Amendment to ease sanctions against India and Pakistan, "in response to positive steps both countries have taken to address our non-proliferation concerns following their nuclear tests in may."[49] Further, US appreciated India's behaviour during the Kargil conflict and impressed upon Pakistan to withdraw its intruders.

In this changing scenario which was slightly more favourable to India, President Bill Clinton's visit to India in March 2000 was a notable milestone in Indo-US relations. During the President's visit, both nations signed a framework document entitled, "The US-India Relations : 21st century in prospect", and decided to forge the new partnership for "lasting, Politically constructive and economically effective" relations, which also provided for : deepening the bilateral relations through systematical dialogue, regular consultation and increasing exchanges.[50] Indian government on its part, regarded President's visit as its significant diplomatic victory. An Indian analyst, termed Clinton's visit "to have brought about a sea-change in the US policy toward South Asia", and "it appears to be tilting towards India", hence, "certainly, a new phase is deemed to have begun Indo-US relations since the visit of President Clinton."[51] Later, the Indian Prime Minister. A.B. Vajpayee paid a return visit to the US in September 2000, and said that both nations due to shared belief in democratic system are 'natural allies'.[52] President Clinton stated : "we have established the firmest and most nature partnership. India's achievements are our common achievements. India and America can change the world."[53] At the economic front, US was India's largest trade partner, and the volume of two-way trade was beyond $ 12 billion in 1999, which was more than double comparing with $ 5.6 billion in 1992.[54] Thus, the Indo-US relations were growing steadily.

An important dimension of bilateral relations was the growing military relations between both nations. The US realized the geo-strategic significance of India in the post cold war framework. In this context, the US Defence secretary, William Perry visit to India in January 1995 was notable development. During Perry's visit, both countries concluded an agreement on the US-India defence relations, which regulated the cooperation in military-to-military group and civilian-to-civilian group, besides the cooperation in defence production and research.[55] One Chinese analyst wrote : "For India, signing of this agreement made it shake off the "shadow" of allied military with the Soviet Union during the cold war, and provided it with good condition to change its weapons supplying source."[56] Be that as it may be, the point needs to be underlined that the post cold war period saw momentous developments in Indo-US relations. India now was more nature, strong nation and managed adroitly the diplomatic adverse situation brought about by the Pokharan II nuclear tests. The improved Indo-US relations was ineloquent testimony to the fact.

The growing Indo-US relations caused some concern in China. As one noted Chinese analyst wrote : "In recent years, while China is being regarded by the US as its potential adversary of the 21st century, US-India relations have witnessed a rapid development. Many Chinese analysts view this remarkable development in India-US relations with concern, wondering if India could really forge an alliance with the United states against China. Although both India and the United States have indicated that the development of India-US relations was not aimed at any third country, China will be on the alert against any changes in its peripheral security environment."[57] The point was also underlined by a western expert who wrote : "China deeply fears Indian alignment with the United States and/or US disengagement from Pakistan that would leave China with complete responsibility for supporting that country. China can accept a nuclear armed India. An India aligned with the United States and cooperating with the United States politically and militarily, is a more troubling prospect."[58] In short, there exists a competitive element in Sino-Indian relations due to development in global political configuration as well. Therefore, both India and China have to tread carefully in managing their relations with the major powers.

India-Russia Relations

During the cold war period, the relationship between India and USSR was extremely close and cordial. In the wake of disintegration of USSR,

India continued to maintain close relations with the most important successor state, Russia. Notwithstanding the problems of supply of military hardware, spare parts and rupee-rouble conversion, as a result of high level political visits the relationship continued to grow.

In addition, the idea of creating a "strategic Moscow-Delhi-Beijing triangle" was proposed by thè Russian Foreign Minister, Evgeny Primakov during his New Delhi visit in December, 1998.[59] But the likelihood of this idea materialising into a concrete reality was not possible due to existence of problems between India-China on the one hand, and the necessity of maintaining close relations with the US on the part of China, Russia on the other hand. While promotion of idea of multi-polarity was in the interest of the large states, i.e., Russia, China and India. As one Russian analyst wrote : "At the end of the 1990's, this idea harbored hopes of creating a system of international relations in Asia that could successfully counteract the west's expansionist strivings, promote stabilisation of the situation in the Balkans, restrain NATO's eastward advance, and soon. It was apparently considered that a Russia-China-India triangle could be formed on an anti-western platform. But after the dramatic events of September 11, 2001 in the US, the situation radically changed, compelling the world community to turn its attention to combating international terrorism and preventing fundamentalists from using weapons of mass destruction."[60]

In the meantime, relations between India-Russia continued to gather upward momentum. Russia continued to be the main source of military supplies of India including advanced Sukhoi fighter planes.

Though Russia was 'alarmed' and 'concerned' about India's nuclear tests in May 1998 and expressed 'deep regrets' over India's actions.[61] At the same time, continuing the tradition of friendly ties with India, Russia stated that the tests would not be a hindrance to Indo-Russian Cooperation, in particular defence cooperation. Later in an important development of the bilateral relations, Russia and India signed a Declaration on strategic Partnership in October 2000. This act demonstrated the close political understanding of Russia-India relations.[62] Among the important political achievements in the bilateral relations were the Moscow Declaration on fighting International Terrorism, Joint statement on bilateral/international issues, Joint statement on strategic Issues and announcement of Eminent Persons Group. Infact, Prime Minister's Moscow visit in November 2001 was a good Indian initiative to "further cement the tradition of high level exchange of visits and reaffirmed the strong bonds of friendship and strategic partnership between the two countries." To strengthen economic relations, during Vajpayee visit both sides concluded agreement between EXIM Bank and Vneshe conombank for extension of credit line of US $ 10 million and MOV on construction of Kundan Kulam nuclear power plant.[63] In short, efforts to broaden the base of India-Russia relations continued to be made in the post cold war phase. Needless to add was the fact of close politico-strategic relations between India and Russia even in the post cold war phase.

Coming of the Bush Administration

After assuming Presidentship in 2001, George W. Bush sought to continue stabilizing of relations with China. However, he and many of his advisers perceived that 'China policy under Clinton had been too weak and overly conciliatory and had tolerated, or even encouraged, PRC actions contrary to US interests'. As such they were determined to pursue a firmer policy towards China. On its part, there was frustration in China throughout the post cold war period 'the US sometimes seemed unwilling to cooperate with China and sometimes was willing to cooperate-but only on terms repugnant to China.'[64] In April, 2001 the Bush Administration announced the largest arms sales package to Taiwan Since the sale of 150 F-16s in 1992.[65] Further deterioration of Sino-US relations occurred in April, 1001 due to US EP-3 incident. From China's perspective, the US 'Spy plane' was engaged in 'aggression' against China. Later, gradually within US administration there was sharp debate and Secretary of State Colin Powell emerged as an advocate of 'stabilizing relations' with China. In short, during initial phase China was perceived as 'strategic competitor'.

Regarding India, President Bush stressed on the importance of strategic dialogue with India, and considered that India was 'a rising country with global status', and the key factor of maintaining Asia's security. Furthermore, the secretary of state, Colin Powell stated in Congress that India was 'a country America's foreign policy should focus increasingly' and 'India has the potential to help maintaining security of the vast Indian ocean and the peripheral area.[66] In April, 2001 the Indian Foreign and Defence Minister visited US to have talks with the new administration. India also supported USA's NMD plan. In President Bush's term, there was an important breakthrough in high level military exchanges. Both nations decided to "fix a time to publish the bilateral agreement on military cooperation, and establish an official dialogue system between the Defence Ministers." The Chairman of US Joint Chief of Staff. Sheldon visited India in August 2001 and symbolically this was the highest level visit the US military officer made to India in post Pokharan II tests. The growing Indo-US engagement caused concern in China. China perceived this development as a subtle approach to contain it. One Chinese analyst specializing on South Asia expressed concern over the US sale of arms to India which "enables it to became the first country to have close military relations with the world's two big powers – the US and Russia."[67] Already in the wake of nuclear tests by India, China's military mouthpiece wrote : "Through 50 years of efforts, India now boasts a mighty army... In light of strategic needs, India has, since the early 1990s focused on developing its naval force... The military strategic targets of India are to seek hegemony in South Asia, contain China, control the Indian ocean, and strive to become a military power in the contemporary world... India has always considered itself to be a "natural successor to the great British empire".[68] Thus, China watched warily the growing Indo-US engagement.

Post 9/11 Developments

After the terrorists attack on New York and Washington on 11 September, 2001, President Bush termed them "acts of war" against the US. Many analysts argued that the attacks pushed world into a new phase of contemporary history. The Chinese President, Jiang Zemin sent a message to his US counterpart conveying 'deepest sympathy and solicitude' over the attacks and stated that 'the Chinese government has consistently condemned and rejected all forms of terrorist violence'[69]. Both India and China cooperated with the US fight against terrorism. China also advised "Islamabad that, in its view, Pakistan's interests would be well served by aligning with the United states, that advice carried considerable weight".[70] At one level, China was happy that after 9/11 significance of Pakistan has enhanced in the US scheme of things. But at another level, the presence of US troops in China's periphery was not a positive development. Though China explicitly did not regard it as a threat but it was uncomfortable. Moreover, as one analyst wrote, "China's initial optimism that Sino-US-Pak triangular cooperation in the aftermath of September 11 will wean Washington away from New Delhi turned out to be wishful thinking as the Bush administration officials went out of their way to assure India that USA's intensifying alliance with Pakistan would not come at India's expense."[71]

Post 9/11 developments brought about a stable relations between China and US President Bush visited China twice after 9/11. From Chinese side, the new leader of fourth generation Hu Jintao visited US in spring of 2002 and President Jiang Zemin met Bush at his Texas ranch in October, 2002.[72]

With India President Bush terminated the economic and military sanctions on 22 September and sped up selling advanced weapon system to India, holding of joint military exercises and strengthening military technology cooperation.[73] Indo-US relations were further strengthened as a result of Prime Minister Vajpayee's visit to US in November, 2001. President Bush stated : "My administration is committed to developing a fundamentally different relationship with India, one based upon trust, one based upon mutual values. After all, the Prime Minister leads a nation that is the largest democratic nation in the world... We lifted sanctions on India, So that our relationship can prosper. We will fight terrorism together."[74] But gradually, there was disappointment in India gradually, there was disappointment in India that for US terrorism against it and cross border terrorism against India was two different things. For that matter even China's response was opaque against cross border terrorism. India was capable of fighting its own war against cross border terrorism and simultaneously maintain close relations with the major powers.

In the face of growing unilateralism on the part of US, in particular after 9/11, Beijing sought to further strengthen its relations with India. It was in this fluid situation that the visits of premiers Zhu Rongji to India in 2002 and A.B. Vajpayee in 2003 happened. Both nations again emphasized on the multipolar world. At the same time, both nations were aware of maintaining close relations with the US both because of political and economic compulsions. But due to growing assertiveness on the part of US especially after its military campaign against Iraq many states including India and China had reservations against the US action of by passing the UN mechanism.

Therefore, during Prime Minister, A.B. Vajpayee's China visit when both nations signed the text of the declaration on principles for relations and comprehensive cooperation, both nations agreed to strengthen multipolarity at the international level and enhance the positive factors of globalisation. They acknowledged the vital importance of the role of the UN and reaffirmed their readiness to work together to promote reform of the UN. Both nations were from developing nations, therefore, they agreed that priority should be given to enhancing representation of the developing countries.[75]

Thus, to conclude it became clear that the evolving global setting shaped the interaction between India and China. The point has already been mentioned that the Sino-Indian relations was conditioned on the one hand, by the evolving nature of politics at the global level, and on the another hand, by both the convergent and divergent interests of both powers. Further, the emerging relations of both nations with USA was a common factor in shaping their bilateral relations. Thus, the competitive element of Sino-Indian relations was enmeshed with emerging Sino-US and Indo-US relations. At another level, to enhance multilateral world, there was talk of China-Russia-India triangle. By 2003, the fact was very clear that both India and China had to deal with the USA. At the same time, due to assertive USA policy in global affairs, both India and China emphasized on the promotion of multipolar world order.

References

1. Yang Xiyue, "Power Relations in Today's World," Beijing Review, 42, 9-10, March 1, 1999, p. 6.
2. *Ibid.*
3. Young Deng, "The Chinese Conception of National Interests in International Relations," China Quarterly, 154, June 1998, p. 326.
4. Samuel S. Kim, "China In and Out of the Changing World Order," World Order Studies Program Occasional Paper No. 21, Princeton University Press, new Jersey, 1991, pp. 25-27.
5. Kaushik Sen, "India, China and the United States," in Kanti Bajpai and Amitabh Mattoo, eds, The Peacock and the Dragon : India-China Relations in the 21st century, Har Anand Publications, New Delhi, 2000, p. 255.
6. Wu Xueqian, "the Post Cold War Era : A Chinese Perspective", World Affairs, 1, 1, January 1997, p. 63.
7. V.P. Dutt, "India-China : Promise and Limitation", in Indian Foreign Policy : Agenda for the Twenty-first century, Vol. II, Foreign service Institute, Konark Publishers, New Delhi, 1998, p. 235.
8. Liu Seqing, "Searching for a New World Order," in Sheng Qurong and Bhabani Sengupta, eds., China Looks at the World, Konark Publishers, New Delhi, 1999, p. 6.
9. People's Daily, December 11 and 12, 1992.
10. Richard N. Haas, "Fatal Distraction : Bill Clinton's Foreign Policy," Foreign Policy, Fall 1997, p. 120.
11. People's Daily, January 26, 1993.
12. See n. 5, p. 260.
13. Cited in US News and World Report, February 22, 1992, p. 33.
14. C.V. Ranganathan and Vinod C. Khanna, India and China – The way Ahead After "Mao's India War", Har Anand Publications, New Delhi, 2000, pp. 90-91.
15. Cited in Ren Xin, "1996 : A year of Diplomatic Feats for China," Beijing Review, 40, 1, January 6, 1997, p. 13.
16. See n. 14, pp. 91-92.

17. See for details, Joint US-China Statement, 29 October, 1997, US Department of state website, http://www.state.gov.
18. John w. Garver, "The Restoration of Sino-Indian Comity following India's Nuclear Tests, "China-Quarterly, 168, December 2001, p. 876.
19. *Ibid.,* p. 877.
20. Cited in Ibid.
21. See the complete text, "Sino-US Presidential Joint Statement on south Asia," 27 June 1998, Beijing Review, 20 July, 1998, p. 17.
22. Ding Kuisong and Niu Xinchun, "Sino-US Relations : A Bumpy Path of Exploring Cooperation", contemporary International Relations, 9. 1, January 1999, p. 6.
23. Cited in Beijing Review, 41, 29, July 20, 1998, p. 11.
24. *Ibid.*
25. See n. 14, p. 93.
26. See n. 5, p. 262.
27. Avery Goldstein, "The Diplomatic Face of China's Grand Strategy : A Rising Power's Emerging Choice," China Quarterly, 168, December 2001, p. 848.
28. Cited in O.N. Mehrotra, "Sino-Russian Strategic Ties, "World Focus, 224, February 2000, p. 22.
29. Cited in ITAR-TASS, no. 28, 13 July, 2000, p. 22.
30. See n. 15, p. 12. See also for details, Fang Yinwan and Yang Guojun, "Beneficial enlightenment for large countries to build a new type of relationship," Xinhua, 25 April 1996, FBIS-CHI-96-082.
31. Cited in n. 14, p. 101.
32. See n. 27, p. 848.
33. See for details, Gilbert Rozman, "Sino-Russian relations in the 1990s : a balance sheet," Post Soviet Affairs, 14, 2, April 1998, pp. 93-113.
34. See n. 14, p. 102.
35. *Ibid.,* pp. 101-02.
36. Cited in *Ibid.,* p. 102.
37. S.S. Mehta, Launching India into the 21st Century, Minerva Press, New Delhi, 1999, p. 115.
38. Chintamani Mahapatra, Indo-US Relations in the 21st Century, Knowledge world, New Delhi, 1998, p. 97.
39. V.P. Dutt, India's Foreign Policy in a Changing World, Vikas Publishing House, New Delhi, 1999, p. 32.
40. Maying, "Development of Indo-US Relations in the Era of the Post-Cold War," in A Presentation Collection for Conference on India in 21st Century: External Relations, SIIS Publication, Shanghai, 2002, pp. 73-74.
41. Cited in *Ibid.,* p. 71.
42. *Economic Times*, May 18, 1994.
43. See n. 5, pp. 264-65.
44. Chintamani Mahapatra, "Pokharan II and After : Dark Clouds Over Indo-US Relations", Strategic Analysis, 22, 5, August 1998, p. 711.

45. Report of the Independent Task Force, After the Tests : US Policy Towards India and Pakistan, pp. 2-3. The task force was co-sponsored by the council of Foreign Relations and the Brookings Institute, Washington, USA.
46. See n. 18, p. 875.
47. *Ibid.*
48. *Ibid.*, p. 879.
49. Cited in n. 5, p. 267.
50. Cited in n. 40, p. 76.
51. Cited in Rajiv Nayan, Vajpayee Visit and Indo-US Relations", Strategic Analysis, 24, 9, December 2000, p. 1709.
52. *Ibid.*, p. 1711.
53. Cited in n. 40, p. 77.
54. *Ibid.*, p. 82.
55. *Ibid.*, p. 84.
56. *Ibid.*, pp. 84-85.
57. Sun Shihai, "China-Indian Relations in the 21st Century," in n. 40, p. 163.
58. See n. 18, p. 889.
59. Cited in Galina Yaskina, "Russia-China-India : Prospects for Trialateral Cooperation," Far Eastern Affairs, 2003, p. 16.
60. *Ibid.*
61. See for details, Jyotsna Bakhsi, "Russia's-Post-Pokharan Dilemma," Strategic Analysis, 22, 5, August 1998.
62. Cited in n. 59, p. 17.
63. See for details and texts of Declaration, Strategic Digest, 31, 11, November 2001, IDSA, pp. 1467-1478.
64. See for details, Quingguo Jia, "Frustration and hopes : Chinese perceptions of the engagement policy debate in the United States,' Journal of contemporary China, 10, May 2000, pp. 321-30.
65. See 'Secret US study concludes Taiwan needs new arms,' New York Times, 1 April 2001. See also 'Bush is Offering Taiwan Some arms but not the best', New York Times, 24 April 2001.
66. Cited in n. 40, pp. 77-78.
67. Rong Ying, "Can India Become a Military Power", in Beijing Review, February 28, 2002, pp. 14-15.
68. Liu Yang and Guo Feng, "What is the Intention of Wantonly Engaging in Military Ventures – India's Military Development should be watched out for," Jiefangjun Bao (Liberation Army Daily), in FBIS-CHI-98-141, May 21, 1998.
69. See for details, Keshav Mishra, 'China's Response To 9/11, Strategic Analysis, December 2001.
70. John W. Garver, "Sino-American Relations in 2001," International Journal, 42, 2, Spring 2002, p. 303.

71. Cited in Washington Times, March 19, 2002. See also J. Mohan Malik, "China, Pakistan.
72. For Chinese perspectives on Asian Security post September 11, 2001, See for details J. Mohan Malik, "Dragon on Terrorism : Assessing China's Tactical Gains and Strategic Losses After 11 September," Contemporary South East Asia, 24, 2, August 2002, pp. 252-93.
73. Cited in n. 40, p. 85.
74. Strategic Digest, 31, 12, December 2001, p. 1637.
75. See the Complete text in Hindu, June 25, 2003.

11

Conclusion

As can be seen from the foregoing chapters, India-China relations which are essentially of a bilateral nature are in a large measure, shaped by a complex interplay of regional factors as well as dynamics of global politics.

Following the conflict of 1962, India-China relations were frozen into a state of hostile coexistence. The years between 1963 to 1975, could be termed as the period of stalemate between India and China. The borders were far from stable and peaceful. The Indian Prime Minister. Mrs. Indira Gandhi adopted a flexible posture vis-à-vis and indicated her willingness to reopen a dialogue with China without any preconditions. In response to India's overtures, during the May Day parade at Beijing on 1 May 1970, Chairman Mao shook hands with the Indian charge d'affaires, signalling China's intention to normalise relations with India. But the hopeful pointers evaporated due to Bangladesh crisis and later on the political crisis in Sikkim. It was in 1976 that the first step towards normalisation was taken by India. India announced the appointment of Shri K. R. Narayanan as India's Ambassador to China and China responded quickly.

With the installation of Janata Party regime in India, the new external Affairs Minister, Shri A.B. Vajpayee visited China in 1979. He identified the border problem as the key obstacle to full realisation of normalisation of bilateral relations. The Chinese assurance of stopping support to insurgency in the north east and the gesture of reopening the holy places of Kailash and Mansarovar to Indian pilgrims was one step forward in the improvement of bilateral relations.

In the beginning of 1980's, Mrs. Gandhi came back to power and the direct contacts at the highest political level began. In May 1980, the Prime Ministers of both countries met at Belgrade and decided to continue the process of improvement in bilateral relations. More substantial talks took place in June 1981, when the Chinese Foreign Minister, Huang Hua visited India and held extensive talks with Indian leaders. Both sides decided to hold official level talks on bilateral problems and issues. The ice had been broken, but the road to rapprochement was a long and tortuous one.

The New Indian Premier, Mr. Rajiv Gandhi evinced keen interest in improving ties with China. In his first meeting with Chinese counterpart, Zhao Ziyang at New York, both agreed that there was need to push forward the efforts to find a solution to border problem and to promote friendship between the two countries. The years 1986 and 1987, however, witnessed a tense atmosphere on the Sino-Indian borders, because of Chinese intrusion in the Ṣumdorong Chu Valley in Arunachal Pradesh. China also lodged a protest against India's decision of granting statehood to the Union territory of Arunachal Pradesh. Both sides, however, did not allow bilateral relations to deteriorate. By the end of 1987, the eight round of official level talks had made little progress, with each side reiterating its stated position.

Indian Premier, Rajiv Gandhi decided in a bold move to visit China in December, 1988. The historic visit of Rajiv Gandhi to China was a leap forward in the process of India-China rapprochement. During his visit, two Joint Working Groups on border and economic relations were constituted. Further, both sides signed three agreements on intergovernmental cooperation in the field of science and technology, civil aviation and cultural exchanges. With a view to keep up the movement generated by the high level contacts at bilateral plane, Chinese Vice-Premier, Wu Xueqian came to New Delhi in October, 1989 and later on Chinese Foreign Minister, Qian Qichen visited India in March, 1990.

In the beginning of 1990's, the combined effect of rapid changing international scenario, regional politics and domestic compulsions, pushed India and China, on a firmer and closer path of rapprochement. Chinese Premier, Li Peng paid an official visit to India in December, 1991 and both sides signed three agreements, i.e., resumption of border trade, reopening of consulates in Bombay and Shangai and cooperation in peaceful applications of outer space sciences and technology. As a result of the summit level talks, India-china relations registered all round improvement. On the border issue, both sides agreed to ensure, peace and tranquility on the Line of Actual control. Now, both sides were following step-by-step approach to resolve this sensitive and complex issue. Further to broaden bilateral relations, India and China moved forward to cooperate in the field of economic, science and technology and cultural areas. As a result of all these developments, the process of India-China rapprochement stabilised firmly by the beginning of the nineties. The enhanced understanding as a result of high level political contacts between the two countries therefore, was a significant step forward in the bilateral relationship.

The South Asian dimension proved an important factor in India-China interaction. The conflicting perceptions of India and China towards South Asia generated tension and further aggravated the bilateral relationship. China, perceived itself as a part of the South Asian region because of geographical contiguity, historical linkage and common heredity with the Mongoloid group of people in India, Nepal and Bhutan. As a result, China considered it natural to get involved in the intra-regional affairs of South Asia. Further, China's interest in the region stemmed from the perception of its security status as well as regional and global roles.

India, on the other hand, had its own perception of its role and status in the region. It perceived China as an intrusive power in South Asia and believed that facts of geography, culture and ethnicity, reinforced by economic compulsions, tied the density of the South Asian nations much more with India than with China. As such, India viewed China's attempts to forge close relations with its South Asian neighbours as hostile acts.

Some significant trends in Chinese South Asian policy deserve mention here. Firstly, it was in a large measure India centred. Secondly, Chinese South Asian policy was pragmatic and devoid of any ideological considerations. Finally, Chinese policy towards the region had a global context. China's regional strategy became a function of its long-term preoccupation with a perceived Soviet threat as also relationship with United States, the other Super Power.

From 1963 onwards, China's regional strategy was characterised by comprehensive efforts to contain India. First, with Pakistan, India's foremost regional adversary, China established an extremely close relationship. In 1963, Pakistan and China signed a border agreement on the area which was illegally occupied by Pakistan in Kashmir. During the Indo-Pak war of 1965, China adopted a hostile attitude and militarily threatened India. During the Indo-Pak war of 1971, China supported Pakistan and indulged in anti-India propaganda on Bangladesh issue. China did not recognise Bangladesh and vetoed its entry to the United Nations till Mujibur Rahman died. Secondly, China played an active role in the Himalayan region providing foreign aid, engaging in strategic road building and giving political support to the monarchy in its power struggle with Nepal Congress. Finally, by supplying military hardware and armaments to Pakistan, China helped in the arms build up in the region. China also questioned India's special relations with Nepal and Bhutan. India perceived China's role in South Asia as of a hostile power which acted to the determent of India's security interests.

However, by the mid 1980's, Chinese South Asian policy underwent a subtle but significant shift. Now, Chinese leaders began to acknowledge

India's role as the leading South Asian power and realised that rather than weakening India, Chinese hostility helped to spur India's transformation into a major conventional military power. Further, Chinese leaders were learning to manage the ambiguous complexities of international relations without making unduly restrictive choices or becoming identified with one side or other side. In this context, Chinese leaders however, emphasised that the gradual amelioration of India-China relations would not take place at the expense of China's existing relationship in South Asia.

The Sino-Pak relationship survived and prospered through numerous changes in domestic regimes and amidst varying international circumstances. The close contacts were maintained at all the higher levels among the political, military and economic establishments. The military intervention of Soviet Union in Afghanistan reinforced he relationship. By late eighties the strategic equation of South Asia slowly changed. By 1989, Soviets had withdrawn their army from Afghanistan and had normalised relationship with China. China, on its part, tried to maintain some kind of balance in its relatinship with India and Pakistan. China urged both sides to solve all the outstanding issues including Kashmir in peaceful way.

Nevertheless, the military dimension of Sino-Pak relationship particularly the sale of missile and nuclear weapons technology was of direct concern to India. India continued to remain wary of the Sino-Pak entente and its impact on India's role in South Asia.

China also sought to maintain close relationship with Nepal and other South Asian nations as a means of partially offsetting the enormous gravitational pull of India. China began to spoke in extremely assertive tones about regional controversies involving India. In seventies, China supported Nepal's proposal of zone of peace. The Chinese advance in participation in projects closer to the Indian border began to cause serious concern in India. To develop relations with Bangladesh in February 1976, China 'condemned India's hegemonic action' regarding Farakka barrage and sharing water of the Ganges. A perceived threat from India soon became the primary factor in the convergence of interest between Bangladesh and China. With Bhutan, China's strategy was to pressurise it, to open direct negotiations on the disputed area north west of Tawang. China vigorously pursued its policy of weaning Bhutan away from India. Similarly, developing close bilateral relations with Sri Lanka was an important element of China's South Asian policy. Close Sino-Sri Lankan relationship had a strategic dimension considering the geo-strategic location of Sri Lanka.

However, by the late eighties, China had moved away from constant encouragement to Nepal and other South Asian nations to stand upto India and emphased peaceful development of relations among all countries in this region. A concrete instance of this was, Nepal's differences with India over trade and transit treaty issues were widening in 1989, Nepal hoped to be bailed by China. But China took the position by making it clear to the Nepalese leadership its inability to help in the matter and advised it to seek a reasonable resolution of its problems with India. However, India was disturbed by Nepal's move to purchase arms from China.

Similarly, China which had earlier supported Bangladesh's stand on the Farakka issue later advised Bangladesh to solve this issue amicably and wound down the anti-Indian campaign. As regards, Sri Lanka's internal politics, Chinese leadership maintained a neutral position and advised the Lankan leadership to find a political solution to the ethnic problem instead of a military one. China cautiously reported the Indo-Sri Lankan Agreement on Tamil question. On Indian Peace Keeping Force Operation in Sri Lanka, the Chinese maintained a muted stance. In sum, China softened the anti-Indian edge in its policy and evinced less interest in fanning any conflictual situation in South Asia. The growth of South Asian Association for Regional Cooperation received enthusiastic response from China.

India, however, continued to remain wary of China's role and influence in South Asia. From 1963 to 1991, the South Asian region saw substantial growth of Chinese influence. The network of relations which China built with other South Asian nations in general, but in particular with Pakistan, the nature of defence relations had security implications for India. India therefore perceived China as an intrusive power in the region. Chinese political influence, military linkages and arms transfer acted in a large measure as a hindrance in the process of India-China Rapprochement. Thus, it can be concluded that South Asian factor was an important input into India-China relationship.

The international political setting affected both India and China. The India-China cold war was enmeshed with the Amrican-Soviet-Chinese triangular relations with in the context of the global cold war. In fact, in early fifties both India and China came closer to each other because of anti imperialist and Pan Asiatic sentiment. India followed the policy of non alignment and China joined the communist camp of Russia against imperialist America. Form late fifties, in a parallel track to deterioration of India-China relations occurred the irreconcilable rift between Sino-Soviet relations. China attacked India at a time when both the superpowers were engaged in Cuban missile crisis. During the Sino-Indian war, both super powers helped India; US supplied arms to India in a bid to contain communism in Asia and Soviets criticised China and urged both the countries to solve the problem amicably. China could not reconcile to the fact the USSR did not support a fellow communist country against India. After the Sino-Indian conflict of 1962, relations between India and USSR became quite close. Consequently, China started attacking the erosion of India's non-alignment policy and its joining the Soviet camp.

Following military clashes in Ussuri area in Sino-Soviet border in 1969, the Chinese tried to normalise their relationship with USA to pressurise the USSR. By forging a strategic relationship with the US, China hoped to effect a US-Pak-China alliance to counterbalance the Soviet-Indian alliance which was further strengthened by Treaty of Peace and Friendship in August 1971. The combined effect of these varied linkages was the freezing of South Asian regional politics in the global pattern. In 1979, US-China Rapprochement was further consolidated by the establishment of normal diplomatic relatinship between two countries. US also was interested in India-China rapprochement as it perceived India was too close to Moscow.

India on its part, had always exercised independence of decision in its relations with China vis-a-vis USSR. One concrete instance was in 1969 when India did not react favourably to Brezhenev's Asian Collective Security Plan. It also sought to normalise its relations worth China in the face of Soviet wariness. It cannot, however, be denied that India's own policies towards China were affected by the changing global alignments and its own relations with the Soviet Union and the United States.

From late eighties, following the USA-USSR rapprochement, and resumption of dialogue between China and USSR, the emphasis in international politics was on resumption of dialogues to resolve all outstanding issues between nations. As the pace of Sino-Soviet Rapprochement accelerated in late 1980s, Soviet Union also encouraged improvement in India-China relations. Hence, we find serious attempts towards India-China Rapprochement following Rajiv Gandhi's China visit in 1988.

Both countries were important developing countries which were engaged in modernising their economic development. Both India and China now emphasised on a world order which was equitable and where there was no international oligarchy, obviously the reference was to USA. India and China had reason to be worried about the unilateralism of the USA in creating a Post Cold War New World Order. The two countries also exchanged views on a wide range of international economic issues, including special 301, GATT etc. Thus, it was apparent that on various international issues, India and China had commonality of interests which was bound to have a positive impact on the evolution of Sino-Indian ties.

It is clear from the foregoing that the combined effect of bilateral factors, regional imperatives and dynamics of global politics remained major inputs into India-China relationship during the years under study.

The fact is evident from the foregoing Chapters that India-China relations which are essentially of a bilaternal nature are also conditioned by a complex interplay of regional factors and dynamics of global politics.

In the post Cold War period, both giants of Asia were compelled in a way by the prevalent circumstances and contemporary historical forces to construct the edifice of rapprochement. The normalisation of Sino-Indian relations was already gathering momentum since the decade of 1980's and in a more substantive way from the historic China visit of the Indian Prime Minister, Rajiv Gandhi in December, 1988. The continuation of high level political interactions contributed in more tangible manner to enhanced understanding between both nations. As a result of the India-China summit level talks of 1993 and 1996, the over all bilateral relations registered all round improvement.

Another notable development in the bilateral relations was the beginning of high level military exchanges with a view to enhance mutual interactions between the military establishments of both nations. On the border issue, the Agreements of 1993 and 1996 were significant developments and both nations agreed to ensure peace and tranquility on the Line of Actual Control on one hand and moved forward on the other hand with Confidence Building Measures. India and China seemingly were pursuing step-by-step approach to resolve the intractable and vexed issue of borders. To broaden the base of bilateral relations, both nations moved forward to cooperate in the areas of economy, trade. Science and technology etc. All these developments in the bilateral relations combined together in a way to construct the architecture of Sino-Indian Rapprochement by the year 1997.

However, the base of rapprochement was raised in weak platform in that there was distrust between both sides. Furthermore, the overall structure of Sino-Indian Rapprochement was tilted more in favour of China much to the detriment of India's security. As a result, India perceived the fact that Sino-Indian relations 'was not a relationship between equals'. Another notable trend which could be discerned in the strategic circles of India was the slow pace of border negotiations and progress in the implementation of confidence building measures has been rather slow. In spite of these drawbacks, India continued to pursue the policy of engagement and acted in a mature way. As a developing nation, India was concerned with development of its economy and as such needed stability of relations with China, an important neighbour.

A combination of factors at the global, regional and bilateral levels brought about brief breakdown in the process of Sino-Indian Rapprochement in the year 1998. India's new government led by the Bhartiya Janata Party and its coalition allies which came to office in March 1998 assigned priority to national security. Due to perceived cumalative disadvantages vis-a-vis China, India wanted to balance the structure of rapprochement in some measure. By this point of time, the global strategic community was talking about Rise of China and some analyses also subscribed to China threat theory. At the regional level, China was pursuing two pronged policy, i.e., engagement and balance of power.

India conducted nuclear tests in May 1998 partly in response to the China factor and China strongly opposed the Indian nuclear tests. China was at the forefront in ensuring tough-line by the Security Council on India. In doing so China was guided by its objective in Asia to prevent rise of a 'peer competitor'. Beijing even in its dealings with Washington pressurised New Delhi and China-U.S.A Joint Statement was an eloquent testimony of the fact. The cumulative effect of Chinese response to the Indian nuclear tests casted a negative spell over the Sino-Indian rapprochement. China also cancelled the Scheduled November, 1998 Joint Working Group meeting in Beijing. India on the other hand, showed its willingness to continue with the policy of engagement throughout the year 1998. India also made 'consistent overtures' and 'conciliatory Statements' to assuage perceived Chinese ruffled feelings in a bid to reduce bilateral tensions.

The process of Sino-Indian rapprochement was irreversible and in spite of brief breakdown, the existence of diverse driving forces at bilateral, regional and global levels brought about reconstruction of the edifice. Gradually from the beginning of year 1999 both nations restored the process of rapprochement in a more substantive and meaningful manner. In this phase, a more Mature India at the official level outlined a friendly framework for the Sino-Indian relations. Similarly, China was a bit more responsive and wanted to put the past behind. The bilateral relations were marked by the resumption of political interactions at the high level and meetings of the bilateral mechanisms.

India pursued a more assertive policy and succeeded in moderate degree by bringing about correlation of forces slightly in its favour vis-a-vis China. As a result from the year 1999 China agreed to the clarification of maps in line of Actual Control and initiation of the security dialogue to address India's security concerns in post-Pokharan phase.

At the political plane, as a result of the prime Ministerial Summits of the years 2002 and 2003, Sino-Indian bilateral relations registered upward trend. The political input to a large extent enhanced the overall quality of bilateral relations. In particular, Prime Minister A.B. Vajpayee's China visit was quite successful and may be put in the same league as earlier Prime Ministerial visit of Rajiv Gandhi in 1988 and Narasimha Rao in 1993. Similarly, the resumption of defence relations and high level defence exchanges enabled the military establishments to enhance mutual trust and understanding.

On the vexed border issue following positive steps could be underlined: Maintenance of peace and tranquility, initiation of various confidence building measures, exchange of maps according to sectors and seeking clarifications on each other's position continued a pace. Furthermore, with the appointment of Special Representatives on the border issue another step forward has been taken in the right direction. It seems that the adoption of political approach would go a long way in resolution of this long standing problem in Sino-Indian relations. Still, the incident of border incursion on the part of China in June, 2003 was a negative episode.

In spite of adoption of step-by-step approach by both India and China, the impression persists among some section of strategic community that China for obvious reasons does not desires to resolve the border issue in a time frame. It could be stated in some ways the perception axists in India that China's dealings with India at times smacks off a degree of hierarchy despite May 1998 nuclear tests. Nonetheless, a look at the larger picture does suggest the positive advancement and China's willingness to address the border issue in a problem resolving manner.

Simultaneously, China's strategic culture, the importance attached to state sovereignty and territorial integrity in the defence policy, signals India to be careful and well prepared with its dealings with China. The political leadership of India should integrate statecraft, real politik dictates, economic development into a fine tuned diplomatic culture and coupled with the evolving strategic culture deal realistically with China and even pragmatically resolve the border issue. At the bilateral level by the summer of year 1998 both nations cooperated in the sphere of economic and trade ties, culture, tourism and science and technology. Thus, the bilateral relation were marked by broadening the base of overall relationship and strengthening the structure of Sino-Indian Rapprochement. In the final analysis, the adoption of declaration on principles for relations and comprehensive cooperation between India and China in 2003 marked the reconstruction of Sino-Indian Rapprochement in a more balanced way. It remains to be seen as to how this is effectively translated into reality.

The regional dimension of India-China interactions assumes significance. One school of thought argues about the dominance of geo-political conflict in Sino-Indian relations. In the post Cold War period. China in a nuanced manner continued to pursue balance of power in the region. The salience of Sino-Pak relations did not diminish despite the end of Cold War, disintegration of Soviet Union and improvement in Sino-Indian relations. Sino-Pak relations were defined as an 'all weather friendship'. Even in the post Cold War period, China reminned Pakistan's principal supplier of all modernised weapons including Conventional and WMD etc. Among the important joint projects MBT Al-Khalid, K-8, FC-1 and Gwadar Port. More dangerously, China's assistance for missiles and nuclear technologies transfers to Pakistan in a way destabilised the strategic equilibrium of South Asia. Even after 9/11 and consequent shift in the global politics the Sino-Pak defence cooperation continued to be special and cordial.

China's continued defence cooperation with Pakistan was central to India's strategic concern. Sino-Pak extermely close relations to a large extent increased inimical approach of Pakistan towards India, this element became one of the important factors in continuation of Indo-Pak conflictual relations. The regional context at one level suggests presence of the competitive element in overall Sino-Indian relations.

Similarly, the evolving military relations between China and Myanmar adversely affected India's security environment. Being a vibrant democracy opinion varied in India about China's linkages with India's smaller neighbours. China viewed military relations with other South Asian nations as legitimate relations but for India it constituted threat to its security. As such, there was difference between India and China on the regional dimension. Following 9/11 and USA's unilateralism, China emphasises on overall stability and peace in the region.

The India-China interaction, which is multidimensional and multilayered is conditioned on the one hand by the evolving nature of politics at the global level and on the another hand by both the convergent and divergent interests and strategies of India and China. In the post Cold War period, China emphasised on multipolar world order and also on the multilateral cooperative mechanism. China in some ways was apprehensive of the US intentions in the Asia-Pacific region. It was in this backdrop that China sought to improve its relations with India, the dominant power in its South Western borders. China's policy of maintaining good-neighbourly relations with India followed from its conscious strategy of seeking peaceful environment in its surrounding areas. Following the uncertainties generated by collapse of the bipolar world, both nations shared similar perceptions of the opportunities and challenges in the post Cold War world. India in early 1990's embarked on the liberalisation programme with the objective of further developing its economy. On a range of issues for instance environment, human rights and search for autonomy in the world order there was convergence of ideas.

The post Cold War period, offered a changed context to India to shape its relations with the major powers. A more confident and mature India, gradually veered towards realism and was no more guided by idealism. India in a more assertive way sought to promote its national interests by restructuring relations with the USA, Russia etc. The USA realised the geo-strategic significance of India in post Cold War framework. The growing Indo-US relations caused some concern in strategic circles of China. As a matter of fact, there exists in some measure a competitive element in Sino-Indian relations due to development in the global political configuration. In near future, therefore, both India and China will have to tread carefully in managing their relations with the major power in particular with USA.

After 9/11 both nations supported USA in the war against terrorism. Later, due to the growing unilateralism on the part of USA especially after military campaign against Iraq both India and China expressed reservations against the US action of by passing the UN mechanism on the use of force. Therefore, during Prime Minister A.B. Vajpayee's China visit in 2003 both nations agreed to strengthen multipolarity at the global level and enhance the positive factors of globalization. The notable trends which could be discerned that the global plane are following : first, the competitive element of Sino-Indian relations at one level was enmeshed with the emerging Sino-US and Indo-US relations. Second, to enhance multilateral world order the preliminary round of meetings of China-Russia-India were held. By the year 2003, it was axiomatic that both India and China had to manage relations with the USA in the face of growing unilateralism on its part. Hence, both nations emphasised on the promotion of the multipolar world order.

Thus, it is apparent from the foregoing that the permutation and combination of bilateral issues, regional context and dynamics of evolving global setting were major inputs in the overall Sino-Indian relationship during the years under study.

Bibliography

PRIMARY SOURCES

India

Lok Sabha Debates, 1963-1991 (Lok Sabha Secretariat, New Delhi).

OFFICIAL PUBLICATIONS

(a) India, Ministry of Commerce,
Report (Submitted Annually to Parliament, New Delhi, 1963-191).

(b) India, Ministry of Defence,
Report (Submitted Annually to Parliament, New Delhi 1963-1991).

(c) India, Ministry of External Affairs,
Documents on China's Ultimatum to India, New Delhi, 1965.
Foreign Affairs Record, 1963-191.
India-China Conflict, New Delhi, 1964.
India: Bilateral Treaties and Agreements, Vol. I-X, New Delhi, 1994-1997.
Notes, Memoranda and Letters Exchanged and Agreements Signed Between the Governments of India and China, White Paper, No. I-XII, 1954-1968.
Report of the Officials of Government of India and the People's Republic of China on the Boundary Question, New Delhi, 1961.
Report (Submitted Annually to Parliament, New Delhi, 1963-1991).

(d) India, Ministry of Information and Broadcasting.
China Disregards the Colombo Proposals: Attempt to Retain Gains to Aggression Against India, New Delhi, 1963.
China's Betrayal of India, Background to the Invasion, New Delhi, 1962.
Chinese Threat, New Delhi, 1963.
India's Fight for Territorial Integrity, New Delhi 1963.
Jawaharlal Nehru, *Pakistan Seeks to Profit from Chinese Aggression*, New Delhi 1063.
______________, *India's Foreign Policy: Selected Speeches,* September 1946-April 1961, New Delhi 1971.
______________, *Selected Speeches, Vol. I to V, New Delhi, 1957 1968.*

Indira Gandhi, *Selected Speeches*, Vol. I to III, New Delhi, 1974-1984.

Rajiv Gandhi, Selected Speeches and Writings, Vol. I to V, New Delhi, 1984-1989.

Narasimha Rao, Selected Speeches and Writings, Vol. I to III, New Delhi, 1992-1994.

China

Mao Ze Dong, *Selected Works*, Vol. I –IV, People's Publishing House, Beijing, 1951-1956.

Deng Xiaoping, *Building Socialism with Chinese Characteristics*, People's Publishing House, Beijing, 1987.

Important Speeches of Deng Xiaoping, People's Publishing House, Beijing, 1987.

Deng Xiaoping and Reform in Contemporary China, Chinese People's University, Press, 1990.

Selected Works of Deng Xiaoping 1975-1982, Foreign Languages Press, Beijing, 1984.

A Selection of Documents and Materials concerning the Tibet Issue, Xinhua New Press, Beijing, 1959.

Documents of the Thirteenth National Congress of the Communist Party of China, People's Publishing House, 1987.

The Question of Tibet, Foreign Language Press, Beijing, 1959.

The Sino-Indian Boundary Question, Enlarged Edition, Foreign Language Press, Beijing, 1962.

SECONDARY SOURCES

Books

Abel, Elie, *The Missiles of October* (London, 1966).

Anne Gilks and Gerald Segal, *China and The Arms Trade* (London, 1985).

Appadoral, A., & Rajan, M.S., *India's Foreign Policy and Relations* (New Delhi, 1985).

Avedon, John F., *In Exile From the Land of the Snows* (New York, 1986).

Bajpayee, U.S., ed., *India's Security: Politico-strategic Environment* (New Delhi, 1981).

Bajpayee, U.S., ed., *India and Its Neighbourhood* (New Delhi, 1986).

Bajpai, K and Matoo, A, ed. *The Peacock and the Dragon, India-China Relation in the 21st Century* (New Delhi 2000).

Banerjee, D.K., *Sino-Indian Borader Dispute* (New Delhi, 1975).

Bartke, Wolfgang, *The Economic Aid of the People's Republic of China to Developing and Socialist Countries*, (London, 1989).

Bartke, Wolfgang, *The Agreements of the Peoples Republic of China with Foreign Countries, 1949-90* (Hamburg, 1992).

Beckman, Peter R., *World Politics In The Twentieth Century* (New Jersey, 1984).

Bhargava, G.S., *The Battle of NEFA: The Undeclared War* (New Delhi, 1964).

Bhasin, As., ed., Nepal's *Relations with India and China; Documents, 1947-92* (New Delhi, 1994).

Bhat, Sudhakar, *India and China* (New Delhi, 1967).

Bhola. P.L, *Pakistan-China Relations, Search for Politico-Strategic-Relations*, (Jaipur, 1986).

Bowles, *Chester, Promises to Keep: My Years in Public Life, 1941-1969* (New York, 1971).

Bradsher, H.S., *Afghanistan and the Soviet Union* (Durham, 1983).

Brecher, Michael, *India and World Politics: Krishna Menon's View of the World* (London, 1968).

Chakravarty, P.C., *India's China Policy* (Bloomington, 1962).

Chakravarty, P.C., *India-China Relations* (Calcutta, 1961).

Chang, Gordon H., *Friends and Enemies: The United States, China and the Soviet Union, 1948-1972* (Stanford, 1990).

Chaturvedi, G. *India-China Relations: 1947 to Present Day* (Agra, 1991).

Choudhary, G.W., India, Pakistan, *Bangladesh and The Major Powers: Politics of Divided Sub Continent* (New York, 1975).

________________, *China in World Affairs: The Foreign Policy of The PRC Since 1970* (Colarado, 1982).

Chih, HLu, *Sino-Indian Border Dispute : A Legal Study* (New York, 1986).

Chopra, Surendra, ed., *Sino-Indian Relations* (Amritsar, 1985).

Chopra, V.D., *Pentagon Shadow Over India* (New Delhi, 1985).

Clarke, D., *Politics of Arms Control* (New York, 1979).

Coelho, V.H., *Sikkim and Bhutan* (New Delhi, 1969).

Cohen, Warren I., *America's Response to China: A History of Sino-American Relations* (Columbia, 1990).

Copper, John Franklin, *China's Foreign Aid: An Instrument of Peking's Foreign Policy* (London, 1976).

Cukwarah, A.O., *The Settlement of Boundary Disputes in International Affairs*, (London, 1967).

Daljit Sen, A., *China and Her Neighbours: A Review of Chinese Foreign Policy* (New Delhi, 1984).

Dalvi, Brigadier J.S., *Himalayan Blunder: The Curtain Raiser to the Sino-Indian War of 1962* (Bombay, 1969).

Das, B.S., *The Sikkim Saga* (New Delhi, 1983).

Das, Nara Narayan, ed., *Contemporary Chinese Politics and Foreign Policy* (New Delhi, 1989).

Dhar, Panna Lal, *India, Her Neighbours and Foreign Policy* (New Delhi, 1991).

Doolin, Dennis J., *Territorial Claims in the Sino-Soviet Conflict* (Stanford, 1965).

Dixit, J.N., *Across Borders: 50 Years of India's Foreign Policy* (New Delhi, 1998)

Dorothy, W., *Himalayan Frontiers* (London, 1969).

Dutt, Gargi & Dutt, V.P. , *China After Mao* (New Delhi, 1990).

Dutt, V.P., *India's Foreign Policy* (New Delhi, 1984).

Eekeien, W.F. Van, *India's Foreign Policy and the Border Dispute with China* (Hague, 1964).

Eisenhower, Dwight D., *Waging Peace: 1956-1961*, (New York, 1965).

Ellison, Herbert J., ed., *The Sino-Soviet Conflict: A Global Perspective*, (Washington, 1982).

Fairbank, John King, *China: A New History* (Harvard, 1994).

Fisher, Margaret, Leo Rose, *Robert A. Huttenback, Himalayan Battleground: Sino-Indian Rivalry in Ladakh* (London, 1963).

Gaddis, J., *The United States and The origins of the Cold War*, New York, 1979.

Gandhi, Arun, *The Morarji Papers* (New Delhi, 1983).

Galbraith, J.K., *Ambassador's Journal: A Personal Account of the Kennedy Years*, (New York, 1969).

Gankshaw, Edward, *The New Cold War: Moscow V. Peking* (London, 1963).

Gardner, L., *The Origins of the Cold War* (New York, 1979).

Garver, John W., *China's Decision for Rapprochement with the United States, 1968-71* (Colarado, 1982).

Ghoble, T.R., *China-Nepal Relations and India* (New Delhi, 1986).

Ghosh, Suchita, *China-Bangladesh-India Tangle Today* (New Delhi, 1995).

Gittings, John, *Survey of the Sino-soviet Dispute 1963-67* (London, 1968).

Glks, Anne and Segal, *Gerald, China and the Arms Trade* (London, 1985).

Griffith, W.E., ed., *China's Foreign Relations in the 1980s* (Yale, 1984).

__________ *The Great Power Triangles* (Cambridge, 1985).

Griffith, W.E., *The Sino-Soviet Rift* (Cambridge, 1964).

Grover, V., ed., *International Relations and Foreign Policy of India*, Vol. 3, (New Delhi, 1992).

Gupta, Karunakar, *The Hidden History of Sino-Indian Frontier* (Calcutta, 1974).

Hanzhang, Ya, *Biographies of the Dalai Lamas,* (Beijing, 1984).

Harrison, Selig S., *The Widening Gulf: Asian Nationalism and American Policy* (New York, 1978).

Hinton, Harold C., *The Sino-Soviet Confrontation* (New York, 1976).

___________., *China's Turfulent Quest* (New York, 1970).

Hoffman, Steven, A., *India and the China Crisis* (California, 1990).

Hussain, Karki, T., *Sino-Indian Conflict and International Politics in the Indian Sub Continent, 1962-66* (New Delhi, 1977).

*****

Jackson, R., South Asian Crisis, London, 1975.

Jain, Girilal, *Panchsheels and After* (Bombay, 1960).

Jain, J.P., *China, Pakistan and Bangladesh* (New Delhi, 1974).

Jain, J.P., China, Pakistan and Bangladesh, New Delhi, 1974.

Jain, R.K., *China-South Asian Relations, 1947-1980*, Vol. I & II (New Delhi, 1981).

Jetly, Nancy, *India-China Relations, 1947-1977*: A Study of Parliament's Role in the Making of Foreign Policy (New Delhi, 1979).

Jha, R.K., *The Himalayan Kingdoms in Indian Foreign Policy* (Ranchi, 1986).

Jha, S.K., *Uneasy Partners: India and Nepal in the Post Colonial Era* (New Delhi, 1975)

Jian, Li, *The Record of New China's Six Counter Invasion Wars* (Beijing, 1992).

Jie, Wu, On Deng Xiaoping Thought, Beijing, 1996.

Kahin, George M, *Intervention: How American Became Involved in Vietnam* (New York, 1986).

_______, Asian-African Conference : Bandung (Cornel, 1956)

Kapur, Harish, The End of an Isolation: China After Mao (Dordrecht, 1985).

Karniak, U.B., *Chinese Invasion, Background and Sequel* (Bombay, 1966).

Kaul, B.M., *Untold Story* (Bombay, 1971).

Kaushik, Devendra, *Soviet Relations with India and Pakistan* (Delhi, 1971).

Keith, Ronald C., *The Diplomacy of Zhou Enlai* (London, 1989).

Kennedy, John F., *Strategy of Peace* (New York, 1961).

Khera, S.S., *India's Defence Problem* (New Delhi, 1968).

Khruschev, Nikita S., *Khruschev Remembers: The Last Testament* (London, 1977).

Kim, Samuel S., *The Third World in Chinese World Policy* (Princeton, 1989).

____________ed., *Chinese Foreign Policy in the 1980s*, (Colaredo, 1984).

Kissinger, Henry, *White House Years* (Boston, 1979).

Klein, Donald W., and Clark, Anne B., *Biographical Dictionary of Chinese Communism, 1921-1965* (Cambridge, 1971).

Klintworth, Gary, *The Practice of Common Security: China's Borders with Russia and India* (Taipei, 1993)

Kodikara, S., ed., *South Asian Strategic Issues: Sri Lankan Perspectives* (New Delhi, 1990).

Kumar, Satish, ed., *Yearbook on India's Foreign Policy* (New Delhi, 1980-89).

Lall, John, *Aksai Chin and Sino-Indian Conflict* (New Delhi, 1988).

Lamb, Alastair, *Sino-Indian Border in Ladakh* (Canberra, 1973).

Lamb, Alastair, *The China-India Border: The Origins of the Disputed Boundaries* (London, 1964).

Lattimore, Owen, *Inner Asian Frontiers of China* (Boston, 1951).

Leo E. Rose, *Nepal's Strategy For Survival* (Delhi, 1970).

Lif Schultz, L., *Bangladesh: The Unfinished Revolution* (London, 1979).

Mac Farquhar, Roderick, *The Origins of Cultural Revolution in China*, Vol. 3, (Oxford, 1997).

Mankekar, D.R., *The Guilty Men of 1962* (Bombay, 1968).

Mankekar, D.R., *The Mcmahon Line and After* (New Delhi, 1974).

Mansingh, Surjit, *India's Search for Power: Indira Gandhi's Foreign Policy, 1966-82* (New Delhi, 1984).

____________, ed., Indian and Chinese Foreign Policies in Comparative Perspective (New Delhi, 1998).

Maxwell, Neville, *India's China War* (Bombay, 1970).

Mehra, Parshottam, *Negotiating with the Chinese, 1846-1987: Problems and Perspectives* (New Delhi, 1984).

Menon, V.K. Krishna, *India and the Chinese invasion* (Bombay, 1963).

Mohan, Ram, *Politics of Sino-Indian Confrontation* (New Delhi, 1973).

Mohanti, Ravindra Nath, *Soviet Union as a Factor in Sino-Indian Relations, 1950-80* (New Delhi, 1985).

Mullick, B.N., *My Years with Nehru: Chinese Betrayal* (Bombay, 1971).

Muni, S.D., *Pangs of Proximity: India and Sri Lanka's Ethnic-crisis*, New Delhi, 1993.

_______________, Foreign Policy of Nepal, (Delhi, 1973).

Murty, T.S., *India-China Boundary: India's Options* (New Delhi, 1987).

_______________, *Paths of Peace: Studies on the Sino-Indian Border Dispute* (New Delhi, 1983).

Nanporia, N.J., *The Sino-Indian Dispute* (Bombay, 1963).

Nayar, Kuldip, *Between the Lines* (New Delhi, 1969).

____________, *India: The Critical Years* (New Delhi, 1971.

Nissanka, H.S.S., *Sri Lanka's Foreign Policy* (New Delhi, 1984).

Palit, D.K., *War in High Himalaya: The Indian Army in Crisis, 1962* (London, 1991).

Palmer, Norman D., *The United States an India* (Prager, 1984).

Panikkar, K.M., *In Two Chinas: Memoirs of a Diplomat* (London, 1955).

Patterson, George, *Tibet in Revolt* (London, 1961).

Pin Lin, Chong, *China's Nuclear Weapons Strategy: Tradition Within Evolution* (Lexington, 1988).

Prasad, Niranjan, *The Fall of Towang* (New Delhi, 1981).

Prassad, Bimal, ed., *India's Foreign Policy: Studies in Continuity and Change* (New Delhi, 1979).

Rajan M.S., and Ganguly, Shivaji, eds, *Great Power Relations, World Order and The Third World* (New Delhi, 1981).

Ramakant (ed.), *China and South Asia* (New Delhi, 1988).

Ranganathan, C.V. and Khanna, V.C. *India and China : The Way Ahead After "Mao's India War"* (New Delhi, 2000).

Rao, G.N., *The India-China Border: A Reappraisal* (Bombay, 1968).

Rasgotra, M & Chopra, V.D. ed., *India's Relations with Russia & China*, New Phase, New Delhi, 1997.

Rey, Hemen, *China's Strategy in Nepal* (New Delhi, 1983).

Rey, Hemen, *Sino-Soviet Conflict over India* (New Delhi, 1986).

Rikhye, Ravi, *The War That Never Was* (New Delhi, 1989).

Robinson, Thomas W. and Shambaugh, David, eds., *Chinese Foreign Policy: Theory and Practice* (Oxford, 1994).

Rose, Leo E., *Nepal : Strategy for Survival* (Delhi, 1973).

Rowland, John, *History of Sino-Indian Relations: Hostile Coexistence* (Princeton, 1967).

Saigal, J.R., *The Unfought War of 1962* (New Delhi, 1979).

Schlesinger, Arthur M., *A Thousand Days: John F. Kennedy in the White House* (Boston, 1965).

Segal, Gerald, ed., Chinese Politics and Foreign Policy Reform, London, 1990.

Sheng, Hu, ed, *A Concise History of the Communist Party of China* (Beijing, 1994).

Sen Gupta, Bhabani, *The Fulcrum of Asia: Relations Among China, India, Pakistan and USSR* (New York, 1970).

Shri Prakash, India-China Relations : A Comparative View of the 1950s and Early 1990s, New Delhi, 1996.

Singh, C.P., *India's Foreign Policy: The Shastri Period* (New Delhi, 1980).

Singh, Jasjit, *The Saga of Ladakh* (New Delhi, 1983).

_______________, India, China and Panchsheel, (New Delhi, 1996)

Soren Sen., T., *Kennedy* (New York, 1965).

Sondhi, M.L. and Nanda, Prakash, *Vajpayee's Foreign Policy: Daring The Irreversible* (New Delhi, 1999).

Stebbins, Richard P., The United States in World Affairs, (New Delhi, 1961).

Sutter, Robert G., China Watch: Toward Sino-American Reconciliation, Oxford, 1978.

Syed, Anwar Hussain, *China and Pakistan: Diplomacy of An Entente Cordiale* (Wassachusetts, 1974).

Tatu, M., *The Great Power Triangle* (Paris, 1970).

Tharoor, Shashi, *Reasons of State, Political Development and India's Foreign Policy under Indira Gandhi, 1966-67* (New Delhi, 1983).

Tieh Tsing Li, *Tibet-Today and Yesterday* (New York, 1960).

Varma, S.P., *Struggle for Himalayas: A Study in Sino-Indian Relations* (New Delhi, 1971).

Vertzberger, Yaacov, *The Enduring Entente: Sino-Pakistani Relations, 1960-80* (New York, 1983).

Vertsberger, Yaacov, China's South Western Strategy: 'Enrichment and Counter Encirclement (New York, 1989)

Vertzberger, Yacov, Y.I., *Misperceptions in Foreign Policy Making, The Sino-Indian Conflict*, 1959-62 (Colarado, 1989).

Whiting, Allen S., *The Chinese Calculus of Deference: India and Indo-China*, (Ann Arbor, 1975).

Willison, Graham, *Essence of Decision (*Boston, 1971).

Cuecheng, Liu, *The Sino-Indian Border Dispute and Sino-Indian Relations*, Washington, 1994.

Yahuda, Michael, *China's Foreign Policy: Towards the End of Isolationism* (London, 1983).

Yasmin, S., *Pakistan's Relations with China* (Islamabad, 1980).

Yingfeng, Lei, My Days as Military Staff in the Supreme Command, Jiang XI, 1997.

Zagoria, Donald S., *The Sino-Soviet Conflict, 1956-61(* Princeton, 1961).

Ziring, Lawrence, ed., *Subcontinent in World Politics: India, its Neighbours and the Great Powers* (New York, 1982).

Articles

Ahmed, Abi Taher Salahuddin, "Bangladesh-China Relations: An Assessment", *BIISS Journal* (Dhaka), 13,2, 1992, 265-298.

Ahmed, N., "China's Himalayan Frontiers: Pakistan's Attitude", *International Affairs* (London), October 1962, 478-84.

Ansari, S., "Chinese Aggression on India: A Selected Bibliography", *International Studies* (New Delhi), July-October 1963, 201-11.

Appadorai, A., "Chinese Aggression and India: An Introductory Essay", *International Studies,* July-October 1963, pp.1-18.

Ashraf, S., Lal., M., and Shrimali, K., "India and Tibet: A Selected Bibliography", *International Studies*, April 1969, 607-25.

Babu, Vithal V., "China's Foreign Trade", *China Report* (New Delhi), November-December 1979, vol.XV, no.6, pp. 39-52.

Bandopadhyaya, J., "China, India and Tibet", *India Quarterly* (New Delhi, October-December 1962), pp. 382-93.

______________, "India-China Relations: Outlook for the 1980s", *Foreign Affairs Reports* (New Delhi) Vol. 29, no. 1, January 1979, 1-14.

Baral, J.K. & Mohapatra, J.K. "Sino-Indian Peace Efforts: Evolution of Variables, *Foreign Affairs Reports*, May 1982, 81-99.

Baral, J.K. & Others, "Rajiv Gandhi's China Diplomacy: Dynamics and Problems", *International Studies*, 26 (3), July-September 1989, 257-70.

Barnds, W.J., "The USSR, China and South Asia", *Problems of Communism,* (Washington) 26(2), November-December 1977, 44-59.

Bhat, Taranath, "Sino-Indian Economic Relations: An Overview", *China Report,* 20(6), November-December 1984, 15-24.

Bhattacharjea, Mira Sinha, "China's Strategy for the Determination and Consolidation of its Territorial-Boundaries: A Preliminary Investigation", *China-Report*, 23:4, 1987, 387-419.

______________, "China : Making and Unmaking of Nehru's Foreign Policy, China Report, 15(2), Mar-April 1979, pp 51-64.

______________, "What's in our China Policy", *Mainstream* (New Delhi), 25(35), May 87, 9-10.

Bhutani, U.C., "What Boundary Question? Sino-Indian or India-Tibetan?" *China Report*, Vol. 21, no. 5, September-October 1989, pp. 427-32.

Chakravarti, Nikhil, "India-China: Real Ahead", *Mainstream*, 4 July 1981, pp.1-3.

Chakravarti, Nikhil, "Chinese Foreign Minister's Visit and After", *India and Foreign Review* (New Delhi), 18(2), 1981, 6-7.

Chakravarti, Sumit., "Rajiv's China Visit", *Mainstream*, December 31, 1988, 25(14), 3-4.

Chauda, Nayan, "Heading for a Conflict", *Far Eastern Economic Review* (Hong Kong), June 4, 1987, p. 46-77.

Chauhan, R.S., "India and Sikkim: The Background to the Merger", *Foreign Affairs Reports*, Vol. 24, no. 9, September 1975, pp. 140-156.

Chauhan, Yadhuvir Singh, "India-China Relations: Future Prospect", *Vikrant* (New Delhi), February 1981, pp. 211-17.

Cheng, Joseph, Y.S., "China's Foreign Policy in the 1980s: From Anti-Hegemony to Modernization Diplomacy", *China Report*, 21(3), 1985, 197-221.

Choudhary, G.W., "Reflections on Sino-Pak Relations", *Pacific Community* (Tokyo), 7(2), January 1976, 248-70.

Dalai Lama, "The International Status of Tibet", *India Quarterly*, July-September 1959, 215-20

Deshingkar, Giri, "India-China Relations: The Nehru Years", *China Report*, 27(2), April-June 1991, 85-100.

Dianzara, "The Vladivostok Challenge", *Asian Defence-Journal*, (Kuallumpur), October 1986, 1-17.

Dixit, Aabha, "Enduring Sino-Pak Relations: The Military Dimesion", *Strategic Analysis,* (New Delhi), 12(9), December 1989, 981-92.

Dixit, Aabha, "Sino-Pak Relations and Their Implications for India", *Strategic Analysis,* 11(9), December 1987, 1067-80.

Dutt, Gargi, "India and China", *International Studies* (New Delhi), July-September 1978, pp.601-11.

Dutt, Sujit, "Sino-India Relations: Some Issues", *Strategic Analysis*, 11(11), February 1988, 1139-64.

Dutt, Sujit, "Sino-Indian Relations: Prospects and Trends", *Strategic Analysis*, 13(5), August 1990, 501-15.

Dutt, V.P., "China and South Asia", *IDSA Journal* (New Delhi), 18(1), July-September 85, 128-47.

Elkin, Jerrold F., and Fredricks, Brian, "Sino-Indian Border Talks: The View From New Delhi", *Asian Survey* (Berkeley), 33(10), October 1983, 1128-39.

Fisher, Mararet, W. and Rose Leo. E., "Ladakh and the Sino-Indian border Crisis", *Asian Survey*, October 1962, 27-37.

Ganguly, Shivaji, "US Military Assistance to India 1962-63: A Study in Decision-Making, India Quarterly", July-September 1972, 216-26.

Ganguly, Sumit, "The Sino-Indian Border Talks, 1981-89: A View from New Delhi", *Aṣian Survey*, 39(12), December 1989, 1123-35.

Garver, John W., "China-India Rivalry in Nepal: The Clash Over Chinese Arms Sales, *Asian Survey*, 31(10), October 1991, 956-75.

Garver, John W., "Chinese-Indian rivalry in Indo-China", Asian Survey, 27, 11, November 1987, 1205-19.

______________, "Indian Factor in Recent Sino-Soviet Relations", *China Quarterly* (London), March 1991, 55-85.

______________, "China and South Asia, Annals of the American Academy of Political and Social Science", 519, Jan. 1992, (Philadelphia), pp. 67-85.

Garver, John W., "The New Type of Sino-Soviet Relations", *Asian Survey*, 39(2), December 1989, 1136-92.

Garver, John W, "China and South Asia, Annals of the American Academy of Political and Social Science", 519, Jan 1992, (Philadelphia), pp. 67-85.

Gengnien, "Sino-Indian Relations: Retrospect and Prospect, South Asian Studies" (Beijing), 3-4, 1981, pp.1-12.

Ghosh, S.K., "The Indo-Soviet Treaty and China", *Journal of IDSA*, V, October 1972, 248-258.

Gill, R. Bates, "Curbing Beijing's Arms Sales", Orbis (Philadelphia), 36(3), Summer 1992, pp. 37-410.

Green L.C., "Legal Aspects of the Sino-Indian border Dispute", *China Quarterly*, January-March 1962, 193-37.

Gupta, Anirudha, "India and the Colombo-Powers", *Far Eastern Economic Review*, (Hongkong), 7 February 1963, 247-48.

Hamrin, C.I., "China Reassesses the Superpowers", *Pacific Affairs*, 56, 2, Summer 1983, 209-31.

Horn, R.C., "Soviet Union and the Sino-Indian Relations", *Orbis*, XXVI (4), Winter, 1983, 889-906.

Hussain, Karki, T., "Modernization: A Long March, *World Focus"* (New Delhi), May 1987-5-9.

Hussain, Karki, T., "Whether Relations With China", *World Focus*, November-December 1987, 67-71.

Hussain, T. Karki, "India, China and the Soviet Union: A Triangular Interaction", *Journal* (July 1973), 15-31.

Jain, B.M., "South Asia and China: Some Issues and Options", *Political Science Review* (Jaipur), 26(3-4), July-December, 1986, 106-17.

Jetly, Nancy, "Indian Opinion on the Tibetan Question", *International Studies*, April-January 1969, 564-83.

Jetly, Nancy, "Sino-Indian Relations: A Quest for Normalization", *India Quaterly*, 42(1) January-March 1986, 53-68.

Kabir, Mohammed Humayun, "From Non-Relation to Negotiation: Prospects for Normalisation of Sino-Indian Relations", *BLISS JOURNAL* (Dhaka), 6(1), January 1985, pp.130-50.

Kaiser, Karl, "The Interaction of Regional Subsystems: Some Preliminary Notes on Recurrent Patterns and the Role of Super Powers" (Baltimore), *World Politics,* 211, October 1968, 34-107.

Kanjilal Tanmany, "US Interests in the Sino-India Rapprochement", *Asian Studies* (Manila), 5(2), April-June 1987, 1130-39.

Kapur, Harish, "India-China Dialogue: Framework for Inquiry, China-Report", May-June 1974, 56-62.

Kaul, T.N., "Taking with China: No Room for Sentiment", *Illustrated Weekly of India* (New Delhi), 20 June 1982, pp.19-21.

Khan, Waheidmurtaza, "Whither Sino-Indian Relations: A Highlight over Border Dispute", *Indian Journal of Politics* (Aligarh), June 1983, pp.73-80.

Kharbanda, UP, "Scope for Sino-Indian Agreement on Science and Technology", *China Report,* 25(2), April-June 1989.

Kohli, Manorama, "Bhutan-China Border Talks", *China Report*, 20(3), May-June 1984, 3-5.

Levi, W., "The Sino-Indian Border War Current History", (Philadelphia), September 1963, 136-43.

Levine, Steven, I., "China and South Asia, *Strategic Analysis"*, 12(10), January 1989, 1107-26.

Loomba, Joanne F., "US Aid to India 1951-1967: A Study in Decision-Making", *India Quarterly 28* October-December 1974-305-31.

Mahaptra, Chintamani, "Nepal in China's South Asian Strategy: Some Reflections", *Strategic Analysis,* 12(6), September 1988, 613-28.

Malhotra, V.K., "Sino-Indian Relations: Problems and Prospects", *Journal of Political Studies* (Jullandhar), February 1986, pp.4-55.

Man Singh, Surjit and Levine, Steven I., "China and India: Moving beyond Confrontation", *Problem of Communism*, 38(2-3), March & June 1989, 30-49.

Maxwell-Neville, "Deadlocked Deadlock: Sino-Indian Boundary Dispute," *Economic and Political Weekly* (Bombay, 19 September 1981, pp.1545-58).

Mehra, Parshottam, "Elusive Triangle: Tibet in India-China Relations", *China Report*, 26(2), April-June 1990, 145-156.

Mehra, Purshotam L., "India, China and Tibet, 1950-54", *India Quarterly,* January-March 1956, 3-22.

Mishra, Pramod K., "China and South Asia", *China Report*, 21(5), September 1985, 403-13.

Misra, G.S., India-China Relations: Appraisal, *Mainstream*, 25(27), 21 March 1987, 15-21.

Mohanty, Manoranjan, "India-China Relations: A Positive Frame", *India Quarterly,* 41(1), January-March 1985, 17-22.

Norbu, Dawa, "Tibet in Sino-Indian Relations", *Asian Survey*, 11 November 1997, 1078-94.

__________, "Chinese Strategic Thinking on Tibet and The Himalayan Region", *Strategic Analysis*, 12(4), July 1988, 371-95.

__________, "Strategic Development in Tibet: Implications For its Neighbours", *Asian Survey*, 13(3), March 1979, pp. 252-63.

Palmer, Norman D., "Trans-Himalayan Confrontation", Orbis, Winter 1963, 513-27.

Panikkar, K.M., "The Himalayas and Indian Defence", *India Quarterly*, April-January 1947, 127-34, July-September 1947, 233-37.

Parmanand, "China's Nepal Policy", *IDSA Journal*, 17(1) July-September 1984, 71-86.

Passon, Herbert, "Sino-Indian Cultural Relations", *China Quarterly*, July-September 1961, 85-100.

Patterson, George N., "China and Tibet: Back-ground to the Revolt", *China Quarterly*, 1 January-March 1960, 87-102.

Rajan, M.S., "Chinese Aggression and the Future of India's Non alignment", *International Studies*, July-October 1963, 115-32.

Ram, Mohan, "Trade Ties Set to Grow", *Far Eastern Economic Review* (Hong Kong), 113 (29), July 10, 1981, 45-48.

Ram, N., "India and China for a Fresh Equation", *Frontline* (Madras), 6(1), January 7-20, 1989, 4-12.

Ramachandran, K.N., "Sino-Indian Relations: Problems and Prospects", *China Report*, 15(1), January-February 1979, 7-12.

Ramachandran, K.N., "India, China and the Super Powers", *IDSA Journal*, 19(1), July-September 1986, 140-152.

Ramachandran, K.N., "Moscow and Sino-Indian Relations", *China Report*, Vol. 15, no. 2, March-April 1979, 40-43.

Rmachandran, K.N., "Problems and Prospects of Li Peng's Visit", *Link* (New Delhi), 34(17), 8 December 1991, 4-6.

Rose, Leo E., "Sino-Indian Rivalry and the Himalayan Border States", *Orbis*, October 1961, 198-215.

Satyapalan, C.N., "The Sino-Indian Border Conflict", *Orbis*, 8, 2, Summer 1964, 374-90.

Sen Gupta, Bhabani, "A Maoist Line for India, China Quarterly", January-March 1968, 3-16.

Seth, S.P., "Sino-Indian Relations: Changing Perspectives", *Problems of Communism*, March-April 1974, 14-26.

Seth, S.P., "Sino-Indian Relations: Problems and Prospects", *Asia Pacific Community* (Tokyo), Fall 1984, 66-85.

Shelvankar, K.S., "China's Himalayan Frontiers: India's Attitude", *International Affairs* (London), 38, 4, October 1962, 472-47.

Shelvankar, K.S., "Non Alignment and the Sino-Indian Conflict", *Indian Yearbook of International Affairs*, 12, 1963, 435-45.

Sidky, Mohammed Habib, "Chinese World Strategy and South Asia: the Chinese Factor in Indo-Pakistan Relations", *Asian Survey*, 16(10), October 1976, pp. 956-80.

Siegal, Richard L., "Chinese Efforts to Influence Soviet Policy to India", *India Quarterly*, 24, 3 July-September 1968, 213-38.

Singh Gurnam, "China's Normalization Diplomacy Towards India: *China Report*, 19(3), May-June 1983, 19-22.

Subrahmanyam, K., "India-China Relations: Some Basic Consideration", *World Focus*, August 1981, 3-6.

Tewari, B.C., and Phadnis, "Urmila, India-China Border Areas Dispute: A Selected Bibliography", *India Quaterly*, April-June 1960, 155-69.

Upadhyaya, R.K., "India-China: Rejuvenating Economic Ties", *Mainstream*, 39(51), October 22, 1991.

Vaidyanath, R., "Some Recent Trends in Soviet Policies Towards India and Pakistan", *International Studies*, January 1966, 429-47.

Varma, S.P., "Chinese Aggression: Impact on India's Domestic Politics", *Political Science Review*, October 1963, 31-41.

Varma, S.P., "Sino-Indian Frontiers: A Study in Origins", *Political Science Review*, October 1964, 12-29.

Venkatasubbiah, H., "Approach to Sino-Indian Relations", *Asian Affairs*, (Manila) January 1973, 140-50.

Vertzberger, Y.I., "China's Diplomacy and Strategy Towards South Asia: From Benign Neglect to Prominence", *Strategic Digest*, July 1987, 1300-20.

Vertzberger, Y.I., "India's Border Conflict with China: A Perpetual Analysis, *Journal of Contemporary History* (London), October 1982, 607-32.

Vohra, Sahdev, "China-India Rapprochement", *Strategic Analysis*, 17(5), Aug. 1994, 641-46.

Vijay Kumar, "Sri Lanka's Sino-Indian Tangle: An International Retrospect", *Indian Journal of Politics*, September-December 1984, 47-54.

Wang, Hong U, "Sino-Indian Relations: Present and Future", *Asian Survey*, 35(6), June 1985, 546-54.

Waria V. Walla, Bharat, "Improving Relations with China: India's Gains", *China Report*, 15(2), March-April 1979, 65-68.

Weiwang, Hong, "Sino-Nepal Relations in the 1980s", *Asian Survey*, 25(5), May 1985, 512-20.

Whiting, Allen S. and Liao, Kuang Sheng, "Indo-Chinese Border Crisis of 1962", *China Quarterly*, March 1976, 117-19.

Yachhun, Chang, "Impact of the Border Issue on Peiping New Delhi Relations", *Issues and Studies* (Teipei), 19(1), January 1983, 52-71.

Zheng, Ruixiang, "Shifting Obstacles in Sino-Indian Relations", *Pacific Review*, 6(1), 1993, 63-70.

Journals

Annals of the American Academy (Philadelphia)
Asia Pacific Community (Tokyo)
Asian Defence Journal (Kualalumpur)
Asian Strategic Review (New Delhi)
Asian Affairs (Manila)
Asian Survey (Berkeley)
Beijing Review (Beijing)
BIISS Journal (Dhaka)
China Quarterly (London)
China Report (New Delhi)
Current History (Philadelphia)
India Quaterly (New Delhi)
International Affairs (London)
International Affairs (Moscow)
International Defense Review (Surrey)
International Studies (New Delhi)
Orbis (Philadelphia)
Pacific Review (Vancouver)
Pakistan Horizon (Karachi)
Problems of Communism (Washington)
Strategic Analysis (New Delhi)
Strategic Digest (New Delhi)

South Asian Studies (In Chinese, Beijing)

Periodicals

Asian Recorder (New Delhi)
Economist (London)
Far Eastern Economic Review (Hong Kong)
Frontline (Madras)
India Today (New Delhi)
Link (New Delhi)
New Times (Moscow)
Time (Hong Kong)

Newspapers

Pravda (Moscow).
Renmin Ribao – People's Daily (Beijing).
China Daily (Beijing).
Hindu (Madras).
Hindustan Times (New Delhi).
New York Times (New York).
Patriot (New Delhi).
Statesman (Calcutta).
Times of India (New Delhi).
Tribune (Chandigarh).
International Herald Tribune (Hong Kong)
Times (London)
Pakistan Times (Islamabad)
Muslim (Islamabad)
Bangladesh Observer (Dhaka)
Times of India (New Delhi)

Press Releases and Miscellaneous

Current Digest of Soviet Press
Department of State Bulletin
Foreign Broadcasting Information Services.
Izvestia
New China News Agency
News Review on China, Institute for Defence Studies and Analyses.
SIPRI Year Book
Summary of World Broadcasts, BBC.
Survey of China Main Land Press
Tass
Xinhua News Agency Report

Index

C

D

E

I